# THE STAGE AND THE SCHOOL

## About the Author—

KATHARINE ANNE OMMANNEY has taught dramatics in American high schools for more than twenty-five years and has lectured at many colleges and universities throughout the country. Her wide experience in the theater includes study at the American Academy of Dramatic Art and the Royal Academy of Dramatic Art, acting with the Triangle Players and the WPA Federal Theater, and directing hundreds of amateur productions. Miss Ommanney has contributed numerous articles to *Theatre Arts* and other professional and educational periodicals.

# THE STAGE

**third edition**

**WEBSTER DIVISION, McGRAW-HILL BOOK COMPANY**

*Katharine Anne Ommanney*

# AND THE SCHOOL

t. *Louis*    *New York*    *San Francisco*    *Dallas*    *Toronto*    *London*

47669

*Library of Congress Catalog Card Number: 59–13213*

11121314 HDMM 7543210

# Permissions and Acknowledgments

We wish to thank the following authors, publishers, and agents for
granting us permission to include copyrighted materials:

Walter H. Baker Company for the following: the excerpts from *Neighbors*
by Zona Gale; copyright, 1914, by B. W. Huebsch; copyright in renewal ✖ the
scene from *Sham* by Frank G. Tompkins; copyright, 1950, by Walter H. Baker
Company ✖ the excerpt from *Riders to the Sea* by John Millington Synge;
copyright, 1951, by Walter H. Baker Company.

Brandt & Brandt for the excerpt from *Golden Boy*\* by Clifford Odets and the
excerpt from *The Time of the Cuckoo*† by Arthur Laurents.

Coward-McCann, Inc. for the scene from *Our Town*,† a play in three acts,
by Thornton Wilder; copyright, 1938, by Coward-McCann. Published by
Coward-McCann, N.Y. Used by permission.

Curtis Brown Ltd. for the scene from *The Barretts of Wimpole Street*\* by
Rudolf Besier.

Dodd, Mead & Company for the extract from "Work" published in *The
Hour Has Struck* by Angela Morgan.

Dramatists Play Service, Inc. and Ronald Alexander for the scene from *Time
Out for Ginger*\* by Ronald Alexander; copyright, 1953, by Ronald Alexander
(Revised); copyright, 1948, by Ronald Alexander (under the title *Season with
Ginger*).

Ernst, Cane & Berner for the excerpt from Ketti Frings' adaptation of *Look
Homeward, Angel*† by Thomas Wolfe; copyright, 1958, by Edward C. Aswell
as Administrator C.T.A. of the Estate of Thomas Wolfe and/or Fred W.
Wolfe and Ketti Frings.

---

\* This selection is intended for classroom use only and may not be performed publicly
without written permission from Dramatists Play Service, Inc., 14 E. 38th Street,
N.Y. 16, N.Y.

† This selection is fully protected by copyright. All rights in this selection, including
professional, amateur, motion pictures, recitation, public reading, radio and television
broadcasting, and the rights of translation into foreign languages, are strictly reserved.

Putnam and Company, Ltd. for the scene from A *Night at an Inn*† by Lord Dunsany and the excerpt from *Spreading the News*† by Lady Gregory.

G. P. Putnam's Sons for the scene from A *Night at an Inn*† published in *Plays of Gods and Men* by Lord Dunsany and the excerpt from *Spreading the News*† by Lady Gregory.

Random House, Inc. for the following: the scene from *The Fabulous Invalid*\* by Moss Hart and George S. Kaufman; copyright, 1938, by Moss Hart and George S. Kaufman ✖ the excerpt from *Golden Boy*\* by Clifford Odets ✖ the scene from *The Rainmaker*† by N. Richard Nash; copyright, 1955, by N. Richard Nash ✖ the scene from *Sabrina Fair*\* by Samuel Taylor; copyright, 1954, by Samuel Taylor ✖ the excerpt from *The Time of the Cuckoo*† by Arthur Laurents. All reprinted by permission of Random House, Inc.

Charles Scribner's Sons for the following: the excerpt from *Mary Rose*† by James M. Barrie ✖ *Poor Maddalena* from *Magic Lanterns* by Louise Saunders; copyright, 1923, Charles Scribner's Sons; renewal copyright, 1951, Louise Saunders ✖ the scene from *Quality Street*† by James M. Barrie; copyright, 1918, J. M. Barrie; renewal copyright, 1946, Cynthia Asquith and Peter L. Davies. All reprinted with the permission of Charles Scribner's Sons.

The Viking Press, Inc. for the scene from *Years Ago* by Ruth Gordon and Garson Kanin; copyright as an unpublished work, 1944, by Ruth Gordon; copyright, 1946, 1947, by Ruth Gordon and Garson Kanin. Professionals and amateurs are hereby warned that *Years Ago*, being fully protected under the copyright laws of the United States of America, the British Empire including the Dominion of Canada, and all other countries of the Copyright Union, is subject to royalty. All rights, including professional, amateur, motion picture, recitation, lecturing, public reading, radio broadcasting, and television, are strictly reserved. All inquiries should be addressed to the author's representative, William Morris Agency, Inc., 1740 Broadway, New York 19, N.Y. These excerpts may not be reprinted in any way without obtaining written permission from the author's publishers, The Viking Press, Inc., 625 Madison Avenue, New York 22, N.Y.

✖✖✖✖

We wish to express our gratitude for the many excellent photographs of student dramatic activities generously contributed by the following teachers: Jean J. Barrett, Westchester High School, Los Angeles, California; Carolyn Cremeens, Shorewood High School, Shorewood, Wisconsin; Mina Cubbon, Leon High School, Tallahasee, Florida; Dorothy Day, Bronxville High School, Bronxville, New York; Winifred N. Gahagan, New Trier Township High School, Winnetka, Illinois; C. Gernerd, Toms River High School, Toms River, New Jersey; Melba Day Sparks, Jefferson High School, Portland, Oregon; and Richard J. Warye, West High School, Columbus, Ohio.

The author wishes to express her appreciation of the invaluable aid afforded by theater people and educational leaders, in the United States and in many other countries, who assisted her in obtaining material for this edition. Among them she wishes to acknowledge especially the services of Ernest V. Theiss, Manager of Program Administration, NBC; Doris Ann, Producer of Religious and Public Affairs Programs for NBC; Miss Maisie Cobby, Inspector of Drama for the London County Council; Signora Flavia Paulon, Executive Director of the Venice Film Festival; John Meston, distinguished television writer; and Robert Montgomery, star of stage, screen, television, and radio.

# Contents

## PART FIVE: Motion Pictures, Radio, and Television

# Scenes for Classroom Use

# Preface

New ideas animate today's theater. In high school and college theaters and workshops, as well as on the professional stage, recent experiments in acting, staging, and playwriting have yielded results of first importance to all students of drama. This completely revised edition of *The Stage and the School* makes many of these new developments in the theater arts available for the first time in a high school textbook. Discussions of such topics as the Stanislavski method, theater-in-the-round, and epic theater bring the new into clear and understandable relation with the traditional. Chapters on motion pictures and television help the student to see the possibilities as well as the problems of these twentieth-century art forms. New sections on lighting and stage equipment provide practical, non-technical information needed by producers of amateur plays.

An attractive new format with hundreds of photographs and drawings, including a fifteen-page picture essay on the production of a play from reading rehearsal to opening night, lend to this book about the theater much of the glamour of the theater itself.

Stage terms are explained or defined when they first occur within the text. A comprehensive glossary of stage terms on pages 504 to 513 gives the student additional help in mastering the vocabulary of the stage.

*The Stage and the School,* Third Edition, is designed to make the student feel at home in the theater—on either side of the footlights. It teaches him the fundamentals he needs as a participant and gives him the background he needs as a spectator. In whichever role he finds himself, the student will benefit from a first-hand knowledge of the actor's problems, a clear understanding of the structure of plays, and a thorough acquaintance with the history and literature of the stage. This new edition of *The Stage and the School* was written to provide these three prerequisites for a successful approach to drama.

This book treats fully the fundamentals of acting technique. Careful explanations, immediately applied, build skill in character interpretation, voice control, stage movement, and pantomime. The comprehensive coverage of such topics as choosing a play, conducting tryouts and rehearsals, selecting costumes, and designing and constructing scenery make *The Stage and the School* a practical handbook for amateur stage production.

The play as an art form receives careful attention. Types and styles of plays are described and analyzed, and abundant examples are given to show their application in the modern theater.

*The Stage and the School* introduces the student to the history and the people of the theater. The development of drama is traced from its beginnings to the present with special attention to architectural forms and styles, stage equipment, scenery, and costumes. This material, together with discussions of the contribution of the world's great playwrights, actors, and scenic artists, provides illuminating insights into the social and intellectual history of the Greek, Medieval, Elizabethan, and modern periods.

In addition to teaching the student how to understand plays and how to put them on, the author hopes to show him that nations express their values and ideals through their drama. Her recent tour of the great theaters of Europe and Asia reaffirmed her conviction that words spoken on stages in Moscow, Paris, or Tokyo may be as important to world understanding as the words spoken at conference tables. She believes that knowing what other peoples have in their hearts is as important as knowing what they have in their arsenals and on their drawing-boards. Drama is one way toward this understanding.

To her task of making the student aware of drama as a cultural force as he learns to act, the author brings a varied experience in the theaters of the world, an understanding of young people, and a contagious enthusiasm for the drama in all its forms. Whether the student makes the theater his life or only a part of it, he will find *The Stage and the School* an indispensable guide to a fascinating new world.

THE PUBLISHERS

# To the Student

*The Stage and the School* introduces you to the fascinating world of the theater. If you look through the table of contents and read the introductions to the five parts, you will realize that in its pages you will contact all phases of the drama. I originally wrote this book because my students felt the need of having all the material we had so enjoyed in class put into a concrete form which they could keep. Since then, other editions have enlarged upon the first book, and now you have the latest volume in your hands to use as a background for your course in dramatics.

Naturally, you will get from the course what you put into it, but the great satisfaction in dramatics is that you can see immediate results from your daily classwork and home practice. You will soon find you are reading more intelligently in all your classes because acting demands that you know the exact meaning of every word. In addition, you will find you are adjusting yourself more easily to people and situations as you study and rehearse plays demanding an analysis of character and plot. As you master the tools of the actor—body and voice—you will find your voice, diction, and poise are improving and you are much more at ease everywhere you go. At the same time, your creative imagination will be stimulated as you put on plays and work out the problems of production under varying conditions. Thus you will know that all phases of your personality are being utilized and you will enjoy a sense of real achievement.

An enthusiasm for the theater can give added meaning to the challenging experiences that lie ahead for you in the world of tomorrow. Seeing plays and pictures will help you to understand the people of our own and other countries and provide insight into many of the world's crucial problems. Whatever your career may be, dramatics will help you to develop your full potentialities. I hope *The Stage and the School* will enrich your life experience now and in the future.

*Katharine Anne Ommanney*

xiv

# THE STAGE AND THE SCHOOL

*Part One*

# Enjoying the Drama

Because the drama is the most exciting of the arts, it has always been, in one form or another, also the most popular. Today millions of people watch television plays, live and on film, listen to radio shows, gaze at colossal motion pictures, and see performances of living actors on the stages of the world.

Perhaps you are starting to study dramatics at school because you have become interested in drama through television plays. You will soon find that the work you do for this class will greatly increase your pleasure in the television plays you see because you will learn to appreciate all the work and talent that lies behind their production.

In addition, you will discover that there are more stimulating and absorbing ways of enjoying drama than sitting inertly in front of fleeting scenes on a screen. At school you will soon be acting parts and at home you will be surprised to find yourself reading

2

plays of far greater variety and interest than those you ordinarily see on television. You will undoubtedly go more often to the many fine motion pictures being produced all the time. Best of all, you will be encouraged to see every stage play possible and thus be introduced to the magic world of the theater which has captivated people throughout history. Being part of a responsive audience that watches living actors and actresses is the most exciting of dramatic experiences.

When you leave school, you may be able to travel and see plays of other countries, not only in city theaters, but also in the byways and along the roadsides of European and Asiatic countries. You will also have an opportunity to work with a local dramatic group and have the fun and satisfaction of pursuing drama as an avocation. Your experience in this class and on your school stage may well lead you to a deep and lasting source of enjoyment.

*Chapter 1*

# You and the Theater

For the first time in history, during the middle years of the twentieth century, drama has come into the home. Until recent times, people had to go somewhere to see a play. They climbed a hillside to look down on the performers in ancient Greece, crowded in the pit around the Elizabethan stage, or went out to a show in a theater or motion-picture house. Now you can sit in front of your television screen and see any number of plays; the characters in the live or filmed scenes come into your home to share their experiences with you.

Thousands of people are perfectly satisfied to accept the drama seen in the home as their one contact with the realm of the theater, where humanity has expressed its dreams for countless generations. You, however, have decided to widen your interest by studying dramatics. Through your class-work you may well become an amateur—a theater lover—who finds great joy in the living drama, as well as in television and films.

## THE WORLD OF THE THEATER

You will very probably discover that there is a community or a college theater within driving distance of your home. There you can see the best plays of the past and present. These productions are usually given by non-professionals, but these amateurs may be more inspired and enthusiastic about their work than actors who make their living on the stage. Of course, you should try never to miss the opportunity of seeing professional casts, if you are lucky enough to have them appear on tour in your neighborhood.

4

Your first contact with the living theater can literally give you the thrill of a lifetime. That exciting moment after the house lights are dimmed and just before the curtain rises, as you wait to catch your first glimpse of the world behind the footlights, is unlike any other experience.

In a sense the curtain is rising on the world of the theater for you as you enter this class; you may even feel the same kind of excitement that you would have before a performance. You will make many new friends in the plays you read and act. New lands and imaginative regions will open to you. Best of all, a wealth of stimulating ideas will crowd upon you to broaden your thinking for the rest of your life.

## THIS COURSE

You are probably wondering what lies ahead in this course and textbook. You will soon find that your school is actually bringing the stage to you, and you will have the fun of being both an actor and a spectator. At the same time, as you do each assignment, you will be developing yourself into a more effective, sensitive, and understanding person.

You will be enjoying simultaneously three phases of the classwork. In the first place, the world of the theater will be opened to you as you read the plays of all periods and countries and as you learn about the intriguing personalities who have spent their lives in this exciting atmosphere. In the second place, you will be acting and producing plays—even writing them if you wish—and, in the process, learning how to use your voice and body effectively. In the third place, you will be developing yourself physically, mentally, socially, and spiritually in a group activity demanding constant adjustment to other people. Thus, this course will not only give you the acting experience you are looking forward to but it will also encourage wide knowledge, critical judgment, and deeper enjoyment of plays. As a result, many of your leisure hours will be happily spent, both at home and in school, in reading and seeing plays with growing appreciation.

You will particularly enjoy being in a class where, in shared activities, friendships blossom quickly. Working together in scenes and plays may lead to watching television with some of your classmates in your home and attending the best motion pictures and plays available with them. As a result, you will become as deeply interested in the development of their abilities as of your own. No class encourages such obvious improvement as do the various phases of theater study. Work in dramatics demands more self-control, ability to accept criticism, good sportsmanship, tact, and plain good nature than any other school activity. You must be prompt, dependable,

in Bali . . .

on Broadway . . .

Photo by George E. Joseph

to the magic of a play . . .

Courtesy of ANTA

in a school auditorium . . .

and even on a showboat.

Courtesy of ANTA

and helpful, if a play is to succeed. In this course you will also have technical exercises to improve your voice and speech and to make your body movements effective and graceful. From these activities you will acquire poise and vitality in appearing before the public. You will learn to memorize, concentrate, and control your emotions more easily as the class advances. You should dress in better taste after studying costuming, move more gracefully after studying pantomime, and express yourself more effectively after studying acting. Certainly your imagination, the foundation of all impersonation, will be stimulated in every phase of your work.

The cultivation of the emotions is one of the chief values of a class in dramatics, for you must lose yourself in the feelings of others if you are to act successfully or, for that matter, watch and read plays wholeheartedly. Feeling, moving, and speaking like someone else will broaden your sympathy and understanding of other people's problems, enlarge your capacity for friendship, and enrich your whole life.

*Discussion*

1. Why, in your opinion, has dramatics been put into the curriculum of many of the high schools in the United States? What were your reasons for taking this course? What do you hope to gain from it?

2. In what ways can your activities in dramatics affect your other classes and experiences in school?

3. Why is the use of leisure time a serious problem today, both to you as an individual and to people throughout the country? How can the training you receive in dramatics affect the way you spend your leisure time now and in the future?

4. How do you explain the appeal that drama has had for more than 2,500 years?

5. Why do you think so many people wish they had gone on the stage? Do you wish to do so? Why?

6. Why shouldn't dramatics in high school be primarily a course to train professional actors? In what ways should such a course assist a student who does wish to become a professional actor?

7. Which of the three phases of drama study sounds most appealing to you? Which do you think will mean the most to you in the future?

8. What television plays, movies, or stage plays have given you practical ideas on adjustment to your personal problems? Why is it important for you to be a well-adjusted individual?

9. What line of work do you expect to follow after leaving school? Do you think that dramatics can be of any special value to you in that field? In what ways might it be helpful?

# FOR THE RECORD

Ideas, which are the most vital things in the world, are also the most intangible; unless you organize the material you use in a course, you will lose many of its real values. In this course, you should record information concerning plays, for instance—the *who, where, when,* and *how* of each one read or seen—and refer to it not only for your work in dramatics, but for other classes, both in high school and college. Some sort of record, probably in notebook or card-index form, can be a source of pride, information, and pleasure long after the course is completed. It should be a distinctly individual record for your own benefit, but its value depends largely upon careful organization. The following suggestions may be of use to you.

## Notebooks

The notebook should be an ordinary loose-leaf one, divided into sections to be filled as the classwork develops. It should have a title page, a table of contents, and a bibliography.

Part 1—Class notes. These should be brief reports of lectures, suggestions, directions, assignments, and reviews given in class by the teacher and students.

Part 2—Reports of plays studied in class.

Part 3—Reports of plays read out of class.

Part 4—Reports of plays seen in or out of the class throughout the period of the term's work.

Part 5—Reviews of books and articles read dealing with all phases of the theater—biography, play production, stage settings, acting, make-up, dramatic criticism, and kindred subjects.

Part 6—Vocabulary—words, their meaning and pronunciation.

Part 7—Exercises for vocal and bodily improvement.

## Scrapbooks

The scrapbooks can be as simple or elaborate as you desire, but a large loose-leaf book is recommended. When your eyes are open to all the interesting pictures and articles constantly appearing about the theater or pertaining to some phase of staging and acting plays, you will be amazed at the amount of material you can gather from newspapers, magazines, advertisements, and programs. The following sections are suggested:

Part 1—Personalities of the stage, screen, television, and radio. These may be pictures and clippings about actors and actresses, producers, directors, playwrights, critics, and scenic artists.

Part 2—Stage settings. This section may include pictures of the various types of stage settings, period furniture, pictures that suggest possible sets, outdoor and indoor scenes of unusual beauty or interest, and stage and lighting equipment.

Part 3—Costuming. This section may include a series of pictures illustrating the historical development of clothing, striking examples of the various periods, appropriate clothes for all types of characters, modern clothes for definite types and occasions, and attractive combinations of line, color, and materials.

Part 4—Facial expression and make-up. This section may include pictures from magazine covers, illustrations, and advertisements which emphasize the lines of the face, expressions under the stress of different emotions, coloring, headdresses, types of faces of the various nationalities and races, or actual make-up and care of the skin.

Part 5—Color combinations. This section need not pertain exclusively to the theater but may illustrate any pleasing or striking color combinations which might be used in staging and costuming plays.

Part 6—Personality development. Include here clippings, pictures, poems, slogans, and so on which deal with improvement of character, appearance, and personality.

Part 7—Miscellaneous section. This section may include anything you care to put in it—programs from theaters, advertisements of plays and pictures, and anything else that you think will be of value to you in your study of the stage.

*Discussion*

1. Mention all the present and future values a good notebook and scrapbook might have for you as a student of the drama.

2. What makes a really fine notebook or scrapbook?

3. What are some arguments in favor of requiring students in the course to organize these books?

4. What are some of the problems involved in keeping notebooks? Make some practical suggestions as to how these difficulties may be overcome.

5. What are some ways in which you can best express your own individuality in a notebook and scrapbook? Why is it important that you do so?

# *A play is born . . .*

A *Touch of the Poet*, Eugene O'Neill's last complete play, goes into rehearsal in a vacant theater. Stage manager Joseph Brownstone, assistant stage manager Norman Kean, director Harold Clurman, and star Kim Stanley read the script.

The assistant stage manager works out an important bit of stage business with Eric Portman and Curt Conway, while Kim Stanley, Helen Hayes, and Harold Clurman look on.

Mr. Clurman discusses a fine point of interpretation with Helen Hayes. The chalk marks on the floor are to show the dimensions of the set and the positions of stage furnishings which will be used in the actual production.

While the actors rehearse in New York, carpenters are busy building the set in a Brooklyn scene shop. The set, which re-creates one room of an early nineteenth-century New England inn, is at the rear of the shop.

Designer Ben Edwards and his assistant inspect the backdrop.

Mr. Edwards selects appropriate period furniture.

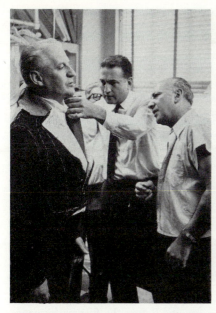

(Left) Ben Edwards, who designed both scenery and costumes, adjusts the collar of Eric Portman's coat. (Right) A seamstress pins up the hem of Helen Hayes's costume. To give the dress an aged and worn appearance, the material was washed and bleached many times.

The fittings completed, tailors make the necessary alterations on costumes.

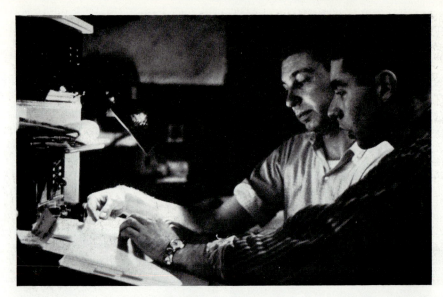

After a month and a half of rehearsals, the play goes to the Shubert Theatre in New Haven for a series of out-of-town tryouts. Before the first performance, the stage managers go over their master script to check lighting, sound, and property cues.

The assistant stage manager then runs through sound and lighting effects with the technician to see that everything is in working order and timed to the second.

The master of properties and his assistant make a last-minute check to be absolutely sure all the hand props are on the table. As the actors get ready to make their entrances, they will pick up their props from this table.

Downstairs in his dressing room, Eric Portman applies the finishing touches to his make-up while his valet adjusts the wig.

Curtain time draws near, and the assistant stage manager makes warning rounds.

Actors about to go on wait in the wings for their entrance cues.

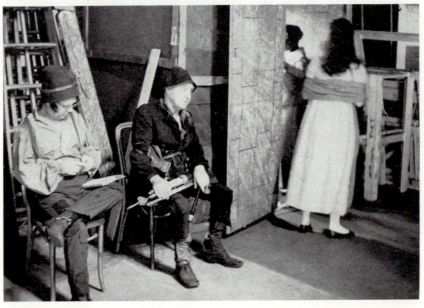

The curtain goes up and for the first time the story unfolds uninterruptedly before an audience. (Above) Eric Portman makes an impressive entrance as Major Cornelius Melody. (Below) Kim Stanley and Helen Hayes, as Melody's daughter and wife, console one another while they wait for him to return from a duel.

Finally Melody comes back, and the play draws to a dramatic close.

After this first performance, the director, stage managers, cast, and production crew gather onstage to work out acting and technical problems. Such "post-mortems," held throughout the tryout period, are essential to the polished production eventually seen by Broadway audiences.

From New Haven the play goes to Boston for more tryouts and then returns to New York for its grand opening at the Helen Hayes Theatre. A few days before the opening the set comes in by truck.

(Left) Inside the theater, electricians mount the spotlights on battens. (Right) A view of the fly gallery and stage before stagehands bring in the set.

Opening night arrives and so do first-nighters and curious spectators.

The audience—including New York's drama critics—waits for the lights to dim and the curtain to go up.

The final curtain rings down, and the entire cast returns for curtain calls before an enthusiastic audience.

Exhausted, veteran actress Helen Hayes relaxes in her dressing room.

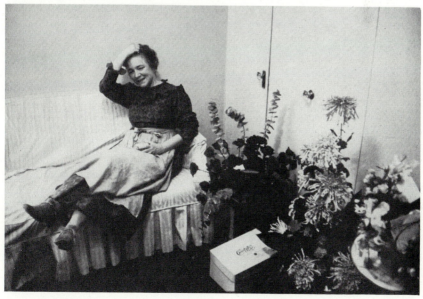

(Above and below) Director Harold Clurman goes backstage to congratulate the anxious stars. (Opposite) A few hours later, reviews appear in the metropolitan papers, praising both play and performance. After its months of preparation, A *Touch of the Poet* is launched on a distinguished run.

All the photographs in this section were taken by George E. Joseph especially for *The Stage and the School.*

*Chapter 2*

# Plays and Players

Watching plays has provided universal entertainment since the beginning of civilization, but never before have so many people been able to watch so many plays. Literally thousands of television dramas are performed each year. If you also consider all the old and new films being shown regularly, you will realize that drama is readily available today in the American home. There is a vast difference, however, between merely watching a play and truly enjoying it.

## SEEING PLAYS

You will find that one of the lasting values to be gained from a study of the drama is learning to watch plays appreciatively. Your pleasure in doing so will increase as the course advances and as you learn more and more about the fundamentals of acting, playwriting, and production.

### Judging Plays

There are four considerations to keep in mind when you watch any type of play: the play itself, its interpretation by the actors, its staging, and its reception by the audience. Your background in these areas will increase as the course advances, but a brief discussion of them now will help you to choose and judge the theatrical fare on which you spend your precious leisure time.

*The first consideration is the play itself.* Right up to the last line, you should want to know what will happen next. The dramatist must place ex-

Photo by Friedman-Abeles; courtesy of J. D. Proctor

One of the theater's highest awards is the New York Drama Critics' Circle Award, given each year to the best play of the season. Pictured here is a scene from Lorraine Hansberry's A *Raisin in the Sun*, recipient of the 1959 award.

citing people in exciting situations leading to an exciting *climax*—the highest point of interest—in order to keep you in suspense. The series of events is known as the *plot*, and the plot centers about the leading *characters*, in whom you should be deeply interested. If the playwright has done his job well, you will really care what happens to the characters as you watch them struggle for what they want or believe in.

In every plot the leading character is faced with a *conflict* which he strives to resolve. The conflict may be serious or comic but it must be of vital significance to the character and, as a result, to you also. Many of the films you have seen may make you think that conflicts are always physical, involving much violence. This is not true, for many great plays center around an emotional, or mental, or social conflict which can be of much more importance than physical combat. People have always been willing to give their lives for ideas, feelings, and traditions; playwrights often build their plots around such moving forces. The end of a play should find the hero (or heroine) either solving his conflict through his own efforts, or failing to do so because of personality weaknesses, the stronger influences of other charac-

Photo by Vandamm

Alla Nazimova (1879–1945), shown here in the role of Hedda Gabler, won world-wide acclaim as one of the finest actresses of her day.

ters, fate, or circumstances. The ending must satisfy you by being logical and believable, even though it is not necessarily happy.

The dramatist has only *action* and *dialogue* with which to tell his story. He must create characters who act and speak in such a way that they stir you emotionally and/or intellectually. Gradually, you will learn to note the skill of the playwright in developing action and in writing dialogue. You will see how he makes clever lines or beautiful passages the expression of the characters, not himself.

What must be the dramatist's, however, is the central idea or *theme* about which he has built the entire play. This theme determines the style of his writing and the actions of his characters, and he should bring it out so clearly by the end of the play that you will want to discuss it with your friends.

*The second consideration is the acting.* After only a little work in dramatics, you will find that you are developing some ability as a critical observer of acting. A good actor creates a role which is convincing all the

A delighted audience watches actors plunge into the pool in *Wish You Were Here,* produced at the Cape Cod Melody Tent in Hyannis, Massachusetts. Front-row spectators are protected by plastic sheets.

time; he is always an inherent part of the action. He avoids attracting attention to himself and, by speaking and listening in character, he helps to bring out the center of interest at every moment of the play. He builds up a personality in which you can believe by being natural and spontaneous and identifying himself with the period and spirit of the play. In this way, he makes you think of him not as an actor but as a person really involved in the action taking place.

*The third consideration is the production.* You will study this phase of dramatics in detail in Part Four of this book. You will come to realize the importance of the director and the way he uses all his tools—actors, lights, setting, and costumes—to create mood and background. The scenic artist and the backstage crew are also important to a well-produced play. The sets should be correct for the period and place, and the lighting should help to establish the desired mood.

*The final consideration is the reaction of the audience.* This depends upon many things and is not too reliable a criterion for the success of a play. It is largely a matter of *empathy,* or the emotional identification of an individual with some object or person outside of himself. In the theater, empathy is most important because the average person watches a play to lose himself in the lives of the characters. He wishes to be lifted temporarily into another world, to become identified with the life on the stage and to experience the emotions portrayed there. A poor audience reaction— lack of empathy—may be due to overacting, settings which are too dark or cluttered, poorly memorized lines, or the use of actors unsuited to their parts and to each other. If the theme of a play is not acceptable or convincing, a poor response on the part of the audience is inevitable. Of course, the individual backgrounds of the onlookers and their states of mind also affect their reactions to a play.

*Discussion*

1. Are there any elements not mentioned in this section which have appealed to you as you have watched plays on the stage, on the motion-picture screen, or on television?

2. Had any of the ideas or considerations mentioned in this section been familiar to you previously? If so, which ones?

3. Have any themes struck you with special force as you have watched plays? What are they?

4. Do you agree with the comments about acting in this section? Can you think of any actors or actresses who fulfill these requirements? Who are they?

5. Explain *empathy.* Give some examples of plays where you have been able to identify emotionally with the characters and their life situations.

## Watching Television

With only thirty, sixty, or ninety minutes in which to tell his story, the television playwright cannot create as intricate plots or as subtle characters as the stage playwrights. Under the constant pressure of time, the television dramatist establishes characters and their problems rapidly and proceeds to the resolution without delay. Another important influence on the writing of television drama is the consideration that television audiences vary widely as to their ages and backgrounds. This diversity, plus economic pressures demanding that television be understood by large numbers of people, tests the writer's skill in selecting material and writing dialogue.

As a student of the theater, you should soon learn to distinguish between live television and "canned" entertainment. A live show often has an appeal which one on film may lack. A live show is shot in complete sequence and the actors thus have an accumulated emotional response not possible in

A mother and daughter relax in front of their television set and watch Gloria Vanderbilt and Jean Pierre Aumont in a "U.S. Steel Hour" drama.

the short, disconnected scenes taken for a film. This immediacy produces spontaneity and freshness in live shows. Of course, in such shows you may see little errors not apparent in films—an actor's hesitancy over a line, a camera or microphone extending into the set, shadows hiding a face— which are, unfortunately, talked about longer than the rest of the play. As is true for a stage play, no scenes can be cut or actors shifted once a live television production starts. In films, or canned programs, each short bit is shot and reshot many times and from varying angles and then edited and cut so that something near technical perfection is possible. Also, the settings for films are unrestricted by time, or place, or even reality, since the world of fantasy is limited only by the imagination of the director and the skill of the cameraman. The wide open spaces of land and ocean, foreign countries, the realms of dreams and ideas, are possible, practicable settings. In contrast, the television studios in which live shows are produced are so restricted that the sets often must be limited to a single tree for a forest or a section of a room with distinctive furniture for a house. The changes in scenes are made by having the actors move from one set to another in a split second. You can see that the whole technique of producing a live show is very different from that used for a filmed show.

In applying to live television plays the four considerations discussed on pages 26 to 30, you have the right to expect a well-knit plot, one or two carefully drawn characters, and a really exciting climax. The photography should be clear-cut against uncluttered sets, and the acting should be natural and spontaneous. As you judge the actors in a live television play, keep in mind the fact that their rehearsal time before microphones and cameras is very short. Even though the action and interpretations have been worked out in previous rehearsals, there is a strain in adapting to the sets, lights, and cameras. It would be unfair to expect the actors to give the kind of finished performances you see in some televised films.

In judging either live or filmed television dramas, it is important to keep in mind the special values of each. Live television offers immediacy and freshness combined with the rapid action of a condensed plot centering around a few characters. Filmed shows can provide more complicated and polished productions, as well as greater variety and dramatic interest.

*Discussion*

1. Do you prefer live or filmed television shows? Give the reasons for your preference.

2. Have you seen any errors in production on live television shows? Have they spoiled your enjoyment of the play? If so, in what way?

3. What spectaculars have you seen? Which have you enjoyed the most? Why? Have you been disappointed in any of them? Why?

4. Can you give any examples of television shows which you felt had been "written down" to the audience? Any that have been too "highbrow"?

5. Have you noticed any differences between the acting on live shows and that on film? What were they?

6. What are some of the great films of the past which you have seen at home? Have you become emotionally involved in them, or have they seemed too old-fashioned?

7. What actors and actresses have you seen in old films on television looking years younger than you are accustomed to seeing them? Can you explain why they are still popular in current motion pictures?

8. Has color television spoiled black-and-white programs for you? Why?

## Shopping for Films

You probably do not attend movies as frequently as did young people before 1950, since seeing films at home on television is so much simpler now and opportunities are so frequent. However, as a drama enthusiast, you probably do go to the movies more often than the average high school student. The effort and money involved nowadays has naturally led to a more critical attitude on the part of potential motion-picture audiences who can now literally shop for films and select only those which will give them more pleasure than television films do.

Immense screens, colossal scenery, use of color, and marvelous photographic and sound effects certainly provide our theaters with many pictures well worth making an effort to see. Many magazines and newspapers carry reviews of important productions. These reviews can help you determine which films are worth seeing and which are not. Exceptionally good movies are "musts" for the student of dramatics; your whole class may wish to attend such films together and then discuss them later in class.

Long ago Gilbert Seldes said, "The movie is the imagination of mankind in action." For half a century millions of people in rural areas and isolated villages and in towns and cities the world over have flocked to the movies. It is a universal form of theater, one which reaches untold numbers of people. Many nations are producing good films, and the "dubbing in" of languages makes possible their presentation in all countries. In Europe today the American traveler can see his screen favorites apparently speaking fluent French, Italian, German, or Spanish, depending upon where the movie is being shown. Likewise, audiences here have the opportunity to see and understand the best foreign films.

In addition to the four considerations for judging all plays (see pages 26 to 30), you should keep in mind the peculiar art values of the cinema,

A scene from the 1959 Academy Award winning film *Gigi*. In addition to being judged the best picture of the season, *Gigi* won Oscars for its direction, its screen play, its costumes, its film editing, its musical score, its color photography, and its art direction.

Courtesy of MGM

especially in the wide-screen productions. Fundamentally, a motion picture is movement in light, and the camera is the most potent element in production. Films are being produced all over the world with the actual settings of far-off places making them truly authentic. The camera can show you what characters are seeing and feeling and can take you into their past and future as well as their present experiences. It can permit you to live with them on every plane, even in their dreams and secrets.

You should follow closely the work of the motion-picture director, for he bears the burden of a film. He coordinates the thousands of human and mechanical details of the production into an artistic whole. He decides how best to communicate the meaning of a story. He selects the cast and inspires the actors and hundreds of other helpers to their highest effort. He works personally with the cameraman, art director, sound expert, costume designer, and all the technicians to create a unified whole. His use of color for emotional effects and of music as a psychological influence contributes to the total production. It is the director's responsibility to create a unique screen product in which mental processes can be visualized, settings of reality or fantasy can be depicted, and any action can be presented—unhampered by time, place, or human limitations.

*Discussion*

1. What are the five pictures you consider the best you have ever seen? State your reasons for liking them.

2. What do you think are the standards by which the average person determines his favorite movies?

3. Bring in a list of your favorite directors. Describe the individual techniques you have noted in their pictures.

4. Do you think a familiarity with the techniques of film production would help or hinder your enjoyment of movies? Why?

5. Do you enjoy going to a movie more than to a play? Why?

6. What do you think will be some of the innovations in the motion-picture industry in the future?

7. Do you prefer the new wide screen to the older type? Why or why not?

8. Are you now going to the movies more than you did when you first got your television set? Explain why or why not.

9. Do foreign films and stars appeal to you? Which do you like most or least? Why?

10. Do you find musical accompaniments to films distracting or helpful in stirring your emotions? Describe several scenes to which you reacted strongly.

11. What magazine reviews of new movies do you read? Do you usually agree with them? Do you make a point of seeing highly recommended films?

## Going to the Theater

The greatest pleasure a drama enthusiast has is going to the legitimate theater, to plays presented on the stage by living actors and actresses. Even in these casual days, it is a thrilling experience to dress up for a matinee or evening performance, arrive at the lobby full of well-groomed people in a holiday mood chatting about actors and plays, enter the illuminated auditorium, and settle back to look through the program while waiting for the play to begin. Then comes the ecstatic moment when the house lights dim, the footlights come up, and the curtain rises on the first act. Going to the theater can be a real adventure, if you are in a receptive mood, ready to lose yourself in another world.

No matter what degree of mechanical perfection screen drama may attain, it can never take the place of the legitimate theater. It can never create that intangible, magnetic quality which passes across the footlights from actor to audience. It can never become the unity—light and color, voice and movement, mass and perspective, imagination and reality—which is a play produced by living actors before a living audience. Living actors can stir an audience as their pictures on a screen can never do. As you watch the fleeting expressions on their faces, their meaningful gestures and spontaneous movements, and as you listen to their beautifully modulated voices and significant speeches, you are really enjoying the drama at its best. If you are fortunate enough to see a fine play, beautifully acted and produced, you will probably remember it for the rest of your life.

Similarly, a stage set dressed with real furniture and appropriate properties artistically selected and arranged under atmospheric lighting creates a mood that a television or motion-picture play cannot achieve. You can enjoy seeing how the director has used contrast in casting, staging, and costuming; planned action to create a balanced stage picture and a definite center of interest; created various moods through lighting. Most of all, you can see how he has built the entire production around the theme so the playwright's message is not left in doubt when the final curtain falls.

It is at a legitimate play that the audience's reaction really counts. Actors respond quickly to an enthusiastic reception and give their best, often overcoming inherent defects in a play by their clever technique. If a play deals with fundamental human emotions, presents a definite phase of a universal theme, and is produced in an adequate manner, it is certain to give you real pleasure. Much of your enjoyment can come from listening to comments between the acts and at the end of the performance and seeing how your own reactions compare with those of others in the audience.

As your class studies the various phases of theater work, you will get more and more enjoyment from watching plays. Go to every play you possibly can. Even failures can teach you something. Analyze the characters and their reactions to their situations and decide how you feel about the theme. Perhaps the most important contribution a fine play offers is insight into the lives of human beings. In real life, you are seldom able to follow the intricate patterns in the lives of people around you. However, in the theater you can see the exact results of decisions and deeds. Thus, your interest in humanity and the problems common to all can be intensified and clarified, and you can begin to grow into a truly understanding person.

*Discussion*

1. Describe a play you have seen to the class, pointing out the difference between it and movie versions of the same play. Explain your reactions to both.

2. What plays have your parents or grandparents seen and greatly enjoyed? Which actors and actresses?

3. Name several Broadway actors who have become famous "overnight." Have you seen the plays in which they appeared or read about them? Why do you think they became famous so rapidly?

4. At this point in the course, what do you think will interest you most when you see your next play?

## READING PLAYS

Reading plays is one of the most exciting and satisfying ways to spend your leisure hours. Today more opportunity is afforded for reading plays than ever before, because most plays produced in New York, London, Paris, and other theatrical centers are promptly published in book form for the benefit of the vast audience of drama lovers who may never have the opportunity to see them on the stage.

*Theatre Arts*, an excellent monthly magazine, covers the entire theatrical field. Each issue contains the complete text and fine photographs of a current play. Your class or club may even wish to subscribe to this magazine. You can also look up copies, new and old, at your school and public library and use them to keep up to date on the theater. The Sunday issues of *The New York Times* and some other newspapers, as well as the theater sections of all the good magazines, can also keep you informed concerning the world of the drama. Very often they list the titles of plays which have recently been published in book form.

Do you realize that reading plays is less time-consuming than reading novels? The playwright must condense his wordage; he must find the exact

A bookstore displays some of the many plays published in book form and available for personal libraries.

word or phrase to serve his many purposes of characterization, plot advancement, and theme development. He has no time for the long descriptive or philosophical passages which a novelist may employ to explain his thoughts. The playwright's characters must come to life and sparkle in stimulating circumstances if he is to hold his audience. As you read plays, the secret is to visualize the persons, settings, and actions in your mind's eye.

If you go to the library and look at the drama and theater collections, you will find thousands of fascinating books. The plays themselves cover shelf after shelf and include everything from English translations of the old Greek dramas down to current productions. There are hundreds of anthologies containing various types of plays by many different dramatists. By browsing a while you should always be able to find a play you will enjoy reading.

It may be a good idea to begin with a play you have seen on television or in the movies so that you have the memory of the scenes to clarify the action for you. It will be interesting to find changes in characters, sequence of events, and especially in the ending. You may also want to read other plays by the same author.

Your English textbooks, particularly the literature anthologies, are another good source of excellent and carefully edited plays. After you get used to the telling of a story in play form, you will want to read all the different types of plays you will be meeting as the course advances. You will find that you want to own some of the plays yourself so you can read and reread favorite scenes aloud for practice and pleasure. Soon you will have started a library which will give you lasting joy. You can go beyond reading plays alone; occasionally you can meet with a group of friends and read plays aloud together. Perhaps you can find a rumpus room, a garage, or even an attic in which you can dramatize the plays as you read them. After a while, you may be inviting other friends to come and hear the play readings.

As you read to yourself, you have time to think about what is being said without the necessity of keeping pace with the rapid action. You can decide what is accomplished for the plot in every incident, analyze the characters and their problems, and, best of all, take time to relish the humor and enjoy the fine writing in the dialogue. The greatest satisfaction in reading a play lies in the fact that you can retrace the theme, check the dramatist's methods of pointing it up and really understand what the heart of his meaning is. You may even find yourself moved by the impact of a good play. After so many years of watching the fleeting impressions of television and movies, you will thoroughly enjoy quietly living with the lines and savoring them. You will probably find that you much prefer reading a good play to watching a poor one. An outline to help you analyze a play after you have read it is given on page 83.

*Discussion*

1. What form of literature do you prefer for leisure reading—a novel, a play, a short story, a poem, an essay, a newspaper, or a magazine? Give reasons for your answer.

2. Explain the statement, "Reading a play is less time-consuming than reading a novel." Give examples if you can.

3. Have you heard lines in plays, on television, or in the movies which you wanted to remember? Did you then try to get a copy of the play to read and look up the lines you liked? What were the lines?

4. Cite an example of a play you have first seen and then read. What were some of the things you discovered about the play in reading it which you did not notice while it was actually being performed?

*Chapter 3*

# Beginning to Act

For centuries human beings have loved to act. In primitive times, when men were recounting tales of their adventures, they imitated animals, the other people they encountered, and even spirits and gods —often disguised behind grotesque or hideous masks. Today children dramatize many phases of the life they see around them, and adults like to play charades and other dramatic games which enable them to assume new personalities. Men, women, and young people, who would not dream of acting in formal plays, love costume parties and spontaneous shows.

Perhaps, when you are telling about an experience, you like to imitate the different people involved. If so, you already appreciate the kind of thing an actor has to do when playing a part. You know how important it is to notice the way people talk and the kinds of mannerisms they have.

Opportunities for this kind of acting practice are unending. The people you meet every day provide a steady source of material for impersonations. Soon after meeting or getting to know a particularly interesting person, you can go off by yourself and try to re-create that personality through action and dialogue. Let your memory recall your over-all impression of the person, his physical appearance, his gestures, and his speech patterns. Then, using your imagination, try to feel his emotions in a specific situation and speak and act as he would. If you keep up such practice, you should see a definite improvement in your acting ability. You will gradually gain skill in expressing emotions effectively with your voice and body, and you will find it easier to create different kinds of characters.

## READING SCENES ALOUD

The actor must visualize in detail the person whose character he is assuming —his age, size, clothing, and movements. He must also study the part until he understands the moods, aspirations, and reasons for the character's doing and saying what he does.

The first and easiest step in learning to act is to read aloud play scenes in which people have strong feelings and express themselves convincingly. As the course advances, you will have the opportunity to study the skills related to the actor's art. For this first experience, however, you can forget about such techniques and have the fun of finding out how your voice, aided by your posture and spontaneous facial and bodily responses, can create a personality different from your own.

The selections on pages 42 to 51 are all suitable ones to start with because they present people reacting realistically to situations of interest. Read them all over carefully, using your imagination to help you decide how each character looks and feels. Select a scene you like and a character you feel you can interpret successfully.

Prepare the scene for reading aloud with classmates who seem suited to the other parts in the scene. Perhaps your teacher may prefer to assign the roles for this first exercise. He may expect you merely to express the meaning of your character's lines as you understand it. Decide with your teacher whether you will read the scene from your seat, attempting only the vocal interpretation, or take several days to work on it and then read your scene in front of the class. Whichever way your class and your teacher decide to handle the assignment, this is your first chance to prove that you can forget yourself and make another person come alive. At the end of the term, if there is time, it will be interesting to do exactly the same scene and see how much you have improved.

In preparing your role, the first thing to do is to get acquainted with it by reading the entire scene and, if possible, the whole play. Then let yourself go; read the lines aloud, trying to sound as much like your character as you can. Move about if you want to, as you get into the spirit of the situation, and let your face and body help you express the emotion the words suggest. Next, sit down and do some good hard work on the part. Remember that sharing an idea with your audience is your only excuse for speaking or reading aloud. Before you can do this, you need to find out exactly what the lines mean.

There are four vital words you should memorize at once and put into practice in every assignment in dramatics. They are *think, see, feel, speak.*

To *think*, you first look up the meaning and pronunciation of every un-familiar word in the scene. Then you read the lines aloud again, thinking as you read, "What am I saying?" You can make the thought clear, when you understand it, by emphasizing important words and minimizing unimpor-tant ones. Put words together in phrases or thought groups and get your breath between them so you will not run ideas together. You break the thought if you breathe just because you have to, with no regard for mean-ing. By breathing between thought groups, you can use your breath to clarify rather than confuse the meaning of the passage. It is also helpful to take time enough to make the thought clear instead of rushing through the lines. This is an error beginners often make, and you should try to avoid it.

To *see*, you visualize your character in detail, imagining exactly how he looks, what he is wearing, how he stands and moves. It may help, at this early stage, to imagine some actor you think would suit the part or some person in real life who is like your character and to see him in the part.

To *feel*, you put yourself in the place of the character emotionally, asking yourself what mood he is in and why, as he speaks his first lines. Then you decide whether he changes his mood during the scene and at what point and for what reasons he does so. Try to sympathize with his feelings and to understand them in relation to his situation and to the other characters.

Only when you have thought the meaning out with greatest care, visual-ized the character, and felt the emotions involved, are you ready to *speak* the lines effectively. Then your voice, probably to your great surprise, will approximate the right tone. Reread the lines aloud, moving about again, if you want to, until you feel you are one with the role. Then stop worrying about it until you have a chance to read the scene with the others.

It will be exciting to get the reactions of others to your interpretation. If they think you are all wrong, explain how you have thought the passage out carefully and then decide for yourself whether or not to follow their suggestions. You undoubtedly will get some new ideas to take home and try out, but do not change your interpretation unless you feel it is right to do so. If you have decided to move about as you read, you can add to your four key words a fifth one, *move*. Many beginners find that moving about as they read and rehearse is helpful in memorizing a part. Practice in this way until you feel at ease with the lines but not tired of them.

After you have rehearsed with the others again, come to class ready to do your best. If you are nervous, try not to think about it. Instead, focus on your character and concentrate on how he feels. You are simply having fun interpreting your first part, not hunting a job or proving that you are a great actor or actress. Pick up your lines quickly on your *cues*—the actions or speeches of other characters which immediately precede your own speeches. Remember to take time to read clearly and to feel the emotion before you speak. Relax, for you will want to change your voice as the scene proceeds and you cannot do so with a tense, tight throat. Don't worry about your grade. For this assignment it will not be vital, although, of course, you will be eager to see how your teacher and classmates feel about your interpretation of the part.

Don't be discouraged, however, if you and they are not satisfied with this first attempt. Your voice will seldom react as you expect it to at first, and you easily may become too excited to do as well before the class as you did when rehearsing by yourself. On the other hand, with the stimulus of an audience, you may perform far better than you expect and have the glorious experience of moving your hearers to a definite emotional response. If they look startled, or laugh in the right places, or actually applaud, you can be really thrilled. If they don't respond at all, talk your reading over with the teacher and get his reaction so you can improve with the next assignment. Keep his suggestions in mind as you work on the part again, incorporating them until you are satisfied that you are reading the part as well as you can.

*Scenes to Read Aloud*

1. *Time Out for Ginger* by Ronald Alexander

*The scene is the living room of a modern American home. Jeannie and Joan, teenagers, are discussing their embarrassment over their fourteen-year-old sister, Ginger, who has recently humiliated the captain of the school track team by challenging him to a race and beating him. Now she is playing football, and her two sisters regard this as shocking. Agnes, the mother, tries to explain why Ginger's activities are her own business.*

JEANNIE. Hello, darling.
AGNES. Hello.
JOAN. How's the play going to be tonight, Miss Bernhardt?
JEANNIE. Guy says I look better than Helen did dress rehearsal night.
AGNES. Helen who?
JEANNIE. Helen Hayes, Mother.
AGNES. Excuse me.
JEANNIE. He's the most fascinating man.
AGNES. He is? Just a week ago you hated him.
JEANNIE. That's before I understood the theater. He wasn't being mean, he was simply being caustic.
AGNES. Oh, I see.

Jeannie, Agnes, and Joan talk over Ginger's athletic activities in the Broadway production of *Time Out for Ginger*. Ginger's photograph, as it appeared on the cover of *Life* magazine, hangs behind them.

JEANNIE. He says I have all the makings of a great actress.
AGNES. He does?
JEANNIE. He says I should come to New York.
AGNES. Don't lie down on that pink cloud with those dirty shoes on.
JEANNIE. Don't you think I'll be a great actress, Mother?
AGNES. I'll come backstage tonight and tell you, Jeannie. One thing I do think is that you and your sister show very poor taste in not being at the football game today.
JEANNIE. Oh, no.
JOAN. Nobody goes to the games this year.
AGNES. You're wrong. Your father tells me the stands are packed every week, and most people come just to see your sister kick the ball around before the game begins.
JEANNIE. They'll get tired of that when she doesn't play.
AGNES. Are those grapes terribly sour, girls?
JEANNIE. Anyway, it's all Daddy's fault we can't see the games.
AGNES. What?
JEANNIE. If he hadn't let Ginger play, we Juniors would be allowed to go.
JOAN. That's right.

AGNES. Now, listen, just a minute, girls. Joan, when you thought gym was being abolished your father allowed you to give up the part in the play,
didn't he?

JOAN. Yes.

AGNES. Jeannie, he allowed you to play in *Victoria*, didn't he?

JEANNIE. Yes, Mother.

AGNES. So basically you were both permitted your free pursuits. Is that right?
Then why do you feel that your father is wrong in not denying Virginia
the same right you had?

JOAN. We don't believe a girl should be allowed to play football.

JEANNIE. It's just not right, Mother.

AGNES. In other words, anything you disagree with is wrong and should be
stopped, is that it?

JOAN. Well, not exactly.

JEANNIE. Well, we feel Ginger should be allowed to do whatever she wants to
do, as long as it's not playing football.

JOAN. That's the resolution passed by the girls of the senior and junior classes.

AGNES. By majority vote?

JEANNIE. Of course, Mother.

AGNES. I see. By democratic procedure, you have both decided to tear up the
Bill of Rights. That's very interesting.

JOAN. Mother, we haven't.

AGNES. If you hadn't, you'd defend Virginia's right to play whether you dis-
agreed with it or not. Any questions? You know you could both take a
very good lesson from your father. He stands to lose his job but he'd
rather take that chance than to deprive your sister of the freedom of her
choice.

JEANNIE. Gee, Daddy is a kind of Joan of Arc character. Isn't he?

AGNES. Yes, voices and all!

JEANNIE. Well, from now on I'm going to the games.

JOAN. Jeannie!

JEANNIE. I'm going over to Ginger's side, and if Eddie Davis makes one more
remark about her or Dad, I'll kick him all over school.

JOAN. What?

JEANNIE. He started the whole thing about the boycott because he was mad
at Ginger.

JOAN. Well, why shouldn't he be?

JEANNIE. Why should he be?

JOAN. She ruined his prestige as captain of the track team.

JEANNIE. From now on, I go along with Ginger.

JOAN. How dare you!

JEANNIE. You're upsetting me emotionally, and I have a performance tonight.

JOAN. She's are traitor toward American womanhood, per se.

**2.** *The Maker of Dreams* by Oliphant Down

*The scene is the kitchen of an old cottage, lit by moonlight shining through a casement window and the glow from a fireplace. Pierrot, a clown, is dressed in the classic costume—white pantaloons and a large white jacket with big buttons. A mysterious stranger, dressed in a green frock coat, knee breeches, and bright shoes, has entered. His air and manner is that of someone not quite real. Knowing Pierrot's fickleness and his poor treatment of Pierrette, the stranger speaks of dreams, and tries to show Pierrot that he really does love Pierrette. The play is a fantasy and has no specific period in time.*

MANUFACTURER. Pierrot—I am a maker of dreams, little things that glide about into people's hearts and make them glad. Haven't you often wondered where the swallows go to in the autumn? They come to my workshop and tell me who wants a dream and what happened to the dreams they took with them in the spring.

PIERROT. Oh, I say, you can't expect me to believe that.

MANUFACTURER. When flowers fade, have you never wondered where their colors go to, or what becomes of all the butterflies in the winter? There isn't much winter about my workshop.

PIERROT. I had never thought of it before.

MANUFACTURER. It's a kind of lost property office, where every beautiful thing that the world has neglected finds its way. And there I make my celebrated dream, the dream that is called "love."

PIERROT. Ho! Ho! Now we're talking.

MANUFACTURER. You don't believe in it?

PIERROT. Yes, in a way. But it doesn't last. If there is form, there isn't soul, and, if there is soul, there isn't form. Oh, I've tried hard enough to believe it, but, after the first wash, the colors run.

MANUFACTURER. You only got hold of a substitute. Wait until you get the genuine article.

PIERROT. But how is one to tell it?

MANUFACTURER. There are heaps of signs. As soon as you get the real thing, your shoulder-blades begin to tingle. That's love's wings sprouting. And, next, you want to soar up among the stars and sit on the roof of heaven and sing to the moon. Of course, that is because I put such a lot of the moon into my dreams. I break bits off until it's nearly all gone, and then I let it grow big again. It grows very quickly, as I dare say you've noticed. After a fortnight it is ready for use once more.

PIERROT. This is all most awfully fascinating. And do the swallows bring all the dreams?

MANUFACTURER. Not always; I have other messengers. Every night when the big clock strikes twelve, a day slips down from the calendar, and runs away to my workshop in the Land of Long Ago. I give him a touch of scarlet and a gleam of gold, and say, "Go back, little Yesterday, and be a memory in the world." But my best dreams I keep for today. I buy babies and fit them up with a dream, and then send them complete and carriage paid— in the usual manner.

PIERROT. I've been dreaming all my life, but they've always been dreams I made myself. I suppose I don't mix 'em properly.

MANUFACTURER. You leave out the very essence of them. You must put in a little sorrow, just to take away the over-sweetness. I found that out very soon, so I took a little of the fresh dew that made pearls in the early morning, and I sprinkled my dreams with the gift of tears.

PIERROT. The gift of tears! How beautiful! You know, I should rather like to try a real one. Not one of my own making.

MANUFACTURER. Well, there are plenty about, if you only look for them.

PIERROT. That is all very well, but who's going to look about for stray dreams?

MANUFACTURER. I once made a dream that would just suit you. I slipped it inside a baby. That was twenty years ago, and the baby is now a full-grown woman, with great blue eyes and fair hair.

PIERROT. It's a lot of use merely telling me about her.

MANUFACTURER. I'll do more. When I shipped her to the world, I kept the bill of lading. Here it is. You shall have it.


3. *Sabrina Fair* by Samuel Taylor

*The scene is the Larrabee mansion, Long Island, New York. Sabrina, a young lady in her middle twenties, is the daughter of the Larrabee's chauffeur. She has grown up on the estate, along with the Larrabee sons, Linus and David. Now she has just returned from school in Paris, and the two young men see her as a charming and beautiful woman. They both fall in love with her, but Linus, believing that being in love exposes one to heartaches, is unwilling to tell Sabrina. In this scene, his Aunt Julia scolds him for his caution and foolishness.*

LINUS. I should hate to see you domesticated, Sabrina. There are so many wonderful things you want to do.

SABRINA. Were you afraid I might be forgetting?

LINUS. Stand still and choose, Sabrina. You're so excited by the things you learned in Paris that you're galloping off in all directions If you want to see everything and do everything and live an active life in a passive world, you'd better get used to the idea that you have to live it alone.

SABRINA. Why? Why? Suddenly I find you know me better than anyone else in this world—but why this terrible compulsion to make me into your own image? If you are the cat that walks alone, must I walk alone too?

LINUS. Sooner or later you learn that there's a conspiracy of little people to cut you down to their size. And then you grow up and make your choice: to live on their terms or your own—

**David, Aunt Julia, and Linus listen while Sabrina argues with one of her suitors in the Broadway production of *Sabrina Fair*.**

SABRINA. And what is the next step?—Never to let anyone impose his terms on me? Not even you?

LINUS. That's right.

SABRINA. And how shall I prevent it?

LINUS. By imposing your terms on others.

SABRINA. That takes power. I see. It is the most exciting game in the world, isn't it? With life-size figures. And the one who loves is captured.

LINUS. The answer is: not to love.

SABRINA. And be without love? (AUNT JULIA *enters.*) Have you made your choice, Linus? And is it irrevocable? Power corrupts, you know. And absolute power corrupts absolutely.

LINUS. Where did you get that? Out of a book?

SABRINA. I beg you to think that you may be mistaken.

JULIA. Why don't you hit him? It's the only thing he'll understand. What are you trying to do to this girl?

LINUS. How do you know I am trying to do anything?

JULIA. I have a room with a view! You're afraid to take her and you're afraid to lose her, so you're warning her off the rest of the world.—You want to own her without being owned. You can't unbend, you won't give in.

You're stiff-necked, self-sufficient, autocratic. (*She begins to cry.*) And you've been my favorite man since the day you were born.

LINUS. Aunt Julia—

JULIA. If you come near me, I'll kick you!—(*She turns to Sabrina.*) And as for you! You listen to me! If anyone tries to tell you that she travels the farthest who travels alone, believe me, when you get there you'll find it wasn't worth the trip. (*To Linus*) Get into her life or get out of her life! But don't stand around playing God!


4. *Life with Father* by Howard Lindsay and Russel Crouse

*The scene is the morning room of Clarence Day's home at 420 Madison Avenue, New York City, in the late 1880's. Mr. Day is an elegant, somewhat pompous gentleman; he is also an amusing tyrant who rules his wife, Vinnie, and their four sons with thunderous roars and oaths. However, Vinnie defeats him constantly with her naiveté and charm. In this scene, he is trying vainly to instruct her in how to keep her household accounts on a sound business basis.*

VINNIE. Clare, dear, I'm afraid I'm going to need some more money.

FATHER. What for?

VINNIE. You were complaining of the coffee this morning. Well, that nice French drip coffeepot is broken—and you know how it got broken.

FATHER. Never mind that, Vinnie. As I remember, that coffeepot cost five dollars and something. Here's six dollars. And when you get it enter the exact amount in the ledger downstairs.

VINNIE. Thank you, Clare.

FATHER. We can't go on month after month having the household accounts in such a mess.

VINNIE. No, and I've thought of a system that will make my bookkeeping perfect.

FATHER. I'm certainly relieved to hear that. What is it?

VINNIE. Well, Clare, dear, you never make half the fuss over how much I've spent as you do over my not being able to remember what I've spent it for.

FATHER. Exactly. This house must be run on a business basis. That's why I insist on your keeping books.

VINNIE. That's the whole point, Clare. All we have to do is open charge accounts everywhere and the stores will do the bookkeeping for me.

FATHER. Wait a minute, Vinnie—

VINNIE. Then when the bills come in you'd know exactly where your money had gone.

FATHER. I certainly would. Vinnie, I get enough bills as it is.

VINNIE. Yes, and those bills always help. They show you just where I spent the money. Now if we had charge accounts everywhere—

**Vinnie and Clarence Day go over the household accounts in the Broadway production of** *Life with Father.*

FATHER. Now, Vinnie, I don't know about that.

VINNIE. Clare, dear, don't you hate those arguments we have every month? I certainly do. Not to have those I should think would be worth something to you.

FATHER. Well—we'll see how it works out.

5. *The Fabulous Invalid* by Moss Hart and George S. Kaufman

*The action of this play, a fantasy about theater people, takes place in the Alexandria Theatre, New York City. Laurence and Paula, a famous husband-and-wife acting team, are dead; they have returned to haunt the theater in which they were appearing when they died. The time is around 1900.*

PAULA. Why, Larry—

LAURENCE. Yes, darling.

PAULA. We're still in the theater.

LAURENCE. Why, yes, we are, aren't we? Curious.

THE DOORMAN. Good evening!

PAULA. Good evening..

THE DOORMAN. Don't be frightened. It's all right. I'm dead too, you know.

PAULA. Oh!

LAURENCE. I don't think I quite understand.

THE DOORMAN. It's all right. I've been dead for years.

LAURENCE. Well—well, then what are you doing *here?* What are *we* doing here?

THE DOORMAN. Well, what it comes down to is—you're ghosts. So am I.

LAURENCE. But—why are you in this theater?

THE DOORMAN. I came around for the opening. I go to them all. You see, I used to be an actor, just like you.

LAURENCE. But—but that doesn't explain—

THE DOORMAN. I never got to be a star, exactly, but I was a good actor. I played with your father, Miss Kingsley, before you were born.

PAULA. Did you? Larry, think of that!—What was he like then? What was he playing?

LAURENCE. Paula, please!—Won't you explain all this, sir?

THE DOORMAN. There's no hurry. You'll be dead a long time. Now, let me see, what was I saying? Oh, yes—I was a good actor.—Well, this is the only way I can explain it. You see actors aren't like other people, are they? You know that yourself. As a matter of fact, they're like nothing on God's green earth. And I think God realizes that, because even when an actor dies, it's different.

PAULA. It is?

LAURENCE. How?

THE DOORMAN. Well, when anybody else dies—ordinary people—they go to heaven, don't they? I mean, if everything is all right. Well, when an actor dies, he doesn't *have* to go to heaven. Not if he dies right in the theater.

PAULA. But—why wouldn't anybody want to go to heaven?

THE DOORMAN. I'll tell you something about heaven.

PAULA. What?

THE DOORMAN. There isn't any theater there.

PAULA. Oh, Larry!

LAURENCE. Please go on.

THE DOORMAN. Oh, heaven's all right. I liked it for a while. It's restful, and—the music is good. But after a while I began to get restless. I didn't know what was the matter with me. After all, there I was in heaven—you'd think I'd be satisfied. And then suddenly I knew what it was. I missed the theater. I kept wondering what kind of season they were having, if any new stars had come along, what kind of plays they were doing now—I was downright unhappy. And of course they *noticed* it, and then they explained to me that there's a special rule for actors if they die in the theater. That I could come back here and hang around.

PAULA. Oh, Larry!

THE DOORMAN. And that's what you can do. Of course, you can go to heaven if you want to—don't let me talk you out of it—but you'd be back here in no time at all. I know real actors when I see them.

LAURENCE. Then the choice is up to us?

THE DOORMAN. That's right.

LAURENCE. Paula.

PAULA. Yes, dear?

LAURENCE. I offer you the Kingdom of Heaven—or the Theater. Which shall it be?

PAULA. Oh, Larry! The Theater.

THE DOORMAN. Good! You won't regret it—you'll have a wonderful time. You can go everywhere, see everything—all through the years. Why, I've been in a dozen theaters tonight. Saw *your* play, took a look at Bernhardt, even jumped out on the road and caught a little bit of Joe Jefferson. Heaven was never like that.

PAULA. Larry, it *is* heaven!

THE DOORMAN. Oh, I forgot to tell you one thing. There's only one chance that you might have to go up there.

LAURENCE. Oh!

PAULA. What is it?

THE DOORMAN. Now don't be frightened—it never can happen. But here it is. If the theater ever dies, we've got to go back.

LAURENCE. I don't understand.

PAULA. There'll always be the Theater.

THE DOORMAN. Of *course* there will, but I'm just telling you what they told me. If anything ever happens so that there's no more theater—if the theater ever dies—we go back. That's all I know.

PAULA. Then—we've got Eternity!

LAURENCE. Paula, it hasn't been taken away from us. Think of it, Paula! Think what lies ahead! Plays yet unwritten, stars that haven't been born yet. We'll see it all, Paula—we'll see it all.

THE DOORMAN. Yes, sir!

PAULA. All the magic and wonder that we love! This isn't death, Larry—it's life!


## IMPROVISING SCENES

In your classwork, putting on impromptu scenes is one of the best ways to gain confidence and get acquainted with the other students. It is usually more fun than more formal acting and an excellent way to learn some of the fundamentals of stage work. Since you must make up both the words and the action, doing spontaneous scenes takes more imagination than reading scenes aloud, but it is excellent practice.

With the class divided into groups of not more than four each, select one incident around which to build your scene and decide whether it will be the opening event, the climax, or the conclusion. Decide on the main idea you want to put over and on the general mood. You may do any kind of scene you want—comic or sad, fanciful or realistic—but each character must be a distinct type, totally different from the others. You should avoid such scenes as those involving girls in a dormitory or boys as members of a baseball team. The greater the difference in age, personality, and type of the characters, the more contrast your scene will contain. Work out your stage setting carefully, knowing just where the real or imaginary entrances will be. You probably will have nothing more than a table and a few chairs to work around. You will not use any doors, windows, or heavy props, but you can explain what they are and where they would be located before the action starts. Even better, suggest entrances and major props by your acting. You may carry any small articles you need, since this is not pantomime. You may even use costumes and make-up, if the class as a whole decides to do so. In turning the classroom into a street, ballroom, theater dressing room, office, or whatever you choose, you are developing not only your own imagination but also that of the rest of the class. They will see whatever you make clear to them, first by your explanation and then by your performance.

You can get your material from any source you wish. Some suggestions are newspaper clippings, cartoon captions, and anecdotes from magazines; events in your own or your parents' and friends' lives; or historical and literary sources. The suggestions at the end of this section may be of use.

In preparing your part, make use of the suggestions on page 40 for reading your first scene. Visualize your character in detail and try to feel his emotions. Consider the relation of your character to the others. Which characters do you like? Dislike? Admire greatly? Fear? Make up dialogue which you feel will be appropriate to your character and to the situation he is in, though it will not necessarily be the exact wording to use before the class. Before you enter, take on the physical attitude of your character in accordance with his age, size, and mood. Walk in character as you enter and remember that your audience is out front. Talk loud enough to be heard and don't hide behind other people or pieces of furniture. Try not to stand with the others in groups on one side of the stage or in straight lines; instead, keep your stage well balanced. Take plenty of time to speak and move so you can create a definite impression. Most important, keep in character all the time—listen and speak as he would in the situation, and lose yourself in his actions and reactions.

After working in groups, you can try to develop individual characters in definite situations reacting to imaginary persons, or crowds, or showing particular moods. It is harder to work by yourself than in a group, but you can take more time to create a personality by yourself and to feel more deeply.

As you get more practice in improvising scenes, you can begin to learn some of the subtleties of acting. You will find that you can stand still without fidgeting and you can make definite gestures when you feel the need, avoiding the little, aimless ones. When you must move to a chair or toward another person, learn to go straight there without rambling. If you are to pick up an article, actually see it before you touch it. In improvised acting, unlike more formal acting, you don't have to worry about giving the impression that you are doing something for the first time, for that is exactly what you are doing.

In these improvisations, keep relaxed and have fun. Don't make the scenes a chore or feel embarrassed at the reactions of the other students. Remember they are on the same spot! Don't let classmates who seem to fall right into a character without apparent effort discourage you from trying to do the same thing. If you keep practicing all sorts of characterizations on the spur of the moment at home, you will find doing so in class much easier. Try being all sorts of people—Joan of Arc at her trial, a star during a television interview, an Olympic champion after a big event, and so on. Get yourself into all sorts of emotional states, laughing out loud and even crying if you can. With no one around, you will not feel silly, and the practice will show in your classwork because you will be more responsive and sensitive to changing moods and situations. You will find your voice and body becoming more flexible and expressive and your impersonations much better. Every now and then, you will realize that you have caught another personality, if just for a moment, and know what it is to feel like an actor!

*Suggestions for Improvisations*

Current Situations

1. Two shopgirls are discussing a floorwalker they especially dislike; he appears and accuses one of them of having stolen a necklace which has disappeared. Work out your own solution.

2. A father meets his fifteen-year-old daughter in the hall at midnight on her return from a party which ended at ten-thirty. Show what happens when the two meet.

3. An elevator is caught between two floors. Work out your own characters, their reactions, and the conclusion.

**4.** A group of strongly contrasted tourists are waiting for their plane to take them back to the United States and are telling what they thought of Paris. An airlines attendant tells them the flight has been canceled. Show the reaction of each person when he finds he must go back to Paris for the night.

Literary Sketches

**1.** Improvise a scene from *The Devil and Daniel Webster* by Stephen Vincent Benét.

**2.** Do a modern version of a scene from any of Shakespeare's plays.

**3.** Improvise situations from Coleridge's *The Rime of the Ancient Mariner* or any other poem which interests you.

**4.** Work up a scene about two modern girls in a foreign country similar to one from *Our Hearts Were Young and Gay* by Cornelia Otis Skinner and Emily Kimbrough.

**5.** Prepare a scene similar to one from *No Time for Sergeants* by Mac Hyman about an army basic training camp of today.

Historical Sketches

**1.** Imitate Joan of Arc trying to tell her mother and father about the voices she has heard commanding her to save France.

**2.** Do an imaginary scene between President Washington and President Eisenhower based on the similarity of their problems as leading generals and presidents involved in disagreements with their Congresses.

Newspaper Clipping Backgrounds

**1.** Use newspaper clippings of exciting situations in the following ways to stimulate your imagination:

    **a.** Take an item and outline several plays based on it, using it in turn as preliminary situation, initial incident, climax, and conclusion.

    **b.** Place two people in one of the situations you have developed and make them talk to each other as naturally as possible.

**2.** Have each member of the class put one clipping into a box from which you can draw items to be dramatized.

## PRODUCING MEMORIZED SCENES

Producing memorized scenes in class will give you a greater sense of accomplishment than either reading or improvising them. You will be able to create a role, memorizing the exact words which the playwright has written, and then giving a fairly accurate interpretation of what he wishes to say. If you take the time to produce a scene carefully, you will have the satisfying feeling of having presented a finished performance. You will find, as you do these assignments, that acting is hard work and demands a sacrifice of time and effort. However, the fun of doing it so far outweighs the exertion that hours spent in rehearsing by yourself and with the group pass quickly.

The importance of exact memorization of lines cannot be stressed too much. Until you are letter-perfect, you cannot really act a part, for your mind is thinking "What do I say next?" instead of creating a character. The first step, as in all reading, is to understand the meaning of the passage perfectly so you are memorizing ideas, not just words. The words will then make sense to you and be easier to fix in your mind, and you will not learn incorrect pronunciation, false emphasis, and poor phrasing.

Always use the "whole" method of memorizing. Repeat the entire part orally over and over again, if the scene is as short as those suggested at the end of this section. Learn a long part by scenes, allowing the unity of a piece of action to determine the length of each scene. Get the entire scene fixed in your mind, then polish it off speech by speech (stanza by stanza if you have a poetic selection) and sentence by sentence. Moving about while memorizing keeps both the body and mind alert. Sitting down in a comfortable chair, with your brain and body relaxed, and reading over dialogue word by word silently is the worst way to memorize. Don't use it!

Select one of the scenes from pages 56 to 67 or one of similar length. If possible, you should read the entire play from which you have selected a scene. Meet with your group, if you have not chosen a one-person scene, and read the whole selection aloud, discussing the characters, the meaning of the lines, any kinds of dialect needed, possible action, necessary furniture and props, and the costuming and make-up you will use.

Then go home and study your role imaginatively. Spend more time than you have before in determining the character's background and his reasons for feeling and acting as he does. Imagine his parents and his childhood; ask yourself whether he might have had experiences similar to any you have had. Decide how you yourself would act if you were in his situation. Try to discover the author's intention in the scene and use this as the basis for your interpretation. Go over the scene many times aloud, noting any changes that creep into your reading. Then begin memorizing.

At the next rehearsal with the group, keep your script in hand but use it only when absolutely necessary. Walk through the action. Use your props in rehearsal as soon as you can give up the script, but be careful not to block yourself with them. Talk to the others in the scene without staring at them every minute. Work toward a presentation that shows real people in real situations.

Try not to get wrapped up in details. Your primary aim is to get the scene over to the class clearly and effectively, making them understand and enjoy it. If you play your part simply and well, you will experience the satisfaction of knowing you have done a good job, and your classmates will react enthusiastically.

*Scenes to Memorize*

1. *Quality Street* by James M. Barrie

*The scene is the charming, orderly sitting room of the Misses Susan and Phoebe Throssel, refined ladies of Quality Street, London. Valentine Brown, a gentleman who is the ladies' friend and counsel, has come calling to announce his enlistment in the army—disappointing news to the Misses Throssel who had thought that Mr. Brown had called to propose marriage to Miss Phoebe. The play takes place during the time of the Napoleonic Wars.*

PHOEBE. Susan, what Mr. Brown is so obliging as to inform us of is not what we expected—not that at all. My dear, he is the gentleman who has enlisted, and he came to tell us that and to say good-bye.

MISS SUSAN. Going away?

**Valentine Brown says good-by to Susan and Phoebe Throssel in the movie** *Quality Street.*

PHOEBE. Yes, dear.

VALENTINE. Am I not the ideal recruit, ma'am: a man without a wife or a mother or a sweetheart?

MISS SUSAN. No sweetheart?

VALENTINE. Have you one for me, Miss Susan?

PHOEBE. Susan, we shall have to tell him now. You dreadful man, you will laugh and say it is just like Quality Street. But indeed since I met you today and you told me you had something to communicate we have been puzzling what it could be, and we concluded that you were going to be married.

VALENTINE. Ha! Ha! Ha! Was that it?

PHOEBE. So like women, you know. We thought we perhaps knew her. We were even discussing what we should wear at the wedding.

VALENTINE. Ha! Ha! I shall often think of this. I wonder who would have me, Miss Susan? But I must be off; and God bless you both.

MISS SUSAN. You are going!

VALENTINE. No more mud on your carpet, Miss Susan; no more coverlets rolled into balls. A good riddance. Miss Phoebe, a last look at the garden. (*He takes her hand and looks into her face.*)

PHOEBE. We shall miss you very much, Mr. Brown.

VALENTINE. There is that other little matter. That investment I advised you to make, I am happy it has turned out so well.

PHOEBE. It was good of you to take all that trouble, sir. Accept our grateful thanks.

VALENTINE. Indeed, I am glad you are so comfortably left; I am your big brother. Good-bye again. This little blue and white room and its dear inmates, may they be unchanged when I come back. Good-bye. (*He goes. MISS SUSAN looks forlornly at PHOEBE, who smiles pitifully.*)

PHOEBE. A misunderstanding; just a mistake. (*She lifts the wedding gown and puts it back in the ottoman. MISS SUSAN sinks sobbing into a chair.*) Don't, dear, don't—we can live it down.

MISS SUSAN. He is a fiend in human form.

PHOEBE. Nay, you hurt me, sister. He is a brave gentleman.

MISS SUSAN. The money; why did you not let me tell him?

PHOEBE. So that he might offer to me out of pity, Susan?

MISS SUSAN. Phoebe, how are we to live with the quartern loaf at one and ten-pence?

PHOEBE. Brother James—

MISS SUSAN. You know very well that James will do nothing for us.

PHOEBE. I think, Susan, we could keep a little school—for genteel children only, of course. I would do most of the teaching.

MISS SUSAN. You a schoolmistress—Phoebe of the ringlets; everyone would laugh.

PHOEBE. I shall hide the ringlets away in a cap like yours, Susan, and people
will soon forget them. And I shall try to look staid and to grow old quickly.
It will not be so hard for me as you think, dear.

MISS SUSAN. There were other gentlemen who were attracted by you, Phoebe,
and you turned from them.

PHOEBE. I did not want them.

MISS SUSAN. They will come again, and others.

PHOEBE. No, dear; never speak of that to me any more. I let him kiss me.

MISS SUSAN. You could not prevent him.

PHOEBE. Yes, I could. I know I could now. I wanted him to do it. Oh, never
speak to me of others after that. Perhaps he saw I wanted it and did it to
please me. But I meant—indeed I did—that I gave it to him with all my
love. Sister, I could bear all the rest; but I have been unladylike.


2. *The Boor* by Anton Chekhov

*The scene is the parlor of a Russian country estate. Mrs. Popov, mistress of
the estate, is a spirited young widow who "enjoys" her mourning. Today she is
visited by Smirnov who demands immediate payment of a debt owed him by
her late husband. As this scene opens, Mrs. Popov has just told Smirnov that he
is an ill-bred boor who doesn't know how to behave in the company of ladies.*

SMIRNOV. Madam, in the course of my life I have seen more women than you
sparrows. Three times have I fought duels for women, twelve I jilted and
nine jilted me. There was a time when I played the fool, used honeyed
language, bowed and scraped. I loved, suffered, sighed to the moon, melted
in love's torments. I loved passionately, I loved to madness, loved in every
key, chattered like a magpie on emancipation, sacrificed half my fortune
in the tender passion, until now the devil knows I've had enough of it.
Black eyes, passionate eyes, coral lips, dimples in cheeks, moonlight whis-
pers, soft, modest sighs,—for all that, madam, I wouldn't pay a kopeck! I
am not speaking of present company, but of women in general; from the
tiniest to the greatest, they are conceited, hypocritical, chattering, odious,
deceitful from top to toe; vain, petty, cruel with a maddening logic and
(*He strikes his forehead.*) in this respect, please excuse my frankness, but
one sparrow is worth ten of the aforementioned petticoat-philosophers.
When one sees one of the romantic creatures before him he imagines he is
looking at some holy being, so wonderful that its one breath could dissolve
him in a sea of a thousand charms and delights; but if one looks into the
soul—it's nothing but a common crocodile. (*He seizes the arm-chair and
breaks it in two.*) But the worst of all is that this crocodile imagines it is
a masterpiece of creation, and that it has a monopoly on all the tender
passions. May the devil hang me upside down if there is anything to love
about a woman! When she is in love, all she knows is how to complain

and shed tears. If the man suffers and makes sacrifices she swings her train about and tries to lead him by the nose. You have the misfortune to be a woman, and naturally you know woman's nature; tell me on your honor, have you ever in your life seen a woman who was really true and faithful? Never! Only the old and the deformed are true and faithful. It's easier to find a cat with horns or a white woodcock, than a faithful woman.

MRS. POPOV. But allow me to ask, who is true and faithful in love? The man perhaps?

SMIRNOV. Yes, indeed! The man!

MRS. POPOV. The man! (*She laughs sarcastically.*) The man true and faithful in love! Well, that is something *new!* (*Bitterly*) How can you make such a statement? Men true and faithful! So long as we have gone thus far, I may as well say that of all the men I have known, my husband was the best; I loved him passionately with all my soul as only a young, sensible woman may love; I gave him my youth, my happiness, my fortune, my life. I worshipped him like a heathen. And what happened? This best of men betrayed me in every possible way,—and in spite of everything, I trusted him and was true to him. And more than that: he is dead and I am still true to him. I have buried myself within these four walls and I shall wear this mourning to my grave.

SMIRNOV. (*Laughing disrespectfully*) Mourning! What on earth do you take me for? As if I didn't know why you wore this black domino and why you buried yourself within these four walls. Such a secret! So romantic! Some knight will pass the castle, gaze up at the windows and think to himself; "Here dwells the mysterious Tamara who, for love of her husband, has buried herself within four walls." Oh, I understand the art!

MRS. POPOV. (*Springing up*) What? What do you mean by saying such things to me?

SMIRNOV. You have buried yourself alive, but meanwhile you have not forgotten to powder your nose!

MRS. POPOV. How dare you speak so?

SMIRNOV. Don't scream at me, please. Allow me to call things by their right names. I am not a woman, and I am accustomed to speak out what I think. So please don't scream.

MRS. POPOV. I'm not screaming. It is you who are screaming. Please leave me, I beg of you.

SMIRNOV. Pay me my money and I'll leave.

MRS. POPOV. I don't care what you do. You won't get a kopeck! Leave me!

SMIRNOV. As I haven't the pleasure of being either your husband or your fiancé please don't make a scene. (*He sits down.*) I can't stand it.

MRS. POPOV. (*Breathing hard*) You are going to sit down?

SMIRNOV. I already have.

MRS. POPOV. Kindly leave the house!

SMIRNOV. Give me the money.

MRS. POPOV. I don't care to speak with impudent men. Leave! (*Pause*) You aren't going?

SMIRNOV. No.

MRS. POPOV. Very well. (*She rings the bell.*)

(*Enter LUKA, an old manservant.*)

MRS. POPOV. Luka, show the gentleman out.

LUKA. (*Going to SMIRNOV*) Sir, why don't you leave when you are ordered? What do you want?

SMIRNOV. (*Jumping up*) Whom do you think you are talking to? I'll grind you to powder.

LUKA. (*Puts his hand to his heart*) Good Lord! (*He drops into a chair.*) Oh, I'm ill, I can't breathe!

MRS. POPOV. (*To SMIRNOV*) Leave! Get out!

SMIRNOV. Kindly be a little more polite!

MRS. POPOV. (*Striking her fists and stamping her feet*) You are vulgar! You're a boor! A monster!

SMIRNOV. (*Steps toward her quickly*) Permit me to ask what right you have to insult me?

MRS. POPOV. What of it? Do you think I am afraid of you?

SMIRNOV. And you think that because you are a romantic creature you can insult me without being punished? I challenge you! We'll have a duel.

MRS. POPOV. Do you think because you have big fists and a steer's neck I am afraid of you?

SMIRNOV. I allow no one to insult me, and I make no exception because you are a woman, one of the "weaker sex"!

MRS. POPOV. (*Trying to cry him down*) Boor, boor, boor!

SMIRNOV. It is high time to do away with the old superstition that it is only the man who is forced to give satisfaction. If there is equity at all let there be equity in all things. There's a limit!

MRS. POPOV. You wish to fight a duel? Very well. My husband had pistols. I'll bring them. (*She hurries away, then turns.*) Oh, what a pleasure it will be to put a bullet in your impudent head. The devil take you! (*She goes out.*)

SMIRNOV. I'll shoot her down! I'm no fledgling, no sentimental young puppy. For me, there is no weaker sex!

LUKA. Oh, sir! (*Falls to his knees*) Have mercy on me, an old man, and go away. You have frightened me to death already, and now you want to fight a duel.

SMIRNOV. (*Paying no attention*) A duel. That's equity, emancipation. That way the sexes are made equal. I'll shoot her down as a matter of principle. What can a person say to such a woman? (*Imitating her*) "The devil take you. I'll put a bullet in your impudent head." What can one say to that?

She was angry, her eyes blazed, she accepted a challenge. On my honor, it's the first time in my life that I ever saw such a woman.

LUKA. Oh, sir. Go away. Go away!

SMIRNOV. That *is* a woman. I can understand her. A real woman. No shilly-shallying, but fire, powder, and noise! It would be a pity to shoot a woman like that.

**3.** *Sham* by Frank G. Tompkins

*This play, a modern social satire, takes place in the home of Clara and Charles. A thief has broken in, and, instead of being frightened at having been caught, proceeds to scold the young couple about their pretenses.*

THIEF. Good evening. (*Pause*) Good evening, good evening. (*Pause*) Can't say I expected you home so soon. Was the play an awful bore? (*Pause*) We-e-ll, can't one of you speak? I can carry on a conversation alone, but the question-and-answer method is usually preferred. If one of you will ask me how I do, we might get a step farther.

CLARA. You—you—You're a thief!

THIEF. Exactly. And you, madame? The mistress of the house, I presume. Or are you another thief? The traditional one that it takes to catch the first?

CLARA. This—this is our house. Charles, why don't you do something? Don't stand there like a—Make him go away! Tell him he mustn't take anything. What have you taken? Give it to me instantly. How dare you! Charles, take it away from him.

CHARLES. I say, old chap, you'd better clear out. We've come home. You know you can't—come now, give it up. Be sensible. I don't want to use force—

THIEF. I don't want you to.

CHARLES. If you've got anything of ours—We aren't helpless, you know. (*He starts to draw something black and shiny from his overcoat pocket.*)

THIEF. Let's see those glasses. Give them here. Perhaps they're better than mine. Fine cases. Humph. Window glass. Take them back. You're not armed, you know. I threw your revolver down the cold-air shaft. Never carry one myself—in business hours. Yours was in the bottom of your bureau drawer. Bad shape those bureau drawers were in. Nice and neat on top; rat's nest below. Shows up your character in great shape, old man. Always tell your man by his bureau drawers. Didn't it ever occur to you that a thief might drop in on you some night? What would he think of you?

CHARLES. I don't think—

THIEF. You should. I said to myself when I opened that drawer: "They put up a great surface, but they're shams. Probably a streak that runs through everything they do."

**4.** *The Barretts of Wimpole Street* by Rudolf Besier

*The scene is Elizabeth Barrett's living room. Elizabeth, an invalid, is confined to a bed-sofa. She and Robert Browning have admired each other's poems for some time, and from afar, a warm friendship has developed between them. Today they meet for the first time as Mr. Browning visits the Barrett house. The time is 1845, London.*

BROWNING. Directly after I read your brave and lovely verses I was greedy for anything and everything I could get about you.

ELIZABETH. You frighten me, Mr. Browning!

BROWNING. Why?

ELIZABETH. Well, you know Mr. Kenyon's enthusiasms run away with his tongue? He and I are the dearest friends. What he told you about poor me I quite blush to imagine!

BROWNING. You mean, Miss Barrett, about you—you *yourself?*

ELIZABETH. I feel it would be hopeless for me to try to live up to his description.

BROWNING. He never told me anything about you—personally—which had the slightest interest for me.

ELIZABETH. Oh?

BROWNING. Everything he could give me about your surroundings and the circumstances of your life I snatched at with avidity. But all he said about *you* was quite beside the point, because I knew it already—and better than Mr. Kenyon, old friend of yours though he is!

ELIZABETH. But—Oh, Mr. Browning, do my poor writings give me so hopelessly away?

BROWNING. Hopelessly—utterly—entirely—to me! I can't speak for the rest of the world.

ELIZABETH. You frighten me again!

BROWNING. No!

ELIZABETH. But you do! For I'm afraid it would be quite useless my ever trying to play-act with you!

BROWNING. Quite useless!

ELIZABETH. I shall always have to be—just myself?

BROWNING. Always.

ELIZABETH. Oh!—and you too, Mr. Browning?

BROWNING. Always—just myself! But really you know, Miss Barrett, I sha'n't be able to take much credit for that! Being myself comes to me as easily as breathing. It's play-acting I can't manage—and the hot water I've got into in consequences! If life's to run smoothly we should all be mummers. Well, I can't be mum!

ELIZABETH. Yes, I can well believe that now I know you. But isn't it extraordinary? When you are writing you never do anything but—play-act.

BROWNING. I know—

Robert Browning warmly greets Elizabeth Barrett in the Broadway production
of *The Barretts of Wimpole Street.*

ELIZABETH. You have never been yourself in any one of your poems. It's always somebody else speaking through you.

BROWNING. Yes. And shall I tell you why? I am a very modest man. I am really!

ELIZABETH. I didn't question it, Mr. Browning.

BROWNING. So modest, I fully realize that if I wrote about myself—my hopes and fears, hates and loves, and the rest of it—my poems would be intolerably dull.

ELIZABETH. Well—since we are pledged to nothing but the truth, I won't contradict that—until I know you better!

BROWNING. Bravo!

ELIZABETH. Oh, but those poems, with their glad and great-hearted acceptance of life—you can't imagine what they mean to me! Here am I shut in by four walls, the view of Wimpole Street my only glimpse of the world. And they troop into the room and round my sofa, those wonderful people of yours out of every age and country, and all so tingling with life! life! life! No, you'll never begin to realize how much I owe you!

BEGINNING TO ACT    **63**

**5.** *Outward Bound* by Sutton Vane

*The scene is aboard ship. Tom, a young man, has been baffled by the strangeness of the ship, apparently bound for an unknown port. He has just discovered that all on board are dead; he questions Scrubby, the steward, about this. The play, being a fantasy, is without time.*

TOM. I am right, aren't I, Scrubby?

SCRUBBY. Right, sir, in the head, do you mean?

TOM. You know what I mean.

SCRUBBY. No, I don't, sir. Right about what, sir?

TOM. You—I—all of us on this boat?

SCRUBBY. What about all of us on this boat, sir?

TOM. We are—now answer me truthfully—we are all *dead, aren't we?*

SCRUBBY. Yes, sir, we are all dead. Quite dead. They don't find out as soon as you have, as a rule.

TOM. Queer!

SCRUBBY. Not when you get used to it, sir.

TOM. How long have you been—you been—oh, you know?

SCRUBBY. Me, sir? Oh, I was lost young.

TOM. You were what?

SCRUBBY. Lost young, sir.

TOM. I don't understand.

SCRUBBY. No, sir, you wouldn't, not yet. But you'll get to know lots of things as the voyage goes on.

TOM. Tell me—tell me one thing—*now.*

SCRUBBY. Anything I can, sir.

TOM. Where—where are we sailing for?

SCRUBBY. Heaven, sir. (*Pause*) And hell too. (*Pause*) It's the same place, you see.

**6.** *Years Ago* by Ruth Gordon

*The scene is the dining room of the Jones family's home in the small town of Wollaston, Massachusetts. Ruth, the daughter, has only one semester left of high school and her father has decided that she should go on to college and become a gym teacher. Mr. Jones is very determined about this and is in the process of filling out her college application when Ruth finally has to reveal where her true ambition lies. The time is January, 1912.*

MY MOTHER. Clinton, Ruth is upset—

MY FATHER. What about?

MY MOTHER. She doesn't want to be a Physical Culture teacher.

MY FATHER. Why the—Why not?

MY MOTHER. Clinton, some people get inspired over some things, others over *others.* Now *you* got inspired to be a sailor. Not a carpenter like you said your father was—

MY FATHER. Ruth doesn't know what she's inspired over, at *sixteen!*

MY MOTHER. Now be patient, Clinton—

MY FATHER. Well, what do you think you're inspired over?

ME. I don't know—

MY MOTHER. Why, yes, you do too, Ruth. You tell Papa.

ME. I don't want to be a Physical Culture teacher.

MY FATHER. What do you want to do?

MY MOTHER. Tell Papa, Ruth. He wants to know.

ME. I don't want to be a Physical Culture instructress.

MY FATHER. Why don't you?

ME. Because I'd rather be dead.

MY MOTHER. Ruth, don't say that. God will hear you.

MY FATHER. God's listenin' to harps and trumpets and watchin' sparrows fall.

MY MOTHER. God's listening to *everybody*—

MY FATHER. God's listenin' to everybody, but *I'm* listening to her!

MY MOTHER. Tell Papa!

ME. I have to do my homework.

MY MOTHER. Why, no, you don't, it's Friday night.

ME. Well—

MY MOTHER. *Ruth!*

MY FATHER. Don't sit there like a dyin' calf. If you got somethin' to say, spit it out!

ME. I want to go on the stage.

MY FATHER. What makes you think you got the stuff it takes?

ME. I don't know.

MY FATHER. What give you the idea?

ME. I don't know, Papa. Maybe I got to be rovin' like *you* felt.

MY MOTHER. And, Clinton, she has a chance to. Ruth got a telegram today. Well, tell Papa about it, Ruth. He wants to know.

ME. I got a telegram from Miss Doris Olsson, the leadin' lady of the whole Castle Square Theatre stock company, sayin' there's a part openin' up there and Mr. John Craig will see me *tomorrow*—

MY FATHER. John Craig of the Castle Square Theatre?

ME. Yes, Papa.

MY FATHER. He wants *you* to be in the company?

ME. There's a *chance!*—and Miss Olsson says for me to go see him at two-thirty in the afternoon. Oh, Papa, I *wish* I could be like what you want me to be, but it's like you asked me to be a giant and I'm not a giant and I'm not a Physical Culture person *either!*

MY FATHER. What makes you think you're a *actress?*

MY MOTHER. She's not statuesque, of course, but she looks all right when she remembers to stand up straight. And when she smiles and doesn't look like a thundercloud, Ruth can be very appealing. She has all *sorts* of artistic leanings. And *mercy*, Clinton, I guess *some* things you got to trust in the Lord.

7. *The Rainmaker* by N. Richard Nash

*The scene is a farm in a western state, during summer drought time. Starbuck, a poetic liar and "confidence man," has come to the farm and promised to bring rain for $100. As yet, he has not done so, but his charm and vitality have changed everyone's life, especially Lizzie's—she has fallen in love with Starbuck. Her father, Curry, and her brother, Noah, try to discourage her.*

NOAH. Where's Starbuck?

LIZZIE. In the tack room. He wanted to come in and talk to you, Pop, but I said let me do it first.

NOAH. What's he want to talk about?

LIZZIE. Well—I—we—You know I think I saw a wisp of a cloud.

NOAH. You're seein' things.

LIZZIE. No! The smallest wisp of a cloud—floating across the moon—no bigger than a mare's tail.

**Noah warns his sister about Starbuck in the Broadway production of** *The Rainmaker.*

Photo by Alfredo Valente

NOAH. You're talkin' like him.

LIZZIE. Yes—I am—yes.

NOAH. Whyn't you comb your hair?

LIZZIE. I like it this way! I'm going to wear it this way all my life. I'm going to throw away the pins. There! I've got no more pins! But I've got something else!

CURRY. What, Lizzie?

LIZZIE. Pop—Oh, Pop, I've got me a beau!

CURRY. Have you, honey?

LIZZIE. Not an always beau—but a beau for meanwhile. Until he goes! He says he'll go in a few days—but anything can happen in a few days—anything can happen, can't it, Pop?

CURRY. Yes—it sure can.

LIZZIE. Oh, Pop, the world's turned clear around!

NOAH. Why don't you tell her, Pop?

LIZZIE. Tell me what?

CURRY. Lizzie, you were right about that fella. He's a liar and a con man.

LIZZIE. But there's nothing bad about him, Pop. He's so good—and so alone— he's so terribly alone!

NOAH. That's what he deserves to be.

LIZZIE. No—nobody ought to be that. And I'll see that he's not any more. I'll be with him every minute he wants me.

NOAH. Lizzie, come here.

LIZZIE. What?

NOAH. I'm sorry, but you better look out this window.

LIZZIE. What are they here for? What are they doing to his wagon, Pop!

CURRY. They're gettin' evidence against him, Lizzie. The Sheriff's here to lock him up.

LIZZIE. No!

NOAH. Stay here, Lizzie.

LIZZIE. Let me go, Noah! They've got no right to arrest him!

CURRY. I'm afraid they have.

NOAH. He cheated and swindled everywhere he went.

LIZZIE. Pop, we've got to help him!

CURRY. Lizzie, quit it! There's nothin' we can do for him.

LIZZIE. Not for him—for me! I love him!

NOAH. You're out of your mind! He'll be gone in a day or two. He'll never even remember he saw you.

LIZZIE. No—that's not true!

CURRY. You think he'd marry you, Lizzie?

LIZZIE. I don't know—

NOAH. Well, you won't marry *him*, I'll tell you that!

*Part Two*

# Understanding

# the Drama

An important phase of work in dramatics is a knowledge of the elements that make plays what they are. To gain the most from your experiences with drama, you should know as much as possible about its history, its structure, and its various types and styles. Studying plays in this way will demand more than reading or seeing them for pleasure alone, but the rewards will prove well worth the effort. You will find your appreciation of plays that you see enhanced many times over, and you will have greater insight into those that you read. This insight will carry over to help you understand many other different kinds of literature.

A knowledge of the history and forms of drama will also benefit you in your participation in school plays. Your increased under-

standing will enable you to interpret your role or perform your backstage work with greater effectiveness. Even if you never do any theatrical work after you leave school, you will have developed an interest in many different aspects of the enchanting world of the theater.

Throughout history, plays have reflected current conditions; they have been and are today a kind of showcase exhibiting the customs, ideals, and problems of people the world over. As you come to understand the drama on a more than surface level, you will be taking a big step toward understanding life itself. A play, with its representation and condensation of human experience, can help you gain a universal outlook and perception which will be of great importance to you now and in the future.

# Chapter 4

# Structure of Drama

The *structure* of a play is its form; its shape and development; the manner in which characters, conflicts, action, and resolution are presented. Play structure is relatively flexible, changing to correspond with different themes and historical periods. Most well-written plays, however, do follow certain traditions laid down by the first drama critic and teacher, Aristotle (384–322 B.C.). In his *Poetics*, he implied that the plot of a play should consist of a beginning which is compelling, a middle which sustains interest, and an ending which is plausible. Everything from the opening of the play up to the critical point he called the *complication*. Out of the complication came the change in fortunes in which the hero might "fall from happiness to misfortune or rise from misfortune to happiness." The events which take place from the change of fortunes to the end of the play are termed the *denouement*. Aristotle believed that a play should center about one series of episodes, all of which were necessary to the plot and linked together in a probable and inevitable sequence. He also thought that drama was the imitation of life and that, therefore, the characters should be true to life in the sense that they were neither too good nor too bad. Their misery or happiness should result from their actual deeds.

In the past there was a well-defined tradition which divided plays into three or five acts, sometimes including a prologue at the beginning and an epilogue at the end. Now plays are often divided into two parts with a single intermission—the assumption being that the fewer the intermissions, the more concentrated will be the audience's attention. Another innovation is the "open stage" which projects into the auditorium without a *proscenium*, the frame of the stage through which the audience ordinarily views a play. Though this open stage is affecting the structure of our plays somewhat, most people still prefer three-act plays on a conventional stage.

70

# PLOT

To isolate plot from other elements of the drama and to define it accurately is difficult. However, it is generally considered to be the series of situations and incidents through which characters move and thereby tell a definite story.

In reading this section, it is important for you to remember that no one exact formula can be applied to all plays in the same way. Since action is vital to any plot, it must be carefully controlled by the playwright. Though there may be several conflicts and climaxes in a play, in most cases there should be one of each which stands out as being the major one. Around the *major conflict* of a play should revolve all of its action. Often this conflict is physical, but it does not have to be. Spiritual forces, government policies, and various ideologies are just a few of the many pressures which can stir leading characters into action. Many great dramas show the hero facing inherent tendencies in himself and in others from which an outer struggle eventually arises. Whether physical or mental, the opposing forces should be evenly balanced, and growing suspense should be aroused as to what the final outcome will be. In the *major climax*, or highest point of interest, the action culminates, dramatically revealing the outcome of the conflict and pointing toward the conclusion of the story.

## Exposition

When a play begins, the audience must be told a number of things. It must be led to understand the *preliminary situation*—the action preceding the first scene which explains the plot of the play and relates directly to it. It also must clearly see what kind of play is being presented, where and when it is taking place, who the leading characters are, what their backgrounds are, and in what situation they are being placed. This presentation of the *why, where, when,* and *who* is called the *exposition,* and it should be as brief and unobtrusive as possible.

Besides establishing the characters, time, and place in the exposition, the playwright must explain the immediate situation and arouse the audience's interest in what is going to happen. The audience wants to meet the chief characters quickly and learn whether the play is serious or light in intent. In addition to dialogue and action, lighting and scenery can assist in clarifying the mood of the play and creating the appropriate atmosphere.

Modern dramatists use all sorts of devices to handle the exposition. Prologues, telephone conversations, narrators, and ingenious scenic effects are just a few of these devices. In *The Night of January 16th, The Caine*

Caesar and Cassius are stopped in the street by a soothsayer who warns Caesar to "beware the ides of March." (Initial Incident in *Julius Caesar*)

On the steps of the Senate House, Caesar is stabbed to death by the conspirators. (Rising Action in *Julius Caesar*)

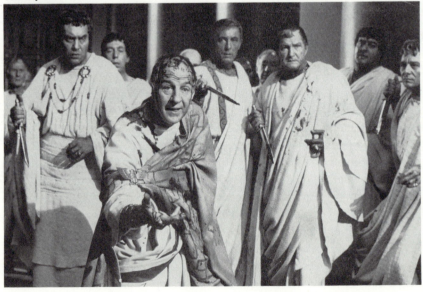

Mark Antony delivers Caesar's funeral oration, which turns the people of Rome against Brutus and the other conspirators. (Crisis in *Julius Caesar*)

*Mutiny Court-Martial,* and the *Trial of Mary Dugan,* which are dramas about court trials, front curtains are not used and the audience becomes a part of the courtroom action, while the clerks, attorneys, and attendants casually explain the case. In *The Diary of Anne Frank* and *I Remember Mama,* the young heroines are shown or heard writing about themselves and their lives in their journals at the opening of the plays and between the scenes.

## Initial Incident

The *initial incident* opens the plot. It is the first important event to take place on the stage, and the point from which the rest of the plot develops. All the action of the play starts with the initial incident, and the audience begins to ask, "What will happen next?" Do not confuse the initial incident with the events introduced by the author to bring the preliminary situation before the audience. For example, the first scene of *Julius Caesar* where the people and the patricians are discussing the war between Caesar and Pompey presents the situation in Rome. The initial incident comes when the soothsayer cries out to Caesar, "Beware the ides of March." At that point, the future danger to Caesar is foreshadowed.

Cassius and Brutus prepare to battle the forces of Mark Antony and Octavius. (Falling Action in *Julius Caesar*)

## Rising Action

The *rising action* is the series of events which builds excitement toward the most dramatic scene of the play, the major climax. Involved in the major climax is the *crisis*, or "turning point," which reveals whether the leading character will win success or fail to solve his problem. The audience should react emotionally with him in his joy or sorrow.

## Falling Action

The *falling action*, or series of events following the major climax, may be drawn out or condensed, but it must always sustain audience interest until the final curtain falls. Sometimes this is done by including minor characters in interesting subplots which also must be concluded before the

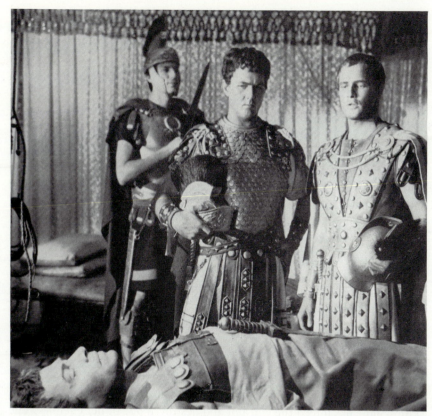

Mark Antony pays tribute to the dead Brutus in the famous lines beginning: "This was the noblest Roman of them all." (Conclusion in *Julius Caesar*)

end of the play. At other times, the settlement of the various complications of the main plot serves to hold audience attention.

## Illustration of Plot Development

*Two Crooks and a Lady* by Eugene Pillot has held its place as one of the best one-act plays for high schools largely because its exciting plot meets the requirements mentioned above. In the exposition, we learn that Mrs. Simms-Vane, a completely paralyzed old woman, owns a diamond necklace which Lucille, her parlormaid, and Miller, Lucille's friend, have decided to steal. They arrange to get Miss Jones, the old lady's companion, out of the house; then they confront Mrs. Simms-Vane in the room where the necklace is kept.

The initial incident occurs when Miller demands that Mrs. Simms-Vane give them the "thirty-three," as the necklace is called because of the thirty-three diamonds it supposedly contains. As the rising action begins, she declares that she will not tell where the necklace is and warns them that they have made a mistake in trying to take advantage of her.

The conflict starts when Miller threatens to shoot Mrs. Simms-Vane. She merely smiles, telling him that death would be a welcome release for her. She then adds that the noise of the shot would force him to flee so that he could not continue his search for the necklace. Miller decides that she is right about the noise of the gun and tries to make her talk by squeezing her hand with pliers. Mrs. Simms-Vane endures this torture, saying that pain will never be her master. Finally Lucille becomes hysterical at the sight of blood and makes Miller stop.

Mrs. Simms-Vane sends Lucille out of the room to get some hot milk from the kitchen. While Lucille is gone, she flatters and bribes Miller. She makes him promise that if she lets him take the necklace, he will not tell Lucille and will allow her to buy it back from him later for $40,000. She also tricks Miller into admitting that Lucille is not his only girl. When Lucille returns, she whispers that Miller has the necklace and has put his gun on the table. Lucille grabs it and tells Miller she will shoot him. However she begins to weaken when he cries out that he loves her. Seeing this, Mrs. Simms-Vane says, "Oh, Lucille, you little fool! The other woman is the one." Lucille fires and Miller falls. This is the climax of the play. Mrs. Simms-Vane has forced the gunshot and destroyed one of her enemies. The front door bell rings and Lucille begs for protection. Hoping that the girl is not really bad, Mrs. Simms-Vane agrees to save her, but insists that she put the revolver in her lap and count into her hand the diamonds Miller had picked from their sockets. She watches Lucille in the mirror and sees her hide one of the diamonds. Voices are heard offstage. Lucille is amazed to find that she has thirty-three stones; she had feared there would be only thirty-two. Police officers enter with the invalid's companion and Mrs. Simms-Vane turns Lucille over to them, saying that there were thirty-four, not thirty-three, stones in the necklace and that Lucille has stolen one. Miller proves to have been only wounded and the two crooks are taken off to jail.

The problem of the play is, of course, that the elderly and helpless lady must overcome two strong young crooks by her intelligence and poise. The conflict is one of wits as well as character. Mrs. Simms-Vane's cleverness and understanding enable her to destroy her opponents through their own traits of jealousy, greed, cruelty, and insecurity.

# CHARACTER

Nothing in the world is as interesting as people. Since a play represents life as we know it, as it has been, or as we might like it to be, the characters should be interesting people who are inextricably related to the plot.

The character whom we want to win the conflict or solve the major problem in a play is called the *protagonist*, and the person opposing him is the *antagonist*. They are usually the two leading characters, at odds with each other, and the interest is evenly divided between them. There are also secondary characters important to the development of the plot, and in a well-written play they are as truthfully and as carefully drawn as the principals. As a matter of convenience, playwrights sometimes resort to easily recognizable stage types, such as the proud butler, the brash detective, the fussy mother-in-law, or the old maid aunt. In the best plays, however, all the characters are individuals, not mere stereotypes. One of the reasons why Shakespeare holds his position as the world's greatest dramatist is that he created real human beings. His plots were seldom original or particularly unusual, but his characters live on as some of the most humorous, most tragic, most fascinating people in all theater literature.

## Methods of Characterization

A playwright reveals his characters in three major ways—by their conversation, their actions, and what other characters say about them. Especially in using the latter method, the playwright must be careful to create a consistent picture of a given character.

Shakespeare and the classic dramatists used the simple method of soliloquy, in which a character talked aloud to himself revealing his innermost thoughts and motives. Contemporary playwrights have also used the soliloquy for characterization. This method requires great skill in writing and in acting or it will appear "stagey" and unrealistic. Examples of the successful use of soliloquy in contemporary drama can be found in Thornton Wilder's *Our Town* and Tennessee Williams' *The Glass Menagerie*.

## Motivation of Action

One of the most important phases of characterization is the *motivation of action*. Every action must be based on the inner nature of the character. As you read or see a play, you must be able to ask, "Why did he do this?" or, "Why did this happen to him?" and find a logical answer in the nature of the person. Lack of proper motivation is a fatal flaw in a play or motion picture.

In *The Glass Menagerie,* contemporary playwright Tennessee Williams made effective use of the soliloquy. He had the character Tom (above) talk directly to the audience, telling about himself and his memories of his mother and sister. Each of these informal talks led directly into one of the play's episodes.

## Examples of Convincing Characterization

Many characters in plays are so magnificently conceived and delineated by the playwright that they become living people for many generations of theatergoers. Mrs. Malaprop is one of these immortal stage people. In Sheridan's comedy *The Rivals,* she uses long words without understanding their meaning. Edmond Rostand's Cyrano, the glorious poet-soldier with the monstrous nose, who expresses his beauty of spirit by enriching the lives of others is another immortal. Some of the Shakespearean characters —Iago, the arch villain; Romeo, the eternal lover; Beatrice, the scoffing spinster; and Falstaff, the buffoon—are equally unforgettable.

Contemporary dramatists have also created characters who will continue to challenge actors and fascinate theatergoers. Among these are Eugene O'Neill's Emperor Jones, James M. Barrie's Peter Pan, George Bernard Shaw's Saint Joan, Arthur Miller's Willie Loman, and Sean O'Casey's Captain Boyle.

# THEME

The *theme* is the basic idea of a play which the author dramatizes through the conflicts of characters with one another or with life-events. It expresses a special phase of the fundamental philosophy indicated by the characters. Sometimes the playwright states his theme in a sentence spoken by a character, but often he leaves it to the interpretation of the audience. The discussion of his purpose in writing the play furnishes one of the chief points of interest in a worthwhile production.

You may find it difficult to determine the theme of a play as you read or see it, but you should enjoy analyzing the plot and characters and finding what the author has expressed through them. Remember that there may be many good ideas presented in a play, but don't be misled into mistaking a minor truth for the theme of the play as a whole. The theme is the specific idea which gives unity and purpose to everything that happens; it should be an interesting phase of the particular problem, rather than a general principle which could apply to dozens of plays.

For example, two well-known plays, found in a number of collections, are Dunsany's *A Night at an Inn* and Pillot's *Two Crooks and a Lady*, the latter discussed earlier in this chapter. Since both plays deal with the stealing of jewels and both end disastrously for the thieves, the general idea that

Two of the drama's unforgettable characters: Edmond Rostand's **Cyrano de Bergerac** (Left) and Eugene O'Neill's **Emperor Jones** (Right).

Courtesy of New York City Center of Music and Drama, Inc.

Photo by Frank Chapman

criminals are punished for their crimes is brought out in both. However, the theme of each play is far more specific.

In *A Night at an Inn*, three sailors under the direction of the Toff have stolen the ruby eye from an idol in India and have been pursued to England by priests who have slain two of their comrades in a horrible manner. As the play begins, they have sought refuge in an isolated and deserted inn on the moors of England, where they are surprised by the priests. Due to the Toff's cleverness, the sailors are able to kill them one by one; but in the midst of the celebration of this victory, the idol himself arrives, takes his eye, and departs. Immediately each sailor is drawn to his destruction by a magnetic force he cannot resist. Even the Toff, who has a fine intelligence, is powerless against the idol. The theme is, therefore, that human power, either physical or mental, is useless in a struggle against a supernatural force.

In *Two Crooks and a Lady*, Mrs. Simms-Vane—old, paralyzed and ill—because of her trained intelligence, inherent refinement, emotional control, and spiritual courage is able to play two crooks against each other, so that they not only fail to get the jewels but are taken by the police as a result of their own dishonesty. The theme of this play is that a trained mind and fine character can overcome brute strength.

Do not confuse the theme with a moral. Many plays have no moral; they are written to show how a certain type of individual would react under certain circumstances, or to portray an interesting phase of life. While it may or may not be a profound truth or teach a lesson, the theme should be an interesting idea which has wide appeal and which is clearly set forth by the characterization and plot development.

## DIALOGUE, ACTION, AND SITUATION

The success of a play depends upon the writer's skillful use of dialogue and action, since they are the sole means by which he can portray his characters, set forth his theme, and develop his plot.

In writing the dialogue or lines of the play, the dramatist must be sure that his characters speak as the men and women of the class, community, and experience they represent would speak in real life. At the same time, he must advance the plot, motivate the actions of the characters, and place them in exciting or amusing situations. Of course, a great writer is bound to inject his individual style into the dialogue, but a dramatist cannot always instill his own brilliance into every sentence as other authors may do. He must often sacrifice beauty of language to naturalness of speech, yet his characters cannot talk aimlessly as people do in real life, for every word must serve to develop the play. Clever lines in themselves are valuable in a comedy, but they should be consistent with the character of the person speaking them. Sparkling dialogue may actually be injurious to the play if it is not in harmony with the over-all aim of the playwright. Words, figures of speech, and epigrams, although witty in themselves, may be completely unsuited to the play. We can hardly speak of dialogue apart from action and situation. When we refer to a playwright's style, then, we mean the cleverness or beauty of his lines in relation to the mood and characterization of his plays.

Action is the lifeblood of drama: something must happen constantly to hold the undivided interest of the onlookers. Events must not only be talked about, they must occur on the stage. Each situation should build to higher and higher points of interest. These points may be diagramed to show the series of minor climaxes leading to the major climax and the falling action.

As you attend films and plays, note how the situations are always presented in dialogue and action. The characters may be placed in embarrassing predicaments, melodramatic moments of great danger, tense emotional upheavals, or in any other combination of circumstances. We must see the characters solve one difficult situation after another. The play should be a related series of logical incidents building to a climax, which is followed by other situations leading inevitably to the conclusion.

The ability to place characters in exciting, tragic, comic, or pathetic situations is what makes a playwright successful. Occasionally one situation alone can be so striking that it helps to make the play a hit. The next time you are at the theater, watch especially for the opening situation, the climax, and the closing event.

## Discussion

1. What do you think Aristotle meant when he called drama an imitation of life? Give your reasons for agreeing or disagreeing with this idea.

2. What do the following terms mean: exposition, preliminary situation, initial incident, suspense, conflict, denouement, motivation of character, consistent characterization, atmosphere, theme, protagonist, situation?

3. Select for analysis a motion picture or televised play which the majority of the class has seen. What was the initial incident? The climax? How were suspense and interest maintained during the rising and falling action? Did the drama end as you expected it would? What was the problem presented? Did it entail mental or physical conflict? State the theme in one sentence and then tell how the actions of the protagonist emphasized the theme.

**4.** Give examples of the following: a play or film in which you found it difficult to decide on the climax, one in which you lost interest long before the end, one in which the theme was not clear. Point out where the weakness lay in each case.

**5.** Summarize, in not more than four sentences, the plot of a play or film with which the rest of the class is not familiar.

**6.** What are the chief differences in the structure of plays written for the stage, screen, radio, and television?

**7.** In his famous play *Saint Joan*, George Bernard Shaw added an epilogue showing what happened to Joan and the leading characters in later centuries. Do you think the play should have ended with her death at the stake instead? Why?

**8.** In the motion picture *Anastasia*, it is implied that the heroine and the villain fall in love with each other at the end. In the stage play another man, who was scarcely introduced in the movie but was an important character in the play, carried her off to be his wife in America and live a normal, active life. Which do you think is the more logical conclusion?

**9.** The popular play *The Rainmaker* by N. Richard Nash has an ending in which a heavy rainstorm comes opportunely to satisfy the hero's spiritual need as well as the other characters' physical need for rain on the parched prairie farmland. Do you think the author was justified in using such an ending?

**10.** When *Winterset* by Maxwell Anderson was transferred from the stage to the screen, a happy ending was given to it by having the young lovers escape death by a very convincing and logical maneuver. In the original stage version, they were both shot by the antagonist and died in each other's arms. Considering the theme, which shows how lives are blighted by a miscarriage of justice, which ending is the better? Why?

**11.** State the themes of the following plays: *Macbeth, Hamlet, Julius Caesar, Outward Bound, Life with Father, Pygmalion, Mrs. McThing, Teahouse of the August Moon*, or other plays or films with which you are familiar.

**12.** What plays or films have caused you to think deeply about their purpose? Do you like dramas that make you do this? Why?

**13.** Which do you prefer, plays emphasizing plot, or character, or situation? Why? Give at least one example of each kind.

**14.** What are three ways in which a dramatist can reveal his characters? Give examples of each method from modern plays.

**15.** Discuss a movie most of the class has seen recently and decide whether the characters were lifelike, consistent, and interesting.

**16.** Are the lines in the average movie well written, in your opinion? Give examples to prove your point.

**17.** What are some of the most dramatic situations you have seen in motion pictures? The most humorous ones? The most pathetic?

**18.** Who are some of the important writers of stage, screen, and television dramas? Do you ever make a point of seeing a play or film because it has been written by someone whose work you know and enjoy? Name a few productions that have attracted you for this reason.

## Applications

1. This form may be followed to outline in your notebooks the plays you read in and out of class. Choose a play and outline it as suggested here.

Title and Author

I. Exposition
   A. Time
   B. Place
   C. Preliminary situation
II. Plot
   A. Initial incident
   B. Rising action—summarized briefly
   C. Crisis
   D. Climax
   E. Falling action—summarized briefly
   F. Conclusion—final outcome for each major character
III. Characters—described in one sentence
   A. Protagonist
   B. Antagonist
   C. Secondary
   D. Minor—listed
IV. Theme—stated in one sentence
V. Personal reaction—a brief paragraph stating honestly what you think about the play
VI. Quotations—lines, or passages, or phrases which clearly illustrate the author's style or express ideas you wish to remember

2. Tell briefly the preliminary situation, climax, conclusion, and theme of the five best films you have ever seen.

3. Bring to class examples of dialogue from plays by several of the following playwrights: William Shakespeare, Oscar Wilde, Maurice Maeterlinck, Somerset Maugham, Christopher Fry, John Van Druten, George Bernard Shaw, Ferenc Molnar, Thornton Wilder, Robert E. Sherwood, Maxwell Anderson, Eugene O'Neill, Clifford Odets, Tennessee Williams, Arthur Miller, William Saroyan, Lillian Hellman, Moss Hart, George S. Kaufman, and Philip Barry. Discuss the distinctive characteristics of the style of each playwright as it is revealed in your dialogue samples.

4. From the plays of Shakespeare, select and bring to class examples of the following: a dramatic situation, a tragic situation, a moving love scene, five figures of speech, and humorous dialogue.

5. Use *How Not to Write a Play* by Walter Kerr as the subject for a round-table discussion. In this book, Mr. Kerr gives a vivid and amusing picture of modern American drama. His humor is obvious in the chapter titles, some of which are "The Day the Shopgirl Got Her Notice," "Act Before You Think," "Anything Happen Next?" and "Worst Foot Forward."

6. Prepare three- to five-minute talks on the following topics:

Why the Drama Has Universal Appeal

What Constitutes a Successful Play

How a Knowledge of the Structure of a Play Increases (or Decreases) Your Enjoyment of the Theater

The Part of the Playwright on the Modern Stage

Differences in the Writing Problems for Stage, Screen, Radio, and Television

My Favorite Playwright

7. Go to a play or motion picture or watch a television play, and write a brief dramatic criticism of the script, apart from the acting and production. Ask such questions as the following:

a. Is the setting interesting?

b. Is the exposition clear but unobtrusive?

c. Is the climax exciting?

d. What is the problem presented and how is it solved?

e. Is interest sustained to the end?

f. Between what forces does the conflict take place?

g. Are the characters consistent throughout the action?

h. How is the atmosphere maintained?

i. Is the dialogue consistent with the characters and locale?

j. Are there any especially clever lines?

k. What are the best situations?

l. What is the theme?

m. How is the theme set forth and do you agree with it?

n. Do you think the play is a good one? Why?

o. Do you want to see other plays by the same writer?

p. Did following the structural elements of the play add to or detract from your enjoyment of it?

8. Study the scenes in exercise 9 and answer these questions:

a. What do we learn about the rest of the play from this selection?

b. Which selections are pure exposition? In them, what is the preliminary situation? Pick out the sentences in which the playwright has presented the *who, when, where,* and *why* of the play.

c. Do you think you would enjoy reading the rest of the play? Why?

d. What do you learn of the characters, the problems facing them, the fundamental idea, the mood of the play, and the purpose of the title? Select specific lines and situations to prove your point.

e. Is any important part of the plot presented in any of the selections; for example, the initial incident, climax, or conclusion? What events actually take place?

f. Are you more interested in the characters or in finding out what will happen next?

g. What can you tell about the author's style? Do you like it?

h. Pick out all the figures of speech, explain their meaning, and discuss their effectiveness. Are there any fine passages?

i. Pick out any examples of humor, suspense, brilliant dialogue, fine characterization, colloquial or period language.

j. Describe the stage setting, the appearance of the characters, the appropriate lighting for each passage.

k. Outline the plot of the play, as you imagine it may be.

9. Read aloud or dramatize each of these scenes carefully by yourself; characterize the people by changing your voice to bring out the meaning of the lines. Present one of them before the class, either reading all the parts yourself or working in a group.

### a

PETER. You don't think she—she wouldn't want anything this morning, would she, Mis' Abel?

MIS' ABEL. Who's she? Who you talking about?

PETER. Why, Inez.

MIS' ABEL. I thought it was Inez. Why didn't you say so in the first place? I hate di-plomacy in man or beast.

PETER. Well, then, I'll say it now. Mis' Abel! Why don't she treat me right?

MIS' ABEL. Treat you right? Why, I don't see how she can. Near as I can make out, you never open your head when you're with her.

PETER. It's funny about me, Mis' Abel. Honest, I dunno what to do about me sometimes.

MIS' ABEL. Well, stop thinkin' about you so much.

PETER. I do try to. But when I try to think how to stop myself thinking about myself there's myself thinkin' about me.

MIS' ABEL. Think about somethin' else, then! You can stand and talk to me all day. I don't see why you can't talk to her.

PETER. I could talk all right enough. But my tongue won't. I could but my tongue, it won't. Why, some girls I know I can jolly like the dickens. But Inez—when she comes along, Mis' Abel, I can't remember anything I know. History now—I know a real lot about history. And about birds and things. I'd like to talk with her about them. But last week, when I took her to the picnic, I couldn't think out any of 'em to say no more'n a hen.

MIS' ABEL. Well, don't ask me to tell you how to court. Men that don't know history from a coach-and-four can court successful. But you can't expect Inez to know whether she likes you or not if you sit like a block. Say something—do something, so's she'll know you're alive.

PETER. I know it. I ain't much. An' what little I am don't show through somehow. Honest, Mis' Abel, I wouldn't care much what happened to me.
(GRANDMA *suddenly laughs out, an old woman's laugh, shrill, but not unkindly.*)

PETER. I guess I am a joke.

GRANDMA. Joke nothin'. You're a human. You're a human an' don't know it. I see a-many in my day.

MIS' ABEL. Well, a body needn't be a fool if they are human.

Neighbours by Zona Gale

b

GEORGE. Emily, why are you mad at me?

EMILY. I'm not mad at you.

GEORGE. You've been treating me so funny lately.

EMILY. Well, since you ask me, I might as well say it right out, George,— (*She catches sight of a teacher passing.*) Good-by, Miss Corcoran.

GEORGE. Good-by, Miss Corcoran.—Wha—what is it?

EMILY (*Not scoldingly, finding it difficult to say*). I don't like the whole change that's come over you in the last year. I'm sorry if that hurts your feelings, but I've got to—tell the truth and shame the devil.

GEORGE. A *change?*—Wha—what do you mean?

EMILY. Well, up to a year ago I used to like you a lot. And I used to watch you as you did everything—because we'd been friends so long—and then you began spending all your time at *baseball*—and you never stopped to speak to anybody any more. Not even to your own family you didn't—and, George, it's a fact, you've got awful conceited and stuck-up, and all the girls say so. They may not say so to your face, but that's what they say about you behind your back, and it hurts me to hear them say it, but I've got to agree with them a little. I'm sorry if it hurts your feelings—but I can't be sorry I said it.

GEORGE. I—I'm glad you said it, Emily. I never thought that such a thing was happening to me. I guess it's hard for a fella not to have faults creep into his character. (*They take a step or two in silence, then stand still in misery.*)

EMILY. I always expect a man to be perfect and I think he should be.

GEORGE. Oh—I don't think it's possible to be perfect, Emily.

EMILY. Well, my *father* is, and as far as I can see *your* father is. There's no reason on earth why you shouldn't be, too.

GEORGE. Well, I feel it's the other way round. That men aren't naturally good; but girls are.

EMILY. Well, you might as well know right now that I'm not perfect. It's not as easy for a girl to be perfect as a man, because we girls are more—more—

nervous.—Now I'm sorry I said all that about you. I don't know what made me say it.

GEORGE. Emily,—

EMILY. Now I can see it's not the truth at all. And suddenly I feel that it isn't important, anyway.

GEORGE. Emily—would you like an ice-cream soda, or something, before you go home?

EMILY. Well, thank you.—I would.

*Our Town* by Thornton Wilder

c

RICHARD. Well, what's the news? Been left a fortune?

CRAWSHAW. Yes—By a Mr. Anthony Clifton. I never met him and I know nothing about him.

RICHARD. Not really? Well, I congratulate you. To them that hath—But what on earth do you want my advice about?

CRAWSHAW. There is a slight condition attached.

RICHARD. Oho!

CRAWSHAW. The condition is that with this money—fifty thousand pounds— I take the name of—ah—Wurzel-Flummery.

RICHARD. What?

CRAWSHAW. I said it quite distinctly—Wurzel-Flummery.

RICHARD. Mr. Robert Wurzel-Flummery, M.P., one of the most prominent of our younger Parliamentarians. Oh, you—oh!—oh, how too heavenly!

CRAWSHAW. Shall we discuss it seriously, or shall we leave it?

RICHARD. How can we discuss a name like Wurzel-Flummery seriously? "Mr. Wurzel-Flummery, in a few well-chosen words, seconded the motion"— " 'Sir,' went on Mr. Wurzel-Flummery"—Oh, poor Robert!

CRAWSHAW. You seem quite certain that I shall take the money.

RICHARD. I am quite certain.

CRAWSHAW. Would *you* take it?

RICHARD. Well—I wonder.

CRAWSHAW. After all, as William Shakespeare says, "What's in a name?"

RICHARD. I can tell you something else that Shakespeare—*William* Shakespeare—said. Who steals my purse with fifty thousand in it—steals trash. Trash, Robert. But he who filches from me my good name of Crawshaw and substitutes for it the rotten one of Wurzel—

CRAWSHAW. As a matter of fact, Wurzel-Flummery is a very good old name. I seem to remember some—ah—Hampshire Wurzel-Flummeries. It is a very laudable spirit on the part of a dying man to wish to—ah—perpetuate these old English names. It all seems to me quite natural and straightforward. If I take this money I shall have nothing to be ashamed of.

RICHARD. I see.

*Wurzel-Flummery* by A. A. Milne

Bess. Don't do you no good, sighin' an' takin' on.

Lissie. I'm sick an' tired of it all.

Bess. If you'd set yourself out to try an' find what's really the matter with him, 'stead of moanin' about it, you'd be better off.

Lissie. Ain't I tried to find out? Ain't I asked him time an' time again? Ain't I almost gotten down on my knees to him? I can't do no more.

Bess. It ain't like Nathan to be so stubborn. It ain't like Nathan a tall. Maw allus said that she could do with Nathan more than with any of us children. I remember how maw uster say, "Nathan, do this," an' "Nathan, do that," an' he'd go right along an' do it without no back-talk or nothin'. He was never close with his tongue, neither. He allus told everything. Why, I remember the night he asked you to marry him. It was the night of the awful black frost. He came right in an' says, "Maw, I hev asked Lissie Hartwell to marry me"—jest simple, like that. He's altogether different now.

Lissie. Yes. He ain't the same Nathan who stood up so straight beside me in the church. Of course, you're all thinkin' it's my fault.

Bess. No, thar ain't no tellin' whose fault it is. The winter was so hard an' he had the trouble with the horses—an' then what happened two years ago—

Lissie. He didn't love our baby no more than me! Why, when they was buryin' her, didn't he stand an' look cold-like, his eyes hard as rocks, not a tear in 'em? He walked clear back to the house, right after, an' I had to ride on Roger's hoss, I was that weak.

Bess. Still we oughter be patient with him.

Lissie. Patient with him! Patient with a man who's took to drinkin'?

Bess. It ain't like Nathan to drink. He hated it so in paw. He uster say to us, "Thar's one thing I don't do an' that's drink." Allus he said that. Besides thar ain't no likker around here.

Lissie. I've smelled it on him. He must have a jug of it somewhere hid. He was stumblin'—

Bess. He works so fast, that's why. He wants to git that seed in the worst way. Seem's like something's walkin' behind him, tellin' him to git that seed in.

Lissie. All that's on his mind is work. He talks work in his sleep, plowin' an' gettin' that seed sowed. In the evenin's he uster be so nice with me— he'd read to me, sometimes, if he wasn't too tired.

Bess. Nathan larned himself to read. He wanted to larn me but I never had no time what with cookin' an' helpin' maw.

Lissie. He was larnin' me but all of a sudden he stopped. I wanted to larn. I liked it, but when I'd ask him, he'd git mad. Waal, thar ain't no use in talkin'.

*In the Darkness* by Dan Totheroh

# Chapter 5

# Varieties of Drama

As you read and see more and more plays, you will find yourself affected by them in different ways. Beyond the fact that each playwright has his own distinguishing characteristics as a writer and his own views on life, you will recognize that the plays themselves fall into categories.

Plays are classified into a variety of types of which comedy and tragedy are the two chief categories. In addition, there are farce, romantic drama, fantasy, melodrama, comedy of manners, sentimental comedy, and social drama. None of these is absolute or entirely separate. Each may, and often does, overlap another. It is often difficult or impossible to identify a play as a specific type.

Classification is further complicated by a consideration of the various styles in which a play may be written. Some of them are naturalism, realism, romanticism, symbolism, expressionism, and allegory. Like types, styles are neither absolute or entirely separate from each other. Furthermore, there is no hard and fast rule about just what constitutes a type and a style.

## TYPES

Remember that classification is rather arbitrary. Still, the following introduction to types should challenge your critical faculties and imagination and give you some knowledge of the terms used to describe plays.

### Comedy

The word *comedy* is derived from a Greek word, *komos*, meaning festivity or revelry. *Comedies* are usually light, written with sparkling dialogue, and peopled by amusing characters who are involved in funny situations

Moss Hart and George S. Kaufman's *The Man Who Came to Dinner.* (Comedy)

Judith Anderson in the Robinson Jeffers adaptation of Euripides' *Medea.* (Tragedy)

which they solve by their wits, their charm, and sometimes by sheer good fortune. Throughout the history of the theater, the greatest and most enduring comedies have taken situations and characters from life and therefore contain certain timeless human truths. Molière, Shakespeare, and Shaw are considered three of the world's best comedy writers. Their comedies have had lasting appeal because they are based on universal human experiences.

## Tragedy

In *tragedy*, the protagonist is defeated because of intellectual or spiritual flaws within himself, or because of the pressures of inescapable destiny. Even after making great sacrifices, his fate may be death or ruin without any of the success and satisfaction obtained by the protagonist in a comedy. The tragic hero is a man of stature, struggling mightily against dynamic forces. He is never commonplace; his will and character put him beyond the ordinary, and his sufferings are more than mere pathos.

There are several reasons why the greatest dramas have been tragedies rather than comedies. One is that only through suffering and sacrifice can human beings achieve true nobility. An enduring play must be concerned with profound emotions, for they have an appeal which is universal. Every person in an audience can appreciate the renunciation of self for others and can understand the fundamental urges of love, ambition, jealousy, and revenge by which the characters in tragedies are motivated.

Comedies, on the other hand, often depend upon local, regional, or topical situations. They seem entertaining to us only if our cultural background, temperament, and past experience permit us to respond to them; or if the characters transcend their particular situations and can be related to something or someone we have known. For example, the tragedies of the Greek dramatists still rank among the greatest dramas of the world, while their comedies, with a few exceptions, have little appeal today. We can all understand the despair of the Trojan women awaiting their fate at the hands of the victorious Greeks after the fall of Troy. However, it is the rare person who can appreciate jokes about politicians who died more than 2,000 years ago.

It should be said that many plays which plumb the depths of human experience include elements of both tragedy and comedy. The way in which a play ends is a rough guide to its classification. If the conclusion settles the main issues in a manner satisfactory to the protagonist, a play is usually called a comedy. On the other hand, if the conclusion shows the defeat of the protagonist, it is ordinarily called a tragedy.

## Farce

A *farce* is an exaggerated comedy written primarily to entertain. It usually depends upon practical jokes, broad humor, and implausible situations in which funny people are hopelessly involved. Some of the popular farces that are played year after year are *Charley's Aunt*, in which a young man dresses up as an old-maid aunt; *Nothing But the Truth*, in which the hero wagers he can tell nothing but the truth for a definite period of time; and Shakespeare's *The Comedy of Errors*, in which two pairs of identical twins precipitate many complications.

## Romantic Drama

*Romantic drama* is usually serious but often contains comic elements. Its most characteristic feature is poetic language. The characters are frequently noble and conceived on a grand scale. Shakespeare, Rostand, and, more recently, Maxwell Anderson and Christopher Fry have written plays of this type.

## Fantasy

*Fantasy* is a form of romantic drama in which the setting is generally unrealistic and the characters are fancifully portrayed. Dreams, magic forests, fairyland, or even Heaven and Hell may furnish the background.

**Edmund Gwenn and Jack Benny in Brandon Thomas's *Charley's Aunt*. (Farce)**

Courtesy of Twentieth Century-Fox

Photo by Etienne Weill, Paris

Jean-Louis Barrault and Simone Valère in Jean Giradoux's *Intermezzo*. (Romantic Drama)

Mary Martin and Cyril Ritchard in James Barrie's *Peter Pan*. (Fantasy)

Courtesy of NBC Television

VARIETIES OF DRAMA 93

**George Montgomery in the television series "Cimarron City." (Melodrama)**

The characters may be alive or dead, real or imaginary. Many of these characters have become immortal—Pierrot and Pierrette, Harlequin and Columbine, and the ghosts, giants, elves, and spirits that inhabit the land of make-believe. From Shakespeare's *The Tempest* and *A Midsummer Night's Dream* to James M. Barrie's immortal *Peter Pan*, from Maxwell Anderson's *High Tor* and John Balderston's *Berkeley Square* to Elmer Rice's *Dream Girl* and Jean Giraudoux's *The Madwoman of Chaillot*, we find such drama appealing to every generation.

## Melodrama

The *melodramatic play* is written to arouse immediate and intense emotion by means of exaggeration and emphasis on action rather than on intricate characterization and situations. In fact, close analysis of a character in a melodrama will often prove disappointing because most of the people are stock types. However, the action usually moves so rapidly that the audience does not have time to look at a character as an individual who should have the usual conflicts and complexities in his life.

George Farquhar's *The Beaux' Stratagem.* (Comedy of Manners)

Atmosphere, stress, and emotion-packed action are the primary elements of melodrama, which often deals with murder, revenge, suicide, thwarted or complicated love, and greed. Many fine films and plays have been done in this form. *Angel Street, Arsenic and Old Lace, Night Must Fall, Witness for the Prosecution,* and *Dial M for Murder* are a few of the more outstanding melodramas. Television, with its serials, mysteries, and westerns, offers many opportunities to view melodramas.

## Comedy of Manners

A *comedy of manners* deals with social customs, fashions, prejudices, and trends of a particular time or place. Dialogue is brilliantly clever and often razor-sharp in its criticism of the customs of the day. For example, Restoration drama satirized its time and habits in such plays as William Wycherley's *The Country Wife,* Sir John Vanbrugh's *The Relapse,* William Congreve's *The Way of the World,* and George Farquhar's *The Beaux' Stratagem.* Richard Brinsley Sheridan also wrote in this vein. S. N. Behrman, Noel Coward, and Philip Barry are modern writers of comedies of manners.

## Sentimental Comedy

Many regular television series belong to this type. *Sentimental comedies* center upon the obvious themes of youthful romance, loss of family, patriotism, self-sacrifice, and lost affection. A large proportion of the "soap operas" on television and radio are excessively sentimental dramas, but they do become real to regular viewers and listeners. Many good stage plays can be identified as sentimental comedies. Some of these are James M. Barrie's *Quality Street* and *A Kiss for Cinderella* and John Van Druten's *I Remember Mama*.

## Social Drama

The *social drama* concerns itself with society and its problems. The author of a social drama may write about the relations between management and labor, group conformity, poverty, crime, the causes of juvenile delinquency, or similar problems.

One of the first writers of the social problem play was Henrik Ibsen of Norway. He shocked late nineteenth-century theatergoers by exposing their own hypocrisies to them. In *A Doll's House*, he attacked the idea that a woman should submerge herself totally in household affairs and live according to the whims of a selfish husband. In *Ghosts*, he showed the horrible effects of a father's dissipation and immorality on his son. These themes were thought unfit for the theater and created a heated controversy about Ibsen.

In the United States, Clifford Odets' *Waiting for Lefty*, Sidney Kingsley's *Dead End*, Paul Green's *In Abraham's Bosom*, Eugene O'Neill's *The Hairy Ape*, Arthur Miller's *Death of a Salesman*, and Michael Gazzo's *A Hatful of Rain* are all examples of social drama.

## STYLES

The term *style* refers to the way in which a play is written, acted, and produced. It is usually appropriate to the material and theme of a play and to the kind of response hoped for from the audience. Styles are given labels such as *realism, romanticism, allegory*, and *expressionism* in accordance with their distinguishing features. In some plays several styles are blended together. Ferenc Molnar's *Liliom*, which is called *Carousel* in the musical version, is a good example. This play goes from the realism of Julie's love for the scoundrel Liliom to the allegory of the Heavenly Court which tries Liliom after his death. Other dramas are done in a style, or styles, which cannot accurately be given any specific label.

Courtesy of CBS Television

James Donald and Siobhan McKenna in James Barrie's *What Every Woman Knows*. (Sentimental Comedy)

Sidney Kingsley's *Dead End*. (Social Drama)

Photo by White; courtesy of the Theatre Collection, New York Public Library

VARIETIES OF DRAMA     97

## Realism and Naturalism

The *realistic play* presents life as it is. "Holding the mirror up to nature," it strives to create the effect of actual reality on the stage. Natural dialogue is used, and the characters are involved in the ordinary problems of life, which may be sordid, ugly, and unhappy. The realistic drama began with Ibsen in the modern era and remains the style of most of our contemporary plays.

*Naturalism* is the term frequently applied to the extremely realistic play, especially one in which environment or heredity plays an important part. No detail is spared in the pursuit of reality in this style of play, and theatergoers are often shocked into a response.

## Romanticism

*Romanticism* is a style of writing which often presents life as it would be if everything were ideal—if people were noble and almost always good. In the nineteenth century, this style of writing and method of presentation

**Arthur Miller's adaptation of Henrik Ibsen's *Enemy of the People*. (Realism)**
Photo by Richard Dean

reached a peak which resulted finally in the turn to realistic drama. Today few dramatists are writing in the romantic style.

## Symbolism

In *symbolic drama,* we enter the area where abstract ideas and concepts are personified or objectified. For example, in Maurice Maeterlinck's *The Blue Bird,* the characters and the physical properties of the play suggest elements of man's eternal search for truth and happiness. Mytyl and Tyltyl are Woman and Man engaged in this search. Truth is represented by the diamond in Tyltyl's cap; when he turns it, he can see things as they really are. Happiness, when it is finally found in their own home, is represented by the blue bird.

Symbolic events and figures are often seen in combination with other styles and types. Though *Death of a Salesman* would not be considered a symbolic drama, Willie Loman, its chief character, has become a symbol of man's need to find his real place in society.

Claude Debussy's opera *Pelléas and Mélisande,* based on Maurice Maeterlinck's play. (Symbolism)

Photo by Sedge LeBlang; courtesy of the Metropolitan Opera

Robert Ardrey's *Thunder Rock*. (Expressionism)

*Everyman*, as performed on the steps of Salzburg Cathedral. (Allegory)

## Expressionism

Abstract ideas and concepts are also visualized in *expressionistic plays,* often by means of distortion or sensationalism in staging and scenery. For example, in Elmer Rice's *The Adding Machine,* the leading character, Mr. Zero, represents all men who have labored at mechanical jobs until they have lost the power to be more than machines themselves. The use of a number for his name is expressionistic and so is the tremendous size of the machine. In the scene where Mr. Zero rebels and kills his employer, his wild hysteria is expressed by the whirling of the stage, swirling lights, and general chaos. The audience actually feels that it is experiencing the situation in the person of Mr. Zero.

## Allegory

An *allegorical play* usually personifies human or animal qualities and teaches a lesson through the use of imagery and implied meanings. In *Everywoman,* written in imitation of the medieval drama *Everyman,* we see the woman going forth to meet Love. On the journey she meets Passion and other personifications of the phases of romantic life. Karel Čapek's *The Insect Comedy,* which concerns the lives and struggles of insects, is an implied allegory.

### OTHER FORMS

New types of drama are constantly springing up, and in our own time we shall no doubt see many exciting theatrical experiments. More and more, our dramatists are breaking away from the standardized three-act play, and no one can foresee exactly what new form or style will be revealed in any season. To know what is going on you must keep abreast of dramatic news and criticism.

## One-act Plays

Sometimes plays are classified by their length, as the one-act play, the full-length play—which usually means three acts today—or the four- or five-act play often found in classical works. Of course, the length has nothing to do with the type, which may be any of those just discussed. Because the one-act play furnishes much material for discussion and presentation by the class in dramatics, it will be considered as a unit in itself here.

The one-act play became a serious dramatic form nearly fifty years ago, largely due to the critical acclaim given to Eugene O'Neill's early dramas, which were written in this form. Also important in the development of the one-act play is the fact that it was well suited to the needs of the little-theater movement which started just after World War I. Inexperienced actors in the many little theaters were able to sustain parts in one-act plays while they could not do so in longer ones. Sometimes one-act plays were given in groups of three or four. This kind of program offered more opportunities for people to work in the theater than did the full-length type of production.

Today the one-act play is still popular. It is seen in professional groups, in little theaters, and in the classroom. Over the years, well-known writers have utilized this form. Some of these writers are Anton Chekhov, Gertrude Stein, Christopher Fry, William Saroyan, Tennessee Williams, Noel Coward, Eugene Ionesco, and Terence Rattigan.

In the one-act play, the action and dialogue concern one incident and are condensed to lead directly to the climax and the conclusion. The exposition must be brief and concise, arousing immediate audience interest.

## Musical Plays

The use of music in the theater is as old as the dramatic impulse itself. Its applications vary from mood music used in straight dramatic plays, masques, pantomimes, and variety shows to music in operettas, operas, musical comedies, and musical dramas.

The distinctive qualities of a musical drama, as opposed to most of the other musical forms, are that it has a strong story line and is peopled with characters who are real and true to life. Singing and dancing in musical drama are integral parts of the play and are used in conjunction with dialogue and action to advance the movement of the story dramatically.

When *Oklahoma!*, with its original choreography, delightful music, and spontaneous charm, opened in 1943, the modern musical drama became a very important medium of expression in our theater. It has since been followed by a continuous succession of hits. Many of these have been based on great plays. *Kiss Me Kate* was based on Shakespeare's *The Taming of the Shrew*; *Carousel*, on Molnar's *Liliom*; *The Most Happy Fella*, on Howard's *They Knew What They Wanted*; and *My Fair Lady*, on Shaw's *Pygmalion*. Some, like *South Pacific*, have been derived from novels or short stories and others have had appealing original plots.

## Symphonic Dramas

The *symphonic drama* is also becoming a part of our contemporary theatrical scene. Reminiscent of the historical and local pageants of twenty-five years ago, it goes far beyond any other form of community drama in re-creating the life of America.

Julie Andrews and Rex Harrison in Alan Jay Lerner and Frederick Loewe's *My Fair Lady*. (Musical)

Paul Green's *The Common Glory*. (Symphonic Drama)

VARIETIES OF DRAMA 103

**Richardson and Berney's** *Dark of the Moon.* **(Folk Play)**

Paul Green has been the greatest exponent of this type of musical drama, which uses huge casts against actual or constructed historical backgrounds and features music characteristic of a particular region. Green's *Lost Colony* at Roanoke Island, North Carolina, and *The Common Glory* at Williamsburg, Virginia, are seen every year by thousands of tourists.

*Ramona*, which is presented annually in California, is another very popular symphonic drama. This is a dramatization of Helen Hunt Jackson's love story about the Indian maiden Ramona and the Indian hero Alessandro. It is staged on the slopes of Mt. San Jacinto, in the lovely valley where many of the events recorded in the novel actually took place. The more than 350 people who make up the cast are residents of the area. Undoubtedly the next quarter century will see many such productions becoming theatrical traditions in various places all across our country.

## Folk Plays

A *folk play* presents the language, the customs, the attitudes, and the problems of a particular locale and its people. Paul Green is our most successful writer of this kind of play. *In Abraham's Bosom*, his play about the folkways of the South, won a Pulitzer prize and is a notable example of the folk play.

Bertolt Brecht's *Mother Courage.* (Epic Theater)

### Epic Theater

The *epic theater* is a reaction against emotionalism and naturalism in both the writing and staging of plays. Mordecai Gorelik, the eminent scenic artist, in his distinguished book *New Theatres for Old*, explains that this type of theater objectively sets forth events in broad phases of human experience rather than showing individual relationships. The author and scenic artist work together to present an important sociological study, using all the mechanical devices of the theater—lantern slides, motion pictures, loudspeakers, lights—to create clear, illustrative episodes. Light is used for illumination—not to create atmosphere. Settings are purely functional, never realistic in any sense.

Mr. Gorelik prophesies that theaters of the future will have large mobile units which will enable settings to revolve, hang in space, and tilt at angles, thus being "tokens of environment" rather than copies of real scenes.

The typical epic play does not attempt to involve the spectator in the problems and emotions of its characters as most plays do. Instead, it presents a problem—usually a social problem—and asks the spectator to find a solution. Entertainment is a secondary goal for epic theater. Its primary purpose is to instruct.

*Discussion*

1. In what does the universal appeal of *Othello, Hamlet,* and *Macbeth* lie?
2. Classify the following plays, giving your reasons:
   a. *Alcestis* by Euripides is the story of a queen who dies voluntarily in place of her husband. Through the intervention of Hercules, her soul returns to earth.
   b. *Death Takes a Holiday* by Casella and Ferris shows Death coming to earth to learn why people hate him and cling to life. He falls in love with a highly spiritual girl who chooses to die and go with him, and so he finds that only love is stronger than he.
   c. *The Scarecrow* by Percy MacKaye tells of a scarecrow who is brought to life as a gallant young man. He uses many humorous tricks to win the love of a beautiful girl. However, when he finds out who he really is, he destroys himself and thereby gains a soul.

3. Using the type and style classifications given in this chapter as a guide, try to find a movie you have seen lately to fit each classification. Be prepared to discuss the reasons for your choices.

4. Name a television play you have seen which can be classified as a tragedy; also name one which you consider a comedy. Give your reasons for classifying each. Which type is seen more often? Why?

5. It has been said that melodrama is "the backbone of television serials." Do you agree?

6. As mentioned in this chapter, types and styles are often combined in a single play. Give an example of a naturalistic tragedy, a social satire, a symbolic tragedy, an expressionistic melodrama, a romantic comedy, and an allegorical fantasy. Use as sources plays you have seen on television, in the movies, or on the stage and explain why you selected each example.

7. Have you heard the term *propaganda play* used? What do you think it means? Give some examples of plays which could be labeled in this way.

8. Explain the amazing development and popularity of the musical play in the United States. What are some of the popular songs which come from musical plays?

9. If you have any, explain your preferences for particular types or styles of plays. (For example, would you rather see movies and plays that represent life as it is or those which show life as you wish it were?)


*Applications*

1. From current newspapers, select items which you think could be developed into good farces, melodramas, social comedies, and sentimental plays.

2. In your notebook start a list of the plays you read and see. Give the name of the play, the author, and the type and style whenever possible.

3. To become familiar with good one-act plays of different types, read the following, which should be easy to obtain at your library. Outline them in your notebook.

Farce—*A Wedding* by John Kirkpatrick
Melodrama—*Two Crooks and a Lady* by Eugene Pillot
Sentimental comedy—*The Old Lady Shows Her Medals* by James M. Barrie
Social comedy—*The Twelve Pound Look* by James M. Barrie
Satire—*Wurzel-Flummery* by A. A. Milne
Fantasy—*Will o' the Wisp* by Doris Halman
Allegory—*The Slave with Two Faces* by Carolyn Davies
Folk play—*The Last of the Lowries* by Paul Green
Epic theater—*The Caucasian Chalk Circle* by Bertolt Brecht
Realistic comedy—*The Camberly Triangle* by A. A. Milne
Romantic comedy-fantasy—*The Wonder Hat* by Goodman and Hecht
Realistic tragedy—*Judge Lynch* by J. W. Rogers
Romantic tragedy—*Torches* by Kenneth Raisbeck

4. Prepare a series of one-act play readings, which will illustrate the various types of drama, to present before English classes.

5. Make a careful class study of *Poor Maddalena* by Louise Saunders in Appendix A. This drama has been selected because it successfully combines elements of tragedy, comedy, realism, and romance against a background of fantasy. Although it has many of the characteristics of a long play, it is no longer than a one-act play and can be read or presented in one class period.

The questions following the play, on pages 465 to 467, should assist you in appreciating the play's values as you read. These questions are typical of the kind of approach you should use in all your reading, especially in play reading, and should help you to reach a greater understanding of the drama.

*Chapter 6*

# History of Drama

The history of the drama is closely related to the history of mankind. When the first hunters recounted their adventures by means of vivid pantomime, when the first storytellers told their tales in rhythmic chants, when the first priests prayed to the gods by means of ceremonial dances, the dramatic impulse was manifesting itself. The use of a mask to hide the identity of the performer in the representation of god or animal, and the expression of emotion in the pantomimic intricacies of the hunting, war, and love dances are outstanding phases of the earliest drama. As civilization developed, drama took definite form in the worship of heavenly gods and the glorification of earthly rulers. Drama, as we think of it today, really owes its birth to the fundamental religious and dramatic urges inherent in human beings. The Book of Job and The Song of Songs in the Old Testament are dramatic in form.

## THE BEGINNINGS THROUGH THE RENAISSANCE

### Beginnings in Egypt

The earliest record of a theatrical performance comes from Egypt, the birthplace of much of the world's art. Carved on a stone tablet some 4,000 years ago, this account tells how Ikhernofret arranged and played a leading role in a three-day pageant made up of actual battles, boat processions, and elaborate ceremonies which told the story of the great god Osiris' death and resurrection. Also in Egypt, carvings and murals on the walls of the ancient temples and tombs show highly theatrical pictures of dancing

108

Masks, similar to those used in ancient Greek dramas, are worn in the Canadian Stratford Festival's production of *Oedipus Rex.*

girls and triumphal processions. Cecil B. De Mille's movie *The Ten Commandments* brought some of these early theatrical spectacles to life.

An early form of dramatic literature existed in the emotional religious hymns of the Egyptians. Around 1350 B.C., Ikhnaton, one of the greatest of all the pharoahs, was responsible for the creation of a hymn to the sun which is still held in high respect in the field of dramatic religious poetry.

### Greek Drama

Markedly similar to the worship of Osiris in Egypt were the beginnings of drama in Greece. Rituals were dedicated to the god Dionysus in the sixth century B.C., and an altar was erected to him in an open spot at the foot of a hillside. Around this altar centered the dancing and chanting of the goat singers, a chorus of citizens from nearby villages. The goat, sacred to Dionysus, was sacrificed as the climax of the festival commemorating the god's death.

The Dionysian festivals evolved into great dramatic contests, the first of which was won in 534 B.C. by Thespis, who stepped from the chorus to recite previously composed lines. In doing this he created a dialogue between the chorus and himself. He is often called the world's first actor, and the term *Thespian* is still applied to actors the world over.

The greatest writers of Greek tragedy were Aeschylus, Sophocles, and Euripides. Aeschylus (525–456 B.C.) introduced dialogue between two persons. His *Oresteia* and *Prometheus Bound* are perhaps his most famous plays. Sophocles (497–406 B.C.) was the most revered of the three and made the largest number of innovations. He not only introduced a third actor to make the dialogues truly dramatic, but he also introduced dramatic action leading to a definite plot structure. His characters were lifelike human beings. Oedipus, of *Oedipus Rex*, and the two young sisters in *Antigone* are amazingly modern in their words and reactions. Euripides (480–406 B.C.) has been called *the first modern* because he developed the human interest element. His plays *Trojan Women, Hecuba*, and *Medea* still rank among the most poignant portrayals of women in dramatic literature.

The conflicts in Greek tragedies evolved from the clash between the will of the gods and the ambitions and desires of men; they showed the futility of human efforts to circumvent fate. These plays dealt with crucial events in the lives of rulers as told in myths and legends. The language in them expresses sublime ideas in exquisite poetic form, and the characters are magnificent in their simplicity, dignity, and courage.

Greek tragedy had certain definite conventions which were rarely violated. Among these were the three unities. The *unity of time* limited the action to successive events which followed each other without lapse of time. The *unity of place* limited the action to one locale. The *unity of action* restricted the play to one series of closely related events. The typical Greek tragedy included the following elements: a *prologue*, the opening explanatory speech by the chorus, setting forth the situation; *episodes*, or dramatic scenes presenting the important action; *choral interludes*, in which the chorus and leaders discussed the main action; a speech by the chorus preceding each episode; and an *exode*, the closing action following the last choral interlude.

In Greek comedy, the outstanding name is that of Aristophanes (450–380 B.C.). He was a skilled satirist and a keen observer of the foibles of mankind. His plays, *The Frogs, The Birds*, and *Lysistrata*, are remarkably modern in concept and treatment and contain much that is humorous and delightful to contemporary audiences.

Described as simply as possible, a Greek theater looked rather like an enormous bowl built into a hillside. Seats were cut into the hillside in tiers so that the theater resembled a modern football arena. In the center was a circular space called the *orchestra*, containing an altar and a playing space

© D. A. Harissiadis, Athens; courtesy of *Theatre Arts* Magazine

*The Thesmophoriazusae* of Aristophanes, as performed at Epidaurus in 1958.

"An Audience in Athens." (A painting by Sir W. B. Richmond)

By permission of City Museum and Art Gallery, Birmingham, England

Model of the Theater of Dionysus in Athens as it probably appeared in ancient times.

The Theater of Dionysus today. This theater is still used every summer for productions of the Greek classics.

for the chorus and actors. Near this space was a sort of hut called the *skene*, which was first used as a dressing room for the actors. Later the skene was expanded into a permanent, heavily decorated architectural backing for the playing area, with steps and columns. In front of this skene the action took place. Eventually side wings, known as the *parascenia*, were added. In the parascenia were doors to facilitate entrances and exits. The most famous of the Greek theaters was the Theater of Dionysus at Athens. The drama festivals were held here, and each dramatist presented three plays in competition for the cherished ivy wreath and accompanying high honor.

Three pieces of stage equipment are credited to Greek ingenuity. One of these was the *machina*, a cranelike device operated from the roof of the skene. Actors playing the gods were lowered by means of this machine to confer with mortal men and to settle their affairs. It was an appropriate piece of equipment in the ancient dramas where the will of the gods predominated over the wills and deeds of men. From the use of this machine came the expression *deus ex machina* which, translated literally, means a "god from a machine." Today this term is used to describe an artificial device introduced to resolve a problem in the plot of a play or story.

The *eccyclema* was a movable platform rolled or pushed into the playing area in order to show interior action. In the early Greek theater the audience was not permitted to watch violence, so the eccyclema was often used to show a tableau of a murder, a suicide, or a battle after it had occurred offstage. The *periaktoi* were three-sided pieces of scenery placed on both sides of the stage. Different scenes were painted on each side, permitting an easy change of place.

Because there was no system of artificial lighting, dramatic performances had to be held between dawn and dusk. They were attended by enthusiastic crowds, many of whom came great distances. At no time in its long history has the drama played a more vital part in the life of the people than it did in this brilliant early period in Greece. This is undoubtedly one very good reason why the Greek theater still influences the dramatic ideals of the Western world.

## Roman Theater

The Roman theater was a decadent imitation of the Greek, deteriorating at last into sensual interpretative dances called *pantomimes*, vulgar farces called *mimes*, and colossal gladiatorial contests in which the slaughter of human beings and beasts furnished the emotional thrill. In structure, the theater gradually became an arena surrounded by towering tiers of seats. The cruelty of the great spectacles and the coarseness of the dramatic entertainment at last aroused the moralists. As the Christian Church became a public force, the drama in all its forms was ostracized. During the Dark Ages following the decline of Rome only wandering players kept the drama alive with their dancing, singing, juggling, and marionette shows.

*Discussion*

1. What do you think is meant by the Greek idea that man is powerless against his fate, or destiny? Do you believe each of us has a destiny which cannot be changed? Why?

2. Have you seen plays which observed the three unities? Name the plays and tell whether the unities affected the impact of the play. If the unities did have some effect, explain what it was. Do you think the unities should be observed in modern drama? Explain your reasons.

3. Have you seen or read about a Greek play recently produced by either amateurs or professionals? If so, describe its production and tell how the audience reacted to the performance.

4. Explain some of the reasons why Greek plays are revived each year.

*Applications*

1. Plan a program for your dramatic club on the subject of early drama. From the books listed in Appendix C and material in encyclopedias give reports on such subjects as the following:

> Ceremonials of an American Indian Tribe
> Pageantry of the Aztecs
> The Religion and Hymns of Ikhnaton
> The Murals in Egyptian Tombs
> The Architecture of the Greek Theater
> Costumes and Masks in Greek Drama

2. Working in groups of two and three, prepare scenes from early dramas to read aloud.

3. In the *Readers' Guide to Periodical Literature* in your library, look up accounts of contemporary productions of Greek dramas and report on them, showing photographs if possible. Look especially for accounts of the production of *Medea* in which Judith Anderson starred and Tyrone Guthrie's production of *Oedipus Rex*.

4. Read a Greek play and outline it in your notebook.

5. As a group, visit a nearby museum to see the theatrical exhibits. Also look for theatrical material in exhibits of costumes, paintings, sculpture, and implements.

6. Make some masks like those you find pictured in books on primitive and ancient drama. Display them in class.

7. Present scenes from Greek plays out of doors or before a columned building. Perhaps this could be your contribution to a community celebration.

## Medieval Drama

The drama owed its revival, like its origin, to religion. During the period extending roughly from the fifth to the fifteenth centuries, drama developed along slightly different lines in the various European nations. In each case, however, its rebirth came about through the Christian Church. Priests introduced into their rituals dramatic representations of great Biblical events. They did this to inform the masses of people who could neither read nor write. From brief tableaux before the altar, Church dramas evolved into elaborate productions which called for presentation out of doors. Latin was used, as in the Masses, and the performers were priests and monks. In the tenth century, the German nun Hrosvitha wrote little playlets for the moral instruction of her companion nuns in the convent.

Gradually Church drama expanded to illustrate more and more of the Bible stories. These were called *mystery plays.* The first mystery play of real literary as well as dramatic value was *Adam,* written in the twelfth century. Another kind of religious drama, the *miracle play,* depicted the lives of the saints. Eventually, the parishioners began to take part in the productions, and the plays were translated from Latin into the native languages. Presentations of plays on festival days became the civic undertakings of various associations of merchants, called *guilds.*

With the presentation of plays by the guilds came the cycles. Each guild had a pageant wagon divided into two parts. The lower level was curtained and used as a dressing room. The upper level became the stage. These wagons were moved about the towns in processions. On each wagon a different religious play was performed. The entire sequence of plays was called a *cycle.* Each guild produced an appropriate Biblical scene. The goldsmiths, for example, presented the story of the Three Wise Men. The guilds vied with one another to see which could stage the most elaborate production. These cycles were highly developed in England at Chester, York, and Coventry. Manuscripts of the plays are still in existence today.

The *morality play* was the next form of the drama to develop. Still distinctly ethical in purpose, it dealt with the principles of right and wrong, dramatized by symbolic characters who represented abstract qualities. The best-known example of this type of play is *Everyman.* In this play, God sends Death to fetch Everyman and demands a strict accounting of his life on earth.

Later, wandering groups of professional players began presenting miracle and morality plays. These players were descendants of the strollers who had kept the dramatic spark alive in the Punch and Judy shows and pantomimes of the Dark Ages. Setting up their crude stages in public squares and at

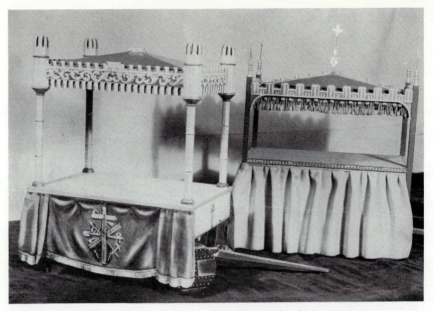

Models of pageant wagons used by the guilds for their religious plays.

country crossroads, they eked out a precarious living from the voluntary offerings of the common folk. These players were the originators of the first dramatic companies. Many of these groups were later taken under the patronage of the nobility.

Other transitional dramatic forms developed in the fifteenth century. They included *interludes*, short bits of humorous action usually performed between serious plays; *chronicle plays*, secular dramatizations of historical events; and *masques*, highly artistic spectacles presented at court entertainments. The latter were usually written and performed for the glorification of the nobility and were often presented against gorgeous backgrounds designed by great artists.

*Discussion*

1. Which Biblical passages do you think would be most effective in play form? Why?

2. Have you recently heard or seen religious plays that are similar to miracle and mystery plays? Tell the class about them.

3. How do our pageants of today differ from those given by the guilds?

4. Describe a modern play that you have seen or read which you feel closely resembles a form of medieval drama.

*Applications*

1. Prepare a report on both early and modern productions of *Everyman*.
2. Read and summarize the account of medieval stage effects in Lee Simonson's book *The Stage Is Set*.
3. Explain why drama and religion have been so closely identified with each other.
4. Read and report on a religious play written for a special church occasion such as Christmas or Easter, or based on a Biblical theme or character.
5. Give reports on the following topics:
   The Passion Play of Oberammergau—Its Performers and Performance
   American Passion Plays
   The Place of Strolling Players in Dramatic History
   Life in the Middle Ages
6. Read an old miracle or mystery play and work up a dramatic sketch from it.
7. Give a dramatic reading of *Everyman*, after analyzing its theme, humor, dramatic power, and theatrical possibilities.
8. Read and compare the Book of Job with its modernized version *J.B.* by Archibald MacLeish.

## Effects of the Renaissance

The historical period known as the Renaissance (meaning rebirth) began in Italy in the early fourteenth century. During this period, which extended into the sixteenth century, man's artistic endeavors were given new life, not only in Italy but throughout most of Europe. Men found enlightenment through intensive study—particularly the study of classical art and literature—as well as experience. They sought to express their new ideas and concepts in an individualistic manner. Painting, architecture, philosophy, and literature moved away from sterile imitations of old forms and new modes of expression were developed.

Drama changed too. Under the patronage of the royalty and nobility of various nations, the professional theater came into its own. Plays were performed in palace halls or specially erected buildings, and sufficient funds made it possible to employ superior artists, actors, and dramatists. Different nations contributed their own special theatrical ideas to the glory of the stage. Italy, for example, developed theater architecture and stage equipment, introducing sets with perspective and colored light. Italy also stamped the European theater permanently with the influence of the *commedia dell' arte*.

The *commedia* was made up of traveling troupes of players who, from the sixteenth into the eighteenth centuries, appeared in Italy (and later

*Commedia dell' arte* **players in a comic scene. (An engraving by J. B. Probst)**

in most of Europe) improvising plays from traditional stories. There were no written lines, and the plays were produced from an outline posted backstage. This outline gave a few incidents which led to a definite climax. The actors made up lines as the situations developed, or adapted set speeches to the scene. One predictable element of a *commedia dell' arte* performance was that the characters would be recognizable "stock" types such as clowns, foolish old men, giddy young women, boastful soldiers, and faithful sweethearts. The characters were called by familiar names, and the actors wore masks or clothing which identified them for the audience. You have probably met some of these stock characters under their more contemporary names of Pierrot and Pierrette, Harlequin, Columbine, and Punch.

The climax of the renaissance in drama came during the Elizabethan Age in England. This was a period in which the drama expressed the nation's soul and the theater was a vital force in the lives of the people. Poet-dramatists in this resplendent period included John Lyly, George Peele, Thomas Nashe, Robert Greene, and Thomas Kyd. Later came Ben Jonson with his comedy *Every Man in His Humour,* Beaumont and Fletcher with *Two Noble Kinsmen,* and Thomas Dekker with his farce *Shoemaker's Holiday.*

Christopher Marlowe (1564–1593) was one of the most outstanding Elizabethan dramatists. Although he only lived for twenty-nine years, he accomplished a great deal in his brief lifetime. He is remembered today for his extraordinary command of language and for his marvelous use of blank verse. His tragedies, *Tamburlaine the Great, Doctor Faustus, The Jew of Malta,* and *Edward II,* are still widely read and frequently performed.

The greatest of the Elizabethan dramatists and certainly one of the greatest dramatists who ever lived was William Shakespeare. For more than three centuries the theaters of the world have presented his plays. The foremost actors in every country have interpreted his roles. His plays have been seen, talked about, and written about endlessly. The finest minds of modern civilization have acknowledged his genius. Shakespeare is more than a historical figure of the drama. He is a contemporary playwright. The world has long accepted the verdict of Ben Jonson who said: "Shakespeare was not of an age but for all time." Shakespeare lived from 1564 to 1616 and for about twenty of those years he pursued a career as playwright, actor, and stage manager. In that time he wrote thirty-six plays and made a fortune which permitted him to retire to the country at the age of forty-seven. (Chapter 7, on pages 154 to 163, will tell you more about the man and his plays.)

**(Left) The title page for the first edition of Christopher Marlowe's** *Doctor Faustus.* **(Right) Troupes of players performed in innyards like this before the first public playhouses were built.**

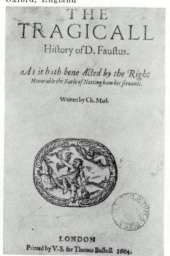

The first public playhouse in London, the Theatre, was built in 1576 by James Burbage. He was the manager of the company later housed in the Globe Theatre, with which Shakespeare was associated as actor-playwright. These theaters were modeled upon inn yards, with open courts surrounded by galleries, and upon bear pits, which were small circular arenas. The stage extended into an open space called the *pit*, permitting spectators who paid the smallest fee to stand on three sides. The higher priced seats were in the balconies or on the stage itself. There was no stage curtain, but a small inner recess could be draped off and used to present interior scenes. Performances were held in the afternoon, weather permitting, and were announced by a flag flying from the theater roof. Because women were not permitted to act, all feminine roles were played by boys. Set pieces, representing rocks and trees, were used together with essential pieces of furniture. Costumes were often very beautiful, since they were furnished by wealthy patrons who competed with one another in the elaborate clothing of their players. No attempt was made, however, to costume the actors with historical accuracy. For example, the Roman citizens in *Julius Caesar* appeared in the gorgeous satins, velvets, and plumes of the sixteenth century.

Seldom in the history of the world has the theater found so congenial an atmosphere as that of the Elizabethan Age. Actors and playwrights were often liberally paid by their noble patrons. The nobility, in turn, sponsored new dramas with the hope of gaining the approving glance of Queen Elizabeth, who showed a lively interest in the theater. It is not surprising that romantic drama reached its peak during her reign.

*Discussion*

1. Why was the Renaissance an exciting era for artists?
2. What does "improvisation" mean? Describe its use by the *commedia dell' arte*.
3. How do you account for the continuing popularity of Shakespeare's plays?
4. Do you think Shakespeare would enjoy having his plays produced in the new mediums? Do you think he would be writing for the movies and television, as well as the stage, if he were alive today? Why?

*Applications*

1. Prepare reports on the following topics:
   The *Commedia dell' Arte*
   Drama in Shakespeare's Boyhood (as depicted in *Kenilworth*, a novel about Elizabethan England, by Sir Walter Scott)
   Christopher Marlowe and His Contribution to Drama
   Leading Pre-Shakespearean Dramatists in England

A reconstruction of the stage of the Globe Theatre. (From a model of the Globe by Dr. John Cranford Adams)

Shakespeare's Contemporaries on the Continent

The play *Will Shakespeare* by Clemence Dane

2. Check the dates of dramatists mentioned in this section and then think back over any movies, plays, or stories which have told you something about their periods. What is the relationship between the lives and works of the playwrights and the historical events taking place around them?

3. Read a pre-Shakespearean play and outline it in your notebook.

4. Read and make a written report on one of Shakespeare's plays which you have not previously read.

This section briefly treats theater activity as it has developed during the last 350 years. The story of drama in the United States follows in a section of its own.

## In England

Kindled by the artistic enthusiasm of the Renaissance, drama in England had flamed into a mighty conflagration, only to die down rapidly and be extinguished by the Puritans. The Puritans had always opposed the theater, as had many of the citizens of London. Their protests were somewhat justified on the grounds that lawless and unsanitary conditions prevailed in the playhouses. Even during the height of Elizabethan enthusiasm, theaters had been condemned as breeders of the plague and actors as instruments of the devil. Preachers and pamphleteers finally succeeded in arousing civic authorities, and in 1642 an edict was issued for the suppression of stage plays. Plays given in secret and performances at county fairs were the only things that kept the drama alive until 1660 when it was allowed to come out of hiding and continue its development. Responsible for this regained freedom was an event which gives its name to the period; the popular and fun-loving Stuarts were *restored* to power on the throne of England, and so the period is called the *Restoration*.

Important innovations in theater were made during the Restoration. Women were allowed to appear as players and elaborate scenery and mechanical equipment, introduced into England by Inigo Jones, came into general use. It is interesting to note that the English Royal Patent of 1662 gave leave that "all women's parts should be performed by women" and provided that plays and acting might be esteemed "not only harmless delights but useful and instructive representations of human life."

The drama of the Restoration reflected the cynical immorality and polished insincerity of the courtly audience to which it catered. These characteristics are easily detected in such plays as William Wycherley's *The Country Wife*, George Farquhar's *The Beaux' Stratagem*, and William Congreve's *Love for Love*.

In England during the eighteenth and nineteenth centuries, the actors and actresses were generally more outstanding than the playwrights. The most brilliant actor was David Garrick (1717–1779), who did a great deal to advance the art of acting. In his characterizations, he sought always to create real human beings who talked and acted naturally. He succeeded so thoroughly that the fame of his interpretations of great roles still lives on. Among the actresses of that time, the tragedienne Sarah Kemble Sid-

The English actor Edmund Kean in the role of Othello. (A drawing by F. W. Gear)

dons (1755–1831) ranks with the all-time stars of the theater. The lovely Peg Woffington, the romantic Edmund Kean, John Philip Kemble, William Charles Macready, and George Frederic Cooke all flourished on the London stage at the same time. Of the playwrights, two are outstanding. They are Oliver Goldsmith, author of the delightful comedy *She Stoops to Conquer*, and Richard Brinsley Sheridan, who wrote social satires. Sheridan's *The Rivals* featured the immortal Mrs. Malaprop, the world's greatest misuser of words, and his *The School for Scandal* centered around the naughty Lady Teazle.

The last decade of the nineteenth century, the nineties, was a significant period in the theater. Oscar Wilde's *The Importance of Being Earnest* was first produced in 1895 and has been performed continuously ever since by both amateurs and professionals. It is one of the funniest plays ever written and brilliant in its epigrammatic style. The most distinguished recent revival is the one done by John Gielgud.

In the mid-nineties, George Bernard Shaw (1856–1950) began his career as the most notable dramatist since Shakespeare. Year after year, he was the titan of the theater, and today his sardonic wit and philosophical insight continue to attract audiences the world over. His *Pygmalion*, on which the popular musical *My Fair Lady* was based, has also been remarkably successful as a motion picture. Perhaps you have seen the film version of *Caesar and Cleopatra* with Claude Rains and Vivien Leigh playing the leads. The historical drama *Saint Joan* has often been deemed Shaw's finest play and it certainly ranks among the world's great dramas. Joan has been played by such stars as Sybil Thorndike, Winifred Lenihan, Katharine Cornell, and recently by Siobhan McKenna. In addition to providing excellent acting material, Shaw's plays make very good reading; their prefaces are quite as amusing and thought-provoking as the dramas themselves.

James M. Barrie (1860–1937) entered the dramatic field in 1897 with *The Little Minister*. This was followed by the whimsical comedies *Quality Street, What Every Woman Knows, A Kiss for Cinderella,* and *Peter Pan*. The late, beloved American actress Maude Adams scored her greatest successes in these Barrie comedies. Other plays by Barrie which are especially suited for high school production include *The Admirable Crichton, Dear Brutus,* and *Mary Rose*.

Also in the nineties, Henry Irving, the first actor to be granted a knighthood, was finishing his great career. He and Ellen Terry, his leading lady, enchanted audiences at the Lyceum Theatre for twenty years, playing largely in elaborately staged classical dramas. Other famous actors of this era include the tempestuous Mrs. Patrick Campbell, who created the role of Eliza in *Pygmalion*; Wilson Barrett, a great actor-manager; Lily Langtry, a celebrated Rosalind; and Johnston Forbes-Robertson, another knighted actor.

Since 1900 British dramatists and players have become familiar to American audiences. John Drinkwater, an Englishman, was the first playwright to eulogize Abraham Lincoln. Such popular players as Rex Harrison, Eric Portman, Julie Andrews, Noel Coward, Michael Redgrave, Alfred Lunt and his wife Lynn Fontanne, and Peter Ustinov have been equally at home on both New York and London stages. You are probably as familiar with Laurence Olivier, Vivien Leigh, John Gielgud, Ralph Richardson, and Alec Guinness from their television and motion picture appearances as you are with American stars.

England's influence on modern theater is very great. The Arts Council of Great Britain promises to be one of the most significant cultural forces in the world today. Plans for its development were originated before the dust of London's World War II rubble had settled. The committee included Tyrone Guthrie, John Gielgud, and Sir Harry Jackson. The Arts Council is financed by an annual grant-in-aid from the British government and by an 8 million dollar foundation set up by Edward S. Harkness, an American. Its purpose is to assist with the promotion and performance of all the arts. The theater section organizes touring companies to take fine plays into the provinces, provides information on the theater, and works in association with Covent Garden, the Old Vic Theatre, Sadler's Wells, the Shakespeare Memorial Theatre at Stratford, festivals, and provincial theater repertory companies. Though it has not yet created a real national theater—the dream of Englishmen for years—the organization does give financial aid to various theaters and theater groups. In almost every large English town there is a repertory theater of professionals presenting weekly runs of the classics and modern plays. Amateur dramatic societies, the British equivalents of our little theaters, also flourish.

In Ireland around the turn of the century, William Butler Yeats and Lady Augusta Gregory, with other Irish writers, founded the Irish Literary Theatre to encourage and develop a national Irish drama. Some of the first plays presented were Yeats' *The Countess Cathleen*, Edward Martyn's

**Alec Guinness in** *Lavender Hill Mob*, **one of the many films which have brought him fame in America.**

Courtesy of Ealing Films, Ltd.

A scene from Edmond Rostand's *Le Chantecler*.

Molière's *Le Misanthrope* as performed by the Madeleine Renaud–Jean-Louis Barrault Company.

*The Land of Heart's Desire,* and Lady Gregory's *Spreading the News* and *The Rising of the Moon.* The movement gained momentum with the opening in 1904 of the Abbey Theatre in Dublin. When they began, Abbey Theatre actors were untrained, but after working together they developed into some of the best actors in the contemporary theater. The Abbey Theatre group became the producing and acting organization of the Irish national drama. It produced some of the greatest plays in dramatic literature, national in feeling and in portrayal of life, but universal in truths presented. Some of the writers associated with the group are John Millington Synge, Paul Vincent Carroll, St. John Ervine, Lennox Robinson, and Sean O'Casey, its most distinguished playwright. This movement, often referred to as "the Irish Renaissance," lasted about forty years, or up to World War II.

## On the Continent

On the mainland of Europe, the theater has flourished for the last three centuries.

France developed its professional theater under the patronage of princes and government ministers and produced such great plays as *Le Cid* by Pierre Corneille (1606–1684) and *Phèdre* by Jean Racine (1639–1699). The Comédie Française was founded by Louis XIV in 1680 and has continued to be the center of French drama. The acting of this famous group followed the comic tradition laid down by Molière (1622–1673), the supreme dramatist-actor-manager of the French theater.

The humor and the rich satire of such Molière plays as *The Imaginary Invalid, The School for Husbands, The Would-Be Gentleman,* and *Tartuffe* are as entertaining to modern audiences as they were to the court of Louis XIV. Molière wrote the comedy *The Imaginary Invalid* while he himself was dying and played the title role shortly before his death. Voltaire, Victor Hugo, and Alexandre Dumas were popular playwrights of the late eighteenth and nineteenth centuries, a period which produced such great stars as Talma, Rachel, Bernhardt, and Réjane. Edmond Rostand (1868–1918) created an immortal character in his Cyrano de Bergerac, the poet-warrior with the huge nose. The role of Cyrano was originally played by Constant Coquelin, a great French actor. Several years ago José Ferrer played Cyrano on the stage, in the movies, and on television.

In recent years the Barrault Company has made the French theater live for Americans in its performances here of plays representing the best in both classical and modern traditions. The term *total theater* is sometimes applied to M. Barrault's type of presentation because he uses all of the resources of dramatic expression—speech, dancing, pantomime, singing, and movement—in a framework of scenery, light, and music. The Barrault Company's all-star cast, headed by M. Barrault and his wife, Madeleine Renaud, creates a living theater which oversteps the boundaries of language and wins the acclaim of everyone fortunate enough to experience it. Barrault's methods may foreshadow some of the developments in the theater of the future. Another group bringing fine theater to the United States is the Théâtre National Populaire.

Today's outstanding French playwrights include Jean Giraudoux, Jean Anouilh, and Jean Cocteau. Translated and adapted by fine contemporary English and American dramatists such as Christopher Fry and Lillian Hellman, their brilliant dramas are well known in London and New York.

In Germany the great dramatists include Gotthold Ephraim Lessing (1729–1781), Johann Wolfgang von Goethe (1749–1832), and Friedrich von Schiller (1759–1805), writers of such world-famous plays as *Minna von Barnhelm*, *Faust*, and *Wilhelm Tell*. Today many state theaters flourish in Western Germany, presenting the classics of all nations in a tradition established by Max Reinhardt, the great pre-war director.

Norway contributed the figure of Henrik Ibsen (1828–1906), the father of modern realistic drama, who dominated and completely revolutionized the dramatic history of the world. At a time when practically all plays were of the Romantic school, he depicted the harsh realities of nineteenth-century life. He aroused a storm of criticism everywhere but produced a new form of dramatic literature. Ibsen's later work moved from realism into a spiritual realm in which profound truths were conveyed by means of poetic symbolism. Plays by Ibsen which every student of the theater should know are *A Doll's House*, *Peer Gynt*, *The Master Builder*, *Ghosts*, and *Hedda Gabler*. After his reluctant acceptance, greatly assisted in the English-speaking world by George Bernard Shaw, Ibsen was imitated by playwrights in every country and will probably continue to be.

The Moscow Art Theatre, founded in 1898, became the home of the most famous group of players of the next quarter century. It was under the direction of Constantin Stanislavski (1863–1938), the founder of a school of acting frequently referred to today as "the Method." Stanislavski and his actors brought to the world the plays of Anton Chekhov, whose dramas of old Russia are played extensively today—especially *The Three Sisters*, *The Cherry Orchard*, and *The Sea Gull*. Maxim Gorki's *The Lower Depths*, Leonid Andreyev's *The Life of Man*, and Nikolai Gogol's brilliant satire *The Inspector General* were also in their repertoire. Vsevolod Meyerhold, another outstanding Russian director, pioneered in constructivism

A scene from *Ghosts,* one of Henrik Ibsen's realistic dramas.

The Moscow Art Theatre in a performance of *Armored Train No. 1469* by Vsevolod Ivanov.

(see page 328), a type of staging which utilizes platforms and skeletal frameworks as settings. Today the Russian theater has lost much of the vigor which once gave the theatrical world many new playwrights and ideas. However, in the big cities, especially in the Moscow Art Theatre and the Maly Theatre of Moscow, excellent productions of the standard dramas are being presented to packed houses all the time.

Many other European countries have produced playwrights whose works you would enjoy reading and seeing. From Belgium come the delightful fantasies *The Blue Bird* and *The Betrothal* by Maurice Maeterlinck. From Czechoslovakia come Karel Čapek's *R.U.R.*, which portrays a world taken over by robots, and *The Insect Comedy*, a fantasy in which the characters are insects with distinctly human traits. Spain has given the world a number of fine playwrights, among whom the seventeenth-century writers Miguel de Cervantes, Lope de Vega, and Pedro Calderón de la Barca are outstanding. José Echegaray's *The Great Galeoto* is a well-known Spanish play about the tragic effects of jealousy upon a marriage.

Two world wars and the physical destruction of many of the great theaters have not succeeded in killing the love of drama on the Continent. For two centuries most governments have subsidized the theater. In every great city and in many small ones, a fine theater building houses a permanent group of players who present a repertory of classical and popular plays each year. Almost every national theater also supports an academy which trains talented young people and gives them an opportunity to join the regular company. In many cases, after twenty years of service, the actors are given a pension for the rest of their lives. The theaters are run at low cost and any deficit is paid by the government, a method which affords security for the theater and the actor. This is quite different from Broadway, where the money is provided by "angels" (investors), who may risk a fortune on one expensive production.

Today there are many independent producers and acting groups all over Europe who are contributing new blood, keeping the theater very much alive. Groups often center around one fine producer or writer who is able to attract a steady supporting audience. It is truly inspiring to go to the theater in Europe, where enthusiastic audiences seek intellectual stimulation and emotional release as well as entertainment.

### In Asia

To the Westerner, the appeal of the drama in the Far East lies largely in the gorgeous costumes which are complemented by masks or elaborate make-up, in the brilliant color, and in the grotesque and expressive pantomime. Everywhere the drama is presented in a highly traditional manner inherited from the distant past, and the subject matter deals with historical and religious legends not easily understood by a foreigner. The length of the performances, the high-pitched voices, and the discordant music are often very wearing, but there is an exotic charm in every program, and the audiences are always interesting to watch.

In India, legends from the epic poems *Ramayana* and *Mahabharata* afford much of the material for both the stage and screen drama. Biographies and historical incidents are also used as source materials. The performances are full of brilliant color, tinsel, and gold. Elaborate transformation scenes and miraculous effects delight the audiences who sit enthralled for hours, chewing betel nut mixture and coughing loudly. Women, if they attend at all, sit in balconies which are covered with heavy gauze curtains.

Purely literary drama performed by highly trained actors and actresses has been the entertainment of the courts in India for many generations. The work of three poet-dramatists is available in fine translations. Examples are Kalidasa's *Shakuntala*, King Sundraka's *The Little Clay Cart*, and

Students at the King-Coit School re-create the classic *Nala and Damayanti*, using traditional Oriental dance movements and Indian hand gestures.

Balinese dancers in one of their famous dance-dramas.

Sir Rabindranath Tagore's modern poetic dramas, which are lasting memorials to a great mystic whose death was a loss to the entire world. Tagore's plays, produced under his personal direction at his "International University," were a lyrical delight. The new India is already reaching out internationally in drama; its National Academy of Dance, Drama, and Music, in New Delhi, recently joined The International Theatre Association.

The most dramatic spot on earth is the little island of Bali, south of Java, where theatrical productions are staged day and night, year in and year out. Every village has its own gamelang (an orchestra of beautifully made instruments featuring chimes, gongs, and drums) and a wardrobe of magnificent costumes. The villagers themselves appear as actors and dancers in colorful, entertaining, and delightful productions of the Hindu legends. Although the various types of dance-plays are religious in purpose, the humor is definitely secular. The actors wear amazing masks and make-up and glorious costumes of gold brocade and brilliant colors, topped by marvelous headdresses featuring flowers of gold. They perform before the fantastically carved temples or under banyan trees. From children to old men and women, the villagers follow all the detailed pantomime with the same enthusiasm. To all of them the drama is one of the most important experiences in life.

In Thailand the drama is based on formalized dances, depicting stories from Hindu literature. Characters are traditional and charming. There are, for example, the Monkey and Elephant gods, fairies who fly through the air on stiff little wings, and princesses with heavy white make-up, tapering fingers, and tiny feet. Grotesque masks cover the heads of the actors who, adorned with jewel-encrusted costumes, appear as the gods and legendary characters. Thailand keeps alive the traditions of the theater, music, and dance by means of a National Library and a School of Fine Arts where young people are trained in the meticulous methods of acting and in the highly formalized dances.

The Burmese theater is far less formal. In the capital of Rangoon and along the Irrawaddy River, movable stages of woven reeds are set up casually so that a *pwe*, or play, can be given. When the word gets around that a *pwe* is to be presented, ox carts filled with girls with their flower-piled hair come lumbering along from nearby villages, children clamber over the stage and sit on the edge, and booths filled with strange-looking food are set up. These plays have many scenes and the humor evokes raucous laughter. To the foreigner, they often seem a haphazard mixture of story, singing, and dancing. The scenery is quite ornate and varied. The costumes, though less resplendent than those in some Eastern countries, are distinctive and colorful.

The Chinese theater, using the same symbolism and techniques as it has for centuries, can still be seen in Hong Kong and occasionally in Honolulu. Historical plays featuring the actions of generals, long journeys by characters, and many battle scenes predominate. In all of them, the nonchalant property man is always a delight. He is dressed in black or blue and is therefore "invisible" to the audience. He lays down pillows when the heroes die, hands out the tasseled stick "horses" for the warriors to ride, sprinkles bits of paper for snow, hangs curtains, holds up branches for trees, and moves simple furniture into place. The movement, properties, and make-up are highly symbolic. Some characters wear a separate make-up on each side of their faces. In historical plays, the generals wear many heavily embroidered robes, four huge winglike banners on their backs, tremendous headdresses, and chains of colored beads. They carry one or two old-fashioned swords. In duel scenes, they leap about in strictly formalized but energetic dance movements, after which they turn their backs, thus becoming "invisible" to the audience. While the generals are facing the rear of the stage, the property man's assistants open their bulky costumes for them, fan their perspiring bodies, and provide refreshing cups of tea. The other actors who face the front of the stage carry on the action.

The Doll Theater's puppets and "invisible" attendants. (From the movie *Sayonara*, a William Goetz production for Warner Brothers)

Model of a *Kabuki* theater and its revolving stage.

Japan is known for three forms of drama—the Nō, the *Kabuki*, and the Doll Theater. The latter uses marionettes which are about four feet high and gorgeously gowned. These marionettes are so realistic that not only the bodies but even the fingers, mouths, and eyelids can be made to move. Each doll is manipulated by three attendants who wear black clothes and gauze masks to symbolize their invisibility. The lines are spoken and sung in turn by five narrators who wear elaborate costumes. This remarkable form of theater was brought to Japan from Korea in the sixth century. The traditional movements of the *Kabuki* plays originated in the Doll Theater.

The Nō plays go back 600 years and in all this time they have adhered to strict rules of performance and content. The traditional forms are handed down from generation to generation. The temple-like theater used for these plays contains an 18-foot square stage which extends into the audience and is supported by four pillars, which are essential to the action. A pine tree and bamboos are always painted on either side of the wooden panel at the rear of the stage and serve as the only stage decoration. A 50-foot corridor at the upper stage right leads to the dressing room, and through it the actors make their stage entrances. Musicians sit at the back of the stage and the chorus on the left. The characters, wearing magnificent symbolic costumes, are all masked rather than made up; they move in rhythmic patterns, using their fans instead of facial expressions as a means of showing emotion. The characters—all of whom are men—include an old man, an old woman, a young man, a child, a monster, a formidable god, a gentle god, and an animal. One actor often plays several parts. Every word has a subtle meaning, and the members of the audience follow the book closely, as if savoring every syllable. Though Nō plays were originally intended for a wide variety of people, they are now performed chiefly for the highly educated.

The *Kabuki* came into being in the sixteenth century and was originally an imitation of both the Doll and Nō Theaters. Today it is the popular entertainment of Japan. Although a woman, O-Kuni, originated the *Kabuki* with an all-woman cast, today only men are the players. The actors spend their lives in the theater. They begin as children and continue to act in historical and domestic plays and dance-dramas until they are in their seventies. The infinitely detailed pantomime and superlative acting, enhanced by elaborate costuming and make-up painted with brushes, are true theater. The stage is very wide and shallow. Actors enter the stage by way of a long, narrow platform, which is known as the "flower path." This platform extends from the back of the auditorium to the stage at the left of the spectators. It is an inherent part of the acting area. The continually changing backgrounds, frequently set up on a revolving stage, are magnificent in artistic detail. Seven narrators at stage left chant many of the lines. The action starts with the clapping of boards as the red, green, and black striped curtain slowly opens. The first tour of the *Kabuki* players in Europe and America in 1956 was very successful. If possible, try to see this exotic form of theater which combines realism, symbolism, tragedy, and farce in every performance.

The famous Takarazuka girl operas are the most popular shows in Japan. The four troupes of carefully chosen and trained young artists appear in their own huge, ultra-modern theaters. Each performance includes versions of *Kabuki* dramas, authentic folk dances, and a Western-style musical comedy modeled upon those of Paris and Broadway. The beautiful girls, known as "Zukettes," are stunning. They wear costumes ranging from exquisite kimonos to the latest in tuxedos and evening gowns. Their productions are a fascinating mingling of the theater of the East and West. If you saw *Sayonara*, a 1957 film made in Japan, you saw sequences in which the girl operas, the *Kabuki*, and the Doll Theater were featured.

There is a distinctly Western drama developing in Japan; it began in 1947 with *The Defeated*, a play written by Teruaki Miyata and translated into English by Dr. Earle Ernest of the University of Hawaii. In fact, throughout the Orient, Western drama has been played for several decades by amateur groups who produce adaptations of Shakespeare, Shaw, O'Neill, Ibsen, and selected current plays of London and Broadway.

## Discussion

1. From this brief survey of theater around the world, in which country would you like to be a theatergoer? In which country would you like to be an actor or actress? Explain your answers.

2. The phrase "a national Irish drama" is used in reference to developments in the Irish theater. What do you think the characteristics of a national drama are?

3. If you have seen movies or read books describing any of the foreign dramatic activities mentioned here, tell the class about them.

4. Between the European and Oriental theaters which seems the most truly theatrical? Give your reasons.

5. Many of the plays mentioned in this section have intriguing titles. Which titles have made you curious enough to want to read the plays?

6. Look up *malapropism* in a dictionary. Then study this typical line by Mrs. Malaprop in Sheridan's *The Rivals* and explain what she meant to say.

"If I reprehend anything in this world, it is . . . a nice derangement of epitaphs."

7. Shaw never permitted any tampering with his plays. Judging from the show itself, the fine recording, or what you have heard about it, do you think he would have approved of the musical *My Fair Lady?* Why or why not?

8. In what ways can the exchange of plays between countries and tours of artists and productions contribute to world understanding which is so necessary today?

*Applications*

1. Give reports in class on the lives of the following people: Ibsen, Bernhardt, Stanislavski, Goethe, Barrie, Tagore, Sheridan, Inigo Jones, and Mei Lan-Fang.

2. Look up and report on interesting events in the careers of: David Garrick, Peg Woffington, Ellen Terry, Henry Irving, Sybil Thorndike, Noel Coward, John Gielgud, or Laurence Olivier.

3. Find out as much as you can about one of these theaters or artists and report to the class.

> Colon, a theater in Buenos Aires, Argentina
> Habimah, the national theater of Israel
> Théâtre Libre, a theater in Paris
> L'Odéon, a theater in Paris
> Die Freie Buhne of Berlin
> The Sadler's Wells Theatre in London
> The Abbey Theatre in Dublin
> The Hanekoms of South Africa
> Gabriele d'Annunzio
> Eleonora Duse
> Gerhardt Hauptmann
> Max Reinhardt

4. Make a list of famous foreign plays which have recently been revived in New York. What stars appeared in the leads? Report on the direction, acting, setting, and press criticism.

5. Read as many of the plays mentioned in this section as you can and outline them in your notebooks. You will especially enjoy those by James M. Barrie, Edmond Rostand, Maurice Maeterlinck, and Oscar Wilde.

6. Browse among the shelves of dramatic literature at your public library, and familiarize yourself with translations of foreign plays. The appendix in this book may help you find plays that will appeal to you. Begin a list or a 3- by 5-inch card file for use with your personal library. In one section, list and evaluate the books you now have. In another, do the same for books you plan to buy.

7. Work out a program of short sketches or scenes taken from world drama.

# DRAMA IN THE UNITED STATES

## Colonial America

British origins were as clearly reflected in our early drama as they were in other phases of colonial life. Plays and players were imported from abroad. Famous acting companies such as the Hallams, toured the colonies with the classics. Williamsburg, Virginia, where the first playhouse was built in 1716, was one of the theatrical capitals. Charleston, South Carolina, with its Dock Street Theatre, built in 1736, was another. Philadelphia, Pennsylvania, where the Southwark was erected in 1766, was a third center of the theater.

As the first stirrings toward independence were felt throughout the colonies, native American actors and playwrights began to develop. In 1765 Thomas Godfrey wrote *The Prince of Parthia*, the first play written by an American to be given a professional production in this country. *The Contrast* by Royall Tyler, produced in New York in 1787, was the first American play of real literary merit. It was concerned with national problems and situations, and it introduced the shrewd, wholesome humor of the Yankee to the stage.

## Nineteenth Century

By the middle of the nineteenth century, one of our most popular plays had been produced; this was *Fashion* by Anna Cora Mowatt. (Her biography, *The Lady of Fashion*, by Eric W. Barnes, was published in 1954.) The play itself is still seen in revival today. In 1852 a dramatization of *Uncle Tom's Cabin* was presented in New York; later the play toured the country. It remained popular for fifty years. Our first musical production was *The Black Crook* in 1866. This extravaganza received a sensational revival by Christopher Morley in 1929 in Hoboken, New Jersey.

As the country developed, American actors came into prominence. The first American-born star was Edwin Forrest, who feuded bitterly with the English actor William Macready over the question of who was the better actor. America's greatest romantic actor is acknowledged to have been Edwin Booth (1833–1893), whose portrayal of Hamlet is regarded as one of the finest interpretations of that role. Booth was virtually forced into retirement when his brother, John Wilkes Booth, assassinated President Lincoln. Though he did return to the stage later, he never again appeared in the nation's capital. The most beloved character actor of the time was Joseph Jefferson (1829–1905). A recent biography of his life is listed in Appendix C.

Photo by Bender; courtesy of William Dempsey

Anna Cora Mowatt's *Fashion* in a recent revival at the Royal Playhouse in New York.

Edwin Booth as Hamlet.

Courtesy of the Theatre Collection, Harvard College Library

In the late nineteenth century there were many fine actors on the American scene, some of whom continued to play into the twentieth century. The list is so long that only the following names can be given here: Louisa Lane Drew, a fine actress and theatrical manager whose daughter Georgiana became the mother of the famous Barrymores—Lionel, Ethel, and John; Otis Skinner; Sothern and Marlowe; Maude Adams; Eleanor Robson; Mrs. Fiske; Richard Mansfield; and Henry Miller. Theatrical managers, such as Augustin Daly, Lester Wallack, Charles Frohman, and David Belasco produced many plays during this period and created many stars.

Some important American plays were written around the turn of the century and shortly after. Among them were *Shore Acres* by James A. Herne, *The Piper* by Josephine Preston Peabody, *The Girl of the Golden West* by David Belasco, *Kismet* by Edward Knoblock, *The Great Divide* by William Vaughan Moody; *Romance* by Edward Sheldon, *Beau Brummell* by Clyde Fitch, and *The Scarecrow* by Percy MacKaye.

## Twentieth Century

The American drama in the twentieth century is a remarkable story of fifty years of *challenge, transition,* and gradual *growth* toward the creation of a national drama. Here it must be treated briefly, but you can refer to Appendix C for books with greater detail on the history of the American theater.

**Challenge.** At the turn of the century, American playwriting was something less than distinguished. Many of our plays were decidedly second-rate, though this is not to say that there were no effective dramatists. The emphasis in our theater during the nineteenth century had not been on the play but on the player—that actor or actress, European or American, who could command adoration and respect by his mere presence on a stage, no matter how inadequate the vehicle. The public wanted to see stars. From New York, the theatrical capital of the United States, managers sent companies of stars on tour throughout the country to satisfy this demand. These tours were, and still are, referred to as "going on the road."

The vitality of the road and the volume of plays seen in communities, large and small, brought the living theater close to many people. However, in 1903 the theater, and more specifically the road, faced a strong threat to its survival. In that year, the first silent feature film, *The Great Train Robbery,* was presented. Theatergoers flocked to see the new miracle of motion pictures.

Unable to withstand the competition, many legitimate houses closed. Though it still managed to survive, the road became less profitable and never again was as popular as it had been in the nineteenth century. Perhaps the invention of motion pictures had one positive effect on the legitimate theater. The new medium did force the improvement of playwriting standards.

Though the silent films presented a serious problem for the theater, even greater challenges were to arrive later. Talking pictures came in 1927, and television spread phenomenally in the late forties.

**Transition.** Near the end of World War I, a group of young people, summer residents of Provincetown on Cape Cod, formed an acting company. It was this group which produced the first Eugene O'Neill play to be staged —*Bound East for Cardiff*, a one-act play about life on the seas. The Provincetown Players later moved to a playhouse in Greenwich Village in New York City. There they continued to present short plays by O'Neill, whose realistic characters and situations had already gained a great deal of attention from critics.

The first full-length O'Neill play to be produced on Broadway was *Beyond the Horizon*, a haunting study of a man who longs for the life of the sea but is doomed to disappointment. This play won a Pulitzer prize for the 1920 season. In 1921 O'Neill wrote *The Emperor Jones*, a psychological drama about human fear. When, in 1921, *Anna Christie* won a second Pulitzer prize for O'Neill, it became apparent that something unique had happened in the drama of the United States: a genuinely American dramatist of genius had appeared, a dramatist of realism and truth.

**(Left) Eugene O'Neill.**
**(Right) A scene from the Theatre Guild's production of Eugene O'Neill's** *Mourning Becomes Electra.*

Photo by Cecil Thorne                                                                                    Photo by Vandamm

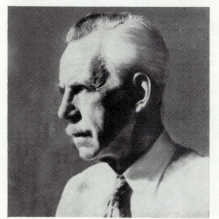 

O'Neill's work launched a kind of revolution in playwriting which extended to all other phases of theater—acting, staging, production methods, and directing. New experiments in types and styles of plays were made in the search for truth. The emphasis shifted from the player to the play, and with this shift came a rediscovery that "the play's the thing."

Two other significant events took place in the American theater at this time. One was the formation of the Theatre Guild and the other was the Actor's Strike of 1919. By striking in protest against unfair working conditions, which often left actors without payment for their services, American actors forced the managers to accept their protective organization, Actors' Equity Association. Equity set up terms for the employment of actors, safeguarding their salaries and providing better working conditions.

The Theatre Guild, organized in 1919, has been the forerunner of much that is important in our theatrical history. (*The Magic Curtain,* the story of the Theatre Guild, by Lawrence Langner, appeared in condensed form in the October, 1955, *Theatre Arts.*) Mr. Langner, with Miss Theresa Helburn, has been the guiding spirit of the group, originally called the Wash-

**The Lunts in a recent Broadway production of Friedrich Duerrenmatt's *The Visit.***

Photo by Vandamm

ington Square Players. Producing plays of artistic merit, the Theatre Guild has brought to the American stage an astonishing number of distinguished European and American dramatists and actors. For example, the Lunts began their long series of "couple" plays with the Theatre Guild. These included *The Guardsman, There Shall Be No Night, Elizabeth the Queen, The Sea Gull,* and *The Taming of the Shrew.*

The Guild has presented many of George Bernard Shaw's plays and opened their own Guild Theatre with his *Caesar and Cleopatra.* They also were bold enough to produce in its entirety his lengthy *Back to Methuselah,* which expounds Shaw's ideas on evolution. Shaw's magnificent *Saint Joan* also had its première with the Guild.

Another history-making venture by the Guild was the production of Eugene O'Neill's extraordinary nine-act play, *Strange Interlude.* The characters in this play not only spoke to each other but also spoke their secret thoughts aloud, allowing the audience to know the difference between their surface appearances and their real selves. In 1931 the Guild produced *Mourning Becomes Electra,* which is regarded by many as O'Neill's greatest play. Here the dramatist utilized the Greek tragic theme of inescapable fate, transferring the action to an American setting—post-Civil War New England.

Other notable American plays of the twenties were Elmer Rice's *The Adding Machine,* 1923; Sidney Howard's Pulitzer prize winning *They Knew What They Wanted,* 1924; S. N. Behrman's *The Second Man,* 1927; Maxwell Anderson and Laurence Stallings' *What Price Glory,* 1924; Marc Connelly and George S. Kaufman's *Beggar on Horseback,* 1924; Philip Barry's *Paris Bound,* 1927; George S. Kaufman and Edna Ferber's *The Royal Family,* 1927; and Paul Green's *In Abraham's Bosom,* 1926.

Native American drama was born during the twenties. However, there still remained an opportunity for growth and maturity.

**Growth.** The thirties, which included the Depression years, were full of idealism and fervor. New experiments in production techniques were made, and stylized methods of staging were utilized. The director became increasingly important in the theater. Perhaps one of the most lasting influences on the growth of native American drama was the formation of several producing companies, two of which were the Group Theatre and the Playwrights Company.

The Group Theatre, an acting and producing company, was founded in 1931 by Harold Clurman, Lee Strasberg, and Cheryl Crawford. The members of this company were dedicated to applying the ideas of Stanislavski to the American drama. As stated by Clurman, the purpose of the Stanislavski

Method, which they employed, was "to enable the actor to use himself more consciously as an instrument for the attainment of truth." Many fine plays were produced by the Group; notable playwrights whom it introduced are Clifford Odets and William Saroyan. Among those who achieved great fame based on early Group training are Elia Kazan, one of the finest directors in our theater today, and Franchot Tone, a motion picture and stage actor. Mordecai Gorelik, the brilliant scenic artist, also worked with the Group Theatre. Economic pressures eventually caused the Group to disband in 1941. Six years later, Lee Strasberg and Miss Crawford founded the Actors' Studio, from which have come such actors and actresses as Marlon Brando, Ben Gazzara, Eva Marie Saint, Kim Stanley, and Julie Harris.

The Playwrights Company, formed in 1938, included Maxwell Anderson, Robert Sherwood, S. N. Behrman, Sidney Howard, and Elmer Rice. Their purpose in creating the organization was to produce their own works independently. This fine organization has made many important contributions to our theater.

During the Depression, many theater people were unemployed; the Federal Theatre was established to provide them with work. Functioning from 1935 to 1939, it introduced a number of new dramatic forms and started many actors on successful careers.

Eugene O'Neill continued during the thirties with plays such as *Ah! Wilderness,* his only comedy, in 1933; and *Days Without End,* a serious drama which some people liked very much and others disliked just as much, in 1934. In 1936 O'Neill was awarded the Nobel prize for literature.

Another development of the thirties was the formation of The American National Theatre and Academy (ANTA). This is the only organization devoted to the performing arts to be granted a Federal charter, which was received on July 5, 1935. Though chartered by the Federal government, ANTA (located at 1545 Broadway, New York City) receives no subsidy. It is supported by voluntary subscriptions, memberships, and donations. Its membership extends to theater groups and individuals in all of the states, including Hawaii, and the Canal Zone.

ANTA exists for the express purpose of extending drama "beyond its present limitations, bringing the best in the theater to every state in the union." It is dedicated to stimulating public interest in drama and furthering the study of it in universities, colleges, and schools. Designed to serve all facets of the American theater—professional, community, and educational—ANTA acts as coordinator, consultant, and guide. Through its National Theatre Service, ANTA provides an information center, which maintains extensive files and reference sources; an advisory service, which

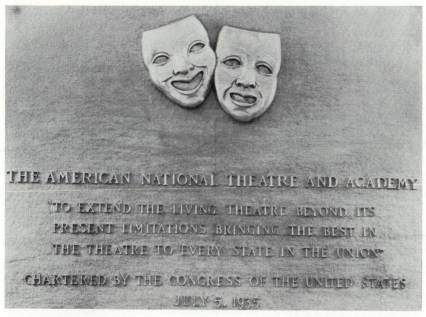

Photo by Roderick MacArthur

The ANTA plaque.

suggests improvements and contributes ideas for new theater projects; guest artist programs, in which professionals appear in local community and university theater productions; a placement service, which has job information for both employee and employer; a job counseling service for aspiring actors; a photographic loan service; and a publication service, which prints pamphlets on specialized subjects.

As the official United States' representative in the International Theatre Institute, ANTA performs many functions. One of these is to arrange for the exchange of companies and theater leaders. Another is to assist recipients of theater scholarships in the United States and abroad. ANTA also sends delegates to theater conferences and represents the theater on the National Commission for the United Nations Educational, Scientific, and Cultural Organization (UNESCO). In addition to all of its services, ANTA has also produced plays. Some have been produced as part of its Experimental Theatre and Invitational Series; others as part of its own ANTA Play Series in the ANTA Theatre.

The forties and fifties have witnessed further developments in playwriting, directing, and stage designing. The modern musical drama began with the Theatre Guild's 1943 production of *Oklahoma!* by Rodgers and Hammerstein. The musical attained further recognition as a popular and artistic form in shows such as *Pal Joey, South Pacific, Wonderful Town, Carousel, The Most Happy Fella, My Fair Lady,* and *The Music Man.*

With the increasing number of Broadway stars appearing on television and in motion pictures, you will have the opportunity to see good actors and actresses more frequently than people formerly did. Also, some of our great stars take their plays on tour; among them are Katharine Cornell, the Lunts, Helen Hayes, José Ferrer, Maurice Evans, Judith Anderson, Fredric March, Rex Harrison, Uta Hagen, Paul Muni, Charles Laughton, and Tallulah Bankhead. Broadway plays are being made available in many cities across the country by the American Theatre Society, a collaboration of the Theatre Guild and Shubert system with the Council of Living Theatre. Since 1952 a paid-up subscription audience of thousands has been able to see the best actors in some of the best plays of each season. Recently film actors have formed drama groups and are staging the best current plays and some tryout plays. Such groups include the Pelican Productions at the Coronet Theatre, and the Actors' Laboratory in Hollywood, and The Actors' Company of La Jolla. The Playhouse, the Golden Hind, and the Actors' Workshop in San Francisco, the Arena Stage in Washington, D.C., the Elitch Gardens Company in Denver, Colorado, and the Alley Theatre in Houston, Texas, are other active professional groups.

These television and movie performances, drama groups, and touring plays are fortunate developments for people interested in the theater. However, some of the less happy developments must also be mentioned. One of these is the fact that the professional theater has firmly centered itself in New York City. This means that there is little opportunity to see *name* stars and productions *on the legitimate stage* unless you live in one of the few cities in which professionally produced plays appear, or unless you actually go to New York. Young actors, playwrights, and directors are also handicapped by this, for it means that there are only a few places where they can get professional training in their crafts before going to New York. Another problem today is the rising cost of production, which has limited the number of shows presented each season. Also, the increase in real estate values has made the building of new theaters almost prohibitive.

In recent years a number of young people have become celebrated actors and actresses, and it seems probable that they will stay at the top. A few of them are Julie Harris, Judy Holliday, Susan Strasberg, Jean Seberg, Andy Griffiths, and Anthony Franciosa. Several of the present-day film favorites who got their start on the legitimate stage are Marlon Brando, Yul Brynner, Deborah Kerr, Paul Newman, and Anthony Perkins.

Many fine directors in the professional theater are now being appreciated as never before by American theatergoers. Some of the best known are Elia Kazan, Joshua Logan, Tyrone Guthrie, Harold Clurman, Guthrie McClintic, Joseph Anthony, Norris Houghton, José Quintero, and Carmen Capalbo.

The two most outstanding recent playwrights are Arthur Miller and Tennessee Williams. Eugene O'Neill died in 1953, but he is still considered one of our best contemporary dramatists. His autobiographical play, *Long Day's Journey into Night*, was brilliantly produced in 1956 under the direction of José Quintero.

If you read theatrical columns in newspapers, magazines, *Theatre Arts*, or *Variety* (the weekly paper of the entertainment world), you are likely to see the term *off-Broadway*. This movement started about 1950 for reasons both practical and idealistic. Actors and playwrights who could not get a hearing on Broadway would have a showcase for their talents, and productions and revivals of plays which commercial pressures kept from Broadway itself could be given. Producers, actors, directors, and stage crews are assembled for a particular production in much the same way as they are for a Broadway show. The theaters themselves are scattered all over New York. They are converted movie houses, rebuilt stables, basements, lofts, and, in some cases, restored theaters. Several of the most famous are Circle in the

**The last scene of Tennessee Williams' A *Streetcar Named Desire*, in which Marlon Brando, at the right, played Stanley Kowalski.**

Photo by Graphic House, Inc.

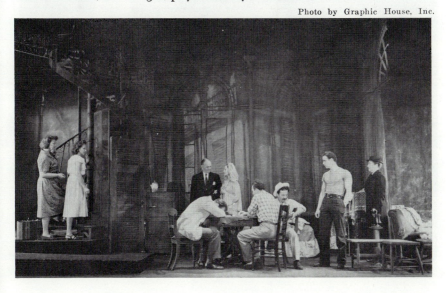

HISTORY OF DRAMA          147

Between acts at the Circle in the Square, a famous off-Broadway theater.

Director, cast, and crew of the Alley Theater, a community theater in Houston, Texas, ready both the play and the stage for opening night.

Square, The Phoenix Theatre, the Cherry Lane Theatre, and the Theatre de Lys. Today off-Broadway is becoming more and more subject to the high costs of production and other commercial pressures which exist on Broadway. However, it is now a firmly established part of American drama, and stars who can command large salaries are often willing to work for little money to gain the artistic prestige of appearing in a distinguished off-Broadway show.

**Nonprofessional theater.** In this country the nonprofessional theater has helped considerably to keep the legitimate stage alive and strong. With the commercial theater centered in New York and few shows undertaking extensive tours, drama-lovers have found an outlet in the little-theater movement. Here small groups of amateurs produce plays largely for the benefit of small, congenial audiences. Many of these little theaters have grown into large-scale community organizations. They draw their acting and production personnel from people in all walks of life and reach large audiences with their productions of period, classical, and contemporary plays. For example, in far-off Honolulu, Hawaii, and Anchorage, Alaska, where no professional companies ever go, current New York hits, splendidly acted and staged, draw crowds for six-week runs of each play. All over America these groups are a vital cultural force. Perhaps some day you will belong to one. The National Association of Community Theatres has been organized to maintain standards of production, assist with various problems, and build cooperation between similar groups throughout the country.

The school theater is also highly regarded in the nonprofessional field. From creative dramatics at the elementary level, through fine high school classes and productions, to the superlative theaters of colleges and universities, the educational theater is an inspiring, constructive, and creative force. Nowhere in the world has public education taken the theater to its heart as it has in this country. Young people in other countries seldom have the chance to meet living drama in their regular classrooms and on the school stage, but in America scarcely a high school, college, or university is without some type of dramatics course and producing group.

In the thirties, Professor Edward C. Mabie of the University of Iowa encouraged the formation of the American Educational Theatre Association. The organization helps solve royalty problems and assists young drama teachers in improving teaching methods. The publications of the AETA cover many new developments in the American schools and theaters. The organization has been enormously influential in improving the quality of dramatics courses and in raising the standards of production in secondary schools.

The National Thespian Society has affiliated groups in over a thousand high schools across the country. For more than twenty years it has encouraged high school dramatics and theatrical productions by sponsoring tournaments, working out organizational problems for its club groups, encouraging outstanding students, and in every way promoting better standards of acting and play production at the teenage level. *Dramatics*, the official magazine of the organization, publishes informative articles and photographs of student productions from the various groups.

At the university level, the growth of courses in drama and acting has been phenomenal in recent years. Someone has referred to the college and university theater as the only endowed theater in America. This is because wealthy alumni and foundations have contributed huge sums for the erection of the finest possible auditoriums and stages, classrooms, rehearsal halls, workshops, libraries, dressing rooms, wardrobe and prop storage rooms, and flexible electrical and lighting equipment. Most of the theater departments have a regular season of major productions. Their activities may include touring companies, children's theater, productions on arena stages, and a repertory of both classical and modern plays.

**A scene from Baylor University's dramatization of Thomas Wolfe's novel *Of Time and the River*. This production, under the direction of Professor Paul Baker, utilized motion-picture projections and multiple stages, in front and on both sides of the audience.**

Photo by Windy Drum: courtesy of Baylor Theater, Waco, Texas

Fifth graders at the Patrick Henry School in Richmond, Virginia, perform *The Pied Piper of Hamelin*.

It is interesting to note that at Harvard University in 1905 the first dramatic theory class for playwrights was organized by Dr. George Pierce Baker; it was the 47 Workshop. Here student-writers had the experience of producing their own plays and receiving constructive criticism. Dr. Baker helped to develop some of our leading dramatists, including Sidney Howard, Eugene O'Neill, and Philip Barry. Later, when Dr. Baker moved to Yale, he continued his course there. Under his influence, Yale built one of the first really adequate university theaters in the world.

Recent years have witnessed increased interest in plays for children, acted and produced by adults. In the United States, children's theater has become an integral part of our national entertainment, creating an interest in plays and giving delight to youngsters everywhere. The Junior League was a pioneer in this field, and today many university and college troupes tour regularly in charming productions of fairy tales, folk dramas, and other suitable and appealing plays. If you have not already done so, you might follow the example of a number of high schools and organize a group from your classes to give plays in neighboring elementary and junior high schools.

Creative dramatics in which children themselves act out stories told to them, spontaneously making up their lines and action, is now an accepted phase of activity in almost all schools. Frequently the young casts put them into permanent form and present them publicly. Winifred Ward's popular book *Creative Dramatics* and Charlotte Chorpenning's charming plays, written for children to present, have greatly influenced this form of theater.

## Discussion

1. Explain why each of the following is an outstanding figure in the history of our drama: Royall Tyler, Edwin Booth, Louisa Lane Drew, David Belasco, Lawrence Langner, Harold Clurman, Elia Kazan, and Robert Sherwood.

2. On the basis of a Eugene O'Neill play, or plays, which you have seen, read, or heard a good deal about, tell why he is considered "a dramatist of realism and truth."

3. Do you think the contemporary American stage exerts as great an influence on today's life as the theater in ancient Greece or Elizabethan England did? Give your reasons.

4. What types of drama do you think are the most popular in the United States today? Give reasons for their popularity.

5. What are some of the recent developments in American drama? What do you think some of the future changes may be?

6. What current American plays do you think may become important in our theater history? Explain your choices.

7. Tell the class about a review of a professional play you have seen in a recent magazine or newspaper.

8. What features of *Theatre Arts* magazine do you enjoy the most?

9. Explain the activities of ANTA to the class.

10. Describe some of the recent productions of nonprofessional theaters in your community or nearby. What plays have been given? Have they been well acted and produced?

## Applications

1. The following groups were important to the development of the theater in this country. After doing research in the drama and history sections of your library, prepare written reports on these groups, describing their contributions and some of the people who have been active in them.

    The Provincetown Players
    The Theatre Guild
    The Group Theatre
    The Actors' Studio

2. Make a list of current issues—political, social, and ethical—upon which you think great American dramas might be built. After each issue, give the particular type and style of drama you think appropriate for it.

3. From this section, select at least two plays to read and outline in your notebook.

4. Look up the April, 1954, issue of *Theatre Arts* and prepare a panel discussion on the article entitled "The Plight of the Living Theatre in the United States." Find materials to bring the many issues it raises up to date so that you can discuss whether or not the situation is improving.

5. Prepare a report on "Maude Adams' Blueprint for a Campus Drama Workshop" by Louise Dudley in the August, 1954, issue of *Theatre Arts*. This is a fascinating account of one of America's most popular actresses in her work as a dramatics teacher at Stephens College.

6. Prepare a debate on the following proposition: "The United States should form a government-subsidized national theater."

7. Bring in a list of American plays which have received a Pulitzer prize or the Critics Award.

8. Read and inquire about some of the famous theatrical families and report on their careers. A few suggestions are the following: Tyrone Power, Sr. and Jr., Helen Hayes and her son James MacArthur, the Barrymores, Osgood Perkins and his son Anthony, James O'Neill and his son Eugene, Norman Bel Geddes and his daughter Barbara, and Lee Strasberg and his daughter Susan.

9. Look up information on one of today's successful young stars (either on the stage or in the movies) and write a biographical sketch of his, or her, life. Include such points as what type of role he plays most often, what films or plays he has been in, what the causes and actual events behind his rise to fame were, and whether you think his popularity will continue.

10. Prepare reports on the following topics:
> The Federal Theatre and Its Role in American Drama
> The Building of a National Cultural Center of Performing Arts in Washington, D.C.
> Women in the World of the Theater Today
> Outstanding Community Theaters in the United States
> The Activities of ANTA
> Opportunities for Young People in the Theater World
> The Lincoln Center for the Performing Arts in New York City

*Chapter 7*

# Shakespearean Drama

Shakespeare's popularity is at a new high today throughout the world. As Henry Hewes, an editor of *The Saturday Review*, states in the July 13, 1958, issue, "Today we have entered the greatest renaissance of Shakespeare-performing the world has ever known." Notable Shakespeare festivals are held every summer at Stratford-on-Avon, England; Stratford, Ontario, Canada; and Stratford, Connecticut. In Central Park in New York City, a professional company has been presenting "free Shakespeare" for several summers. Season after season there are productions of Shakespeare on Broadway and off-Broadway. Every year university and community theaters all over the country give excellent and original productions. The Antioch Area Shakespeare Festival in Ohio has presented all of the plays in a five-year cycle, and annual productions are held on the campuses of the universities of Colorado, Illinois, Oregon, and Utah— to mention only a few. For many years the Old Globe Theatre in San Diego, California, has drawn crowds to see its streamlined versions of the plays.

Shakespeare has furnished the contemporary mediums of motion pictures, television, and the newer recording techniques with quantities of material. Perhaps you have seen some of the following films: Laurence Olivier's *Hamlet, Henry V,* and *Richard III; Julius Caesar,* featuring Marlon Brando; Orson Welles' *Macbeth;* and Maurice Evans' television versions of *Twelfth Night, The Taming of the Shrew, Macbeth,* and *Richard II.* Old films of Shakespeare's plays are often seen on television. For example, Max Reinhardt's *A Midsummer Night's Dream,* the Leslie Howard–Norma Shearer *Romeo and Juliet,* and *As You Like It* have all been shown. Long-playing recordings have been made of scenes and entire plays by such actors as Laurence Olivier, John Gielgud, Claire Bloom, Alec Guinness, Maurice Evans, and Judith Anderson.

154

Photo by George E. Joseph

In the heart of New York City, a free, outdoor production of *The Taming of the Shrew* plays to a capacity audience.

Maurice Evans and Judith Anderson rehearse for the television version of *Macbeth*.

Courtesy of NBC Television

SHAKESPEAREAN DRAMA     **155**

William Shakespeare. (A portrait by Sir Godfrey Kneller)

London in Shakespeare's day, with the Globe Theatre in the center foreground. (Set design for *Henry V*, a Rank Organization film)

# SHAKESPEARE, THE PLAYWRIGHT

As you begin your study of Shakespeare, there are a few things you should remember. The ideal way to become acquainted with Shakespeare is to *see* his plays, not merely to read them or read about them. The plays were written by a practical man of the theater who wrote them to be seen—not read—by a loud, boisterous audience accustomed to yelling its approval or hissing its displeasure. A play had to be exciting, moving, and violent, filled with fury, humor, and truth, in order to keep such an audience interested. The characters Shakespeare wrote of were moved by emotions that are as universal today as they were 350 years ago—love, jealousy, ambition, joy, and grief. It follows that Shakespeare can be vital to you.

Although you may apply to the plays of Shakespeare many of the standards that you use to analyze contemporary plays, you must remember that Shakespeare lived in another age. You will need to accustom yourself to the archaic speech, exaggerated situations, and flowery language of the sixteenth century. Shakespeare was an Elizabethan, and his plays are full of the slang, colloquialisms, and allusions of those times. The wonder is that plays so distinctly Elizabethan in tone and language have appealed to people of the eighteenth and nineteenth centuries alike and are more than holding their own in the twentieth century.

In the school, Shakespeare is useful in three ways. Of all dramatic literature, his plays offer the richest reward for intensive study. His roles afford the finest opportunity for impersonation. His texts furnish the most varied material for practice of vocal and pantomimic technique.

## THE PLAYS THEMSELVES

Thoughtful study of Shakespeare's plays (first collected and published by his actor friends, Heminge and Condell) reveals his great humanity and artistic power. The scholar Edward Dowden has said of Shakespeare's plays that they were composed in the workshop, in the world, and in both the depths and the heights of feeling. In other words, Shakespeare was a skilled craftsman who worked from his experiences and his emotions.

### Structure

Shakespeare did not divide his plays into acts and scenes; his characters came and went, explaining in their conversation where they were as well as who they were. In the Elizabethan theater, there was no curtain to be drawn, so there were no dramatic curtain lines—each scene blended into the next. However, Shakespeare often used a rhymed couplet to show

"Groundlings," who paid only a penny to get in, occupied the pit of the Globe Theatre. Here they are shown crowding around an actor delivering the Prologue to *Henry V*. (From *Henry V*, a Rank Organization film)

when a scene was over, and this is one clue that producers and editors have used in dividing the plays into acts and scenes.

His plays are famous for their openings in which the master dramatist did so much to set the characters, the preliminary situation, and the mood of the play as a whole. The exposition usually takes several scenes because the action is invariably complicated.

The rising action begins in the first act and reveals the main problem of the play, the opposing forces, and the conflict, which may be between two groups of people or in the soul of the leading character or characters. The crisis usually comes in the third act, when the eventual outcome of the play is definitely foreshadowed. The crisis of *The Taming of the Shrew*, for example, comes in Act III, Scene 2, for after Petruchio has married Katharine he must proceed to tame her. The third act often brings together all the main groups of characters in a single dramatic situation.

The action is built, often by the use of minor plots, to the high point or climax in the fifth act. The play concludes with the resolution, and the ending is usually as effective as the beginning. Note how the closing scene helps to make a complete unit of the play.

The theme, or underlying idea of the play, may be found by analyzing the leading characters and the way they solve, or fail to solve, their problems. The motivation of the main character often provides the theme. Jealousy, for instance, impels Othello, and jealousy is the theme of the play.

## Characters

It is, of course, in his unsurpassed power of characterization that Shakespeare's genius most brilliantly expresses itself. His stories were seldom original, but when the magic of his hand touched plots and characters, they were transformed into masterpieces which eclipsed the sources from which they sprang. In turn, his masterpieces inspired works of art by the world's greatest composers, painters, and poets.

The characters form the center of the interest of Shakespeare's plays. Note exactly how each is introduced and how well defined his personality becomes immediately. Pick out all the crucial remarks in which he reveals his own individuality and note what the other characters say about him. Shakespeare used the soliloquy and accurate descriptions by other actors to delineate his characters; there were no programs to make any printed explanations. Look for lines in which the actions of the leading characters are motivated and see if the final result is not inevitable. Notice how clear-cut the minor characters are, defining themselves in their few lines as vividly as do the main characters in their thousands of lines. Often Shakespeare used two characters or two sets of characters in direct contrast or comparison, each making the other more interesting as the result.

Among the hundreds of immortal personages waiting to greet you in Shakespearean plays are mirthful Gratiano, dashing Mercutio, mischievous Maria, jovial Sir Toby, imbecilic Sir Andrew, outspoken Emilia, generous Antonio, engaging Touchstone, and devoted Adam. You will learn much of the tragedy and horror of life from Lady Macbeth, Richard III, Othello, Shylock, and Cardinal Wolsey. You will laugh with Falstaff, the merry wives, and all the fools. You will weep with Prince Arthur, Hermione, and Cordelia. In the world of fantasy Ariel, Puck, Caliban, Oberon, and Titania will enchant you, and in the world of romance you will meet the immortal lovers—Romeo and Juliet, Beatrice and Benedick, Katharine and Petruchio, Portia and Bassanio, Rosalind and Orlando, Miranda and Ferdinand, Perdita and Florizel, and Antony and Cleopatra. You will come to know and appreciate these and many others. And you will find, in spite of blank verse soliloquies and theatrical posturing, that these characters are very human in their strength and weakness, their tragedy and sorrow. It is through his characters that Shakespeare expresses his philosophy of life.

Othello as portrayed by an Iowa State College student.

Oberon, Titania, Bottom, and Puck in a scene from *A Midsummer Night's Dream*, produced by University of Minnesota students.

Proteus and Valentine in the Barter Theatre's production of *The Two Gentlemen of Verona.*

Shylock in the Dallas Theatre's production of *The Merchant of Venice.*

SHAKESPEAREAN DRAMA         161

## Language

As you read a Shakespearean play, its language will strike you with its power and beauty if you do not worry too much about its form. Most school editions of the plays have excellent notes which will help you over the difficulties of Elizabethan speech. You will be amazed, however, to find how modern in spirit the language is. In a recent production of *The Taming of the Shrew* in modern dress, the word *lute* was changed to *uke* for *ukelele* and *thee* and *thou* to *you*, but these were the only changes made. The members of the cast found that they could present the play in exactly the same tempo and manner as contemporary plays. You will, of course, pick out the figures of speech in a play and see how greatly they add to the beauty and force of Shakespeare's ideas. You will also listen to the music of the language and note how the pronunciation and emphasis of words form a definite rhythm. See how the movement of the lines and the choice of words express the spirit of a scene and suggest the manner in which it must be played.

The rhythmic beauty of Shakespeare's poetry and the power of his prose held the noisy Elizabethan audiences enthralled just as they do the politer audiences of today. One of the pleasures of witnessing or reading his plays is to find famous quotations in their original context. Another is to come upon a perfectly expressed idea which you have felt but were never able to put into words.

## Chronology of the Plays

Since the exact dates for the composition of Shakespeare's plays are not known, an approximate chronology has been devised by scholars from available evidence. In the following list, the plays appear in the order generally agreed upon. (The starred titles are those most suitable for use in class reading.)

> 1590—*Love's Labour's Lost*
> 1591—*The Comedy of Errors*
>       *Henry VI*
> 1592—*Two Gentlemen of Verona*
>       *Richard III*
>       *Romeo and Juliet**
> 1593—*King John*
>       *Richard II*
>       *Titus Andronicus*
> 1594—*A Midsummer Night's Dream**

1595—*All's Well That Ends Well*
      *The Taming of the Shrew\**
1596—*Henry IV*
1597—*The Merry Wives of Windsor*
      *The Merchant of Venice\**
1598—*Much Ado about Nothing*
      *Henry V*
1599—*As You Like It\**
1600—*Twelfth Night\**
1601—*Julius Caesar\**
1602—*Hamlet\**
1603—*Troilus and Cressida*
1604—*Measure for Measure*
      *Othello*
1605—*Macbeth\**
1606—*King Lear*
1607—*Timon of Athens*
1608—*Pericles*
      *Antony and Cleopatra*
1609—*Coriolanus*
1610—*Cymbeline*
1611—*The Winter's Tale*
      *The Tempest\**
1616—*Henry VIII*

## Stagecraft

Shakespeare's stagecraft is, of course, sound because he took an active part in the production and acting of plays. His craftsmanship is displayed in the clever manner in which he clears his stage at the end of each scene, his apt use of prose and verse, and his painting of a scene so clearly in words that the need for scenery is eliminated. Practically all the stage directions necessary for producing one of his plays are incorporated into the dialogue, and yet there is room for much interpolated action. The devoted theater-goer enjoys comparing different productions of Shakespearean plays, noting the essential action that is similar in them all and the varied methods by which different companies achieve distinctive effects.

## Discussion

1. What have been your reactions to Shakespearean plays that you have read? How did these reactions change after you actually saw the plays?

**2.** In the plays which you have read or seen, have you been impressed by the ease with which Shakespeare could create many different types of characters? Give some examples to support your answer.

**3.** From Shakespeare's plays, name the following characters: a famous fool, a heroine who disguised herself as a man, a terrible villain, an entertaining old lady, a great lover, a fairy character, a faithful servant, a humorous clown, and a powerful tragic figure.

**4.** Cite some instances where Shakespeare's knowledge of stagecraft has been particularly apparent.

**5.** After reading a good biographical account of Shakespeare, discuss how he proved himself to be a practical man of the theater, a successful businessman, and a capable actor.

**6.** Look up the Baconian theory and then give your own reaction to it. Do you think Francis Bacon might have written the plays ascribed to Shakespeare? Why, or why not?

**7.** Bring to class any information you can gather concerning the number and quality of Shakespearean plays produced in the United States during the last year. Discuss the reasons why Shakespeare's plays are still so important and popular today.

**8.** Who are some of the best-known English and American Shakespearean actors at present?

*Applications*

**1.** In order to clarify your ideas after you have read or seen a Shakespearean play, complete the following activities:

  **a.** Write a brief synopsis of the plot, outline the structure, and in one sentence state the theme.

  **b.** Write character sketches of the leading characters based on what they say and do in the play. Bring out their strong and weak points and point out the elements which give them their charm, universal appeal, or lasting value.

  **c.** Memorize the finest passages, both long and short.

  **d.** Write a brief paper telling whether or not you liked the play. Put down exactly what you feel and give all possible reasons for your reaction. State the ideas you have gathered from the play which you feel will have lasting value for you.

**2.** Prepare reports on the following topics concerning Shakespeare's life:

Shakespeare's Childhood

The Personal Friends of Shakespeare

Shakespeare's Life in London

Shakespeare's Retirement and Later Life in Stratford

Shakespeare's Will and Testament

The Chief Historical Events in Elizabethan England

Queen Elizabeth as a Woman and a Queen

The Great Men of Elizabethan England

A Comparison between Elizabethan England and the United States of To-day

What to See in Stratford-on-Avon

3. If you are just getting acquainted with Shakespeare, choose one of his plays and read it purely for enjoyment. Don't worry too much about the meaning of words, but try to catch the feeling, understand the characters, enjoy the beauty and power of his expression, and realize the value of his ideas.

4. Give reports on the following topics concerning his plays:

The Ghosts in Shakespearean Drama

Shakespeare's Philosophy of Life

Shakespeare's Love of Nature

Why Shakespeare Has Been Identified as Prospero

Shakespeare's Use of Prose and Poetry

Shakespeare's Vocabulary

Why One Should Read Shakespeare

Why Shakespeare Is the World's Greatest Playwright

5. Listen to some of the fine Shakespearean recordings available today. As you play these records for the second time, follow the text. Try to see in your mind's eye the production as it might be acted by the Shakespeare Memorial Theatre group, or any other fine group of Shakespearean players. Compare various recordings of the same speech or scene. Make a disc or tape recording of your own interpretation of a part and play it for the class. Start a collection of Shakespearean recordings for your school or classroom library.

6. Present a written or oral report on Margaret Webster's book on producing and directing Shakespeare, entitled *Shakespeare without Tears*.

7. Start a loose-leaf Shakespearean album for yourself and for the school: include photographs of actors and scenes, clippings, old prints, postcards from Stratford-on-Avon, travel materials from England, old and current programs, and advertisements of recent productions on stage and screen.

8. As a class, attend any and all Shakespearean productions given in your community by professionals and amateurs. Also see any which are presented in the movies or on television. Write criticisms of the performances after discussing them in class and keep them for future reference.

9. Work out your own prompt copy (see page 301) of one of the Shakespearean plays you like best. Get two copies of a cheap edition, cut the pages, and paste them on colored sheets or notebook paper. Make your own costume charts, lighting plan, and stage designs. If you find it possible, these may be used for an actual production.

*Part Three*

# Interpreting
# the Drama

A play is interpreted for an audience by actors. Each actor creates a character in his imagination, but to project that character truthfully and effectively he must master the technique of acting. (Technique is the means or procedure essential to the successful performance of an action.) The actor has two tools—his voice and his body—with which he conveys to the audience the action and dialogue conceived by the dramatist. Acting is, therefore, an art of communication depending upon vocal and bodily skill for its effectiveness. Since a play is a story presented before an audience, you as an actor are responsible for making the action visible at a distance and the lines audible throughout the theater.

Many young people are sincerely afraid of becoming artificial and "stagey" as they begin their study of technique. They set up a mental block concerning grace of body and excellence of speech

Photo by Windy Drum

and rebel against the effort involved in acquiring sound stage training. As you enter this phase of the work, try to be open-minded and responsive. Remember that an actor must be seen, heard, and understood. This ability is the product of careful preparation. Your technique is the means by which you make clear to your audience the character you are portraying and the ideas of the play.

Your classroom is your workshop, but life itself is the best school of drama. An actor must develop an all-embracing sympathy for people and the ability to analyze them and their motives correctly. Your personal background, therefore, will help you to construct a part. Wide experience, keen observation, and broad interests make true characterizations possible. Technical skill will enable you to project the role which the author has created after you have absorbed it emotionally and intellectually.

167

## Chapter 8

# Pantomime

Pantomime, the art of expressing dramatic ideas without speech, demands a responsive and flexible body. Because of the close relationship between physical and emotional attitudes, it is vital that you learn to use your body correctly and effectively by conscious exercise until the right habits are set up and become automatic. All forms of correct physical exercise are important, especially those which develop muscular coordination and freedom of movement.

### PREPARING FOR PANTOMIME

**Relaxing**

The first step in freeing the body is relaxation. The following exercises will help you:

1. Raise, lower, and rotate your head without moving your shoulders. Let it roll freely, without the slightest tension.

2. Rotate your shoulders up and down, forward and back, in circles.

3. Move your arms in wide circles, first close to the body and then at shoulder height.

4. Rotate your lower arms from the elbow, toward and away from the body.

5. Rotate your hands from the wrists.

6. Move your arms horizontally and vertically, with wrists leading.

7. Shake your hands vigorously, keeping them completely relaxed.

8. Open and close your fists, stretching the fingers apart and drawing them together.

168

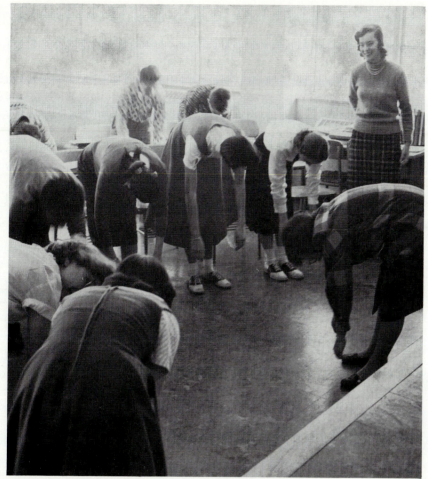
Photo by Hays, from Monkmeyer

**An acting class begins work with a series of relaxing exercises.**

9. Do the five-finger exercises. Alternate your fingers: little, middle, ring, first, and thumb.

10. Bend your body forward, back, and to the sides.

11. Clasping your hands together, push your arms vigorously above your head. Then rotate your body, keeping your head within your arms.

12. Rotate each leg in circles, kick as high as possible, swing forward and back.

13. Rise on your toes, bend your knees, and sit on your heels.

14. Rotate each foot at the ankle.

15. Pick up marbles with your toes.

## Posture

Your posture is fundamental, not only to your health, but to your personal appearance as well. Often good posture offsets a plain face, and certainly in the theater it is of far greater importance. Therefore, the next step in training the body deals with normal posture, movement, and gesture. Gracefulness is the mean between over-relaxation or flabbiness and extreme tension or rigidity. Perfect coordination of all parts of your body is a basic requirement for bodily poise and expressive movement.

To stand properly, hold your body easily erect with chest high, chin up, back flat, and arms and legs straight but not tense. Keep one foot slightly in front of the other, the weight centering on the ball of the forward foot. The following exercises will help you to cultivate good posture. They should be repeated many times a day in sequence.

1. Stand easily erect with your weight on the balls of your feet.

2. Bend forward, perfectly relaxed, with your loosely hanging arms almost touching the floor.

3. Place your right hand on your chest and your left hand at the small of your back.

4. Raise your body, expanding the torso so that you feel your hands being pushed apart.

5. Bring your head to an upright position, with the chin held at right angles to the throat and the mouth closed.

6. Drop your arms to the sides. Shift your weight to the ball of one foot and move forward. Keep your chest high, head erect, and the small of your back flat.

## Walking

In walking, maintain good posture and a sense of exuberant alertness. Face the world squarely with high chest, erect body, and direct glance. "Thinking yourself tall" may help you to carry yourself gracefully. Although the heel strikes the ground a slight fraction of a second before the toes, your movement should spring from the balls of your feet, and it should be easy, poised, and rhythmical.

Systematic exercise, such as regular setting-up exercises or consistent pursuit of some outdoor sport, will keep the muscles of your body supple and responsive. The length of your step will be modified by many elements such as your height, build, and physical energy. However, avoid striding, mincing, plodding, or tottering. Toeing straight ahead with your weight on the balls of your feet is the natural way to walk, and walking in a straight line keeps the moving silhouette narrow. Except when playing parts which call for it, never place your feet more than two inches apart. Your body should swing easily from the hips, and your arms should swing in easy opposition to your legs. Beware of habitually looking at the ground.

When you turn, rotate on the balls of your feet, shifting your weight from one foot to the other. Never turn on your heels or cross one foot over the other, tripping yourself. Turn your entire body, including your head.

Remember to hold yourself easily erect when standing or walking. Avoid the common habits of leaning forward, holding one shoulder higher than the other, looking down as you walk, dragging your feet, walking on your heels, keeping your feet apart as you walk, or tensing any part of your body.

These exercises from daily life are designed to help you to stand and walk in the right way.

Imagine you are standing:

1. At the microphone in your auditorium ready to give a speech
2. In the doorway of your date's living room, waiting to meet her parents
3. In the garden, watching a skylark
4. At the curb, waiting to dash across the street when the lights change
5. At the airport, waiting for friends to arrive

Imagine you are walking:

1. On a sandy beach with a fresh wind blowing over the waves
2. On Fifth Avenue in New York City, with the skyscrapers and church spires rising above you
3. In a forest of tall trees on a lovely fall day
4. On a ballroom floor at a formal dance
5. On the stage, trying out for the part of Petruchio or Katharine in *The Taming of the Shrew*

Walking up and down stairs is an excellent exercise. Place one foot in front of the other and lift your weight from the balls of the feet. Think yourself tall and vigorous, keeping a high chest and head. Try not to look at the stairs.

## Sitting

In sitting, maintain an erect position. Keep the base of your spine at a 90-degree angle to the seat and lean easily against the back of the chair. Your hands will ordinarily rest in your lap or on the arms of the chair. Crossing your arms on your chest or folding them restricts your breathing and looks tense. Avoid playing with buttons, jewelry, or your hair. Just sit easily erect against the chair. Your feet may be crossed at the ankles, or one foot may be placed slightly in front of the other. Avoid crossing your legs, spreading your feet apart, and resting your hands or elbows on your knees.

In rising, let your chest lead, not your head. Keep your weight balanced on the balls of your feet, placing one foot slightly forward and using the rear one as a lever in pushing yourself up. Never hang on to the arms of the chair or push yourself up from them. Take a deep breath while rising. This relaxes the throat, gives a sense of control, keeps the chest high, and leads into a good standing position.

At all times your body should move, or sit, as a whole. From the top of your head to the tips of your fingers and toes, it should be expressive. As a matter of fact, it always is, but not always in the way you might desire. For example, a slovenly walk, a rigid or slouching posture, irritatingly aimless gestures, or a wooden face reveal your personality just as clearly as do purposeful, vigorous movements and a radiant, mobile face. Nine times out of ten, the world will take you at your "face value." You are judged first by your appearance and manner, only much later by what you say and how you say it.

## Crossing and Turning

The center of the stage area is called *center*, the front is *downstage*, and the back is *upstage*. The actor's right is *stage right* and his left, *stage left*. To *cross* means to move from one position to another. On entering the stage, the actor leads with his upstage foot to turn his body toward the audience. Normally all turns are made to the front. In making turns, rotate on the balls of your feet.

Try these exercises in crossing and turning, walking, sitting, and rising:

1. Enter stage right to speak at a microphone downstage center. Cross to center and turn downstage. Stand with your right foot slightly advanced and weight forward. To leave, turn right, shift weight to left foot, and go off right.

2. Enter stage right and cross to center. Remember that you have forgotten something and turn front, rotating on balls of the feet. Go back right.

3. Enter left and walk diagonally upstage to up center where there is an imaginary bookcase. Get a book and go off right.

4. Enter right to wait for someone at a store entrance up center. Turn front and look around. Then turn and pace up and down, looking in the windows on both sides of the entrance. Each time you reach center, turn to look around. Finally give up and go off left.

5. Enter stage right to make a speech. Cross to chair at left center. Without looking at chair, turn front, touching chair with calf of upstage leg.

Shift weight to upstage foot and lower body into the chair keeping head and chest high. Rise, pushing with the upstage leg. Shift your weight to forward foot and step with back one. Move to front center. Then turn and bow to chairman. Turn front with weight on forward foot. Return to chair and be seated. Rise to bow for continued applause and sit again. Rise and go off stage right.

6. Enter a living room. Greet the hostess and be seated on a couch. Rise to greet an older person and be seated again. Rise, bow, and leave.

7. Enter stage left to walk down a path in a park. Be seated on a bench center and watch people pass. Rise and leave stage right.

8. Enter stage right in your graduation procession. Stand before your chair left center and then be seated. Rise and cross down center to receive your diploma. Cross front, turn upstage, and return to chair. Stand and then be seated. Rise and go off stage right.

9. Enter a dining room at a tea party. Cross to table up center and get a teacup on a small plate. Cross down right to meet someone. Cross to another friend across stage. Turn and cross to center. Then go upstage and place plate on table. Cross down center to chat. Then turn and leave.

Diagram of stage areas

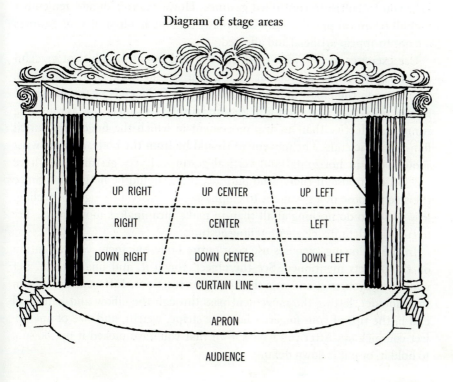

UP RIGHT | UP CENTER | UP LEFT

RIGHT | CENTER | LEFT

DOWN RIGHT | DOWN CENTER | DOWN LEFT

CURTAIN LINE

APRON

AUDIENCE

## Falling

Some roles will require you to fall onstage. Practicing the following steps will enable you to fall safely and convincingly:

1. Relax, and sway or stagger backwards.
2. Sway forward, dropping the hands and arms.
3. Relax from the ankles and drop on the knees.
4. Bend the knees. Pivot slowly and, as you do so, go closer and closer to the floor. Lower the shoulder which is closest to the floor and slide down.
5. Lower the head to the ground.

## Gesture

Gesture is the movement of any part of the body to help express an idea. It may be a lift of the eyebrow, a toss of the head, or a sweeping movement of the arm and hand. A change of attitude is usually expressed first by the eye, then by the response of the mouth and facial muscles, then by the reaction of the torso, and lastly by the motion of the arm, hand, and finger tips. These movements are so rapid that they seem simultaneous, but in training exercises you must try to follow their natural sequence.

A few practical suggestions regarding the use of the arm and hand may help you to cultivate controlled gestures. However, you should remember that all technical practice must eventually become habitual if your gestures are not to appear artificial and affected.

Use exercises to free your tight muscles and establish habits of graceful coordination. Every movement of the arm should begin at the shoulder, pass through the elbow and wrist, and "slip off" the ends of the fingers. It is most important that every arm gesture finish at the finger tips, for nothing is more ineffective than an arm movement in which the fingers are curled flabbily at the ends. The movement should be from the body, and the wrist should lead in horizontal and vertical gestures. Every gesture must have a definite purpose; if there is no purpose, there should be no gesture. Since the sole purpose of a gesture is to emphasize or clarify a thought or feeling, it is better to do nothing at all than to make meaningless movements. Try to cultivate definite, clear-cut, telling gestures.

In the following exercises use your entire body but focus your attention on the objects mentioned. See the object, touch it, and finally react. Let your eyes, eyebrows, and mouth show your reactions. Lift your arms from the shoulder, letting the movement pass through the elbow and hand and end in the tips of your fingers. Show the shape, weight, and size of any object you pick up. After you have shown that you have picked it up, be sure to hold it, or put it down definitely.

1. You are walking in a garden. Pick flowers from plants, bushes, and vines, and pull weeds. Select fruit from a tree, taste it, and throw it away. Select another piece and eat it.

2. You go into the garage and find a flat tire; fix it.

3. You are in a big railroad station, looking in vain for a porter. You are carrying a suitcase, handbag, umbrella, box of candy, and magazines. You drop your handbag and everything spills out. Put down everything else you are carrying in the process of recovering the contents of your handbag. Retrieve everything and lift the suitcase last of all.

4. You are wandering around a department store. You feel the fabrics, smell the perfume, and look at costume jewelry without buying anything. You see a hat bar. Try on several hats. Buy one and wear it out, carrying your old one in a bag.

5. You are showing a small boy how to throw a baseball.

6. You are preparing breakfast. Break eggs into a bowl, showing their size and weight, etc., and the cracking of the shell. Drop one on the floor.

## ACTING WITHOUT WORDS

Pantomime preceded the spoken drama in primitive times, kept pace with it through the Middle Ages and the Renaissance, and threatened to outdistance it in the days of the silent motion picture. In the theaters of the Orient, it is a highly developed art which has survived hundreds of years. In the Western world today, pantomime is a rather specialized entertainment. Perhaps you have seen Marcel Marceau, the great French mime, in person or on television, or the American pantomimist Barton and production of the American Mime Theatre. Pantomimic sequences are often included as an integral part of contemporary choreography; the energetic dances in the stage and screen productions of such musicals as *Oklahoma!*, *The King and I*, and *Brigadoon* are basically enlarged pantomimes.

Your richest source of authentic material for pantomimes is the observation of your associates in daily life. Watch facial expressions, mannerisms, gestures, and ways of walking. You may find it profitable to analyze the movements of television, movie, and stage actors. Also try to check your own bodily responses and note how they reflect your feelings and thoughts.

There are two phases of your work with pantomime. You have studied the first—exercises to relax your muscles and free your body for quick expression of feeling. The second phase is the creation of impersonations in which feeling prompts a bodily response. Both activities demand concentration of thought and interest in detail. You will find it takes a great deal of time and practice to create the exact effect you desire.

Photo by Vandamm

**A pantomimic dance sequence in Rodgers and Hammerstein's musical** *Oklahoma!*

### Physical Principles

There are a few established principles which affect acting because they are based on what people often do in real life as well as on the best way to communicate a feeling or idea. The following are some of these. Try to apply them as you work out your pantomimes.

1. The chest is the key to all bodily action.

2. Positive emotions such as love, honor, courage, and sympathy expand the body and tend toward a high chest and head, free movement, broad gestures, and animated features.

3. Negative emotions such as hate, greed, fear, and suffering contract the body and tend toward a shrunken chest, tense movement, restricted gestures, and drawn features.

4. Facial expression—the use of the eyes, eyebrows, and mouth—usually precedes action.

5. Whenever possible, make all gestures with the upstage arm, the one away from the audience, and avoid all tendency to cover the face while expressing an emotion.

6. Some exaggeration of bodily response is essential to being clearly understood.

7. Always keep the audience in mind and direct reactions to them.

8. Keep the arms away from the body in gesturing. Except on specific occasions when it is necessary for communication purposes, do not gesture above the head or below the waistline.

9. Arms and hands should always be moved in curves, never in straight lines, unless you are deliberately trying to give the impression of awkwardness or being ill-at-ease.

10. All action must be definite in concept and execution, and all movement clearly motivated.

## Showing Emotional Responses

Emotion affects our bodies in various ways. In practicing the exercises below, be sure that *you feel the emotion first*; then *let your face and body respond*. Apply the physical principles given above.

1. You have quarreled with your girl or boy friend. You are standing by a window, looking out, frowning, and biting your lip. Your chest is sunken, your body slumped. The phone rings. Your face lights up, with eyes wide and lips smiling. Your chest is up. You wait expectantly to hear your name called. Then you run to the phone and lift the receiver, holding it in your upstage hand. Let your face reflect the conversation. When you hang up, you show by your movements whether the quarrel is over or not.

2. You are a feeble old man or woman, coming out to sit in the sun. You walk with short, uncertain steps; your head is down and your face drawn. You sit down slowly with great effort and gradually relax as the sun warms you. Someone calls you and you express your irritation by frowning and shaking your head. Then you rise, pushing yourself up from the arms of the chair. Hurry away as fast as your stiffness of limbs will allow, expressing worry and agitation.

3. You are a big bully on the playground. As you look over the whole field, you stand with feet wide apart, hands on your hips, and head thrust forward. You see a smaller boy and beckon him to approach. When he doesn't, you stride over and grab him. Then you see the playground instructor coming. Your face shows your fear. Your aggressiveness melts and you relax your grip on the boy, smile at your instructor, and stroll off.

4. You are a contestant on a quiz show. While your opponent is answering, you show your tension with eyebrows drawn down, lips tight, and body stiff. The master of ceremonies comes over to you, and you try to brace up and smile. After the questioning, you reveal by your face and body whether you have succeeded or failed.

The exercises you have just completed should have shown you that when a person feels strongly his face and body react with definite movements.

As the ghost of Hamlet's father reveals the details of his murder, Hamlet's face and body reflect horror and bewilderment.

It might be helpful to you to make a daily practice of running through a series of movements related to an emotion so that your muscles will become limber and accustomed to reacting in a certain way.

The suggestions below are acceptable pantomimic practices. After you have familiarized yourself with them, choose one that stimulates your imagination and create a character and situation to fit it.

Body as a Whole

1. Feet together, weight on both feet, and body passive represent timidity, indifference, or trained self-control.

2. Weight carried to the front foot with the body leaning slightly forward represents interest, persuasion, sympathy, enthusiasm, and positive emotions.

3. Weight carried to the rear foot represents fear, hesitation, deep thought, amazement, and negative emotions.

4. Shrunken chest and bowed head represent old age, envy, greed, and negative emotions.

5. Feet apart, head high, and arms akimbo represent conceit, scorn, contempt, and self-assertiveness.

Head and Face

1. Head raised, eyebrows lifted, eyes wide, and mouth open represent fear, horror, joy, and surprise.

2. Head raised, eyebrows lifted, and mouth drawn down depict comic bewilderment or a quizzical state.

3. Head down, eyebrows down, and mouth set or twisted by biting lips show worry, meditation, and suffering.

4. Twisted mouth and eyebrows can show petulance, irony, anger, pain, sophisticated attitudes, and various subtle emotions.

5. Raised eyebrows, wide eyes, smiling or open lips may depict innocence, stupidity, or coquetry.

**In *J.B.*, Archibald MacLeish's contemporary play based on the Book of Job, J.B.'s face clearly expresses anguish as he raises his arms and implores God to tell him why he must suffer.**

Hands and Arms

1. Arms extended, palms up, are appropriate for pleading, presenting ideas, and offering sympathy.

2. Arms drawn up or back with palms down are appropriate for negation, refusal, condemnation, fear, horror, and negative ideas.

3. Clenched fists represent anger and effort at control.

4. Pointed finger and extended arm are useful for pointing out, commanding, and directing.

Feet and Legs

1. Feet apart with legs straight denote arrogance or stolidity.

2. Feet apart with legs bent denote lack of bodily control, old age, great fatigue.

3. Tapping the foot depicts irritation, impatience, nervousness.

4. Twisting one foot denotes embarrassment.

**Gigi looks up impishly and somewhat coquettishly at her friend Gaston, whom she has managed, by rather devious means, to beat in every card game. (From the movie** Gigi**)**

Courtesy of MGM

## Characterization

Characterization in pantomime involves placing a character in a situation and showing a change in his mood. This entails two mental processes—imitation and imagination. Many professional actors keep notebooks with them at all times. When they see a person of particular interest, especially if they happen to catch him in a moment of excitement, they jot down notes on his exact expression, gestures, and eccentricities of movement. They draw upon these notes when creating parts to be sure they are being true to life. However, this is only the beginning, for they then use their imaginations to place and maintain themselves in the parts they are playing and so create roles.

After you have put on some comfortable clothes which leave your body free for action, run through the relaxing and other practice exercises. Then imagine yourself in such situations as the following:

1. You are alone in your home. Go to the television set and adjust it. You find that you are watching the climax of a horror picture. Suddenly you hear a sound at the window. As you listen, the sound continues. The window slowly opens and a hand appears. You seize a book and hurl it at the hand, which promptly disappears. You tiptoe to the window, lock it, and fall into a chair, exhausted.

2. Practice falling several times (see page 174). Then imagine yourself in the following situations.

    a. You have been wounded in the shoulder. Fall from loss of blood.

    b. You have stubbed your toe on roller skates left on the floor. Fall, get up, and put away the skates, limping from a sprained ankle.

    c. You suddenly feel faint and fall. Then you recover, get up, and stagger to a chair.

3. Relating each to an imagined situation, show fear, agony, appeal, embarrassment, hate, sympathy, indecision, power, weariness, and joy. First employ your face, next your hands, and then your feet. Finally express these emotions with your entire body.

4. Imitate people you know in the following situations:

    a. A strict teacher in a large study hall called out of the room and then returning

    b. A neighbor working in his garden and being annoyed by an inquisitive child

    c. A woman shopping in a supermarket with her three-year-old boy

    d. An enthusiastic baseball fan in the ninth inning of a close game

    e. An old man or woman friend coming into your living room for a chat

## Individual Pantomimes

Now you can begin working out real pantomimes involving careful planning, rehearsing, and presentation before the class. What you actually present will, of course, depend upon class assignments. The individual pantomimes may well be divided into life studies, imitations of people you know, and into imaginary characterizations.

In your imitation of a real person, you should first determine his chief characteristics. Is he friendly? Timid? Boisterous? Suspicious? Glamorous? Physically vigorous? Discontented? Next, note mentally the details of his habitual facial expression, especially his eyes and mouth. Observe how he holds his head, the kinds of hand movements he makes, and the way in which he walks. Decide what makes him different from any other human

**Marcel Marceau, a contemporary master of the art of individual pantomime.**

being. Then place him in a situation. (You need not have actually seen him in such a situation, but you must be able to imagine how he would react to it.) Take plenty of time to think through his exact reactions to your imaginary situation. Visualize them as if you were watching him on a television screen. Finally, imitate what you have imagined he would do.

In your imaginary characterizations, you should follow much the same procedure. You will, however, have to begin by inventing the details which will characterize the person you plan to play. What is his age? What are his physical traits? How does he dress? What makes him a distinctive individual? Only when you can see him as clearly as someone you actually know will you be able to make him live.

Whether your character is imitated or imaginary, you must work out in detail the situation in which you plan to place him. Have your character enter a definite environment in a clear-cut state of mind and body. Invent something that will change his mood. The conclusion of your pantomime should leave no uncertainty in the mind of your audience about the mental state of the character as he leaves the stage.

You will also need to visualize in detail the setting of your pantomime. Be sure you know the exact position of the doors, windows, furniture, and props you will employ. Last of all, assume the physical appearance of your character as nearly as you can. Feel yourself to be his age and of his size. Let his state of mind take possession of you until your face, hands, and feet are reacting as his would in the imagined circumstances.

While working out your individual pantomime keep the following directions constantly in mind:

1. Set your mental stage in detail, knowing exactly how much space you are to use, the location of the furniture, and the shape, weight, and position of every imaginary prop you will be using. If you move an object, make very clear its shape, weight, and new position. After you have made your audience see your setting and props, you must remember not to break the illusion by shifting an article without clear motivation and action.

2. Visualize the appearance and emotional state of your character in minute detail.

3. Imagine yourself to be dressed in the clothes of your character, making your audience see the weight, shape, and material of each garment and its effect upon you in your particular mood and situation.

4. Remember that in all dramatic work the thought comes first—think, see, and feel before you move. Let your eyes respond first, then your face and head, and finally the rest of your body. This is a "motivated sequence."

5. Keep your action simple and clear-cut.

6. Keep every movement and expression visible at all times to your entire audience.

7. Never make a movement or gesture without a reason. Ask yourself: "Does it make clear who I am, how I feel, or why I feel as I do?" Take time to make every movement absolutely clear and definite.

8. Try out and analyze every movement and gesture until you are satisfied that it is the most truthful, effective, and direct means of expressing your idea or feeling.

9. Make only one gesture or movement at a time, but coordinate your entire body with it and focus the attention of the audience upon it.

10. Rehearse until you know that you have created a clear-cut characterization and that the action has begun definitely, remained clear throughout, and come to a conclusion.

11. Plan your introduction very carefully. It may be humorous or serious, but it must arouse interest in your character and the situation in which he is placed. It also must make clear all the details of the setting and preliminary situation.

12. Plan the ending very carefully. You should either leave the stage in character or come back to your own personality and end with a bow or smile.

*Suggestions for Individual Pantomimes*

If you find it difficult to get started, the following suggestions may help you. At first it is not a bad idea to run through them all in rather rapid succession to get yourself limbered up physically and imaginatively. Then select one and work it out in detail, elaborating on mannerisms and concentrating on details. After creating a single study which satisfies you with its clarity, build up a sequence of events which brings about a change of mood and situation. Finally, build up to a definite emotional climax and conclusion. Such a pantomime will require hours of preparation before it will be ready for class presentation.

1. Standing erect, with your feet close together, suggest the following:
   a. A butler
   b. A model waiting to display a gorgeous evening gown
   c. A dowager contemptuously watching the behavior of the younger generation
2. With legs wide apart and a comfortable posture, represent the following:
   a. A genial gentleman in front of his fireplace beaming at his guests
   b. A football captain addressing a mass meeting
   c. A good-natured hobo stopping to pass the time of day with a fellow tramp
   d. A contented farmer smoking a pipe and standing in his doorway studying the weather

**3.** With alert posture, one foot somewhat ahead of the other and your weight definitely placed on the ball of the forward foot, represent the following:

   **a.** A high school boy watching a football game
   **b.** An energetic cheerleader addressing a mass meeting

**4.** With a similar posture, except that the weight is definitely shifted to the rear foot, impersonate the following:

   **a.** An old lady afraid to cross the street
   **b.** A mother disgusted with the caterpillar her son is showing her
   **c.** A little girl hesitating to ask a favor of her teacher
   **d.** A hunter terrified at seeing a snake swinging from a tree in front of him

**5.** Cross the room, suggesting by your posture and walk the following:

   **a.** A burglar stealing across an unfamiliar, dark room
   **b.** A vigorous athlete walking across the campus
   **c.** An Indian looking for enemies in the forest
   **d.** A murderer stealing up on his victim with uplifted knife
   **e.** A tired soldier marching in a parade
   **f.** A weary father returning from a long, hard day at the office
   **g.** A model displaying evening wraps
   **h.** A criminal awaiting a last-minute reprieve in the death cell
   **i.** A pompous fat man in evening dress in a theater lobby

**6.** Walk across the room, kneel, and kiss a lady's hand in the manner of:

   **a.** A knight in armor of the Middle Ages
   **b.** A cavalier of the court of Charles II, with a long curled wig, a stiff, outstanding coat with ruffled sleeves, and a plumed hat
   **c.** A modern boy burlesquing a romantic lover

**7.** Walk across the room and curtsy in the manner of the following characters:

   **a.** A colonial lady at a formal party in a full-skirted gown and towering headdress
   **b.** A Civil War beauty of the old South
   **c.** A timid country girl at the squire's house
   **d.** A naughty little girl at dancing school

**8.** Cross the room, sit in a chair, and rise as the following characters:

   **a.** A criminal leaving the witness box at his trial
   **b.** A coquettish old lady flirting with a gay young man
   **c.** A miser counting his money and listening for eavesdroppers
   **d.** A middle-aged gossip retelling the latest scandal
   **e.** A mother at the bedside of her sick child
   **f.** A queen dismissing her court
   **g.** A sleepy child trying to keep awake
   **h.** A young man at his first dance

9. By facial expression alone—chiefly a frown—suggest these people:
   a. A mother entertaining a distinguished guest while she can see her little boy in the kitchen eating all the cakes
   b. A frightened substitute teacher in her first class
   c. An angry traffic cop
   d. A spoiled child sulking because he is denied something
10. Suggest, by smiling, the following characters:
    a. A seasick traveler trying to appear sociable
    b. A Sunday school superintendent greeting some new students
    c. A tired salesgirl trying to sell a hat to a fussy customer
    d. A young man during the last course of a dinner when he suddenly discovers he does not have enough money to pay the check
11. Suggest, by facial expression, the following situations:
    a. A boarder opening a spoiled egg
    b. A small boy taking castor oil
    c. A junior high school girl watching a sentimental movie on television
    d. A butler admitting unwelcome guests
    e. A hiker realizing he is about to step on a coiled rattler
    f. A mother encouraging a sick child
12. Assume the following characters as completely as you can. Sit or walk, as you choose, and include enough action to show them in a real situation:
    a. An egotistical, self-confident businessman
    b. A pompous butler
    c. A swaggering bully
    d. A distinguished society woman
    e. A patient trying to gain courage before his turn in a dentist's chair
    f. An energetic and jovial stenographer
    g. A man bothered by a mosquito while trying to read

## Group Pantomimes

Group pantomimes should follow your individual ones and eventually lead you into the acting of a short play. They will, therefore, demand even more careful planning and rehearsal time than you have devoted to your individual pantomimes. They may be based on plays, novels, stories, or such secondary sources as photographic magazines, newsreels, and films. Feel free, also, to draw upon the daily life about you.

Plan your story as you would a one-act play, centering it around one interesting situation that has a carefully worked out exposition, rising action, climax, and a logical and clear-cut conclusion. Create an interesting setting and five or six strongly contrasted characters. Be sure that each one is a real personality. Motivate all entrances, exits, and side action and be sure that all the characters can be seen at all times. Avoid bunching, huddling

The American Mime Theatre in a group pantomime based on *commedia dell'
arte* forms.

behind furniture, or standing in stiff lines. Your stage picture should be
well balanced and attractive, and attention should always be focused upon
the center of interest. Rehearse together until you have a unified whole in
which each character is a living, breathing person. Do not rush your action, for the audience must be able to follow the development of all the
roles; take plenty of time to tell your story effectively and pictorially. Remember that you are limited to visual means of presenting your ideas. Try
to build your plot around an emotional situation with considerable human
interest and avoid trite material. Be original, imaginative, and painstaking.

PANTOMIME     187

## Suggestions for Group Pantomimes

The suggestions below may be useful to you. Be sure you plan the entrances and exits carefully and keep the action clear and unhurried. See that each character is a distinct personality and that the stage picture is well balanced at all times.

1. A jolly fat woman, a thin disagreeable woman, and a silly young girl are having tea with a motherly old lady.

2. A boy and a girl quarrel and make up.

3. Four models display contrasting types of dresses to a rich lady who is helping her daughter choose a trousseau while the father looks on.

4. Several old soldiers recount their adventures in the Civil War.

5. A typical "character" actress, a leading man, and a leading woman await their cues in the greenroom (the room offstage where actors and actresses rest and chat between appearances).

6. Several stenographers apply to a brusque businessman for a position.

7. A small boy is left to take care of a baby while the baby's nurse flirts with a policeman.

8. A photographer takes a family picture of four generations.

9. A crotchety old man, a supercilious middle-aged lady, a young couple, and a traveling salesman watch a thrilling moving picture.

10. A "high-powered" salesman is selling magazines to an irritated housewife.

11. A young man is taking his best girl riding, but cannot start the car.

12. A shy young man pays his first call on a girl who does not know how to put him at ease.

13. A kindly judge interviews a frightened boy brought in by a hard-boiled policeman.

14. A young girl cannot find her ticket, and the conductor becomes angry. A man across the aisle pays her fare, while a middle-aged spinster nearby expresses intense disapproval.

## Applications

1. Write on separate pieces of paper twenty suggestions for pantomimes which can be presented by a single person. Four should show just one mood. Four should reveal a transition from one mood to another. Four should require a definite entrance and exit. Four should necessitate sitting and rising. Four should require falling down and getting up again. Bring these suggestions to class and mix them up. Let each class member draw one and present it in class.

2. Give as many individual and group pantomimes as possible before the class. Analyze each performance to see whether it has convincing characterization, clarity, reality, and effectiveness. These questions, among others, should be discussed:

   a. Has the pantomime been carefully prepared?

**b.** Are the characters interesting, lifelike, and vivid? Do you become emotionally involved with them?

**c.** Do the gestures and movements seem sincere, convincing, clear, and properly motivated?

**d.** Does all of the action help to delineate the characters and their situation for you?

**e.** Is the action clear-cut, realistic, prolonged sufficiently, and exaggerated enough to be seen by the whole audience?

**f.** Can you visualize the setting, the props, and the clothing of the characters?

**g.** Does the pantomime have a definite beginning and ending?

**3.** Work out pantomimic interpretations of some of the old folk tales such as "Little Red Riding Hood," "The Three Bears," "The Three Pigs," and "Snow White and the Seven Dwarfs."

**4.** Turn to *Poor Maddalena* in Appendix A and present the following scenes in pantomime, making the action graceful and expressive. Try to make every movement meaningful in itself and every pose of the characters an effective tableau. Contrast the artificiality of the first and third scenes with the realism and sincerity of the second.

**a.** The opening pantomime of the play (described in the introduction to Scene 1)

**b.** The begging of the key from Bumbu

**c.** The unlocking of the door and the looking upon the world

**d.** The opening of Scene 2, through Paolo's entrance but before Maddalena speaks

**e.** The ending of Scene 2, beginning when Maddalena throws herself on her knees before Paolo

**f.** The return to the land of fantasy, at the beginning of Scene 3

**g.** The end of the play, from the point where Pierrot says, "Still, the pantomime of love, you'll admit, is enchanting."

*Chapter 9*

# Voice and Diction

An expressive voice and clear correct speech are not only indispensable tools for the actor; they are also vital assets in every walk of life. Personnel directors list them among the first considerations for all positions which involve meeting the public and sharing ideas. As Shaw so amusingly points out in *Pygmalion*, a person's social standing and educational background are judged by the way he talks.

In the drama class a simple, practical daily routine of exercises and constant attention to your speech are necessary, but it is in the regular speech classes that you should get your detailed information and concentrated drill work. In many schools a course in phonetics and speech in all its phases is a prerequisite for the course in dramatics. If you have not taken such a course, you should certainly try to do so. However, if you understand the fundamental principles explained in this chapter and practice the exercises with regularity, you can definitely improve your vocal and speech habits.

## DEVELOPING AN EFFECTIVE VOICE

There is nothing mysterious or complicated about developing an effective voice; it depends primarily upon bodily relaxation and good posture. Few people realize the close relationship between the voice, the emotions, and the body. A person who is ill, tired, worried, angry, nervous, hurried, or tense reflects his feelings in his voice. In spite of himself, his voice becomes high-pitched, monotonous, or colorless. On the other hand, a person

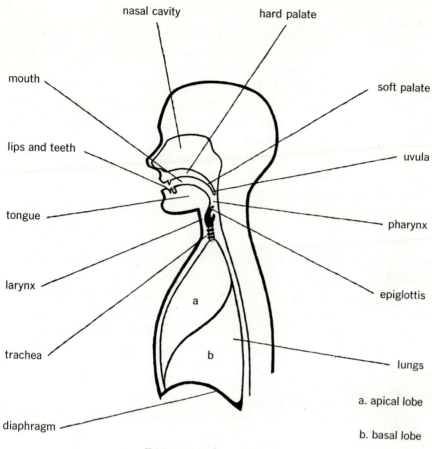

nasal cavity

hard palate

mouth

soft palate

lips and teeth

uvula

tongue

pharynx

larynx

a

epiglottis

trachea

b

lungs

a. apical lobe

diaphragm

b. basal lobe

Diagram of the vocal tract

who is poised, self-confident, and healthy is likely to have a pleasing voice. Consequently, your first efforts should be directed toward building a vigorous, well-controlled body and a cheerful disposition.

Voice is produced by the air from the lungs passing over the vocal cords, thin curtains of muscles with delicate edges. These cords respond instantly and set up vibrations or waves. The vibrations become sounds and are amplified when they strike the resonating chambers of the throat, head, nose, and mouth. Exactly what sounds are produced depends upon the shape of the resonating chambers, and this shape is determined by the position of the tongue, soft palate, lips, and lower jaw. For correct speech and voice production it is necessary for you to have deep central breathing, an open, relaxed throat, flexible tongue and lips, and a relaxed lower jaw.

VOICE AND DICTION 191

## Breath Control

The first rule for achieving an effective voice is to relax; the second is to breathe centrally. No one can teach you how to breathe for you have done so successfully since your birth, and you breathe correctly when you are asleep or perfectly relaxed. There is some difference, however, between regular breathing and breathing for speech. In the former, the inhalation (breathing in) and exhalation (breathing out) periods are of equal length. The latter requires a very brief inhalation period and a slow, controlled exhalation period. This is true because for all practical purposes speech is produced only when the breath is being exhaled. In breathing for speech, therefore, you should inhale through the mouth, since this allows for more rapid intake of breath than does inhalation through the nose. You should work for a prolonged and controlled exhalation so that the outgoing breath will match your needs for sustained vocal tone. Controlled breathing is more important to the actor than deep breathing, for the tone of his voice depends upon it.

The first exercises for you to try in training your voice are those which will focus the breathing process in the center of your body and those which will strengthen and control the breath stream once it has been centered where it belongs. Practice these exercises every night and morning until central breathing gradually becomes automatic:

1. Place your hands on either side of the lower part of the rib cage and pant rapidly, laugh silently, and sniff in the air in tiny whiffs. Lie down and breathe deeply and regularly. Be sure to keep your hands in the same position.

2. Stand straight with an easy and well-balanced posture. Inhale slowly, making sure from the feeling under your hands that the whole rib cage is expanding. Hold your breath without straining for a count of six. Then exhale slowly and evenly while you mentally count, first to fifteen, then to twenty, twenty-five, and thirty. Be particularly careful to avoid muscular tension.

3. Repeat this exercise, gauging the evenness of your exhalation either by whistling or by making a soft sound as you breathe out (as the sound of *s* or *ah*). If the sound is jerky or irregular or fades at the end, repeat the exercise until you can keep it smooth and regular.

4. Use "The Cataract of Lodore" by Robert Southey, which follows, for practice in breath control. Take a deep breath and see how far you can read in the following selection before you have to draw a second breath. Do not strain and be sure to relax after each effort. With practice, your breath control should gradually increase.

The cataract strong
Then plunges along,
Striking and raging
As if a war waging
Its caverns and rocks among;
Rising and leaping,
Sinking and creeping,
Swelling and sweeping,
Showering and springing,
Flying and flinging,
Writhing and ringing,
Eddying and whisking
Spouting and frisking,
Turning and twisting,
Around and around
With endless rebound;
Smiting and fighting,
A sight to delight in;
Confounding, astounding,
Dizzying and deafening the ear with its sound.

Collecting, projecting,
Receding and speeding,
And shocking and rocking,
And darting and parting,
And threading and spreading,
And whizzing and hissing,
And dripping and skipping,
And hitting and splitting,
And shining and twining,
And rattling and battling,
And shaking and quaking,
And pouring and roaring,
And waving and raving,
And tossing and crossing,
And flowing and going,
And running and stunning,
And foaming and roaming,
And dinning and spinning,
And dropping and hopping,
And working and jerking,
And guggling and struggling,
And heaving and cleaving,

And moaning and groaning; . . .

Retreating and beating and meeting and sheeting,
Delaying and straying and playing and spraying,
Advancing and prancing and glancing and dancing,
Recoiling, turmoiling and toiling and boiling,
And gleaming and streaming and steaming and beaming,
And rushing and flushing and brushing and gushing,
And flapping and rapping and clapping and slapping,
And curling and whirling and purling and twirling,
And thumping and plumping and bumping and jumping,
And dashing and flashing and splashing and clashing;
And so never ending, but always descending,
Sounds and motions for ever and ever are blending
All at once and all o'er with a mighty uproar,—
And this way the water comes down at Lodore.

"The Cataract of Lodore" by Robert Southey

## Voice Characteristics

There are four characteristics of the voice which must be used correctly if you are to become an effective and expressive speaker. These are quality, pitch, volume, and rate. Their development constitutes voice training.

**Quality.** *Quality* is the individual sound of your particular voice. Its beauty and richness can be improved by keeping the resonating chambers of your throat and head open. Your daily speech habits are most important. Never speak with a tight throat, and always try to use a low, clear tone. Relax your throat frequently with a yawn, and breathe through your nose when you are not speaking. Never strain your voice.

The quality of your voice depends, for the most part, upon resonance and the correct formation of vowel sounds by the speech organs. *Resonance* is the vibrant tone produced when sound waves strike the chambers of the throat, head, nose, and mouth. A relaxed throat, necessary to a full and pleasing tone, can be obtained by yawning and then keeping the open position. The best practice for resonance is humming. The nasal passages must be kept open for vibrations to be set up in them, so exhale through the nose using the *m-n-ng* positions. The cavities of the head will vibrate automatically if you hum while throwing the voice forward. If the nasal passages are closed by a cold or raised soft palate, the sound is denasalized. The much-criticized nasal twang of many American voices is due to nervous tension which tightens the throat and raises the soft palate, thus closing the nasal cavities, cutting down resonance, and leaving the voice flat.

The vowel sounds are all made with the lower jaw relaxed. The position

A student does her homework in front of a mirror to be sure that she is forming her vowel sounds correctly.

of the lips and tongue determines the sound. In pronouncing all vowels, you must keep the tip of the tongue at the base of the lower teeth. *Ah* is the most open sound, with the tongue flat and lips loose. By rounding the lips you produce the sounds of ŏ (*ŏn*), ô (*lôrd*) ō (*ōh*), ŏŏ (*lŏŏk*) and ōō (*lōōse*). Keep the tip of the tongue at the base of the lower teeth, the jaw and lips relaxed, but allow the middle of the tongue to arch up and forward until it almost touches the roof of the mouth to produce the sounds of ŭ (*ŭp*), ẽr (*makẽr*), ă (*ăt*), ĕ (*lĕt*), ā (*āte*), ĭ (*ĭt*), ē (*bē*). Practice making these sounds without tightening the throat, concentrating on the tone so that it leaves the mouth and passes beyond the lips and is not muffled or "swallowed." In this way you keep a pure tone in every syllable and word that you utter, and the quality of your voice is at its best.

Before doing voice exercises, relax, consciously letting go both mentally and physically. Yawn! Stretch your whole body as an animal does after a nap. (Incidentally, watching a cat relax and move is an excellent exercise in itself for bettering your own reactions.) Feel the big muscles of your back, legs, and arms ease first. Imagine that a warm, relaxing shower is falling over your head. Imagine it passing over your forehead and wiping out the frown lines. Imagine it releasing the tension of the little muscles around your eyes, nose, mouth, and especially your cheeks, so that the lower jaw and lips are loose. Next roll your head forward and backward and to the sides until both the inner and outer throat muscles are relaxed. Then imagine the shower pouring over your whole body, relaxing your arms and finger tips, your chest, lungs, diaphragm, and even your toes. You should be yawning by this time, and that is one of the best voice exercises there is. With practice you can learn to run through this process imaginatively when you are waiting to make a speech or standing in the wings before an entrance on the stage; you will also find it is an excellent cure for stage fright. Also run through the posture exercises on pages 170 to 171 and do the breathing exercises on pages 192 to 194 before you begin vocal work. The importance of an erect, easily relaxed body should not be underestimated.

The simple voice exercises which follow can do wonders for your voice if you practice them regularly every day for ten or fifteen minutes when you are feeling fresh and relaxed.

For Relaxed Jaw

1. Let your head fall forward on your chest. Lift it up and back, letting the jaw remain loose. Drop it again and slowly roll the head over the right shoulder, back, over the left shoulder, and forward, describing a circle.

2. Drop your head forward again. Place your hands lightly on your cheeks and lift your head with your hands, keeping the jaw relaxed and being careful to avoid using the jaw muscles. When your head is lifted, the jaw should hang open. It helps sometimes to try to make your face as expressionless as possible; looking blank will help to relax the muscles.

3. Babble like a baby, saying *dä-dä-dä-dä* and *lä-lä-lä-lä* brightly, and feeling relaxed and happy, moving only the tip of the tongue. (In these and following exercises, refer to the Voice Chart on page 217 for pronunciation of vowel sounds. The diacritical markings are those used in *Webster's New Collegiate Dictionary*.)

### For Open Throat

1. Yawn freely, getting the feeling of an open, relaxed throat.

2. Take in a deep breath, relax your jaw, think of your throat as large, and exhale slowly.

3. Say: "I can talk as if I were going to yawn. Hear me talk as if I were going to yawn."

4. Say *lō-lä-lē-lä-lōō*, gradually increasing the energy for each repetition. Give the vowels fullness and roundness, and relax your jaw. Sing the syllables on one note. Increase your volume by breathing deeply, but do not tighten your throat.

5. Repeat the following expressions, keeping the throat open: *lä-lä-lä-laughs, lä-lä-lä-lose, lä-lä-lä-loaves.*

### For Flexible Lips

1. Say *ōō-ō-ô-ŏ-ä*, opening your lips from a small circle to a large one. Then reverse, saying *ä-ŏ-ô-ō-ōō*. These sounds may be sung with the piano, taking them all on one note. Keep the tongue flat in your mouth with the tip at the lower teeth. Keep your throat well open and your jaw relaxed.

2. Say *mē-mō-mē-mō-mē-mō-mē-mō*, then sing these sounds with the piano.

### For Flexible Tongue

1. Say rapidly: *füd-düd-düd-düd-däh-füd-düd-düd-düd-däh-füd-düd-düd-düd-däh-frill.* Trill the *r* in *frill.*

2. Keeping your jaw well relaxed, repeat the following sounds, watching with a hand mirror to see that your tongue is slowly arched as you go from one position to the next: *ä-ŭ-ēr-ă-ē-ä-ĭ-ē.*

3. Say *ira-ira-ira-ira-ira-very.* Trill the *r* in *very.*

For Resonance

1. To locate your larynx and feel the vibration of the vocal cords, place your fingers lightly on your Adam's apple and say *b* and then *p*, *d* and then *t*, *v* and then *f*, *s* and then *z*. Note the vibration on the *b*, *d*, *v*, and *z*. Also note the vibration on the vowel sounds *ā*, *ē*, *ī*, *ō*, *ū*.

2. To feel the effect of obstructing the resonators, sing the word *hum* and repeat while you pinch your nose closed. Say "good morning," opening your mouth and your throat. Say it as if you were on the verge of tears and were swallowing them. Say it holding your nose closed. Say it with your teeth tightly set. Say it while drawing your tongue back in your mouth.

3. Place your fingers gently on your lips and on your nose and hum, feeling the vibration. Place the palm of your hand on the top of your head and hum; try to feel the vibration. Repeat with your fingers at the back of your head. Repeat the exercise using a piano and noting where on the scale the vibration is strongest.

4. Sing the sounds of *m-n-ng*, using a piano. Then combine each of them with the vowel sounds in exercise 4 of "For Open Throat" and repeat.

5. Say the following words with full resonance: *ring, sing, ding-dong, bells, wind.*

For Speech and Breathing

1. Breathe in, relax your throat and lower jaw; count "one" as you exhale. Repeat and count "one, two"; continue until you can count to twenty on one breath. Be careful not to tighten up. It may take you several weeks before you can reach twenty, but take time so that you can do it without straining. Any tension is bad.

2. Breathe in; relax your throat and lower jaw. Say "Hong-Kong" as you exhale, prolonging the vowel and *ng* sounds.

3. Breathe in; relax your throat and lower jaw. Say "Hear the tolling of the bells—iron bells," prolonging the vowels and the *ng* and *n* sounds.

4. Breathe in; relax your throat and lower jaw. Without straining, try to retain the position of your diaphragm as you exhale, saying, slowly, "Roll on, thou deep and dark blue ocean, roll."

5. Turn back to "The Cataract of Lodore." This time do not try to see how far you can read on one breath, but read it naturally, inhaling as you have to between the phrases. Form the vowels accurately and sound the *m*'s, *n*'s, and *ng*'s carefully.

It is important for an actor to remember that voice quality is definitely affected by emotion. Perhaps you have already realized that your voice responds instantly to your inner feelings. For example, the voice may quiver with fear, sweeten with sympathy, and harden with anger. If you wish to develop a flexible, responsive voice for acting, you must cultivate your imagination to the point where your tone becomes that of your character as he experiences various moods. In addition, the age of your character will affect the quality of the voice appropriate for him. For instance, with old age the vocal apparatus is usually less flexible and the disposition has been obviously affected for better or worse by life's experiences. These things must be made apparent in your characterizations. A good way to help yourself is to listen very carefully as you meet a new person and try to judge his temperament and mood by the tone with which he speaks. Note also the voices of your friends and family under differing circumstances.

## Applications

Practice the following exercises aloud, first feeling the appropriate emotion and then speaking.

1. Repeat an appropriate word—*no, yes, dear, of course, really*—conveying the following emotions: surprise, scorn, irritation, sarcasm, boredom, suspicion, eagerness, love, doubt, weariness, exaltation, determination, horror, pain, despair, and joy.

2. Assume the character of a gay young girl, a cross old man, a dictatorial employer, a discouraged job-seeker, an eloquent minister, a distinguished actor, a plotting criminal, and an hysterical mother. Speak the following sentences as each of these characters would. Change your tone for each character but try not to tighten your throat.

    a. Now is the time to make your choice.
    b. Oh, what a beautiful morning!
    c. Whatever will be will be.
    d. Stop! Think it over before you do anything rash!

3. Say the following words, recalling personal experiences to give them "color," the special tone quality resulting from feeling and imagination: *home, icy, flag, ocean, roar, sunset, welcome, golden, jingle, melancholy, magnificent, dog, star, glamorous, eternal, enemy, splendid, horrible, brilliant, glory, sobbing, autumn, whisper, shot, scream, terrific.*

4. Read the following selections,* concentrating mainly on the vowel sounds. Try to make each vowel in an accented syllable as full and rich as possible. Sound these vowels alone many times and then put them back into the words.

* In these and in all other excerpts and passages the student is urged to read the complete work, if possible, in order to understand fully the mood and meaning of the selection.

a

[THE PRINCE OF MOROCCO:]
All that glitters is not gold,
Often have you heard that told.
Many a man his life has sold
But my outside to behold:
Gilded tombs do worms infold.
Had you been as wise as bold,
Young in limbs, in judgment old,
Your answer had not been enscroll'd:
Fare you well; your suit is cold.

*The Merchant of Venice* by William Shakespeare

b

Why so pale and wan, fond lover,
Prithee, why so pale?
Will, when looking well can't move her,
Looking ill prevail?
Prithee, why so pale?

*Song from Aglaura* by Sir John Suckling

c

[ROMEO:]
Night's candles are burnt out, and jocund day
Stands tiptoe on the misty mountain tops.

*Romeo and Juliet* by William Shakespeare

d

[ZARA:]
Heaven has no rage like love to hatred turn'd
Nor hell no fury like a woman scorn'd

*The Mourning Bride* by William Congreve

e

'Tis not too late to seek a newer world,
Push off, and sitting well in order, smite
The sounding furrows; for my purpose holds
To sail beyond the sunset, and the baths
Of all the western stars, until I die.

*Ulysses* by Alfred Lord Tennyson

f

[MACBETH:]
Ring the alarum bell! Blow, wind, come, wrack!
At least we'll die with harness on our back!

*Macbeth* by William Shakespeare

A scene from *The School for Scandal*. (**A painting by William Dunlap**)

5. Study the following passages. Decide what type of person is speaking, exactly what he is saying, what mood he is in, and why he is saying these lines. Read them aloud trying to convey the exact meaning and mood.

a

[LADY TEAZLE:] Sir Peter, Sir Peter, you may bear it or not, as you please; but I ought to have my own way in everything, and what's more, I will too. What! though I was educated in the country, I know very well that women of fashion in London are accountable to nobody after they are married—and am I to blame, Sir Peter, because flowers are dear in cold weather? You should find fault with the climate, not with me. For my part, I'm sure I wish it was spring all the year round, and that roses grew under our feet!

*The School for Scandal* by Richard Brinsley Sheridan

b

[SHYLOCK:]

> You come to me, and you say,
> "Shylock, we would have moneys"; you say so;
> You, that did void your rheum upon my beard,
> And foot me as you spurn a stranger cur

Over your threshold: moneys is your suit.
What should I say to you? Should I not say
"Hath a dog money? Is it possible
A cur can lend three thousand ducats?" or
Shall I bend low and in a bondman's key,
With bated breath and whispering humbleness,
Say this,—
"Fair sir, you spat on me on Wednesday last:
You spurn'd me such a day: another time
You call'd me dog; and for these courtesies
I'll lend you thus much moneys?"

*The Merchant of Venice* by William Shakespeare

c

[THE GHOST OF HAMLET'S FATHER:]
I am thy father's spirit;
Doom'd for a certain term to walk the night,
And, for the day, confin'd to waste in fires
Till the foul crimes done in my days of nature
Are burnt and purg'd away. But that I am forbid
To tell the secrets of my prison-house,
I could a tale unfold whose lightest word
Would harrow up thy soul. . . .

*Hamlet* by William Shakespeare

**Pitch.** *Pitch* is the relative highness or lowness of the voice at any given time. Each person's voice has a characteristic pitch level from which it moves up and down. Women's voices are pitched on a higher level than those of men, and children's voices are higher than either. Pitch is determined by the rapidity with which the vocal folds vibrate. This vibration, in turn, is influenced by the length of the vocal folds, their elasticity, the degree of tension in them, their thickness, and the amount of breath pressure applied.

Most persons use only four or five notes in ordinary speaking, but a good speaker can use two octaves or more. Many girls and women pitch their voices, consciously or unconsciously, at too high a level, not realizing that a low voice is far more musical and easily heard. As a rule, therefore, girls should do their vocal exercises on the lower pitch levels.

The pitch of the voice gives meaning to speech. When speakers are excited, interested, and enthusiastic in conversation, they unconsciously lift the pitch on important words to emphasize them and lower the pitch on unimportant words to subordinate them. In repeating conversations, they lower or raise the voice in imitation of various people. Pitch gives life to reading aloud and speaking, and depends largely upon a vital interest in living and in what you are saying and doing. For a colorful and interesting voice, keep your mind alert as you talk, read, and think.

As you speak you often alter your pitch. There are two primary ways of doing this. In the first, the *step*, you shift abruptly from one pitch level to another between words, parts of sentences, or sentences to express a distinct break in thought or feeling. In the second, the *inflection*, you gradually raise or lower the pitch level within a word or sentence. A rising inflection shows incompleteness of thought or uncertainty, and is often used in asking a question. A falling inflection indicates completeness and definiteness and is often used in answering a question. The rising-falling inflection is used to convey subtle shades and sharp differences of meaning within words.

Variety in pitch, called modulation or inflection, makes the voice musical. Monotony in pitch, resulting either from speaking continuously on one level or from giving every sentence exactly the same inflection, is a fatal flaw in speaking. Without variety in pitch, a speaker is unable to hold the attention of his audience. Ministers, teachers, and lawyers sometimes fall unconsciously into pitch patterns and monotonous inflections which lessen their influence to a marked degree. Monotony in pitch may be due to two technical deficiencies: a person's inability to hear pitch changes, or a lack of vocal flexibility. The former is probably caused by a defect within the hearing mechanism and should be discussed with a speech correctionist who may administer a test for "tonal deafness." Lack of flexibility, however, can be overcome by practice and conscious attention. It is due largely to lack of vitality and enthusiasm in thought and feeling or in vocal and bodily response.

As a student of dramatics, you must learn to control the number, length, and direction of pitch changes and the modulation of your voice as you interpret a part. In doing exercises for improving your pitch range and flexibility, a tape recorder is of great value, for it helps to train your ears as well as your voice. Today many schools have tape recorders. If you use one you will be able to hear your voice in scenes and check on your skill in doing interpretative work. In any case, you must learn to go as low and as high as you can without straining. Try to notice your own and other people's changes in pitch in normal conversation and how these changes affect the communication of thoughts and feelings. Notice what anger, exhaustion, irritation, worry, joy, and excitement do to the pitch of people's voices. You will find that the pitch is usually higher when a person is angry, that domi-

Photo by Hays, from Monkmeyer

**A student records his voice so that he can hear and improve his speech.**

nant people use falling inflections for the most part, and timid ones use brief, rising inflections. Sneering and sarcasm are often shown by rising-falling inflections which convey inner, subtle meanings.

The reading aloud of plays or strongly contrasted conversations from stories is extremely helpful in daily practice for pitch variation. In reading aloud, you may find that a complete poem or single passage in prose has a predominant mood. An idea which is lofty and inspiring may need little range in pitch and will be best expressed by long, falling inflections. A passage which is gay, exciting, lyrical, and vital will have a wide range with many short, changing inflections. In all interpretative work, keep asking yourself, "What am I saying?" and then answer the question in the author's words.

*Applications*

1. Count from one to ten, beginning as low as you can and going as high as you can without strain. Then reverse the count and come down. Be sure that it is pitch and not loudness that makes the difference in each count.

**2.** Count slowly from one to ten, giving the vowel in each number a long falling inflection. Repeat with a long rising inflection on each. Then alternate the two exercises.

**3.** Using the alphabet, talk as if you were preaching a sermon, explaining a geometry problem, describing a horrible accident you just saw, putting a little child to sleep, and speaking to someone who is hard of hearing.

**4.** Take a nursery rhyme and recite it as a father, an old-fashioned elocutionist, a bored small boy, and a frightened little girl.

**5.** Read these sentences with the widest possible range. Put emphasis on the important words and syllables by raising the pitch, using both the step and inflection shifts. Drop definitely on unimportant words.

    **a.** What a glorious sunset!

    **b.** To speak effectively you must raise your voice on the important words.

    **c.** In direct conversation we change the pitch of the voice constantly.

    **d.** Did you hear what I said? Then go!

    **e.** No, I will not go!

    **f.** Look, that plane is exploding!

    **g.** I shall never, never, never believe you again!

**6.** Stand behind a screen or curtain and give the following lines, having someone check on your variations in pitch:

    **a.** No, never. Well, hardly ever.

    **b.** To be or not to be, that is the question.

    **c.** Do unto others as ye would that they should do unto you.

    **d.** Give me liberty or give me death!

    **e.** Laugh and the world laughs with you;
       Weep and you weep alone!

**7.** Analyze the following selections and decide what inflections to use in order to bring out the predominant mood and inner meaning of each. If possible, use a tape recorder and read the lines aloud. Then study the pitch of your voice and try again, concentrating particularly on inflection and modulation.

**a**

[PETRUCHIO:]
    Good-morrow, Kate, for that's your name, I hear.

[KATHARINE:]
    Well have you heard, but something hard of hearing:
    They call me Katharine that do talk of me.

[PETRUCHIO:]
    You lie, in faith; for you are called plain Kate,
    And bonny Kate, and sometimes Kate the curst,
    But Kate, the prettiest Kate in Christendom.
        *The Taming of the Shrew* by William Shakespeare

**b**

[THE PIPER:]

She was my mother.—And she starved and sang;
And like the wind she wandered and was cold
Outside your lighted windows, and fled by,
Storm-hunted, trying to outstrip the snow.
South, south, and homeless as a broken bird,—
Limping and hiding!—And she fled, and laughed,
And kept me warm; and died! To you a Nothing;
Nothing, forever, oh, you well-housed mothers!
As always, always for the lighted windows
Of all the world, the Dark outside is nothing;
And all that limps and hides there in the dark;
Famishing,—broken,—lost!

*The Piper* by Josephine Preston Peabody

**c**

[MARULLUS:]

Wherefore rejoice? What conquest brings he home?
What tributaries follow him to Rome,
To grace in captive bonds his chariot wheels?
You blocks, you stones, you worse than senseless things!
O you hard hearts, you cruel men of Rome,
Knew you not Pompey? Many a time and oft
Have you climb'd up to walls and battlements,
To towers and windows, yea, to chimney-tops,
Your infants in your arms, and there have sat
The live-long day with patient expectation
To see great Pompey pass the streets of Rome:
And when you saw his chariot but appear
Have you not made an universal shout,
That Tiber trembled underneath her banks
To hear the replication of your sounds
Made in her concave shores?
And do you now put on your best attire?
And do you now cull out a holiday?
And do you now strew flowers in his way
That comes in triumph over Pompey's blood?
Be gone!
Run to your houses, fall upon your knees,
Pray to the gods to intermit the plague
That needs must light on this ingratitude.

*Julius Caesar* by William Shakespeare

**Volume.** *Volume* is the relative strength, force, or intensity with which sound is made. You must not confuse volume with mere loudness, for you can utter a stage whisper with great intensity or you can call across a room with little intensity. Volume depends upon the pressure with which the air from the lungs strikes the vocal folds, and while a certain amount of tension is required to retain the increased breath pressure, this tension should be minimal. If your throat is as relaxed as possible, you will not become hoarse even when speaking with increased volume and your words will be resonant and forceful.

To speak loudly enough to be heard in the largest auditorium without forcing the words from your throat, you must breathe deeply and centrally. Think that you are talking to the person farthest away from you. Such concentration will cause you to open your mouth wider, speak more slowly, and enunciate more clearly. When you use a microphone, remember that no greater volume is necessary than might be used in ordinary conversation —no matter how large the auditorium may be.

Force is of two types. A sudden, sharp breath pressure creates *explosive* force which is useful in commands, shouts, loud laughter, and screams. When the breath pressure is held steady and the breath released gradually, the force is said to be *expulsive*. This type of force is necessary in reading long passages without loss of breath and in building to a dramatic climax.

Like the other voice characteristics, volume is closely related to the expression of ideas and emotions. Fear, excitement, anger, hate, defiance, and other strong emotions are usually accompanied by an explosive intensity. On the other hand, quiet, calm thoughts call for a minimal amount of force. Animated conversation requires an average amount.

Volume is used in combination with other voice characteristics to suggest various feelings. For example, a quiet voice accompanied by a flat quality suggests dullness, indifference, and weariness. A quiet voice with a full tonal quality may express disappointment, shock, despair, bewilderment, and sometimes even great joy.

When you are on the stage, it is important to remember that you must use more energy to convey impressions of all kinds than is necessary off the stage. Thus, if you are merely chatting comfortably at home with a friend, your voice will have relatively little intensity. Put that identical scene on the stage, try to make it equally informal, and you will have to increase your vocal intensity considerably—otherwise the scene will fall flat. Keep the person farthest away from you constantly in mind and talk directly to him, using your jaw, tongue, and lips to enunciate clearly.

Using greater force to emphasize the important words in a sentence is the most common means of clarifying a thought. You can change the meaning of a sentence by shifting the force from one word to another—expressing innocence, surprise, anger, and other emotions. In acting, the entire thought of a line can be clarified or obscured by emphasizing a word or phrase. Key words brought out forcibly can make a character's personality understandable to the audience.

*Applications*

1. Pant like a dog. While you do so, feel the movement of your diaphragm with your hands. Then say "ha-ha" as you pant.

2. Repeat "ha-ha" many times, making the syllables by a sharp "kick" of the diaphragm. Gradually work from a light sound to a shout. Be careful not to allow an audible escape of breath on the *h* sound.

3. Take a full breath and call "one" as if you were throwing a ball against a wall at some distance. Exhale, relax, inhale, and call "two" in the same manner. Count up to ten in this way, but be careful to relax between each effort. Get your power from a quick "kick" of the rib cage rather than from tightening the vocal bands. In the same way, use the words *no, bell, on, never,* and *yes.*

4. Repeat the letters of the alphabet, increasing your energy whenever you come to a vowel. Then reverse the exercise, beginning with a strong, firm tone and gradually reducing the energy involved. Keep all the sounds on the same pitch.

5. Say the sentence "I am going home," as though you were saying it to the following people:
   a. A friend sitting next to you
   b. A person ten feet away
   c. Someone across the room
   d. Someone in the back row of your assembly room, when you are on the platform
   e. A person in the next room
   f. A person across the street
Notice that if you are thinking about the person to whom you are speaking, your voice adjusts itself naturally to the distance involved.

6. Change the meaning of the following sentences in as many ways as you can by using force to emphasize different words. Explain your exact meaning.
   a. I didn't say that to her.
   b. You don't think I stole the book, do you?
   c. Why didn't you warn me before it happened?

7. Read these passages aloud, making the mood and meaning clear by the amount of force you use and the words you emphasize. Use volume sufficient for a large auditorium by getting enough breath, keeping an open throat, and sounding the vowels clearly. Stand correctly.

### a

The earth is the Lord's, and the fulness thereof; the world, and they that dwell therein.

For he hath founded it upon the seas, and established it upon the floods.

Psalm 24:1–2

### b

Swiftly the brazen car comes on . . .
Its eyes are lamps like the eyes of dragons
It drinks gasoline from big red flagons!

"The Santa Fé Trail" by Vachel Lindsay

### c

Boot, saddle, to horse, and away!
Rescue my castle before the hot day
Brightens to blue from its silvery gray
Boot, saddle, to horse, and away.

"Boot and Saddle" by Robert Browning

### d

[PORTIA:]

The quality of mercy is not strained.
It droppeth as the gentle rain from heaven
Upon the place beneath. It is twice blest;
It blesseth him that gives, and him that takes.
'Tis mightiest in the mightiest; it becomes
The throned monarch better than his crown.
His sceptre shows the force of temporal power,
The attribute to awe and majesty,
Wherein doth sit the dread and fear of kings;
But mercy is above this sceptred sway;
It is enthroned in the hearts of kings,
It is an attribute to God himself;
And earthly power doth then show likest God's
When mercy seasons justice.

The Merchant of Venice by William Shakespeare

### e

Out of the North the wild news came,
Far flashing on its wings of flame,
Swift as the boreal light which flies
At midnight through the startled skies.
And there was tumult in the air,
    The fife's shrill note, the drum's loud beat,
And through the wide land everywhere
    The answering tread of hurrying feet;

Photo by Friedman-Abeles

Shylock, Portia, and Antonio in the court scene from Shakespeare's *The Merchant of Venice.*

While the first oath of Freedom's gun
Came on the blast from Lexington;
And Concord, roused, no longer tame,
Forgot her old baptismal name,
Made bare her patriot arm of power,
And swelled the discord of the hour.
And there the startling drum and fife
Fired the living with fiercer life;
While overhead with wild increase,
Forgetting its ancient toll of peace,
   The great bell swung as ne'er before;
It seemed as it would never cease;
And every word its ardor flung
From off its jubilant iron tongue
   Was War! *War!* WAR!
      "The Rising in 1776" by Thomas Buchanan Read


**Rate.** *Rate,* in speech, is the speed at which words are spoken. Each person has a characteristic rate of speech, which is usually more rapid in informal conversation than in public speaking or in work in dramatics. Like quality, pitch, and volume, rate is also an important means of suggesting ideas and emotional states. A steadily increasing speed creates a feeling of tension and excitement, while the deliberate delivery of important passages impresses the hearer with their significance. Light, gay, happy, and lyric passages are usually spoken rapidly. Calm, serene, reverent, tragic, and awesome passages are delivered more slowly. Unemotional ideas are conveyed by an average rate of speech.

Practically all of our sentences in both speaking and reading are divided into groups separated by pauses of varying lengths. The breathing pause is a necessity because we must have breath in order to speak. One of the worst faults a beginner can have is gasping for breath because he needs to do so, thus breaking the thought of a sentence. You must train yourself at once to get your breath between thought groups when reading or speaking in front of an audience. You undoubtedly manage it properly in normal conversation, unconsciously putting into groups words which belong together before you catch your breath. You will find it harder to do this on the stage. The number of words in a group necessarily varies with the thought. A single word may be important enough to stand alone or there may be twelve or more in a group; ordinarily there are four or five. Too many breath groups tend to create choppy speech. Punctuation can be of great assistance for it often clarifies meaning as well as grammatical relationship.

Logical grouping and pausing is a matter of making the thought clear and depends upon your knowing exactly what you are saying. The secret of great interpretative power is the ability to realize an idea—to visualize, emotionalize, and vitalize it for yourself—and then give the audience an opportunity to do the same thing. Logical and dramatic pauses demand thought and feeling on your part or you will not have your audience thinking and feeling with you. Therefore, work out your thought groups very carefully and then remember that pauses are often more effective than words. After the pattern is set, approach each group as if for the first time every time you speak or read aloud. In acting, this is one of the secrets of giving a sense of spontaneity and freshness to every performance throughout a long run.

Go back over the passages you have been reading in the Applications sections in this chapter and decide where the thought groups divide. Then read the passages aloud again, watching your timing. Hold the important words longer than others and slip rapidly over the unimportant ones. Let the idea speed you up or slow you down and take time to feel the emotions and moods. A skillful use of phrasing and pausing is one of your most valuable tools in putting over ideas and arousing emotion, and the more you practice reading aloud, either from prepared selections or at sight, the more effective you will become.

## Using the Voice in Interpretation

*Emphasis* and *subordination* are the light and shadow of interpretation in acting. The key words of every passage must be highlighted to be heard by everyone in the audience so that the meaning may be understood. To stress such words you must first feel their emotional context to give them color. They can be made to stand out in the following ways: by delivering them with greater force, holding them for a longer period, lifting or lowering them in pitch, and giving them a rich resonant quality. They can also be set off by pauses, either before or after, or sometimes both before and after. To subordinate unimportant words or phrases, you can "throw them away" by saying them rapidly at a lower pitch with less volume.

*Stress* also involves tone placement and projection. There are two rather different but not conflicting ideas regarding the matter of placement of tone. One is that tone should be placed in the mask of the face by forming the sounds of speech with the position of the lips, lower jaw, and tongue, thus producing resonance. The other is that the voice should be thrown as far as the size of the auditorium requires. This is accomplished by breathing deeply, opening the mouth, and forming the sounds accurately, while consciously putting attention on the person farthest away. In both cases the throat is never tightened but kept open. The term "swallowing words" is used when the sound is prevented from reaching the resonating chambers because the throat is closed by tension or carelessness in controlling the breath and the vocal folds cannot vibrate to produce sound.

*Climax* is another principle of great value in interpretation. A climactic passage must, of course, be well written by the author before it can be effectively spoken by the speaker. In such a passage, the emotional intensity of the lines is increased to a high point of feeling at the end. Naturally, to reach a high point it is necessary to start at a relatively low one. In a strong emotional passage, begin with a relatively slow rate, deliberate utterance, low pitch, and little or medium energy. Gradually increase the energy and speed and change the pitch until you reach the highest point of interest or feeling.

A flexible, responsive voice is the most valuable asset an actor or speaker can have. Speaking is like painting. In both arts, the main purpose is to express an idea. The painter may use dull grays or he may utilize a great variety of colors, exquisitely blended and harmonized. So, too, the speaker or actor may use a lifeless voice—monotonous in tone, energy, and pitch—or he may utilize all the resources of vocal technique. You will achieve the most effective communication if you first think and feel deeply, understanding and visualizing your ideas. Then express these ideas, making full use of voice and body.

In the Applications which follow, try to use all the suggestions made in this chapter, first thinking and feeling, then using the intonation, inflection, and emphasis necessary to express the ideas back of the sounds and words. Be sure to take the time you need and be careful not to tighten your throat.

*Applications*

1. Tell the story "The Three Bears," stressing the vocal characteristics of Goldilocks and the bears and getting all the contrast possible. Also read Lincoln's Gettysburg Address aloud, doing the same thing.

2. Using the letters of the alphabet instead of words, tell a funny story, a moral tale, a short tragedy, and a ghost story.

3. Say "oh" to suggest keen interest, sudden pain, deep sympathy, utter exhaustion, delight, fear, irritation, anger, sarcasm, hesitation, embarrassment, good-natured banter, polite indifference, horror, and surprise.

4. Address the following sentences first to someone 5 feet away, then to someone 25, 100, and 500 feet away. Keep an open throat but control the breath from the diaphragm. Make full use of the vowel sounds.

a. Run for your life!
b. Fire! Help!
c. Are you all right?
d. Come here at once!
e. Run around the corner for rolls.

5. Read these passages aloud. First carefully analyze their meanings. Then determine the mood, situation, and emotion portrayed. Finally decide what quality, energy, change of pitch, and rate will best suit your interpretation.

a

[PIERRETTE:]
>Pierrot, don't wait for the moon,
>There's a heart-chilling cold in her rays;
>And mellow and musical June
>Will only last thirty short days.
>>The Maker of Dreams by Oliphant Down

b

>Work!
>Thank God for the might of it,
>The ardor, the urge, the delight of it—
>Work that springs from the heart's desire,
>Setting the brain and the soul on fire.
>>"Work" by Angela Morgan

c

[THE PIPER:]
>If I knew all, why should I care to live?
>No, No! The game is What-Will-Happen-Next?
>
>It keeps me searching. 'Tis so glad and sad
>And strange to find out, What-Will-Happen-Next!
>>The Piper by Josephine Preston Peabody

d

During the whole of a dull, dark, and soundless day in the autumn of the year, when clouds hung oppressively low in the heavens, I had been passing alone, on horseback, through a singularly dreary tract of country; and at length found myself, as the shades of evening drew on within view of the melancholy House of Usher.
>The Fall of the House of Usher by Edgar Allan Poe

e

>By Jupiter, he never seems to sleep,
>For, after banquetings when all go home,
>I have observed how often he will keep

An all night vigil in the gloom
Of Diane's temple, cudgeling his head
Until the dawn comes, which he straightway greets,
And, walking off as freshly as from bed,
The labors of another day he meets.
Many before him had no doubt been wise,
And many brave, and many loved truth,
But he, we think, deserves the earliest prize
For making all these beautiful to youth.
    And, too, we youth adore another trait—
He makes talk logical instead of just debate.
        "Athenian Youth Speaks of Socrates" by Eugene Fuller

## IMPROVING YOUR DICTION

There are various definitions of *diction*, but for all practical purposes it means the selection and pronunciation of words and their combination in speech. Because the way in which you speak is an index to your personality and to your educational and cultural background, it may well affect your future social and professional success. To be sure that your speech will be an asset rather than a liability, it is wise to try continually to improve it. If you do wish to improve your speech, or diction, you must consider your vocabulary and grammar, as well as the formation of sounds which make up words. Your aim should be clear, pleasing speech which carries well.

Ear training is almost as important as voice training. Therefore, in order to accustom yourself to good speech you should listen to people who speak well, for there is nothing more contagious than speech habits. Listening to the best speakers on the radio is excellent training because you are not distracted by facial expression and bodily action. Television provides opportunities to hear good actors from the stage and screen and recordings enable you to listen to fine speech by many of today's leading dramatic artists.

For your own benefit, make a recording of your voice in ordinary conversation—better still, get someone to set up a recorder when you don't know it is around—and check it again and again as you work with diction. Keep the recording and do the experiment again at the end of this course, noting the changes.

If possible, you should certainly take a speech course, for such study will help you to distinguish between the styles of speech appropriate for different occasions. In informal conversation, it is natural to use speech patterns that differ somewhat from those you use in formal conversation or platform performances. However, your daily speech should be correct and clear at all times, flexible in pitch and pleasing in tone.

VOICE AND DICTION        215

## Vowel Sounds

The vowel sounds are "unobstructed tones" through the mouth, given characteristic tone by the positions of the lips, tongue, jaw, and soft palate, which necessarily differ for each vowel sound.

The vowel sounds may be classified as front vowels, middle vowels, and back vowels, according to the position of the tongue as each is formed. Look at the diagram of the speech organs on this page and note the parts of the tongue. In the front vowels, the front of the tongue is gradually raised until it almost touches the inner gum ridge, as $\bar{e}$ in *me*. In the middle vowels, the front of the tongue (which is considerably more than the tip) is midway to the roof of the mouth, as $\breve{u}$ in *up*. In the back vowels, the back of the tongue is raised, the jaw relaxed, and the lips rounded, as $\bar{oo}$ in *food*. In all the back vowels, the lips are rounded until only a small opening is left. (*Diphthongs* are combinations of two vowel sounds, as in *how* ($\ddot{a} + \breve{oo}$) or hay ($\bar{a} + \breve{i}$). Prolong the vowel sounds and see how the quality changes from one sound to another.)

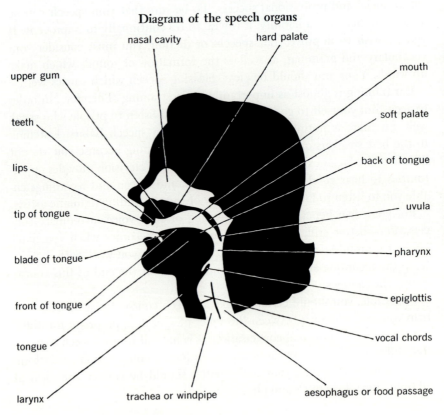

**Diagram of the speech organs**

nasal cavity       hard palate

upper gum

mouth

teeth

soft palate

lips

back of tongue

tip of tongue

uvula

blade of tongue

pharynx

front of tongue

epiglottis

tongue

vocal chords

larynx      trachea or windpipe      aesophagus or food passage

## THE VOWEL SOUNDS*

| FRONT | MIDDLE | BACK |
|---|---|---|
| ē as in ēve | ŭ as in ŭp | ä as in äh |
| ĭ as in hĭm | à as in àlone | ŏ as in ŏccur |
| ĕ as in ĕnd | û as in ûrn | ô as in lôrd |
| ă as in căt | ē as in makēr | ō as in ōld |
| | | oŏ as in hoŏd |
| | | ōō as in fōōd |

## Consonant Sounds

The consonant sounds are made when the air passage is obstructed at some point by the tongue, soft palate, or lips. If there is no vibration of the vocal cords, the consonant is said to be voiceless; if there is a vibration of the vocal cords, it is voiced. You can tell whether a consonant sound is voiced or voiceless by placing your fingers lightly on your throat and feeling whether there is any vibration.

### THE CONSONANT SOUNDS
#### Plosive Consonants
In these sounds the air is stopped and suddenly released.

| VOICELESS | VOICED | AIR STOPPED BY |
|---|---|---|
| p as in pop | b as in bob | Lip against lip |
| t as in tame | d as in dame | Tip of tongue against upper gum ridge |
| c or k as in came | g as in game | Back of tongue against soft palate |

#### Fricative Consonants
In these sounds the air passage is narrowed at some point and a slight friction results.

| VOICELESS | VOICED | AIR PASSAGE NARROWED BY |
|---|---|---|
| f as in fan | v as in van | Upper teeth on lower lip |
| s as in bus | z as in buzz | Front of tongue against upper and lower teeth which are almost closed |
| sh as in sure | zh as in azure | Tip of tongue turned toward hard palate, teeth almost closed |
| th as in breath | th as in breathe | Tip of tongue against upper teeth |
| wh as in which | w as in witch | Rounded lips and raised tongue |

#### Nasal Consonants
In these sounds the mouth is completely closed at some point and the soft palate is lowered. Thus the air is forced to pass through the nose.

| | |
|---|---|
| m as in mammy | Mouth closed by lip on lip |
| ng as in sing | Mouth closed by back of tongue on soft palate |
| n as in ninny | Mouth closed by tip of tongue on upper gums |

* Based on the Guide to Pronunciation in *Webster's New Collegiate Dictionary*.

*Applications*

1. Distinguish between the vowel sounds as you read the words in the following lists.
   a. feel   fill   fell   fall   fail   file   foil   foul
   b. tea   tin   ten   tan   ton   turn   tarn   torn   tune   town
   c. eat   it   at   ought   ate
   d. peak   pick   peck   pack   Puck   perk   park   pock   pork   poke
   pike

2. Distinguish between the consonant sounds as you read the words in these lists.
   a. pen   Ben   ten   den   ken   fen   when   wen
   b. have   cat   gap   quack   land   nag   tap   dash   rat   map   pat
   bat   fat   vat   thank
   c. than   sad   sham   chap   jam   plaid   black   flat   slack   clan
   glad   snack   stand
   d. smack   span   scan   trap   dram   prank   bran   frank   crab   grab
   thrash   shrapnel
   e. strap   sprat   scrap   splash   swam   twang   wag   yap
   f. hood   could   good   look   nook   put   book   foot   soot   should
   brook   crook   wood

## Pronounciation

Good pronunciation entails the use of correct vowel and consonant sounds in words and the placing of the accent on the stressed syllables. A recently edited dictionary should be one of your most valued possessions, for the "dictionary habit" is the only means by which anyone can become reasonably certain of his pronunciation.

The following words are only a very few of those in ordinary use which are being constantly mispronounced.

Place the accent on the first syllable in the following list:

| | | |
|---|---|---|
| ex'qui site | pos'i tive ly | in'flu ence |
| nec'es sar y | gon'do la | the'a ter |
| des'pi ca ble | mis'chie vous | in'ter est ing |
| lam'en ta ble | ad'mi ra ble | hos'pi ta ble |
| ab'so lute ly | req'ui site | for'mi da ble |

Place the accent on the second syllable in the following list:

| | | |
|---|---|---|
| ho tel' | suf fice' | en tire' |
| in quir'y | ro mance' | al ly' |
| gri mace' | ad dress' | a skance' |
| a dult' | a dept' | man kind' |

Drop the silent letters in the words in the following list:

| | | |
|---|---|---|
| often | corps | sword |
| toward | subtlety | heir |
| debt | forehead | indictment |
| blackguard | gnaw | business |

Note the consonant and vowel sounds, as well as the accent marks in the following list of words. Say these words according to the pronunciation spellings which are given within the parentheses following the words themselves; all are taken from *Webster's New Collegiate Dictionary*. The first pronunciation is considered preferable, but the others are also in good usage.

Feb′ru·ar′y (fĕb′rŏŏ·ĕr′ĭ; fĕb′ů·ĕr′ĭ; fĕb′ŏŏ·ĕr′ĭ; fĕb′ŏŏ·ĕr·ĭ)

hearth (härth)

na·ïve′ (nä·ēv′)

vau′de·ville (vô′dĕ·vĭl; vōd′vĭl)

hei′nous (hā′nŭs)

gen′u·ine (jen′ů·ĭn)

I·tal′ian (ĭ·tăl′yăn)

ir·rev′o·ca·ble (ĭ·rĕv′ô·ká·b′l)

har′ass (hăr′ás; há·răs′)

bou·quet′ (bŏŏ·kā′; bō·kā′)

come′ly (kŭm′lĭ)

with (wĭth; wĭth)

ac·cli′mate (á·klī′mĭt; ăk′lĭ·māt)

bade (băd)

fin′an·cier′ (fĭn′ăn·sēr′; fĭ′năn·sēr′; fĭ·năn′sĭ·ēr)

her′o·ine (hĕr′ô·ĭn)

sin·cer′i·ty (sĭn·sĕr′ĭ·tĭ)

or′ches·tra (ôr′kĕs·trá; ôr′kĭs·trá)

col′umn (kŏl′ŭm)

am′a·teur′ (ăm′á·tûr′; ăm′á·tûr; ăm′á·tûr)

chauf·feur′ (shŏ·fûr′; shō′fēr)

ar′chi·tec′ture (är′kĭ·tĕk′tůr)

ab·surd′ (ăb·sûrd′)

says (sĕz)

been (bĭn; bēn)

wom′en (wĭm′ĕn; wĭm′ĭn)

a′li·as (ā′lĭ·ás)

## Vocabulary

Careful diction also involves discrimination in the choice and use of words. A wide and constantly increasing vocabulary, free from an over-use of slang, is a cultural asset you cannot afford to neglect. Standard usage and grammatical structure are, of course, taken for granted by an educated speaker.

### Applications

The following suggestions will help you to improve both your vocabulary and pronunciation.

1. Make a list of one hundred words which you think are commonly mispronounced. Look them up, mark them carefully, and pronounce them correctly before the class.

2. Keep a list of new words you find in books or hear spoken. Look up their meanings and pronunciations and then use them in your own speech.

3. Bring in a list of words to illustrate the use of the following sounds: ā, ă, ạ, ä, ē, ĕ, ê, ī, ĭ, ō, ŏ, ōō, ŏŏ, ū, ŭ.

4. Bring in ten words in which diphthongs are used. Pronounce them carefully.

5. Look up the pronunciation of the following words:

| | | |
|---|---|---|
| diphtheria | gala | incognito |
| maintenance | acrid | Pall Mall |
| tumult | coupon | machinations |
| Leicester | George | promenade |
| civilization | Thames | Yorkshire |
| government | gesture | hostile |
| yacht | fiancé | library |
| exist | escape | finances |
| presentation | absurd | repartee |

6. Read the following as rapidly as you can, keeping the sounds clear:

a. The perfectly purple bird unfurled its curled wings and whirled over the world.

b. Amidst the mists and coldest frosts
With stoutest wrists and sternest boasts,
He thrusts his fists against the posts
And still insists he sees the ghosts.

c. The weary wanderer wondered wistfully whether winsome Winifred would weep.

d. When and where will you go and why?

e. The sea ceaseth and sufficeth us.

f. To sit in solemn silence in a dull, dark dock
In a pestilential prison with a life-long lock,
Awaiting the sensation of a short sharp shock
From a cheap and chippy chopper on a big black block!

g. The queen was a coquette.

h. They know not whence, nor whither, where, nor why.

i. Judge not that ye be not judged, for with what judgment ye judge ye shall be judged.

j. The clumsy kitchen clock click-clacked.

k. Didn't you enjoy the rich shrimp salad?

l. The very merry Mary crossed the ferry in a furry coat.

7. Read these sentences aloud very carefully:

a. The speech of the children over the radio was scarcely intelligible and entirely lacking in spirit and enthusiasm.

b. Some sparks from the largest of the rockets burned holes in her scarlet jacket.

c. The President of the United States of America delivered the dedicatory address.

d. His vocabulary is as meager as when he was in the elementary grades, and he is entirely lacking in intellectual curiosity; this is a sad commentary on his secondary education.

e. His thought that remaining in the automobile would allow them to see over the audience placed them in an awkward position.

f. They quarreled as to whether or not to take the spotted dog on the yacht.

g. Aunt Blanche answered his demand by advancing with her passport.

h. We hope next year to hear that he has started his career as an engineer rather than a mere cashier.

i. He was so boorish that he could endure the lonely moor and the obscure rural life.

8. Such combinations as "Didn't you?" "Wouldn't you?" "Haven't you?" "Shouldn't you?" "Why don't you?" are often run together slightly. Practice them carefully to avoid separating them too much and yet not saying "Didncha?" or "Didn'tchew?"

9. Read the excerpts below, giving full value to the vowel sounds:

a

Water, water, everywhere,
And all the boards did shrink.
Water, water, everywhere,
Nor any drop to drink.
*The Rime of the Ancient Mariner* by Samuel Taylor Coleridge

b

She left the web, she left the loom,
She made three paces through the room,
She saw the water-lily bloom,
She saw the helmet and the plume,
She looked down to Camelot.
*The Lady of Shalott* by Alfred Lord Tennyson

10. Read these excerpts, making the consonants distinct:

a

By the margin, willow-veiled,
Slide the heavy barges trail'd
By slow horses; and unhailed
The shallop flitteth silken-sailed
Skimming down to Camelot.
*The Lady of Shalott* by Alfred Lord Tennyson

VOICE AND DICTION          221

**b**

Great rats, small rats, lean rats, brawny rats,
Brown rats, black rats, gray rats, tawny rats.

*The Pied Piper of Hamelin* by Robert Browning

11. Reread "The Cataract of Lodore" on pages 193 to 194, applying all the suggestions given in this chapter. Change the tempo of your voice to suit the movement of the water and give color to each word by imaginatively seeing and hearing the water. Adapt your pitch, quality, and volume to suit the action back of the poet's words. Be very careful with your pronunciation and enunciation.

12. Select a passage from a play, poem, or book to present before the class. After you have finished, both you and your classmates should evaluate your voice and diction according to the following outline, which gives the qualities necessary for effective voice and diction. It would be a good idea to keep this outline in mind as you engage in your everyday conversations.

I. Voice
   A. Clear—due to proper
      1. Placement
      2. Projection
      3. Volume
      4. Phrasing
   B. Correct—due to proper
      1. Posture
      2. Breathing
         a. Deep
         b. Controlled
      3. Use of tongue
      4. Use of lips
      5. Use of lower jaw
      6. Emphasis
         a. Pitch
         b. Stress
         c. Pause
      7. Subordination
   C. Pleasing—due to expressive
      1. Modulation
      2. Resonance
      3. Emotional response
         a. Sincere
         b. Sympathetic
         c. Vital

II. Diction
   A. Clear—due to proper
      1. Formation of vowel and consonant sounds
      2. Enunciation of key words and phrases
   B. Correct—due to proper
      1. Pronunciation
      2. Choice of words
      3. Grammar
      4. Standard English
   C. Pleasing—due to
      1. Pure vowel tones
      2. Precise consonants
      3. Cultivated rhythm
      4. Easy fluency

## VOICE AND DICTION IN ACTING

A play comes to life by means of the voices and words of the actors; it is their ability to arouse emotion through the playwright's lines that creates the illusion of reality for the audience. Actors must make the meaning of every passage clear to all listeners by the proper projection of the key words. It is their responsibility to avoid spoiling lines by blurring pronunciation, muffling enunciation, or speaking with a nervous rhythm. The inner soul of the characters they are creating must be expressed through clear-cut patterns, suitable to the roles but varied with every change of mood and situation.

The presentation of a character through voice alone is only possible if you can visualize him accurately and feel with him. As in daily life, each character has his own voice quality, pitch, and tempo. However, these must all be varied in keeping with an immediate situation and mood without the loss of the character's individuality.

Recordings of Christopher Fry's play *The Lady's Not for Burning* and *My Fair Lady* are both available. In both recordings, perfect diction, subtle intonations expressing variety of feeling and mood, artful building of climaxes through proper emphasis, and the use of the pause combine to provide a remarkable lesson in voice and diction. Reading Shaw's *Pygmalion*, on which *My Fair Lady* is based, will give you added insight into the importance of good speech.

*Applications*

1. The following play excerpts present two strongly contrasted young women who are speaking in entirely different moods. In the first, Mary Rose is deli-

cately beautiful and utterly charming. She is a young mother trying to coax her rather stolid British husband to say he loves her in a delightful comedy scene. In the second, George Bernard Shaw's Saint Joan is speaking at one of the highest emotional moments of the play; all the men who have supported her in her defiance of the enemy have turned from her saying she is now alone if she persists in further battles. Work with the two passages until you have created two totally different young women, each remarkable in her own right.

a

[MARY ROSE:] Have I been a nice wife to you, Simon? I don't mean always and always. There was that awful time when I threw the butter-dish at you. I am so sorry. But have I been a tolerably good wife on the whole, not a wonderful one, but a wife that would pass in a crowd?

*Mary Rose* by James M. Barrie

b

[SAINT JOAN:] Do not think you can frighten me by telling me that I am alone. France is alone; and God is alone: and what is my loneliness before the loneliness of my country and my God? I see now that the loneliness of God is His strength: what would He be if He listened to your jealous little counsels? Well, my loneliness shall be my strength too: it is better to be alone with God: His friendship will not fail me, nor His counsel, nor His love. In His strength I will dare, and dare, and dare, until I die.

*Saint Joan* by George Bernard Shaw

2. In the same way, work with these two masculine selections. In the first, young Abe Lincoln is grief-stricken at the death of his sweetheart, Anne Rutledge. The second shows a delightful, rather elderly, vicar speaking of his wife.

a

[ABE LINCOLN:] I went through something like this once before! Someone you love—standing helpless—waiting. I set day by day reading Ma parts of the Bible she liked best. On the sixth day she called me to her bed—talked of many strange things—principalities and powers—and things present—and things to come—urged me and Sairy always to walk in paths of goodness and truth—and told us many things would come t'him that served God—an' th' best way t'serve Him was t'serve His people. (*Pause*) She was amongst the lowliest of mankind. She walked the earth with her poor feet in the dust—her head in the stars—(*Pause*) Pa took me down into the woods t' make her a coffin. Pa was sawin' and I was hammerin' the pegs in. The hammer dropped at my feet; it was like someone was drivin' 'em into my heart. It's—just goin' through all that again—now!

*Prologue to Glory* by E. P. Conkle

Uta Hagen in the title role of George Bernard Shaw's *Saint Joan.*

VOICE AND DICTION  **225**

**b**

[THE VICAR:] Every year of my life—of our life—my dear Ann has altered. Only a little of course—a line here, a grey hair there—a point of view every now and then—no one notices these things so quickly as a husband. No one hides his knowledge so closely. Every year of our married life—and they are well over twenty—every year I have started my romance all over again. I shall continue to perform that astonishing miracle until I leave this rather absurd planet altogether; I am inclined to think, if I am lucky, that I shall be allowed, in a future condition, to go on being idiotic about my wife. If harps are to be played, I cannot conceive of anything else but that Ann and myself—however inadequately—will take turns at the same instrument.

*The Lilies of the Field* by John Hastings Turner

**3.** Start a section in your notebook for materials on voice and diction. You will want to include newspaper clippings and articles dealing with voice and personality, listings of new or difficult words with their pronunciation and meanings, descriptions of local types of speech, and pictures illustrating the use of the vocal organs. Listen carefully to people talking and make note of similarities and differences in tone, pitch, and diction.

**4.** Turn to the chapter on pantomime and put words into the mouths of the characters in all the suggested situations. Practice changing your voice completely for each character and coordinating your voice and body as you present each situation.

**5.** Using the following play excerpts, paint voice pictures of each of the characters by employing as much beauty, variety, and effectiveness of voice and speech as you can.

**Romeo and Juliet in the balcony scene. (From *Romeo and Juliet*, a Rank Organization film)**

Courtesy of J. Arthur Rank Productions, Ltd.

**a**

[ROMEO:]

But soft! What light through yonder window breaks?
It is the east, and Juliet is the sun!
Arise, fair sun, and kill the envious moon,
Who is already sick and pale with grief,
That thou her maid art far more fair than she.

*Romeo and Juliet* by William Shakespeare

**b**

[PROSPERO:]

Our revels now are ended. These are actors,
As I foretold you, were all spirits, and
Are melted into air, into thin air:
And, like the baseless fabric of this vision,
The cloud-capp'd towers, the gorgeous palaces,
The solemn temples, the great globe itself,
Yea, all which it inherit, shall dissolve
And, like this insubstantial pageant faded
Leave not a rack behind.

*The Tempest* by William Shakespeare

**c**

[GWENDOLINE:] Ernest, we may never be married. From the expression on mamma's face, I fear we never shall. Few parents nowadays pay any regard to what their children say to them. The old-fashioned respect for the young is rapidly dying out. Whatever influence I ever had over mamma I lost at the age of three. But though she may prevent us from becoming man and wife, and I may marry someone else, and marry often, nothing that she can possibly do can alter my eternal devotion to you.

*The Importance of Being Earnest* by Oscar Wilde

**d**

[ANTONIO:]

Give me your hand, Bassanio; fare you well,
Grieve not that I am fallen to this for you.

*The Merchant of Venice* by William Shakespeare

6. Turn to *Poor Maddalena* and prepare what you consider the ten most difficult passages. Present them with clarity of thought, dramatic power, and emotional understanding. For example, take time to bring out the crucial dramatic pause before Maddalena says, "Paolo, you are quite right," with the resulting contrast in inflections and quality.

7. Memorize the selections in exercise 5 above and the passages from *Poor Maddalena*. Put in the bodily responses appropriate for them.

# Chapter 10

# Acting

One of the best lessons ever given on the art of acting was spoken by Shakespeare's Hamlet to a group of players before their presentation of a play at the court in Elsinore castle.

"Speak the speech, I pray you, as I pronounced it to you, trippingly on the tongue: but if you mouth it, as many of your players do, I had as lief the town-crier spoke my lines. Nor do not saw the air too much with your hand, thus; but use all gently: for in the very torrent, tempest, and—as I may say—whirlwind of passion, you must acquire and beget a temperance, that may give it smoothness. O! it offends me to the soul to hear a robustious periwig-pated fellow tear a passion to tatters, to very rags, to split the ears of the groundlings, who, for the most part, are capable of nothing but inexplicable dumb-shows and noise: I would have such a fellow whipped for o'erdoing Termagant; it out-herods Herod: pray you, avoid it.

Be not too tame neither, but let your own discretion be your tutor: suit the action to the word, the word to the action; with this special observance, that you o'erstep not the modesty of nature; for anything so overdone is from the purpose of playing, whose end, both at the first and now, was and is, to hold, as 'twere, the mirror up to nature; to show virtue her own feature, scorn her own image, and the very age and body of the time his form and pressure. Now, this overdone, or come tardy off, though it make the unskilful laugh, cannot but make the judicious grieve; the censure of which one must in your allowance o'erweigh a whole theatre of others. O! there be players that I have seen play, and heard others praise, and that highly, not to speak it profanely, that, neither having the accent of Christians nor the gait of Christian, pagan, nor man, have so strutted and bellowed that I have thought some of nature's journeymen had made men, and not made them well, they imitated humanity so abominably.

And let those that play your clowns speak no more than is set down for them: for there be of them that will themselves laugh, to set on some quantity of barren spectators to laugh too; though in the mean time some necessary question of the play be then to be considered; that's villainous, and shows a most pitiful ambition in the fool that uses it."

From Shakespeare's day to today, the art of acting has been the subject of spirited argument, perhaps more so now than ever before. One side of the argument favors what is called *the Method*, based on the teachings of Constantin Stanislavski of the Moscow Art Theatre (see page 128). The Method seeks to do two things: enable the actor to use his own personality and life experiences in order to create a truthful character portrayal and

**Constantin Stanislavski.**

enable him to interpret his character in relationship to the other characters in the play. The Method is, therefore, a blueprint to guide the actor in using his own emotional and intellectual resources to achieve these goals in acting. It is a system involving hard work and intensive training, and is far too complex a study to be discussed here in detail. A key to the Method is the word *if*. Stanislavski suggested that the actor ask himself what he would do *if* the events in the play were actually happening and he were involved in them. The actor's answers will help him in gaining an understanding of the inner nature of the character; upon this understanding all vocal and bodily details of his characterizations must be based.

As a result of this approach to acting, Stanislavski's company became known the world over for its magnificent ensemble acting, each actor being important but no one more so than another. In the early twenties, the company visited the United States; this visit greatly influenced the younger generation of directors and actors at that time. Most of Stanislavski's ideas have become an intrinsic part of the contemporary art of acting. Today actors, directors, and teachers who use the Method have evolved their own approaches to it, but, for many, the original inspiration is still Stanislavski and those who directly followed him. Among actors known to you who have trained in the Method are Marlon Brando, Kim Stanley, Kim Hunter, Julie Harris, David Wayne, Ben Gazzara, Eli Wallach, Maureen Stapleton, and Shelley Winters.

Another side of the argument over the art of acting favors what may be called a *theatrical style*. This is not an accurate name since all good acting is theatrical. However, for purposes of pointing up the divisions of thought on acting, the word *theatrical* will have to suffice. This style emphasizes conscious technique rather than emotional involvement. Tyrone Guthrie, the dynamic director popular in England, Canada, and the United States, is an exponent of the theatrical style. His production of *Tamburlaine* by Christopher Marlowe and his Shakespearean productions move with terrific excitement and great variety of tempo. Under his direction, *The Matchmaker* by Thornton Wilder was one of the most hilarious farces ever seen on Broadway.

There are those who think Stanislavski's influence has gone too far. Many theater people, including Tyrone Guthrie, believe that the American theater is due for a revolution in acting styles. They believe that misapplication of the Method has often resulted in slovenly acting, awkward movement, and excessive analysis. Today it is generally recommended that actors combine what is good in the Stanislavski system with the best in theatrical techniques. This is probably the course taken by all good actors.

A scene from Tyrone Guthrie's production of *Tamburlaine the Great*.

As a student of acting, your chief responsibility is to remember that a play comes to life through the actors, who must communicate the play to an audience as truthfully and as effectively as possible. You should be as flexible and as spontaneous as you can, always applying what you know of body and voice techniques to the interpretation of your role and following the supervision of your director.

## CREATING A CHARACTER

### Analysis of a Role

The analysis of your role begins your work in building a characterization. You must first read the entire play carefully several times. Then you will be ready to find out about your character. You will want to know what kind of person you are in the play, why you behave as you do, what you want, and what stands in the way of your achieving your aims. Pay careful attention to the lines your character speaks, for he will reveal himself in his speech and his actions. Take note also of what the other characters say about him. Try to imagine what might have happened to him in his childhood to affect his personality. Note any changes that take place in him during the action of the play.

If the setting is an unfamiliar one, make a study of the place and period. Learn all you can from books, pictures, and travelers so that you may enter into the atmosphere, wear the costumes naturally, and feel a part of the life depicted by the playwright. Where dialect is involved, try to talk with people from the locality or listen to recordings of their voices and notice their inflections and pronunciation.

You will find it helpful to make an outline of the character traits brought out by your own lines and those spoken to and about your character. Use any main headings which seem appropriate such as physical, mental, and spiritual characteristics; individual and social behavior; and emotional, environmental, physical, and intellectual motivations. As soon as you can, visualize your character in detail and begin working out specific ways to clarify him for your audience.

It is wise not to see a motion picture or stage production of the play you are working on, for you are apt to find yourself copying another person's mannerisms rather than developing a sound understanding of the play and role. A better means of getting material for building a characterization is to observe carefully a person in real life who is similar to your conception of the part. This individual is your *primary* source. You may wish to adopt his posture, movements, vocal inflections, and habit patterns. Ordinarily you will combine characteristics from several primary sources. The books you read are your *secondary* sources. They are helpful, but the best actor must always refer to life for his materials and his inspiration.

As you get better acquainted with your part, ask yourself questions: How good is the social adjustment of my character? Is he shy, or uninhibited? How intelligent is he? Is he suffering from major or minor maladjustments? In what way has he been influenced by his environment? What are his particular problems? Is he meeting or evading his responsibilities? How and why? How does he react to all the other characters in the play? Has he developed a defense mechanism to evade the main issues of his situation? What makes him cynical, talkative, rowdyish, tense, aggressive, shy, charming, friendly, fearful, envious, courageous, idealistic? Altogether, you must understand both the social and personal background of your character.

Your character's actions and speech are your means of making him real to your audience. If you have a real understanding of the character, you will be able to create movements which reveal his inner nature. You may want to develop what is called a *master gesture*—some distinctive action that can be repeated effectively as a clue to the personality—a peculiar walk, laugh, or turn of the head. The position of your feet while you are standing, walking, or sitting can help to truly characterize your part.

After a careful analysis of the play and your character, work by yourself to create the various situations in your imagination and feel the emotions your character experiences. Try to let your voice and body react naturally as you read your lines. Be willing to cry, laugh, or go into a stony silence. Try to sense how your character reacts to the strains and tensions he undergoes. When actual rehearsals begin, recall emotions you have had which are similar to those of your character so that you can make your actions spontaneous, colorful, and natural. One of the problems in acting is maintaining a character's continuity of thought and feeling throughout a play. A sensitive director will encourage you in this and at the same time help you to grow into your role.

## Leading and Supporting Roles

Roles in plays usually fall into two main divisions, *leading* and *supporting*. In some plays the leading role is written for a man, as Oedipus in *Oedipus Rex*, Prospero in *The Tempest*, Tartuffe in *Tartuffe*, and Willie Loman in *Death of a Salesman*. The leading role may also be written for a woman, as Antigone in *Antigone*, Nora in *A Doll's House*, Joan in *The Lark*, and Terry in *Stage Door*. A number of plays have two leading roles, as Macbeth and Lady Macbeth in *Macbeth*, Eliza and Professor Higgins in *Pygmalion*, Mio and Miriamne in *Winterset*, and Sabrina and Linus in *Sabrina Fair*. Others include several leading roles, as Con, Nora, and Sara Melody in *A Touch of the Poet*.

Differences between the two types of roles are ones of function and degree. Both are integral to the play and essential to its development; however, the leading role is usually longer and somewhat more important because it is through the lead, or leads, that the playwright illustrates the theme of his play. Also, the leading role usually arouses more audience response than the supporting role.

A mistaken idea about leading roles is that the romantic interest of a play is always found in them. This is often true, but not always. Many people have an equally mistaken concept of what supporting roles are. They feel that supporting roles are usually such characters as disappointed sweethearts, spinster aunts, precocious children, or wisecracking detectives. No such generalizations can be made about either leads or supporting roles. The important thing to remember is that every role is a vital part of the play and that therefore each actor in a play must make his character truly alive.

Young people sometimes fail to realize that supporting roles can afford as much, if not more, opportunity to display dramatic ability and versatil-

Pictured here are three recent Academy Award winners: Burl Ives, who won his Oscar for a supporting role; and Susan Hayward and David Niven, who won theirs for leading roles.

ity than leading roles. They often lose interest if they cannot be leading ladies or dashing heroes. Some girls and boys always wish to be attractive on the stage, adorned in the latest style, and winning the sympathy of the audience. If you are wise, you will seek out the most difficult roles to interpret, ones which are totally different from your own personality so that you cannot play yourself. In this way you will develop versatility.

Leading and supporting roles can be either straight parts or character parts. *Straight parts* are those in which the character to be portrayed resembles the actor in looks and personality. The actor, in effect, plays himself. A *character part*, on the other hand, is one which embodies some degree of eccentricity—physical, psychological, mental, or spiritual. The actor who plays a character part usually is not playing himself.

### Some Special Skills

**Old age characterizations.** Old age offers an especially rich field for intermingling humor and pathos, mixing tragedy and comedy, and drawing forth tears and smiles from the audience. Everyone knows the outstanding characteristics of the aged. There is a slowing down of bodily activity with a resulting uncertainty of movement, lack of vigor, and dependence upon others. The voice is slower in rate and somewhat higher or lower in pitch, with a thinner quality than that of a younger person. There are many mannerisms, gestures, facial expressions, and inflections which have become set through the years. The varying success with which old people have faced the events of a lifetime should stir the imagination of the actors who characterize them. The mellowness or irascibility resulting from the great experience of age gives color and interest often lacking in youthful roles. Careful observation of primary sources will give you the details necessary to create these older characters.

**Dialects.** Characterizations often present interesting problems in dialect. You will find that national and sectional speech differences show themselves in pronunciation, choice of words, and sentence inflection.

If you are assigned a part which calls for dialect, make every effort to hear that dialect spoken, for you will then sense the subtle shifts in inflections and the lilt of the particular sounds of the language. You will find that dialects are the result of changes in pitch, quality, inflection, timing, stress, and rhythm, with occasional substitutions and omissions of sounds.

Through the years certain dialect conventions have been established by actors and entertainers to characterize Yankees, westerners, southerners, Frenchmen, Englishmen, Germans, Italians, Irishmen, and others. These conventions are described in books such as the recently revised *Foreign Dialects* by Lewis and Marguerite Shalett Herman, to which you may wish to refer when creating certain characterizations. Though these dialect patterns provide an effective means of portraying characters from particular regions, it should be remembered that even within a given geographical area people speak differently. All westerners do not speak in exactly the same way, nor do all Frenchmen use the same inflections and pronunciations when speaking their own or the English language. Therefore, whether a given dialect pattern is acceptable or unacceptable depends to a great extent upon the audience's knowledge of just how people from, or in, particular regions actually speak.

Dialects are local in nature. If a dialect is to be done accurately, the actor really must listen to and study the way people talk in the locality from which his character comes. There are several ways of doing this. One, of course, is to talk to people who live in the region. Another is to listen to recordings of people speaking native dialects. Records of this type can be ordered from any record shop. You may also find it helpful to see movies and watch television programs in which people use a particular dialect.

## Applications

1. The following are selections for practice in dialect:

### a

*A very old lady in a small town in Wisconsin has been pushed aside by the energetic younger members of her family and talks to herself by the fireplace.*

[GRANDMA:] Dum 'em. They've gone off to do things. And I'm so old, so fool old. Oh, God! Can't you make us hurry? Can't you make us hurry? Get us to the time when we don't have to dry up like a pippin before we're ready to be took off? Our heads an' our hearts an' our legs an' our backs—oh, make 'em last busy, busy, right up to the time the hearse backs up to the door!

*Neighbours* by Zona Gale

### b

*A middle-aged Irish woman quarrels with another woman.*

[MRS. FALLON:] Is that what you are saying, Bridget Tully, and is that what you think? I tell you it's too much talk you have, making yourself out to be such a great one, and to be running down every respectable person!

*Spreading the News* by Lady Gregory

### c

*An old Irish woman muses to herself after her last son has been drowned at sea.*

[MAURYA:] They're all gone now, and there isn't anything more the sea can do to me. I'll have no call to be up crying and praying when the wind breaks from the south, and you can hear the surf is in the east, and the surf is in the west, making a great stir with the two noises, and they hitting one on the other.

*Riders to the Sea* by John Millington Synge

### d

*A very dominating Southern woman talks condescendingly to her seventeen-year-old son about his girl, who has just jilted him.*

[ELIZA:] Gene. You know what I'd do if I were you? I'd just show her I was a good sport, that's what! I wouldn't let on to her that it affected me one bit. I'd write her just as big as you please and laugh about the whole thing.—Why, I'd be ashamed to let any girl get my goat like that. When you're older, you'll just look back on this and laugh. You'll see. You'll be going to college next year, and you won't remember a thing about it. . . .

*Look Homeward, Angel* adapted by Ketti Frings from the novel by Thomas Wolfe

Anthony Perkins as Eugene and Jo Van Fleet as Eliza in *Look Homeward, Angel.*

e

*Mr. Doolittle, a Cockney dustman, has become a gentleman in London
society due to a benefactor's having left him a great deal of money. He objects
violently to his new position.*

[MR. DOOLITTLE:] It's making a gentleman of me that I object to. Who
ask him to make a gentleman of me? I was happy. I was free. I touched
pretty nigh everybody for money when I wanted it, same as I touched
you, 'Enry 'Iggins. Now I am worrited; tied neck and heels; and everybody touches me for money. It's a fine thing for you, says my solicitor.
Is it? says I. You mean it's a good thing for you, I says. A year ago I
hadn't a relative in the world except two or three that wouldn't speak to
me. Now I've fifty, and not a decent weeks's wages among the lot of
them.—And the next one to touch me will be you, 'Enry 'Iggins. I'll have
to learn to speak middle class language from you, instead of speaking
proper English. . . .

*Pygmalion* by George Bernard Shaw

ACTING    237

### f

*A kindly, old Italian discusses life and its beauties with his friend, Mr. Carp.*

[MR. BONAPARTE:] You make-a me laugh, Mr. Carp. You say life'sa bad. No, life'sa good.—You say life'sa bad—well, is pleasure for you to say so. No? The streets, winter a' summer—trees, cats—I love-a them all. The gooda boys and girls, they who sing and whistle—very good! The eating and sleeping, drinking wine—very good! I gone around on my wagon and talk to many people—nice! Howa you like the big buildings of the city?

*Golden Boy* by Clifford Odets

### g

*A young Englishman of twenty tries to propose.*

[BRYAN ROPES:] I say, look here, I'm not a bit mad, you know. There never has been any madness in my family. I mean that might be important, you know.—Look here, I'm awfully sorry but I love you.—I was awake all night about it. It's frightfully short notice, I know.

*Lilies of the Field* by John Hastings Turner

2. Select one of the following plays and work up several speeches in it for further practice in dialect.

> *Neighbours* by Zona Gale
> *The Emperor Jones* by Eugene O'Neill
> *Anna Christie* by Eugene O'Neill
> *Sun-Up* by Lulu Vollmer
> *Spreading the News* by Lady Gregory
> *The Servant in the House* by Charles Rann Kennedy
> *Welsh Honeymoon* by Jeannette Marks
> *What Every Woman Knows* by James M. Barrie
> *Mary Rose* by James M. Barrie
> *Pygmalion* by George Bernard Shaw
> *Tovarich* by Jaques Deval and Robert E. Sherwood
> *Lady Precious Stream* by S. I. Hsiung
> *Night Over Taos* by Maxwell Anderson
> *Judgment Day* by Elmer Rice
> *The Corn Is Green* by Emlyn Williams
> *Maid of France* by Harold Brighouse

**Laughter.** It is difficult to laugh on the stage, for natural laughter demands a sense of relaxation seldom felt under the strain of a performance. Human beings furnish the only source material for the actor, who must reproduce by art the many different forms of the natural laugh. Therefore, listen constantly for unusual laughs and giggles and form the habit of catching the vowel sounds and inflections employed by different people.

There are uproarious guffaws, artificial simperings, musical ripples, hysterical gurgles, and sinister snorts. For stage work, all types of laughter must have a definite vocal sound. Beginners usually manage merely to grimace and gasp without making a sound.

A laugh is produced by a sudden contraction of the abdominal muscles which forces the breath out in sharp gasps. These gasps must be given sound as they pass through the larynx. The first step in learning to laugh is to pant like a dog, tightening your abdominal muscles as you exhale and relaxing them as you breathe in. You will probably only make faces without sound when you first try, because you will undoubtedly try to say "ha" when you are drawing in the breath instead of when you are expelling it in sharp, quick spurts. As you practice, you will literally "laugh until your sides ache"; it is the continuous, rapid movement of the abdominal muscles which causes this perfectly harmless ache.

In order to master the laugh, you must relax first and then let yourself go. Take such vowel combinations heard in laughter as "ha-ha-ha, ho-ho-ho, he-he-he, hoo, hoo, hoo," and say them in rapid succession with sharp contractions of the abdominal area. Do not stop or become self-conscious. Begin at a high pitch and run down the scale. Begin at a low level and go up the scale. Then use a circumflex pitch pattern and go both up and down, prolonging some sounds and shortening others in various combinations. Be sure to spread the laughter throughout a whole sentence or speech in your part; let it die off as you speak, "Ha-ha-ha, you don't say so! Ha-ha-ho-ho, that's the funniest thing, ha-ha-ha-ha, I ever heard, ho-ho-huh-huh."

*Applications*

1. Read the following passages from Shakespeare, laughing aloud:

a

[GREMIO:]
     Tut, she's a lamb, a dove, a fool to him!
     I'll tell you, Sir Lucentio: when the priest
     Should ask if Katharine should be his wife
     "Ay by gogs-wouns," quoth he; and swore so loud
     That, all amaz'd, the priest let fall the book;
     And, as he stoop'd to take it up,
     The mad-brain'd bridegroom took him such a cuff
     That down fell priest and book, and book and priest;
     "Now take them up," quoth he, "if any list."—
     Such a mad marriage never was before.

                          *The Taming of the Shrew*

**b**

[PORTIA:]
God made him, therefore, let him pass for a man.

*The Merchant of Venice*

**c**

[JAQUES:]
A fool, a fool!—I met a fool i' the forest
A motley fool;—a miserable world!

*As You Like It*

**d**

[CELIA:]
O wonderful, wonderful, and most wonderful, wonderful, and
yet again wonderful!

*As You Like It*

**e**

[MARIA:] Get ye all three into the box-tree: Malvolio is coming down
this walk: he has been yonder i' the sun practicing behavior to his own
shadow this half-hour: observe him for the love of mockery; for I know
this letter will make a contemplative idiot of him. Close, in the name of
jesting.

*Twelfth Night*

**f**

[GRATIANO:]
Let me play the fool
With mirth and laughter let old wrinkles come.

*The Merchant of Venice*

2. Practice all the laughs which can be introduced into *Poor Maddalena*
in Appendix A, especially the one which breaks into tears at the end of
Scene 2. Get a contrast between the laughs of all three characters under all the
different emotions they experience.

3. Laugh like the following people: a giggling schoolgirl on the telephone, a
fat man at a comic television show, a polite lady at a joke she has heard many
times, a villain who has at last captured the hero, a miser gloating over his
gold, a boy when his pal trips over a brick, a minister at a ladies' aid meeting, a
farmer at a motorist whose car is stalled, a charming girl much thrilled over a
date.

**Crying.** It is much easier to cry on the stage than to laugh, although the
technique is much the same. Gasp for breath, using the abdominal muscles
in short, sharp movements. Words are spoken on the gasping breath, but

you must be very careful to keep the thought clear by not obscuring the key words. In sobbing without words, sound the syllable "oh" through the gasps, intensifying and prolonging the sound to avoid monotony. Occasional indrawn and audible breaths for the "catch in the throat" are effective, and "swallowing tears" is achieved by tightening the throat muscles and really swallowing. In uncontrolled or hysterical weeping, your "oh" will be stronger, and if words are needed they will be greatly intensified. Your entire body should react in crying. Facial expression is most important and can be created by puckering the eyebrows, biting the lips, and twisting the features to obtain the necessary effect.

## Applications

1. Sob like a young child put in the corner for punishment, a wife at the bedside of her sick husband who is asleep, a spoiled child putting on an act, an hysterical woman after a serious automobile accident, an old woman alone on Christmas.

2. Read the following passages, crying through the words and being careful to keep the meaning clear:

**a**

*A young girl has just heard that her brother is a thief.*

[POLLY:] I can't believe it. I can't—I can't—He's only a little boy—just a kid.

*Pearls* by Dan Totheroh

**b**

*An American tourist in her thirties has had an unfortunate flirtation with a charming Italian.*

[LEONA:] I'm Leona Samish. I *am* attractive. I'm bright and I'm warm and I'm nice! So *want me!* Want me!—Oh, why couldn't you love me, Renato? Why couldn't you just *say* you loved me?

*The Time of the Cuckoo* by Arthur Laurents

**c**

*A young woman is crying as she recites a poem because she feels her love for Pierrot is hopeless.*

[PIERRETTE:]

> If you meet this maid of a hopeless love,
>> Play not a meddler's part.
> Silence were best; let her keep in her breast
>> The dream of her hungry heart.

*The Maker of Dreams* by Oliphant Down

**Emotional passages.** In passages with rising emotional intensity, you must strike a balance between overacting and underplaying your role. It is best to begin quietly, saving your vocal and physical resources for the most intense moment at the climax of the speech or scene. Try to re-create in your imagination the emotions of the character you are portraying. In rehearsal, recall some similar experience and response of your own and then try to sense how the character would react to the tensions of the situation.

*Applications*

In the following excerpts from plays, rise to the appropriate emotional pitch.

1

*Cyrano, a seventeenth-century poet, swordsman, and philosopher is charming, witty, and bold. However, his huge nose often makes him the object of ridicule. In this speech, he sadly tells a friend that he knows no woman can ever love him.*

[CYRANO:]

    My old friend—look at me,
And tell me how much hope remains for me
With this protuberance! Oh I have no more
Illusions! Now and then—bah! I may grow
Tender, walking alone in the blue cool
Of evening, through some garden fresh with flowers
After the benediction of the rain;
My poor big devil of a nose inhales
April . . . and so I follow with my eyes
Where some boy, with a girl upon his arm,
Passes a patch of silver . . . and I feel
Somehow, I wish I had a woman too,
Walking with little steps under the moon,
And holding my arm so, and smiling. Then
I dream—and I forget . . . .
                 And then I see
The shadow of my profile on the wall!

    *Cyrano de Bergerac* by Edmond Rostand, translated by Brian Hooker

2

*A young prince pleads with his jailors for more consideration.*

[PRINCE ARTHUR:]

    Alas what need you be so boisterous-rough?
I will not struggle, I will stand stone-still.
For heaven sake, Hubert, let me not be bound!
Nay, hear me, Hubert!—Drive these men away,
And I will sit as quiet as a lamb;

    *The Life and Death of King John* by William Shakespeare

## 3

*A very young husband protests a change in diet.*

[HE:]

A change?
You thought
I'd like
a change?
What!
From the godliest of vegetables,
my kingly bean,
that soft, soothing
succulent, caressing,
creamy, persuasively serene,
my buttery entity?
You would dethrone it?
You would play renegade?
You'd raise an usurper
in the person of this
elongated, cadaverous,
throat-scratching, greenish
caterpillar—
you'd honor a parochial,
menial pleb,
an accursed legume,
*sans* even the petty grandeur
of cauliflower,
radish, pea,
onion, asparagus,
potato, tomato—
to the rank of household god?
Is this your marriage?
Is this your creed of love?
Is this your contribution?
Dear, dear,
was there some witch at the altar
who linked your hand with mine in troth
only to have it broken in a bowl?
Ah, dear, dear!

*Lima Beans* by Alfred Kreymborg

## 4

*A middle-aged mother vehemently expresses her views on marriage.*

[MRS. HARDY:] Well, James, aren't you going to say something? Aren't
you a judge? You're not going to uphold these girls in this nonsense

about not being happy, are you? What has happiness to do with marriage, I'd like to know? Marriage means discipline and duty and you know it. Any man and woman can get along if they're willing to sacrifice their own desires once in a while. If one won't the other must. Somebody has to yield. Generally it's the woman.—Now, Myra, you think you'd be better off if you had a more practical man to deal with and Estelle thinks she'd like a little more attention. I don't doubt you would, both of you. I don't doubt that many a woman would like to shake her own husband and get another picked to order. But husbands aren't made to order. You took George and Terrill for better or for worse and even if it's worse than you expected, you'll have to make the best of it! I've raised one family. I'm not going to start in now and raise another. I've had my problems to work out and I've stood it. You can!—Do you imagine my life's been a bed of roses? At times I have been dissatisfied, mighty dissatisfied. I'd have liked a husband who took me to parties and brought me roses and carnations and chocolate creams—but I didn't get them. You never sent me a box of flowers in your life! Sometimes when I've spent the day darning your socks and turning your cuffs and hemming flour sacks for dishcloths, and buying round steak when I wanted porterhouse, and I've seen one of my old chums drive past in her new automobile while I was hanging out the wash—I've been so dissatisfied I could have smashed the whole house down. But I didn't do it. I pitched in and beat up some batter cake and scrubbed down the back steps and worked it off. And so can they!

*Skidding* by Aurania Rouverol

### 5

*Mercutio dies by the sword of Tybalt.*

[MERCUTIO:] I am hurt;—'tis not so deep as a well, nor so wide as a church door; but 'tis enough, 'twill serve; ask for me tomorrow and you find me a grave man. I am peppered, I warrant for this world. A plague o' both your houses! Zounds, a dog, a rat, a mouse, a cat, to scratch a man to death!—Why the devil came you between us? I was hurt under your arm.

*Romeo and Juliet* by William Shakespeare

### 6

*Brutus rebukes Cassius for taking bribes.*

[BRUTUS:]

Remember March, the ides of March, remember!
Did not great Julius bleed for justice' sake?
What villain touch'd his body, that did stab,
And not for justice? What, shall one of us,
That struck the foremost man of all this world

But for supporting robbers, shall we now
Contaminate our fingers with base bribes,
And sell the mighty space of our large honors
For so much trash as may be grasped thus?—
I'd rather be a dog and bay the moon
Than such a Roman!

*Julius Caesar* by William Shakespeare

## One-person Sketches

Presenting sketches—in poetry or prose—which have only one person speaking is an excellent step toward acting a part, for it demands careful analysis of character, visualization of situation, and understanding of meaning. One-person sketches afford a very good opportunity for characterization, for the interpreter alone bears the responsibility of revealing the soul of a human being caught at a crucial moment or in a distinct mood. If possible, see the one-man performances of Charles Laughton, Emlyn Williams, or Cornelia Otis Skinner, for you can learn a great deal from watching such artists. They may people the stage with many characters seen through the eyes of one person, or they may present one interesting personality against a background which is defined in the course of the performance. These actors are so convincing that audiences are held spellbound.

**Emlyn Williams as "A Boy Growing Up," a one-man performance based on stories by Dylan Thomas.**

Courtesy of S. Hurok

For your own presentation of a one-person sketch in class, choose a character who will force you to play against your natural type if you want to use and improve your acting technique. The following are some suggestions for your classroom performance and for your own practice:

1. Poems by Robert Browning, T. A. Daly, Rudyard Kipling, Paul Lawrence Dunbar, John V. A. Weaver, Don Marquis, Robert Burns, Edgar Lee Masters, Edna St. Vincent Millay, Ogden Nash, Dorothy Parker, Vachel Lindsay and other popular poets.

2. Passages, excerpts, poems, and scenes which appear in the Applications sections of this book and are in the first person.

3. Prose selections from "Postscripts" in *The Saturday Evening Post*, the many satirical one-person sketches in *The New Yorker* and other magazines, and any printed selections by Cornelia Otis Skinner, Corey Ford, James Thurber, Bob Hope, Robert Benchley, Earl Wilson, and others.

4. Well-known poems such as the following:

"The Courtin' " by James Russell Lowell

"Little Breeches" by John Hay

"Ben Jonson Interviews a Man from Stratford" by E. A. Robinson

"Lasca" by F. Desprez

"Death of the Hired Man" by Robert Frost

"Chiquita" by Bret Harte

"Patterns" by Amy Lowell

"Vagabond House" by Don Blanding

5. Selections from such publications as:

*Scenes for Student Actors* by Frances Cosgrove

*Play-readings for Schools, Radio and Screen Tests* by L. Frankenstein

*Practice in Dramatics* by Edwin Lyle Hardin

*The One-woman Show* by Marjorie Moffett

*These Mortals among Us* by Clay Franklin

*Dramatic Scenes from Athens to Broadway* by James Lowther

*Life Studies* by Tom Powers

*First Person Singular* by Ryerson and Clements

*The Junior Silver Treasury* by Jane Manner

*A Masque of Queens* by Maria M. Coxe

Once you have chosen your sketch, follow these steps in preparing it for performance. Notice in what ways this procedure resembles the procedure for creating a character.

*The first step is to study the selection carefully.* Look up the meanings of unfamiliar words and expressions. Determine the author's purpose and the mood of the selection. Visualize the character and situation.

*The second step is to analyze the character speaking.* Who is he? How old is he? What are his predominating physical and spiritual characteristics? How did he get into the situation in which we find him? What is his present state of mind? How is he dressed? How does he move? How does he speak? Does he use polished diction? To give validity to your analysis, use a primary source—a real person who resembles the character you are delineating. Study his speech, gestures, and movements.

*The third step is to imagine the stage setting for the character.* It is especially important to visualize the person whom you are addressing and talk to him throughout the selection. Imagine him on a diagonal line downstage, so that you may face your audience. The angle or direction of your glance is a vital consideration; it tells the audience where the other characters are and helps to identify them. For example, a child speaking to an adult looks up, a woman speaking to someone in bed looks down, a man talking with friends around a table looks first at one and then another of them. Visualize, too, the imaginary stage setting with the essential furniture, doors, and windows in set places. Once places are established, you may not move the person to whom you are speaking or the furniture without losing the illusion—unless, of course, such action is necessary in the story. If new imaginary characters enter during the scene, they should receive your attention as you turn to address them. It is not an easy matter to make clear-cut turns toward imaginary characters and still keep the entire audience in view.

*The fourth step is to memorize and rehearse the monologue, using the "whole" method (see page 268).* Memorizing is the final, not the first, step; for until you have studied the selection from every angle, you are likely to fall into errors of emphasis, phrasing, and pronunciation which are almost impossible to eradicate after they have become fixed in your mind. Rehearse out loud and constantly imagine the audience and the setting.

When you present the selection, step to the front of the stage in your own person; include the entire audience in a friendly and confident glance. Give any introductory remarks in a clear voice, using good articulation and speaking unaffectedly and graciously. Then pause for a moment as you assume the bodily attitude of your character. The opening words of the monologue should suggest to the audience the age, sex, personality, strength, and mood of the character. During the performance, keep your character consistent in voice, gesture, and movement. Hold the person to whom you are speaking and the properties clearly before the audience by the position of your body and the direction of your glance. Complete the closing sentence in character; then pause and, in your own person, depart.

## Interpreting Scenes

You are now ready to put into practice what you have learned concerning the analysis and performance of a role in its relationship to a scene as a whole. Interpreting scenes which have some special appeal or strong emotional impact is an excellent way of developing yourself as an actor. Presenting scenes from plays also provides an excellent program for entertaining visiting classes or outside guests. Your selection of a scene will be determined by whether you are trying to arrange an interesting program or to gain experience in acting. Whatever your purpose, select your scene with care, for you will work with it a long time. A scene is not created in a day.

After the scene has been selected, read it with the group and make plans for rehearsals. Decide what the period is, what style of acting is appropriate, and what essential pieces of furniture you will need. Plan an effective stage setting which can be executed easily and simply.

The next step is to apply the techniques of responding to the other actors while creating your own part. With the rest of the cast, decide the relationship of each character to the others by reading the scene together conversationally. Stop to discuss the meaning of words and lines. Then walk through the scene, planning the action or stage business to bring out the values of the scene. Review the chapters on pantomime and voice to refresh your memory about ways of making ideas clear. Especially when you begin working with others, listen carefully and learn to pick up your cues instantly. Get ready to speak during the speech before yours and make your speech right on top of your cue. Keep your stage picture balanced all the time and learn never to move in any way when someone else is the center of interest, for movement attracts attention more quickly than speech.

If all of you work together, you will achieve the joy of the rapid give-and-take of real conversation as you toss the lines back and forth. You will feel the different personalities reacting to each other and realize that acting is a cooperative experience. Discovering how personality plays upon personality in a scene is what makes rehearsing so exciting. It is in rehearsals that you will sense phases of your character you had not fully realized when practicing alone. You will note his prejudices as he reacts to other people, and you will recognize his ideals as they are clarified by his reaction to some remark by another character. In response to a cue, you will suddenly find yourself saying a line exactly as you know it should be said. When this happens, mark the exact inflection and phrasing, for you may forget them. After an especially inspired rehearsal, go home and restudy your lines at once while you are under the spell. You will work out pauses and phrasing you had not thought of before; the same creative force will work out ac-

After an early group rehearsal, the leads work overtime on the interpretation of a difficult scene.

tions, and you will find new physical movements to clarify your role. Remember that all unnecessary, random movement must be eliminated.

Your eyes are your most expressive feature. The speed and direction of a single glance can tell volumes. Always know exactly where you are focusing your attention, but do not make the mistake of keeping your eyes glued to the eyes of the person to whom you are speaking. Remember to include the entire audience in your conversation and avoid looking at the ground or at objects which will throw your voice to the floor.

After establishing your character in clear-cut lines by your bodily attitude and a few striking gestures, use your small muscles in delicate movements to point essential lines but never fidget, wave your arms, or make faces! Coordination of the entire body is essential every moment, and the tone and inflections of your voice, the expression and direction of your eyes, the gestures of your hands, and the position of your body must always create a single impression.

Doing one thing at a time and doing it effectively will help you keep your role clear-cut. Never anticipate what the next line or move is to be by either an uncertain inflection of the voice or the slightest gesture.

It is this single impression that you must work toward, not only in your own part, but in the effect of the whole scene. Watch the timing of your lines and action to see that they build directly to the most important point. Keep the emotion of the scene increasing in intensity toward the climax.

Arranging a program of scenes can be a fascinating class or club project. In arranging such a program you should always have a unifying idea back of your choices. For example, you may select scenes showing different countries or periods, scenes from different plays by the same author, or a group of contrasting quarrels, farewells, or love scenes.

There should be a stage manager for the whole program. He will be responsible for changing the furniture, props, and lights for each scene. He should be given a résumé of the plot, a list of the furniture, props, and effects wanted, and all cues for the curtain and lights.

Your teacher will decide whether or not to have student directors for your scenes, since problems of class procedure must be considered. Someone outside the cast should be the announcer, giving the names of the plays, the writers, and the student actors; he should also give a brief summary of the action leading up to each scene presented.

At the end of the program, if it is presented in class, there should be an evaluation of each scene, either oral or written. The strong and weak points in each characterization and the general effect of the scene as a whole should be analyzed. Suggestions should be constructive, with the aim of improving the acting ability of the performers.

## ACTING IN PLAYS

Acting a part in a play is the culmination of your work in dramatics. There are two distinct phases of dramatic activity in school: the work done in the classroom and the public production. Until the last forty years, the latter was the only form and in some high schools today it still is. Usually employed as a means of raising funds for school activities, a school play naturally tended to exploit clever students. If they were able to "steal the show" they were acclaimed as brilliant, when in reality they had probably violated many principles of stage technique. Spontaneous faking of lines was applauded, and mistakes and disasters were overlooked.

Today, the standards of dramatics are very high in many public school systems. The student has an opportunity in the classroom to engage in theatrical activity based on sound technical training. Casting of public productions varies in different schools, but in more and more schools only students who have done well in daily classes have the opportunity to act in public.

In classroom acting, the student is afforded an opportunity for character development. The emphasis is on personal growth, not personal exploitation. With a number of groups putting on different plays, the casts become cooperative teams. In the friendly atmosphere of a classroom, without the strain of public acclaim to worry them, students gain a proper perspective on acting. They develop good sportsmanship, dependability in gathering props, punctuality in attending rehearsals, and ingenuity in working out productions with limited equipment. Many young people discover they can do well as actors, scenic artists, technicians, and directors. In every case, the student's life becomes richer and fuller in experience and artistic achievements and he gains an added assurance which carries over into all his school activities. The more talented members may be inspired to stage plays in their church and community groups. Many little theaters draw their most capable recruits from school classes in dramatics. In this way, a link is made between the school and the community, and the young people themselves find their leisure time filled with work which is exciting and constructive.

A word of warning might not be amiss here. Too often those brilliant students who are at first the most satisfactory members of the class are later

**Students give a classroom performance of a Greek play.**

Photo by Louise Phillips

completely spoiled by their success and consider themselves finished artists when they are only beginners. As Touchstone says in *As You Like It,* "The fool doth think he is wise, but the wise man knoweth himself to be a fool." One of the advantages of approaching the theater through the school is that young actors gain a solid foundation while they have the wholesome comradeship of the class and the guidance of the teachers. This lessens the danger of the selfish egotism sometimes encouraged by success behind the footlights.

Two distinct types of people like to act. There is the sincere actor who devotes himself to the creative experience of conveying the spirit of the play to the hearts of the audience. He helps to lift people into the rich world of the imagination. The show-off, on the other hand, is the bane of the theater—amateur or professional. He is the clever person, often with good appearance and facile talent, who uses a role as a medium for exhibiting his ability and charm. He cares very little for the meaning of the play or the elements that make up an entire performance. He never learns the great joy of acting, for he is always self-conscious and self-centered. He is apt to be over-sensitive to criticism because he is sure his judgment is best. He belittles the work of the other actors and makes them feel awkward as they struggle for a particular effect. Sometimes he even refuses to learn lines accurately, knowing he can improvise readily and easily pass his own mistakes on to other people. His wisecracking and sarcasm will often kill the inspiration of a fine rehearsal and the enthusiasm of the cast. He frequently misses rehearsals or comes late, confident that he can be a hit the night of the show. In most school drama groups, missing rehearsals without an excuse will result in dismissal from the cast. Exhibitionists spoil any profession, and they have no place in the school theater.

Every actor and speaker must enjoy holding the attention of an audience; it is only when an actor is unwilling to lose himself in a part that he becomes a show-off. One advantage of getting your first theatrical experience on the school stage is that you soon learn to curb purely exhibitionistic tendencies. Remember that the artist loses himself in his role while the exhibitionist merely shows himself off in it.

Stanislavski speaks of "ethics for the theater," telling his company "to love art in yourself, not yourself in art." Amateurs should feel this respect for acting as an art and it should carry over into rehearsals and performances. You are expected to take criticism without comment or bad feelings and improve at once, to be poised and alert and on the job every minute, to be quiet backstage, never to peek from the wings or through the curtain, and never to be seen in costume and make-up except backstage and onstage. Your attitude toward the director and the other members of the company should be helpful and receptive. There should be no side remarks or disparaging comments. You must be prompt at all rehearsals and not ask to leave until the final dismissal. The professional rule of never interfering with the stage crew in handling furniture and changing scenes applies equally to the amateur theater. Unless you are called upon to help backstage after a scene, go straight to the dressing room from the stage. If there is to be a final curtain call, you must stay in costume and make-up in the dressing room until the end of the performance.

## Acting Terminology

There are a number of expressions with which you must be familiar if you are to work on the stage. Those most frequently used in connection with acting are listed here. Technical terms applying to staging and lighting will be found in the sections dealing with those aspects of the theater.

**ad-lib**   To extemporize stage business or conversation.

**back** or **backstage**   The area behind the part of the stage visible to the audience.

**blocking yourself**   Getting behind furniture or actors so that you cannot be seen by the audience.

**building a scene**   Using such dramatic devices as increased tempo, volume, or emphasis to achieve a climax.

**business**   Any action performed on the stage.

**C**   The symbol used to designate the center of the stage.

**countercross**   A shifting of position by one or more actors to balance the stage picture.

**cover**   To obstruct the view of the audience.

**cross**   The movement by an actor from one location to another onstage.

**cue**   The last words or action of any one actor which immediately precedes any lines or business of another actor.

**curtain**   The curtain or drapery which shuts off the stage from the audience; used in a script to indicate that the curtain is lowered.

**cut**   To stop action or to omit.

**cut in**   To break into the speech of another character.

**down** or **downstage**   The part of the stage toward the footlights.

**dressing the stage**   Keeping the stage picture balanced during the action.

**exit** or **exeunt**   To leave the stage.

**feeding**   Giving lines and action in such a way that another actor can make a point or get a laugh.

**getting up in a part**   Memorizing lines or becoming letter-perfect.

**hand props**  Personal properties, such as notebooks, letters, or luggage, carried onstage by the individual player.

**hit**  To emphasize a word or line with extra force.

**holding for laughs**  Waiting for the audience to quiet down after a funny line or scene.

**holding it**  Keeping perfectly still.

**left** and **right**  Terms used to refer to the stage from the actor's point of view, not that of the audience.

**left center** and **right center**  The areas to the left and right of the center stage, again with reference to the actor and not the audience.

**off** or **offstage**  Off the visible stage.

**on** or **onstage**  On the visible stage.

**overlap**  To speak when someone else does.

**pace**  The movement or sweep of the play as it progresses.

**places**  The positions of the actors at the opening of an act or scene.

**plot**  To plan stage business, as to "plot" the action, or to plan a speech by working out the phrasing, emphasis, and inflections.

**pointing lines**  Emphasizing an idea.

**properties** or **props**  All of the stage furnishings, including furniture.

**ring up**  To raise the curtain.

**set**  The scenery for an act or scene.

**set props**  Properties placed onstage for the use of the actor.

**showmanship**  A sense of theater and feeling for effects.

**sides**  Half-sheets of typewritten manuscript containing the lines, cues, and business for one character.

**stealing a scene**  Attracting attention away from the person to whom the center of interest legitimately belongs.

**tag line**  The last speech in an act or play.

**taking the stage**  Holding the center of interest; moving over the entire stage area.

**tempo**  The speed with which speech and action move a play along.

**timing**  The execution of a line or piece of business at a specific moment to achieve the most telling effect.

**top**  To build to a climax by speaking at a higher pitch, at a faster rate, or with more force than in the preceding speeches.

**up** or **upstage**  The area of the stage away from the footlights, toward the rear of the stage.

**upstaging**  Improperly taking attention away from an actor when he is the focus of interest.

**warn**  To notify of any upcoming action or cue.

## Acting Techniques

A number of acting techniques have been discussed earlier in this book. However, a systematic summary of the most important of these as they are used onstage, from your first entrance to your last exit, will be useful as you start to work on a class production.

**Entrances.** Entrances are vitally important. For a good entrance, you must indicate by your action that you come from a definite place for a definite purpose in a definite state of mind. Because the first impression you make on the audience sets the key to your role, you must get into character long before you enter. Many stars start to get into character as soon as they arrive in the theater and will not permit anyone to visit them in their dressing rooms. If brilliant professionals consider it necessary to take time to get into the spirit of a part, how can an amateur expect to dash on the stage at the last moment after gossiping in the wings, primping before a mirror, or feverishly looking over his lines? Plan exactly how you wish to appear, especially in regard to your posture, which will be affected by your character's age, mood, and attitude toward the people on the stage. Be sure that every detail of your make-up, costume, and hand props is exactly right so you will not be worrying about them onstage. As you wait for your entrance, be careful not to cast a shadow onstage by getting in front of a backstage light; also do not block the exit.

You must always plan your entrance so that you have time to come onstage and speak exactly on cue. If the set has steps for you to come down in making your appearance, negotiate them, deliberately or rapidly, in a direct or curved line, depending upon the mood you are trying to establish. Do not look down at the steps and suit your rate of motion to your character. If you enter through a door, open it with the hand nearest the hinges and close it with the other as you step in. A pause in the doorway is effective if the action of the play permits it or if you have a line to say.

In every entrance you should keep the audience in mind without appearing to do so. Enter on the upstage foot, so that your body is turned downstage. If several characters enter together, one of them speaking, the speaker should come last so that he need not turn his head to address the others who can more easily adapt themselves to him than he to them. Be careful not to cover your face when speaking.

**Stage emphasis and balance.** From the moment you enter, emphasize the *center of interest* by giving it your attention. The center of interest is the object, person, or situation upon which the interest of the audience should be focused. The actors must cooperate with the director in emphasizing it. Though the position of actors in conversation on the stage is largely the di-

Although Hamlet is at the far left in this scene, he is clearly the center of interest. The other actors direct attention to him by leaning forward and listening intently to his words.

rector's problem, you can help by being "stage conscious." This means that you know how to get into the right positions of your own accord. Learn to adjust yourself to the stage space and to the other actors. If you are the center of interest, don't hesitate to take the stage, but plan your movement and turns on definite cues which point your lines.

Keep the stage picture constantly in mind and get yourself into the right place as inconspicuously as possible. If other actors cover you, move your position slightly, right or left. The actors must maintain the stage balance which the director has arranged. They should avoid covering each other, huddling behind furniture, moving beyond the curtain line, hugging the backdrop, and standing in rigid lines. No matter how insignificant your part may be, remember that you are a part of the stage picture from the moment you enter until you leave.

You must learn to adjust your position easily to keep the stage picture balanced at all times. Grouping characters onstage in a triangular arrangement with the important speaker at the apex is one method. When the interest shifts from the figure at the apex, the characters show the shift by crossing to new positions. Ideally crossing and countercrossing should have meaningful motivation, but frequently they are used merely to get the central character of the moment into an advantageous position. Sometimes the central character is maneuvered into center stage, sometimes to a higher elevation with the other actors facing him. He may take the stage and move as he pleases, but he should be careful to make his crosses emphasize the meaning of the lines or the emotional impact of the moment.

**Movement and position.** Normally, no movement or gesture should be made without a reason inherent in the script or action of the play—every movement must have meaning or there should be no movement! To keep still without being rigid or disinterested and to be intelligently alert and in character without distracting the attention of the audience from the center of interest is one of the difficult things you must learn to do. A good rule is not to cross on your own or anybody else's speeches. Cross between

**Diagram of a countercross. The boy and girl were originally at the positions marked "X." When the boy moved upstage to pick up something, the girl had to countercross to avoid blocking him in his new position.**

speeches on some definite piece of business and arrange to countercross when you must give way to someone. Then stand still! Above all, avoid aimless movements of the hands and fidgeting of the body. When you do have to gesture, try to follow the usual practice of using the upstage arm and hand in order to avoid cutting the body by an awkward line. When you must move, go straight to the door, chair, or person without ambling about uncertainly.

If two characters are conversing, they stand at angles to the footlights so that both their faces can be seen by the audience. They occasionally look directly at each other to sustain the illusion of real conversation. When you face another character, look directly at him, not over his head, or at his breastbone, or at the footlights. A turn of the eye can spoil an effective line or pause. Be sure to look directly at an object before you move to pick it up or at a person before you address him.

Sitting and rising must be a part of the motivated action and kept strictly in character. Practice crossing to a chair or sofa and sitting down until you don't have to look at the furniture but can make the action a part of your characterization. Do not let yourself get into the habit of grasping chairs before you sit down or rise.

The fairly recent convention that the proscenium opening is the fourth wall of the room in which the action of the play takes place has led to the breaking down of a number of established rules, such as "Never turn your back on the audience." If the wall were there, the characters would frequently have their backs toward it. Therefore, directors often arrange to have characters turn and speak in that position. However, the actor must be heard and amateurs often cannot be heard when talking upstage. Therefore, it is usually best to speak front or diagonally front, except when especially directed to do otherwise by the director, who can test your audibility from all parts of the auditorium. Nothing is more irritating to an audience than not being able to understand and see what is going on. (The use of a loudspeaker is rarely practical because it complicates the actors' problems of establishing sound areas.)

Special lighting also affects your position onstage. In these days of localized lighting, you must be careful to hold your body and face onstage in the exact position assigned by the director. If certain limited areas of the stage are defined by spots and floods, see that your shadow does not fall on the face of another actor and that your own face is in the light when you are the center of interest. The style of illumination, the effectiveness of your shadow, your relationship to the entire stage picture are often as important as your acting.

**Lines and cues.** Effective techniques of movement and position achieve little without equally good speech techniques. Stage conversation must be kept fluent, broken only by the pauses which have been rehearsed. In order to avoid abrupt breaks, have a complete thought worded for every sentence which is to be interrupted and go right on speaking until you are stopped by the other person. Be sure to use as full a voice for these extended lines as you do for those which are a part of the script. In a telephone conversation, write out what the other person is supposed to be saying. Count how many beats it would take him to say it and listen with a responsive face while you count.

Ad-libbing is used in emergencies to avoid a dead silence, and such lines should be spoken as though they were part of the script without any cutting down in volume and inflection. When one actor forgets his lines or gets into a speech ahead of the appropriate point in the action and skips important information, the other actors have to ad-lib the missing facts while carrying on the conversation naturally. Whole conversations are ad-libbed in crowd or social scenes, but they must be subdued to avoid drowning out the lines of the speaker carrying the scene.

A rapid picking up of cues must be established as early in rehearsals as possible. Therefore, cues should be memorized along with the lines. Many amateurs wait until their cue has been given before they show any facial or bodily reaction. Let your face respond during the other person's lines and then you will be ready to speak on cue. One secret is to take a breath during the cue; then speak on the last word of the cue. Failure to pick up cues swiftly causes many amateur performances to drag in spite of painstaking rehearsals, for this loss of a fraction of a second before each speech slows the action.

Of course, there is a common difficulty attendant upon the rapid picking up of cues, especially in comedies: actors must wait for their laughs and applause, holding the action without dropping the tempo. After the laughter or applause has begun to die down, the actor can give the first words of his next line at a slower tempo, speeding up when the sound of his voice has silenced the noise. Amateurs seldom can adapt their words and action to the response of the audience with ease. Thus the presentation of rapid-fire comedies by amateurs is far more difficult than the playing of serious drama.

**Pointing lines.** It is important that you learn to point your lines on the stage, so that the audience will appreciate a joke or be thrilled by an emotional moment. Pointing lines is essential in comedy, where making the audience laugh is the author's aim. The actor giving the cue must not get a laugh himself but he must place the emphasis on his cue line in such a way that the actor to whom he is speaking can get it. This is called "feeding the line," and actors who play together a great deal become masters of the proper timing and pointing of lines. Notice in the regular television programs, played by the same people week after week, how the lines sparkle and the laughs come naturally. This perfection of timing does not just happen; it is the result of careful phrasing, emphasis, and pausing. It is advisable to have a few people unfamiliar with a comedy come to the final rehearsals so you can check their reactions and have some idea of how to point your lines and hold for laughs. Otherwise these lines may be thrown away on the night of the performance.

## Application

Ask another member of the class to work with you in the following excerpt from *The Importance of Being Earnest* by Oscar Wilde and see how well you can point your lines for laughs. You can also use this, just for fun, to try English diction after you have listened to Charles Laughton, Michael Redgrave, Deborah Kerr, Rex Harrison, or other English actors in the movies, on television, or on recordings.

*The scene is the elegant Victorian apartment of Algernon Moncrieff, a young English gentleman. He is visited by his friend Jack Worthing, whom Algy knows as Ernest Worthing. Jack is the guardian of a young lady, Cecily Cardew, who lives in the country with a governess. Knowing Algernon to be something of a man-about-town, Jack has never told Algy about Cecily. In this scene, Algy, by finding Jack's cigarette case, discovers the existence of Cecily and also the fact that Jack uses two names. He wants to know all about the double life that his friend leads.*

ALGERNON. My dear fellow, Gwendoline is my first cousin; and before I allow you to marry her, you will have to clear up the whole question of Cecily.

JACK. Cecily! What on earth do you mean? What do you mean, Algy, by Cecily! I don't know anyone by the name of Cecily.

ALGERNON (*To butler*). Bring me that cigarette case Mr. Worthing left in the smoking-room the last time he dined here.

JACK. Do you mean to say you have had my cigarette case all this time? I wish to goodness you had let me know. I have been writing frantic letters to Scotland Yard about it. I was very nearly offering a large reward.

ALGERNON. Well, I wish you would offer one. I happen to be more than usually hard up.

JACK. There is no good offering a large reward now that the thing is found.

ALGERNON (*Taking case from butler*). I think it rather mean of you, Ernest, I must say. However, it makes no matter, for now that I look at the inscription inside, I find that the thing isn't yours after all.

Jack insists that Algernon return his cigarette case in *The Importance of Being Earnest.*

JACK. Of course it is mine. You have seen me with it a hundred times, and you have no right whatsoever to read what is written inside. It is a very un-gentlemanly thing to read a private cigarette case.

ALGERNON. Yes, but this is not your cigarette case. This cigarette case is a present from someone of the name of Cecily, and you said you didn't know anyone of that name.

JACK. Well, if you want to know, Cecily happens to be my aunt.

ALGERNON. Your aunt!

JACK. Yes. Charming old lady she is, too. Lives at Tunbridge Wells. Just give it back to me, Algy.

ALGERNON. But why does she call herself little Cecily if she is your aunt and lives at Tunbridge Wells? "From *little* Cecily with her fondest love."

JACK. My dear fellow, what on earth is there in *that?* Some aunts are tall, some aunts are not tall. That is a matter that surely an aunt may be allowed to decide for herself. *You* seem to think that every aunt should be exactly like your aunt! That is absurd! For Heaven's sake give me back my ciga-rette case.

ALGERNON. Yes. But why does your aunt call you her uncle? "From little Cecily, with her fondest love to her dear Uncle Jack." There is no objec-tion, I admit, to an aunt being a small aunt, but why an aunt, no matter what her size may be, should call her own nephew her uncle, I can't quite make out. Besides, your name isn't Jack at all; it is Ernest.

JACK. It isn't Ernest; it's Jack.

ALGERNON. You have always told me it was Ernest. I have introduced you to everyone as Ernest. You answer to the name of Ernest. You look as if your name was Ernest. You are the most earnest-looking person I ever saw in my life. It is perfectly absurd your saying that your name isn't Ernest. It's on your cards. Here is one of them. "Mr. Ernest Worthing, B.4, The Albany." I'll keep this as a proof that your name is Ernest if ever you attempt to deny it to me, or to Gwendoline or to anyone else.

JACK. Well, my name is Ernest in town and Jack in the country, and the cigarette case was given me in the country.

ALGERNON. Yes, but that does not account for the fact that your small Aunt Cecily, who lives in Tunbridge Wells, calls you her dear uncle. Come, old boy, you had much better have the thing out at once.

JACK. My dear Algy, you talk exactly as if you were a dentist. It is very vulgar to talk like a dentist when one isn't a dentist. It produces a false impression.

ALGERNON. Well, that is exactly what dentists always do. Now, go on! Tell me the whole thing.

JACK. —Well, old Mr. Thomas Cardew, who adopted me when I was a little boy, made me, in his will, guardian to his granddaughter, Miss Cecily Cardew. Cecily, who addresses me as her uncle, from motives of respect that you could not possibly appreciate, lives at my place in the country, under the charge of her admirable governess, Miss Prism.

ALGERNON. Where is that place in the country, by the way?

JACK. That is nothing to you, dear boy. You are not going to be invited. I may tell you candidly that the place is not in Shropshire.

ALGERNON. I suspected that, my dear fellow.—Now go on. Why are you Ernest in town and Jack in the country?

JACK. My dear Algy, when one is placed in the position of guardian, one has to adopt a very high moral tone on all subjects. It's one's duty to do so. And as a high moral tone can hardly be said to conduce very much to either one's health or happiness, in order to get up to town I have always pretended to have a younger brother of the name of Ernest, who lives at the Albany, and gets into the most dreadful scrapes. There, my dear Algy, is the whole truth, pure and simple.

ALGERNON. The truth is rarely pure and never simple.

**Climax.** Each scene has its own climax; reaching it is a matter of pace and tempo, which are set by the director and carried out by the actors.

*Application*

The following excerpt from the melodrama *A Night at an Inn* by Lord Dunsany provides excellent practice in building a climax within a scene. The two actors playing The Toff and Bill are seated at a table in the center, and

Sniggers enters from right or left. Sniggers must be careful to start at a low enough emotional level to build to the high point and the others must build with him. Sniggers can try out several different methods of saying the words *what I didn't like.* They can be screamed, whispered, spoken amid hysterical tears or in frantic haste; but they must come at the height of his terrific horror.

*The scene is a deserted cottage on the moors of England in the early 1900's. The Toff, Bill, and Sniggers have stolen a precious jewel from a mysterious idol in India and are now hiding from avenging worshippers of the idol. In this scene, they begin to realize that a supernatural power, perhaps the idol himself, has followed them and that there is no escape.*

THE TOFF. Hullo, here's Jacob Smith, Esquire, J.P., alias Sniggers back again.

SNIGGERS. Toffy, I've been thinking about my share in that ruby. I don't want it. Toffy; I don't want it.

THE TOFF. Nonsense, Sniggers. Nonsense.

SNIGGERS. You shall have it, Toffy, you shall have it yourself, only say Sniggers has no share in this 'ere ruby. Say it, Toffy, say it!

BILL. Want to turn informer, Sniggers?

SNIGGERS. No, no. Only I don't want the ruby, Toffy—

THE TOFF. No more nonsense, Sniggers. We're all in together in this. If one hangs, we all hang; but they won't outwit me. Besides, it's not a hanging affair, they had their knives.

SNIGGERS. Toffy, Toffy, I always treated you fair, Toffy. I was always one to say, "Give Toffy a chance." Take back my share, Toffy.

THE TOFF. What's the matter? What are you driving at?

SNIGGERS. Take it back, Toffy.

THE TOFF. Answer me, what are you up to?

SNIGGERS. I don't want my share any more.

BILL. Have you seen the police?—

SNIGGERS. There's no police.

THE TOFF. Well, then, what's the matter?

BILL. Out with it.

SNIGGERS. I swear to God—I swear I saw something *what I didn't like.*

THE TOFF. What you didn't like?

SNIGGERS. O Toffy, Toffy, take it back. Take my share. Say you take it.

THE TOFF. What has he seen?

**Exits.** When you are ready to leave the stage, remember that exits are as important as entrances. Go from the room in a definite state of mind, with a definite purpose, to a definite place, keeping in character until you are completely out of sight. If you go through a door, use the hand nearest the hinges to open it. If you are lucky enough to have a good exit line or a reason to look back, turn on the balls of your feet, still holding the door-knob, and deliver the line or glance pointedly. Otherwise, go right off, closing the door with the hand farthest from the hinges.

## Building Acting Techniques

By the time you go onstage to give an actual performance, the techniques of movement and speech should be automatic. If you are listening to your voice and diction and watching your own movements while onstage, you will be self-conscious and think of yourself rather than your character. Therefore, every detail of characterization and action must be worked out during rehearsals. Nothing should be left to inspiration on the night of the first performance.

To make your movements and speech automatic, you may wish to have a daily practice schedule designed for this purpose. If you devote as little as half an hour a day to practice as it is outlined in the following schedule, you will see a definite improvement in your vocal and physical reactions. (Refer to the exercises in Chapters 8 and 9 for more detailed instructions.)

*Daily Practice Schedule*

1. Setting-up exercises:
   Stretch
   Bend over
   Rotate torso, head, neck, arms
   Bend knees
   Do push-ups
   Rotate legs while lying on back
2. Pantomime exercises:
   Shake out tension from hands and arms
   Open and close fists
   Move fingers—as in five-finger piano exercises
   Turn hands from wrists in circles
   Move lower arms in circles
   Move entire arms from shoulders in circles
   Move arms out, up, and down, with wrists leading
3. Vocal exercises:
   Relax whole body—avoid excess tension in the throat area
   Pant
   Rotate jaw
   Babble
   Say, "The king is moaning and roaming around the room."
   Count on one breath to twenty, sustaining each number
   Sustain a "pure vowel tone" for twenty seconds
   Read "The Cataract of Lodore" aloud (see pages 193 to 194)
   Recite tongue-twisters
   Chant short passages, using a sustained volume level
   Read Portia's speech (see page 209)

**4.** Interpretation exercises:
  Sight-read passages from Shakespeare
  Recite memorized passages from Shakespeare
  Read poetry and prose selections aloud
  Read scenes from plays aloud

## Rehearsing

Rehearsing is like football practice: it determines the success or failure of a performance. Each rehearsal should show decided improvement over the former one, especially in the emotional and technical growth within roles. You should bring a pencil to the early rehearsals and write down each stage direction and suggestion from the director so that you can follow it the next time you do the scene. You must know your crosses and positions and those of the other actors for they are the basis of the director's "stage pictures." Whatever the director's methods of conducting a rehearsal, you must carefully follow his instructions, for he alone knows the purpose of every bit of business. The stage settings, action, and tempo create an artistic whole of which the actors are only one part. If the stage business is altered, even at the last minute, the actor should offer no objection, for the director is privileged to change his mind in his constant effort to improve the production.

In rehearsals, meanings are clarified, characters come to life, business is crystallized, and tempos are developed. Therefore, be sure to be at rehearsals on time and stay to the end. Even attend rehearsals to which you are not called. Learn what to do and what not to do from watching the other members of the cast and listening to the suggestions from the director. Keep yourself imaginatively and emotionally alive during rehearsals, for only then will the right reactions come to you. Never let down, no matter how weary or hungry you may be! Try to be relaxed and poised, as well as alert, for anxiety creates nervous tension. Personal animosities must be ignored, and over-sensitiveness must be corrected. *Spontaneity* and *freshness of approach* at every rehearsal and performance are obligatory; nothing irritates a director more than a bored, listless actor. Remember to say every line and make every gesture as if for the first time. The "illusion of the first time" is difficult to create and harder to maintain, but it is essential to the artist-actor.

**Interpreting a role.** After a play has been selected for production, and you have been chosen a member of the cast, you are expected to read through the entire play and analyze your role in the manner described on pages 231 to 233 in this chapter. The first rehearsal of the play will be a reading re-

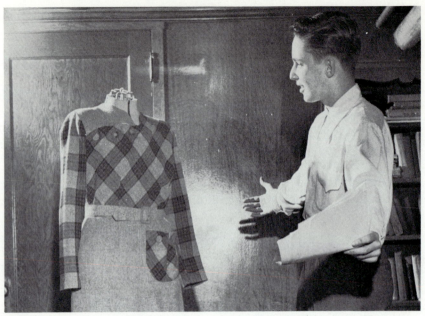

**A young actor rehearses with a leading lady who will not "step on his lines."**

hearsal which everyone attends. During this rehearsal, the director often gives his interpretation of the play and indicates how the actors can best realize this interpretation. This rehearsal will help you to better understand your character and his relationship to others in the play. As you coordinate your part with the whole play, you will see the reasons behind particular lines and pieces of business and so be able to more easily memorize and use them effectively in performance.

After the general business of your part has been given to you by the director, memorize your lines and, at the same time, work out your characterization. You should have a clear conception of your part after a few rehearsals and then begin using techniques to project it to the farthest reaches of the auditorium. Understand every word and idea, visualize your character every moment in your mind's eye, and try to feel as he would feel at any given moment. In other words, always think, see, feel, move, or speak with a reason. Strive for simplicity of characterization so that the role will be clear to the audience; over-elaboration can make it vague or incoherent.

The director will be happy to have you make suggestions regarding your characterization during rehearsals and will incorporate them in the stage business if they fit into his scheme for the entire play. However, never spring innovations on him during a final rehearsal or during a performance. Along these lines, you will find the book *Players at Work* by Martin Eustis a fascinating account of how several of our leading American stars work out their roles and react to directors and production problems.

**Projection.** Successful projection of a character is achieved through practice and conscientious effort. A few hints here will help you learn how to project. First of all, keep far enough away from other actors to enable everyone to gesture freely. Remember that acting requires some exaggeration to be seen and heard at the back of the auditorium. You must, therefore, project your character broadly by means of action, facial expression, and voice. This in no way means that you should lose all sense of a simple, natural reaction to a situation, but it does mean that gestures should be clear-cut, stage groupings uncrowded, and vocal and bodily expressions vigorously alive. One of the duties of the director is to control the degree of this exaggeration; it is your responsibility to follow the director's advice so that all the acting will be "in the same key."

The analysis of your role should follow what you learn from the reading rehearsal, at which the director may give the actors their introduction to the play. You are then expected to study the relationship of your character to all the others in the play. (Look back in this chapter to the section on creating a character.) You must also coordinate your part with the whole play; this over-all concept gives you the proper perspective. When you see the reasons for a line or piece of business, each will become easier to memorize and use effectively in performance.

**Keeping in character.** In order to keep in character during an entire play, you must so absorb the personality of your role that your every gesture and facial expression is in harmony with the mood of the moment. It is easy to do this when you are the center of interest, but it is more difficult to listen in character and react naturally when you are in the background. When someone else is the center of interest, an actor finds it hard to resist the temptation of stealing scenes by attracting the attention of the audience to himself. Any movement can be distracting, and you must learn to sit or stand quietly and concentrate on the action. At the same time, you must not lose your character and start violently or jump back into the role when you hear your cue! A good actor not only acts, he reacts to the other actors. These subtle responses build the play as a whole and are one of the signs of ensemble playing.

**Memorizing.** The enchantment of rehearsals comes after your lines have become second nature and you have grown into your role. Then your voice and body will respond instantly to your emotions, and you will begin to act in the truest sense. Many amateurs seem to think that knowing their lines is knowing the part and that when they are letter-perfect they have attained the heights. In reality, knowing one's lines is a mechanical detail to be taken for granted after the first few rehearsals. An over-eager actor who memorizes his lines before the first rehearsals and then refuses to develop or change his reading may well be as unsuccessful as the actor who always forgets his part. No one can interpret a role until he knows his lines, but it is easier to memorize them after the mechanical business has been worked out and all cuts have been made.

Remember also that the best method is to memorize whole scenes at once by going over the entire unit aloud—cues and all—many times, instead of learning it sentence by sentence and cue by cue. In this way, you learn the continuity of the action. If a sentence or cue is lost, you can think through the whole situation and work back to the exact lines without "blowing up." After the entire scene is practically memorized, you may work on it in detail, taking long passages first and working down to paragraphs, sentences, phrases, and words. Incidentally, it is usually better to memorize while moving about rather than while settled in the most comfortable chair in the coziest spot of the room. When the body is active, the brain will also be alert.

Stage fright is frequently the result of not being sure of one's lines. There is no better remedy than perfect preparation. But even with perfect preparation, very few experienced performers are free from an odd sensation in the pit of the stomach and a quivering of the knees immediately before their first entrance. However, actual appearance before the audience usually ends the trouble. If you are fully prepared and properly costumed in every detail and forget yourself and your technique in your part, you need not fear the eyes of a critical audience.

**Polishing.** Once your lines for each scene are memorized, you can get rid of the script and begin to polish your interpretation of the role. Then you can use furniture, hand props, and costumes to help you characterize your role and point your lines. Learn how to place your foot on a step and kneel on a sofa. Practice glancing over your teacup and using it. Remember, spoons are never left in cups or waved in the breeze—after stirring, they are placed on a saucer. Open your cigarette case or your compact. Use your lorgnette—remember that ladies use them only for momentary concentration on an object, never are they worn continuously. Fold your arms and put your hands in your pockets but don't leave them there forever! Unless it is used for a comic effect, you should make certain that no one else is simultaneously imitating your stage business.

It is best to rehearse in the type of clothes you expect to wear in the play. For example, boys should wear coats or jackets in order to get used to them and to use them for effective bits of action. Girls should also practice in the kind of shoes and skirts they expect to wear. If the final costumes are not available, simulated ones may be used.

The lights and shades which distinguish a fine piece of acting are difficult to classify. A good actor knows how to use restrained action, which is still sufficiently exaggerated to be seen in the top gallery. He has learned the use of the pause, in which emotion pulsates while body and voice are still. He has versatility which surprises and delights. He can use an effective gesture or inflection to exactly convey a subtle meaning. These techniques and skills come only after weary hours of painstaking rehearsal and concentrated study.

**Fundamental suggestions.** Don't be afraid to let yourself go, especially in rehearsals. Overplay until your voice and body are free to make emotional responses. In the beginning it is better to overdo than underdo; a director finds it easier to reduce than induce action. There is always a median point between "ham" acting and underplaying. Though this point may vary with every play and with each role, the rules of thumb for final rehearsals are: avoid extremes which call attention to the acting and let the director be your guide.

Most directors say about the same thing to beginners at the early rehearsals: get your lines, speak up, keep your hands still, don't overact, be natural and easy, don't play to the gallery, hold back, be yourself, don't gag, pep up, use your head, don't put on airs, act like a human being, don't steal the scene from the center of interest.

These suggestions are fundamental but not all-inclusive. Many more will occur to you, whether you are working alone or under direction. The important thing to realize is that imagination, concentration, alertness, and attention to detail are vital. Dependence upon a facile talent and pleasing personality will never take you beyond the exhibitionary stage.

## Putting on a One-act Play

Taking part in a one-act play as a class project gives you the experience of using the techniques you have been studying and practicing. If you care to read ahead in Part Four for help in play production, you will be able to put on a better show; but the one-act play is largely a classroom activity, and you will not have the time or facilities for elaborate stage effects. Aim for a simple setting in keeping with the period, place, and mood of your play. Keep it well balanced and attractive with an appropriate color scheme and sufficient furniture and properties to create the proper atmosphere. Your make-up and costume should be sufficiently accurate to give you the feeling of your character.

This is the opportunity for each of you in the class to play a part before an audience. You must avoid getting tense and nervous, for the performance should be a profitable experience in which you find the emotional release and the sense of creative achievement acting affords.

These suggestions can help you put the play on successfully and learn something about drama in general:

1. Divide the class into groups, and make each group responsible for the production of a one-act play. The teacher should select and cast the plays, so that each member of the class has a part that suits his individual needs. The entire series of plays should include the various types discussed in Chapter 5. A list of suitable plays will be found at the end of this chapter and in Appendix B. A definite production schedule should be posted. If a member of the cast is absent on the day of performance, someone should read the part from a script.

2. Each group should select a student director (preferably an advanced student who is not a member of the cast) to be responsible for calling outside rehearsals, checking on props and costumes, and generally managing the show.

3. Permission to perform any play held under copyright must be obtained from the copyright holder before any definite production plans are made. The copyright holder or play publisher will either provide you with copies of the scripts or tell you how to obtain them. Copying parts and cues from plays in your library is expressly forbidden by copyright laws.

4. Rehearsals usually take about three weeks. Every moment of class time must be used to advantage, with the teacher passing from group to group and directing the action and answering questions. Every group should be allowed sufficient use of the stage or platform to plan the action and setting. It is best to take up the action each day from where it was dropped the day before, rather than to begin at the opening every day. Separate scenes between different characters can be rehearsed at the same time, so that no one has to sit around with nothing to do. One or two intensive rehearsals at the homes of the cast members provide an opportunity to go through the entire play several times without interruption. These meetings foster the friendliness which constitutes one of the greatest joys of amateur work in dramatics. All rehearsals should be handled in a businesslike manner, without waste of time and with every effort made toward a satisfactory result. A prompter should keep a record of directions.

5. The setting cannot be elaborate but it should be in keeping with the mood, atmosphere, and period of the play. Simple lighting effects, costumes, make-up, and all the necessary props should make the action live for the audience. Originality and ingenuity in working out the background should be considered in evaluating the final production.

6. The presentation should be as finished as possible, with lines and cues memorized and the action and tempo developed to create definite emotional reactions. The prompter should be on the job every moment.

7. After each presentation, the group responsible must move all props and leave the stage clear for the next group to take over. Anything brought from home should be returned at once and scripts should be collected and filed for use by other classes in the future. It is helpful to accumulate furniture and props gradually for future use. Store them near the classroom. Food and sources of fire such as candles and cigarettes are usually prohibited in schoolrooms and must be faked. If they are allowed, handle them with care and dispose of all crumbs and debris.

8. Invite guests to see the plays but make it clear to them that the productions are regular classwork and educational in purpose. At the close of each performance, ask the audience to discuss the play and its interpretation in detail, offering constructive criticism of the acting and pointing out the strong and weak points of the production. A skillful teacher can direct this discussion and bring out the structural phases of the play and the methods of judging it so that the students in the audience, perhaps unfamiliar with stage plays, will gain a knowledge of the drama and an incentive to take the course.

9. If some of the plays are sufficiently well produced and likely to appeal to a large audience, they can be repeated in the school auditorium at assembly periods, or for the PTA or community groups. A public production, however, should never be the goal of the classwork, for then the matters of individual development and educational value may be lost in the effort to put the best students into an exhibition of dramatic art. The dramatics club should be the group to present public productions, not the class in dramatics.

10. When the entire series has been presented, a careful discussion should be held, stressing the best characterizations, settings, and emotional appeals. Reasons for any poor productions should be discussed without too much emphasis upon the shortcomings of individual members of the class. Private conferences between the teacher and students concerning their success or failure and their over-all dramatic ability can be very valuable after so important a class activity.

11. See Chapter 14 on dramatic criticism and then write reviews of the plays in which you did not take part.

12. Write an essay on "What the Presentation of One-act Plays in Class Has Meant to Me as an Individual."

*Plays for Classroom Production*

The following plays are suggested because of their literary and artistic value, their variety of good parts, and their adaptability to classroom use. Each of the plays listed is followed by the title of an anthology or collection in which it may be found. To obtain permission to perform these plays outside of the classroom, you must write to the person or organization whose copyright notice appears with the play.

"The Dear Departed" by Stanley Houghton in *Thirty Famous One-act Plays* by Bennett Cerf

"The Florist Shop" by Winifred Hawkridge in *Short Plays* by Edwin Knickerbocker

"The Glittering Gate" by Lord Dunsany in his *Five Plays*

"Good Medicine" by Jack Arnold and Edwin Burke in *Twelve One-act Plays* by Walter P. Eaton

"The Grill" by G. W. Johnston in *Twelve One-act Plays* by Walter P. Eaton

"Joint Owners in Spain" by Alice Brown in her *One-act Plays*

"Juliet and Romeo" by Harry W. Gribble in *Fifty More Contemporary One-act Plays* by Frank Shay

"Lima Beans" by Alfred Kreymborg in *Representative One-act Plays by American Authors* by M. G. Mayorga

"The Lost Silk Hat" by Lord Dunsany in his *Five Plays*

"Maid of France" by Harold Brighouse in *One-act Plays* by H. L. Cohen

"The Maker of Dreams" by Oliphant Down in *One-act Plays* by H. L. Cohen

"Martha's Mourning" by Phoebe Hoffman in *Representative One-act Plays by American Authors* by M. G. Mayorga

"Mrs. Pat and the Law" by Mary Aldis in *Representative One-act Plays by American Authors* by M. G. Mayorga

"Neighbours" by Zona Gale in *One-act Plays* by Marie H. Webb

"Nevertheless" by Stuart Walker in his *Portmanteau Plays*

"A Night at an Inn" by Lord Dunsany in *One-act Plays* by H. L. Cohen

"The Noble Lord" by Percival Wilde in *Short Plays* by Edwin Knickerbocker

"Overtones" by Alice Gerstenberg in *Thirty Famous One-act Plays* by Bennett Cerf

"Riders to the Sea" by J. M. Synge in *One-act Plays* by H. L. Cohen

"Rosalind" by James M. Barrie in his *Half-hours*

"The Slave with Two Faces" by M. C. Davies in *Dramas by Present-day Writers* by Raymond W. Pence

"Spreading the News" by Lady Gregory in *One-act Plays* by H. L. Cohen

"Trifles" by Susan Glaspell in *Dramas by Present-day Writers* by Raymond W. Pence

"The Twelve Pound Look" by James M. Barrie in his *Half-hours*

"Two Crooks and a Lady" by Eugene Pillot in *Short Plays* by Edwin Knickerbocker

"The Valiant" by Holworthy Hall and Robert Middlemass in *Short Plays* by Edwin Knickerbocker

"A Wedding" by John Kirkpatrick in *Short Plays* by Edwin Knickerbocker

"Where But in America" by Oscar Wolff in *Plays of Democracy* by M. G. Mayorga

"Will-o'-the-Wisp" by Doris Halman in *Representative One-act Plays by American Authors* by M. G. Mayorga

"The Wonder Hat" by Ben Hecht and Kenneth Goodman in *Representative One-act Plays by American Authors* by M. G. Mayorga

"Wurzel-Flummery" by A. A. Milne in *One-act Plays* by H. L. Cohen

## Acting in Shakespearean Plays

Acting Shakespearean roles in accordance with Shakespeare's own instructions is the most valuable dramatic experience you can have. A single-volume edition of his complete works should be one of your most cherished possessions. By reading his lines aloud, impersonating his characters, and dramatizing his scenes, you can effectively increase your acting ability. You can enjoy interpreting his fascinating characters, caught at dramatic moments in their lives, and making an intensive study of his minor as well as major roles by way of contrast. Because Shakespeare's plays offer a source of unlimited opportunity to develop dramatic potentialities, all schools of speech and acting stress interpretative work with his roles.

In the classroom, Shakespeare's importance is threefold. Of all dramatic literature, his plays offer the richest reward to intensive study. His roles afford the finest opportunity for acting. His texts furnish the most varied material for practice of vocal and pantomimic techniques. Elizabethan audiences liked broad effects, so a Shakespearean role calls for great vocal and bodily freedom. You will find you can have great fun losing yourself completely in the exuberant acting his plays demand.

In class you will find it challenging to work out and stage a number of dialogues and scenes from different plays. Take speeches from characters which appeal to you, analyze and memorize them, and then interpret them orally, letting yourself go in the creative process of self-expression. Change

**High school students in an outdoor performance of** *The Taming of the Shrew.*

your voice and movement for each character, interpreting your role by laughing, whispering, kneeling, and shouting to your heart's content. When you have caught the flashing humor, fiery hate and anger, fawning subservience, or romantic passion, begin to tone down the emotion, polish up the lines, and improve the inflections.

In preparing scenes, analyze them carefully. Work to bring out the meaning and the mood. Give the scenes simple costuming and make-up and play them against plain backgrounds of screens or curtains. Vigorous gesture and movement, carefully balanced stage pictures, and sharp characterizations of the smallest as well as the most important roles should be your goals in your work with Shakespeare. Shakespearean scenes can also be presented in modern dress against realistic backgrounds. The speech can be made colloquial, rather than rhythmical. The characters themselves can be presented as ordinary persons of daily life caught at exciting moments. It is amazing how such experimentation proves that Shakespeare belongs to all time rather than to a particular era.

After you have acted many parts and scenes, you can use the plays as a source of unlimited material for vocal practice. If you want to overcome poor articulation, select difficult passages with complicated word combinations. First chant them very slowly, using a loud, even tone, avoiding sharp stresses and changes of volume, and prolonging every vowel and voiced consonant. Be sure not to omit such sounds as the *z, d, t,* and the nasals. Then read the passage as rapidly as you can while keeping the meaning clear. Take difficult phrases and repeat them many times. Make lists of all the words that you find hard to pronounce and read them again and again.

If you want to improve your diction, imagine yourself an old-time Shakespearean actor and roll out the lines with exaggerated stage diction, watching the Italian *a*'s, long *u*'s, and short *i*'s and *e*'s. Distinguish carefully between voiced and voiceless sounds. Keep your voice low and use a restricted pitch range.

The iambic pentameter line provides excellent practice for chanting exercises. Select a passage of about four lines which has combinations of *m*'s, *n*'s, *ng*'s, and vowel sounds. Sing each line on one tone, going one note up or down the scale for each succeeding line. Then carry the singing tone in your speaking voice and chant the lines on one pitch, stretch and blend the sounds in long phrases. At last, read them as well as you can. Let the resonance and vocal quality carry over into your voice and make the reading more musical. Your aim should be a musical blending of the meaning with the characterization.

In class, it is good practice to read the lines in unison. The teacher and students can work many passages into exquisite choral readings. Divide the class according to the pitch of the voices and carefully rehearse the timing, reading, and phrasing.

Reading passages and scenes at sight, after you have become familiar with Elizabethan phraseology, is excellent practice, for the lines improve your vocal power and emotional responsiveness. Many actors prefer Shakespeare to all playwrights because they can "sink their teeth" into the lines. It is a good dramatic exercise to take one character and read all of his lines in an entire play, catching his changing moods and his reactions to the other characters. Several students can act out scenes and plays together and in this way learn much from one another.

It is also valuable to use Shakespeare's scenes for practice in pantomime. One person can read the lines, and the rest act them out. Rosalind and Celia planning to run away, old Adam dying in Orlando's arms, Brutus and Cassius quarreling in the tent, the mock duel between Sir Andrew and Viola, Lady Macbeth urging her husband to murder Duncan, Juliet and Romeo dying in the tomb, and the clowns with Bottom rehearsing their play are all first-rate scenes which combine lines, gesture, and strong physical movement.

Such vitalized study of the plays and characters of Shakespeare will be of twofold value to you. The first values are technical. Your voice will increase in range and power and your bodily response will become more expressive. Your enthusiasm for cultured speech and finished platform address will be enhanced. You will improve your ability to interpret the printed page intelligently and sympathetically. This, in turn, will help you gain an appreciation of great literature that will enrich your entire life and encourage you to read other masterpieces. Thus your theatrical taste will be improved a hundredfold. In the second place, William Shakespeare will become a living personality to you, and you will probably begin a lifelong association with him which will expand your understanding and promote your spiritual growth.

*Applications*

1. The following are some recommended Shakespearean scenes for practice to improve your acting ability:

A *Midsummer Night's Dream*—Act I, Scenes 2 and 3; Act II, Scenes 1 and 2; Act III, Scene 2; Act V, Scene 1

As *You Like It*—Act I, Scenes 1 and 3; Act II, Scenes 1, 4, and 7; Act III, Scenes 2, 4, and 5; Act IV, Scenes 1 and 3; Act V, Scenes 1 and 2

*Coriolanus*—Act I, Scene 3; Act V, Scene 3

*Hamlet*—Act III, Scene 2 (to King's entrance)

*Julius Caesar*—Act I, Scene 2; Act III, Scene 2; Act IV, Scene 3

*King Henry V*—Prologue; Act III, Scene 3; Act V, Scene 2

*King Henry VIII*—Act II, Scene 4; Act III, Scene 2 (Wolsey and Cromwell); Act V, Scene 4

*King John*—Act IV, Scene 1

*Macbeth*—Act I, Scenes 1, 3, 5, and 7; Act II, Scene 1; Act III, Scene 2; Act V, Scene 1

*The Merchant of Venice*—Act I, Scenes 1 to 3; Act III, Scenes 1 to 3; Act IV, Scene 1

*Much Ado about Nothing*—Act II, Scene 3; Act IV, Scene 1 (Beatrice and Benedick)

*Othello*—Act III, Scene 3; Act IV, Scene 2

*Richard II*—Act III, Scene 4; Act V, Scene 1

*Romeo and Juliet*—Act I, Scene 4; Act II, Scene 2; Act II, Scene 5; Act III, Scene 5; Act IV, Scene 3

*The Taming of the Shrew*—Act II, Scene 1; Act III, Scene 2; Act IV, Scenes 1, 3, and 5

*The Tempest*—Act I, Scene 2; Act III, Scene 1; Act V, Scene 1

*The Two Gentlemen of Verona*—Act IV, Scene 2

*Twelfth Night*—Act I, Scenes 3 and 5; Act II, Scenes 2 to 5; Act IV, Scene 1

2. Using the material in Shakespeare's plays, make a list of individual speeches you consider suitable for memorized presentation in public. Make another list of scenes you would like to present by yourself. Also list scenes you would like to act out with a group. On the basis of these lists, give class presentations of some of these speeches and scenes.

3. Make a list of sentences which would be good exercises for improving your articulation, volume, pitch, tempo, contrast, and emphasis.

4. List scenes and passages especially good for pantomime practice.

5. As a class, plan a program of Shakespearean monologues to interest others in reading his plays and then present it at an assembly period, over the radio, or in other classes.

6. Working in groups and following a definite idea, present a series of sketches from a number of Shakespearean plays. You may choose to depict great love scenes, Roman heroes, English kings, clown scenes, famous soliloquies, tragic moments, or Shakespearean wives. These can be done as readings or as costumed and memorized scenes.

7. Present a modern dress version of *The Taming of the Shrew* or *Julius Caesar*, both of which have been successfully staged in this manner. If you prefer, choose another Shakespearean play and adapt it to present-day dress and staging.

8. Make a Shakespearean production a class project for the year. Design and make your own costumes and backgrounds. Enlist other departments in arranging for lighting effects, platform backgrounds, and so on. If practicable, an outdoor production is always delightful, especially if your music and physical education departments will cooperate in providing Elizabethan songs and dances.

9. Produce a forty-five minute cutting of one of the plays. You can use the *Globe Theatre Editions*, but it is more fun to do the cutting and production yourselves.

10. Arrange a showing for the school and/or community of some of the great moving pictures such as *Henry V*, *Hamlet*, *A Midsummer Night's Dream*, *Romeo and Juliet*, *As You Like It*, and *Richard III*.

## Acting in the Round

Staging plays in an open space surrounded by seats is an accepted form of play production today. Introduced by Glenn Hughes in 1932 in his Penthouse Theatre at the University of Washington, theater in the round is now used on many campuses and often by professional and little-theater groups to avoid the expense of renting auditoriums and building sets. Hotel lobbies, ballrooms, tents, public buildings, and open-air areas are being used with great success. This form of staging is somewhat similar to that of the Greeks and Elizabethans and creates a close contact between the actors and spectators. You can use it in your classroom, if you do not have a stage, by placing chairs around an open space and leaving one or two aisles for entrances.

Staging plays in the round demands careful planning and rehearsing. The director cannot depend on a set for effects, and the audience is so close that every detail of costumes, furniture, and lighting must be right. The acting area must be lighted by spots which do not hit any of the audience in the eyes. Acts can be ended by blacking out the lights or by incorporating exits into the play's action. Either will take the place of the usual stage curtain. The furniture must not block the action from any side, and scenes must be arranged so that they can be seen from all angles. The director also must plan to keep his actors moving and speaking as they cross and countercross rather than have them seated for too long a time. Keeping the actors in motion allows their faces and voices to carry the meaning of the play to everyone. If possible, the director must plan his action to be seen from all sides at once.

The demands on the actors are much greater in round staging than on an orthodox stage. Each actor must be conscious all the time of being surrounded by spectators who must see and hear him. He must speak very

A scene from Agatha Christie's *Witness for the Prosecution,* performed in the round by the Arena Stage, Washington, D.C. At each performance eleven members of the audience served as the jury.

Lee Salsbery Studios

INTERPRETING THE DRAMA

clearly, projecting his voice so that he can be heard even when he turns away from part of the audience. Very accurate pointing of lines and accenting of key words must be combined with a few clear-cut gestures which are effective from every angle. With the audience so close, any artificiality or exaggeration becomes so apparent that all sense of reality is lost. Also, fidgeting and aimless gestures are far more irritating at close range.

Plays must be selected rather carefully for an arena production. Entrances must permit effective approaches for actors before they speak, and exits must allow for convenient departures. Actions and lines must be suitable for the close attention of the audience. Sofas, benches, and low-backed chairs must be appropriate as a background for the actors since there is no setting. When done well in the round, a suitable play can move the spectators deeply; if it is poorly selected or acted, every fault is enlarged and a production which may be good enough for a regular stage is spoiled.

The following plays are typical of those which can be successfully produced in the round, and you will find it interesting to do one occasionally, either in class or at recreational centers.

*The Caine Mutiny Court-Martial* by Herman Wouk
*Our Town* by Thornton Wilder
*Outward Bound* by Sutton Vane
*Holiday* by Philip Barry
*Years Ago* by Ruth Gordon
*There's Always Juliet* by John Van Druten
*Joan of Lorraine* by Maxwell Anderson
*Dear Ruth* by Norman Kraşna

The plays listed above are all contemporary American or English plays. Almost all classics can be adapted to theater in the round if they do not require balconies, inner stages, and large elevations for the important action.

## PLAY READINGS

Individual and group play readings are rapidly becoming a recognized form of dramatic presentation. For many years, reading plays aloud has been a popular means of arousing interest in the drama in university centers. Charles Laughton has recently made it universal in its appeal. In his one-man shows, he lumbers on the stage laden with books which he dumps casually on a table. He then opens one and begins reading carefully prepared selections, holding his audience enthralled. He has also de-

Charles Laughton, Charles Boyer, and Agnes Moorehead in a reading taken from George Bernard Shaw's *Man and Superman.*

veloped the now-famous play-reading companies, with which he has presented selections from such great works as Shaw's *Man and Superman.* A number of other professional groups have taken up his idea and are making platform readings of plays an accepted form of art.

With the increasing number of suburban communities growing up at a distance from theatrical centers, the reading of plays together in homes and clubs has become a favorite pastime of many people who want to keep up to date on the best plays or to enjoy the classics together. It is one form of dramatic entertainment which you can enjoy for the rest of your life, regardless of how undramatic your career may be!

Select any readings you do yourself with great care; find something that suits you well and that you really admire. Your enthusiasm will be contagious and you can inspire your classmates to enjoy the play with you. The amount of time and energy a first-rate play reading takes to prepare should be spent on something which will give pleasure both to yourself and others.

### Individual Play Readings

Platform readings of a play by one person may take either of two forms: a *play review* or a *dramatic reading.* In the first, the play is presented in selected scenes in conjunction with a well-prepared discussion of the author and the literary values of the play. In the second, the play is read or recited—usually in condensed form—without comments of any kind.

**Play reviews.** The purpose of a play review is to help your audience enjoy the play by showing them the author's reason for writing it. A satisfactory play review might include four categories. One would be a discussion of the author—his life, his central idea in the particular play in relation to his philosophy of life, and his literary style. Another would be a condensation of the plot into a two- or three-minute synopsis. Still other categories might be an interpretative reading of the finest passages and the reviewer's personal reaction to the play, characters, and theme.

As in all forms of public speaking, consider the people in your audience and their particular interests. Make a unified and logical outline of the entire review. Watch your allotted time or you may devote too much attention to one phase and neglect others. Do not talk over the heads of your audience. In organizing your material, refer to Chapters 4 and 5 which deal with play analysis. Also look up the reviews of dramatic critics listed in the *Readers' Guide to Periodical Literature* or *The New York Times Index*. If possible, get pictures of the author, the actors who have appeared in the play, and the sets which have been designed for it. If it is a period play, pictures of the costumes and furnishings of the time, and a brief discussion of the historical background might add interest; this is possible only if you have been allotted an unusually long time for your review. Use of a stereopticon or slide projector is the best method of making visual aids available to the entire class.

It is wise to clarify the theme of the play in your own mind by writing it out in one sentence. Base your presentation on this central idea, showing how the dramatist developed it. Strive to arouse in your audience a desire to discuss the theme with you at the end of your review.

Because the first impression is so important in arousing interest in the play, plan your opening sentence carefully. Write it down and, if necessary, memorize it. Then discuss more or less briefly the author's life and place in literature, illustrating his style with several typical passages from the play.

Many people waste time and bore their audiences by a lengthy and pointless telling of the whole story. Condensing the plot into two or three sentences requires intelligent concentration upon the big issues of the play and is perhaps the most difficult part of the review. However, such effort is very important if you wish to make an effective presentation.

Before you read the scenes from the play, briefly describe the main characters. If possible, quote lines which characterize them; use either their own speeches or those by other characters. In choosing passages for reading, remember that the scenes you select must be interesting in themselves. They should be good examples of the author's style, and they should bring out the personalities of the characters. Of course, they should lend themselves to effective reading. Occasionally it is wise to read one act in its entirety, but usually cuttings from a number of scenes are more interesting.

Your personal reaction to the play will be obvious throughout the discussion and will color your interpretation. Remember that you must appreciate, understand, and enjoy the play yourself, if you are to share it with others.

The manner in which you close your review is important. A fine reading of a brilliant passage with emotional content is the most dramatic kind of conclusion. If you can leave your listeners genuinely moved, you will deserve the applause you receive.

*Applications*

1. Make a list of twenty plays which you have seen or read in your work this term which you think would make good material for platform reviews. List the qualities you consider essential in a play if it is to be reviewed.

2. Organize a series of play reviews for presentation by individual members of the class as the final piece of work for the term. Arrange these reviews in some logical order—chronologically, geographically, or according to the various types of dramatic literature. Allow for plenty of contrast in the entire series. Decide on a definite time limit—one or two reviews in a class period. The shorter the period, the more difficult the planning will be. Make the assignments months before the series is to begin.

**Dramatic readings of plays.** If your review takes the form of a presentation of the play without comments, it becomes a dramatic reading, a more formal type of platform interpretation than the play review.

The arrangement and cutting of a play for such a reading is of paramount importance. Reduce all descriptive material to a minimum, leaving only gripping situations which work up to a dramatic climax. The play selected should have a strong emotional appeal, preferably with an intermingling of humor and pathos against an interesting background. The characters should be strongly contrasted in type so that they will be easily identified after their first introduction. When several persons are presented at the same time, place each one clearly, first in your own mind and then for the audience. Always keep their respective positions clear. When they are supposed to speak, turn enough each time to suggest their locations. Be careful to assume the general bodily set of a character as well as a voice suited to his personality. However, remember that you are reading to the audience—there is no illusion of a fourth wall.

Necessary stage directions and descriptions of the set must be given clearly and positively. Although subordinated to the dialogue, they should never be presented so casually that they seem to have no importance.

Because both the play review and the play reading are forms of interpretation, they involve many of the principles discussed in previous chapters. First, of course, you must understand the main idea of the entire play or selection in order to present the atmosphere. Then be sure you understand every character and passage and the relationship of each to the play as a whole. Interpreting a play demands visualizing every situation and character. You must see, feel, and imagine with the playwright and then re-create what you see and feel for the audience. This means that you must re-create the actions and emotions of the characters at the time you present them to your audience. Full control of the techniques of acting, pantomime, and voice is demanded to make the interpretation a living, breathing creation. Again, "The play's the thing." You have the privilege of being the channel through which the play may become a thing of beauty, bringing joy to those with whom you share it.

## Applications

1. Make a list of twenty plays which you think are particularly adapted to dramatic reading. What qualities do you think are essential for this type of presentation?

2. State the central idea of one of the following plays, imagining that you are going to present it as a dramatic reading:

> The Barretts of Wimpole Street by Rudolf Besier
> Antigone by Sophocles
> She Stoops to Conquer by Oliver Goldsmith
> Awake and Sing by Clifford Odets
> Our Town by Thornton Wilder
> Life with Father by Howard Lindsay and Russell Crouse
> The Skin of Our Teeth by Thornton Wilder
> Le Chantecler by Edmond Rostand
> All My Sons by Arthur Miller
> Ondine by Jean Giraudoux
> The Lady's Not for Burning by Christopher Fry

3. Cut any one of the above plays for a forty-five minute reading.

4. Select three students who are capable of preparing excellent dramatic readings. Have each of them work up a finished reading cut to about forty-five minutes. Let the students present the readings to the class and then, when you feel they are sufficiently polished, arrange for them to be presented before school and community organizations.

## Group Play Readings

A play read by a carefully chosen cast avoids certain involved production details, but it does demand rehearsals and planning. Parts mumbled at sight can ruin a play. When a group reading is well cast and well presented, it is a very popular form of dramatic entertainment.

The first difficulty is securing scripts for the entire cast. Technically, a public reading and the copying of an entire play are prohibited for any copyrighted piece of literature. The proper procedure is to write to the publisher of the play and explain the exact purpose of the reading and the conditions under which it will be given. Since a good play reading is one of the best possible forms of advertising, you will have a good talking point if the play or film is coming to town.

Usually, the play must then be cut to make an interesting evening's entertainment. Keep the main thread of the plot clear by cutting detailed subplots and lengthy speeches. Be sure to include the passages containing the best acting scenes and those essential to the theme. Any introductory or descriptive material should be written out for a narrator to read. When important parts are omitted, they should be summarized if there is any danger of the audience's losing the thread of the plot.

A group reading can be done in several ways. You can place the performers around a table or in a row and have them read in turn, picking up their cues, characterizing their roles, and building the tempo and climax. Plan an attractive background. For example, if you have black or very dark drapes, all the men and women can wear formal black clothes and then be lighted by spots so that only their faces stand out. In planning the lighting, be sure the pages of the readers' scripts are illuminated so they can read without strain.

A more exciting method of presentation is to have the cast move about a stage equipped with the essential furniture. Stage business should be quite simple in order not to detract from the lines. Limited costumes in keeping with the characters and period can bring further reality to the roles. Both settings and costumes should help to create an illusion but they should not be made too striking or realistic.

Of course, if you have the time and energy, you can present a reading of the whole play using costumes, settings, and action as for a regular production. In that case, the rehearsing must be almost as punctilious as for a real performance. The scripts should be as inconspicuous as possible.

A season's program of group readings in a small auditorium or a private home can be a community project which arouses real enthusiasm for plays.

*Applications*

1. Make a list of good plays with small casts and clear-cut characters which would make effective group readings.
2. Cut any one of the plays on your list and write the narrator's lines.
3. Plan five simple backgrounds which would be appropriate for group readings.
4. As a class, plan a series of monthly group play readings. Select outstanding plays and make your plans far enough ahead so that every presentation will be well cast, carefully rehearsed, and effectively read. The series should provide at least one good part for every member of the class. The presentations may be made in class, immediately after school, or before the dramatics club or some other school or community organization.

*Suggestions for Preparing and Presenting Play Readings*

I. Individual play readings
  A. Play reviews
    1. Select a play which you are eager to share with others.
    2. Go to the library and get all the material you can concerning the author and various productions of the play.
    3. Outline this material for presentation to your audience.
    4. Write a brief description of all of the characters you will be interpreting. Analyze their personalities and visualize their appearance and clothing.
    5. Write a brief description of the setting.
    6. Select the passages that you feel you must read aloud to bring out the theme, characterize the people, and show the author's style.
    7. Write a brief synopsis of the essential action of the plot.
    8. Plan your review in its entirety, read it aloud to time it, then cut and rearrange the material and scenes to fit the time allotment. Ask yourself these questions:
      a. What is the central idea of the review?
      b. What is the predominant mood?
      c. How can I best establish this mood for my audience?
  B. Dramatic readings
    1. Select a play which is suited to your particular talents and personality. It should have comparatively few, well-contrasted characters and an entertaining plot.
    2. Cut it to about forty-five minutes. First select the essential scenes and read them aloud so that you will know how long they are. Then choose minor scenes of special value to meet the time requirement.
    3. Write out your introductory remarks if you feel they are necessary to make the setting and characters clear to your audience.

4. Go through your whole reading just as you will present it and check carefully on the time. Remember that it is better to stop ten minutes before your audience wants you to than one minute after they have become tired and bored.

5. If you memorize it, first fix the entire play in your mind, next the important scenes, and then work on individual scenes, speeches, and sentences.

C. Rehearsing for reviews or readings

1. Study your material. Analyze and visualize the setting and characters. Determine the general mood and the delicate shades of feeling in separate passages. Look up all unfamiliar words, checking their pronunciation and meaning. Divide the thoughts into phrases. Mark the pauses and important words.

2. If you are reading the scenes from a book, practice with the book in your left hand, turning the pages at the upper right-hand corner with your right hand. Train your eye to grasp a full line ahead so that you may look directly at your entire audience or in the direction of the character to whom you are speaking. Hold your book at shoulder height.

3. Rehearse out loud. Let yourself be emotionally stirred so that you actually laugh and cry over the lines. Don't feel embarrassed or you may spoil your effectiveness. Of course, in performance you must never lose control of your voice or emotions.

4. Practice your voice and diction exercises but forget them when you are working on the reading itself.

5. Plan your stage setting for each scene so that you can visualize clearly where every character stands in relation to the others. Then you can turn slightly and clarify the positions of the different characters. Also visualize the costumes the characters are wearing and suggest them by your posture.

6. Have the lights and stage decorations properly arranged and rehearse with them at least once. Use the reading stand. Have someone check to be sure that you can be heard in the back of the auditorium.

7. Plan what you will wear. Boys can usually wear a dark suit and an inconspicuous tie. Girls must decide on either an afternoon or evening dress, appropriate hairdo, and make-up.

8. Remember that you are presenting the play, not yourself. Subordinate your appearance and delivery to the reading.

D. Presenting your review or reading

1. Get to the auditorium in ample time to check on all stage details, especially the lighting and acoustics. No externals should upset you during your presentation.

2. Name the author and give any introductory remarks in your own person. Use your best diction and talk directly to your entire audience—simply, naturally, and, above all, distinctly.
3. When presenting a dramatic reading or scenes from the play in a review, assume the personality of your opening character, making a marked distinction between his personality and your own. As you present each new character, make a definite change in order to fix his voice upon the audience so that you will not need to repeat his name before or after his speeches.
4. After your closing speech, reassume your own personality, bow and smile slightly, and leave the stage. Or, if you have it definitely arranged and rehearsed, keep in character and have the curtains drawn on the final line.

II. Group play readings

A. The director must make all arrangements: royalty rights, scripts or books for each reader, and stage setting. He must also decide on the method of presentation before the first rehearsal. Then his explanations will be clear and definite, and the cast can go right to work. He should also cut the play.

B. The first rehearsal should be the long, careful one in which the meaning of the play and individual passages is made clear, pronunciations are set, characters are clarified, and all plans are laid, including costumes.

C. Succeeding rehearsals should build up moods, climax, contrast, and tempos. The lines for the narrator must be carefully written and inserted into the reading as an integral part of the presentation.

D. The actual performance should be a finished whole in which the play comes to life. Every character should be clear-cut, and scripts should be handled unobtrusively.

# Part Four

# Producing
# the Drama

Producing a play is the creative process by which the director, cast, designer, and stage crew transform a play script into a living experience for the audience. A person, class, club, producer, or theatrical angel has the idea of putting on a play. Interested people are brought together and organized into a working unit. A play is written or chosen, the cast selected and rehearsed, the sets designed and built, the costumes planned and acquired. Then all are brought together in the performance. How little this process means to anyone who has not had a share in it and how much to anyone who has!

"The play's the thing," but the kind of thing it is depends largely upon its production—the coordination by the director of actors and mechanical equipment against the background of the stage setting. Before the first curtain rises on any play, the entire production staff—director, designer, stage manager, backstage crew—has been

engaged in planning and executing the countless details necessary to getting a play on the boards. If these details have been welded into a whole representative of the best efforts of everyone involved in the production, then everyone shares in the glory, the backstage people as well as the actors onstage. You may well find there is as great a thrill in working backstage as in acting. In the professional theater, the careers of directors, scenic artists, and stage technicians are often more stable, lucrative, and creative than that of the average actor.

Today ideas concerning the construction of stages and theaters are changing rapidly. Scientific improvements are being made in all phases of architecture and equipment and new technical materials are coming into use. Both playwriting and directing are being affected. In the second half of this century a new kind of theater may evolve in the United States and around the world.

*Chapter 11*

# Fundamentals of

# Play Production

Play production offers many opportunities which you may well find more stimulating and exciting than acting. All the activities involved in the design and construction of sets and costumes, the handling of lighting equipment, and the managing of affairs backstage and in the front of the house are of absorbing interest when a play once gets under way.

At present your interest centers in the plays given by your own school. School stages may range from simple ones in classrooms to theaters having fully equipped switchboard, recording and sound equipment, fine dressing rooms, and ample work and storage space. If your school does not have all these facilities, do not be dismayed. A small stage, crowded backstage area, and the minimum of stage lights are limitations which may challenge your imagination and ingenuity. As a result, your productions may well be superior to those presented more easily with first-class physical equipment. Whatever the size and equipment of your theater, having a share in a big public production is a stimulating experience.

In this chapter your attention is directed to the guiding principles of play production, especially as they pertain to school dramatic groups. Detailed analysis of these principles can be found in the books listed in Appendix C. In them you will find fascinating material for your notebook, as well as ideas which will enable you to work with greater efficiency

**W**orking with a limited budget, a designer shops for bargains in material.

and which may even inspire you to study some special phase of production in detail. Initially, though, you will want to familiarize yourself with all phases of stage work in order to find the particular field you enjoy most.

Putting on a public production of a long play means at least six weeks of intensive work by a large group of people. Before that period much preliminary planning and preparation must be done. In order to get the fullest possible experience, follow all the activities from the beginning, carrying out your own special duties with enthusiasm and responsibility.

In school dramatics, the director usually plans the production in accordance with the schedule for school events. He often works with a student executive committee in the selection of individual production staff members and their assistants. The director and this executive committee also set up special committees to assist in all, or some, of the following production procedures: play reading and selection, casting, costuming, publicity, business management, and backstage work. All of the people chosen should be dependable and enthusiastic, since a great deal of the authority in production rests with them.

# THE PRODUCTION STAFF

The number of people on the production staff will be determined by the size of the production, the availability of capable people, and the needs of the individual school or class. In the school theater, various departmental activities often center about public production. The class in dramatics may furnish the cast and the direction. The art department may design and/or paint the set. The shops may make and handle the scenery and provide stage carpenters. The home economics classes may make the costumes or do alterations. The music department may provide the incidental music. In the case of an operetta or musical, the music department usually furnishes singers, instrumentalists, and musical direction.

A brief discussion of the tasks of each position to be filled will give you an idea of the work involved in producing a play.

## The Director

Though some productions may be assigned to a student, the director is usually the drama teacher in a school situation. His principal aim is to reproduce the playwright's intentions as faithfully as he can. The director must discover the values and meanings of the play. Then he must work

A teacher-director guides his actors as they work out the details of an important scene.

to bring them out through the actors, the scenic artist, and the other resources at his disposal. Ideally, he should be an excellent actor, scenic artist, and stage mechanic, able to handle equipment and human beings with equal skill.

The director is the person upon whom the success or failure of the play most largely depends. He is responsible for the unification of all production elements. He must be able to delegate authority—to the backstage crew, for example, in order to be out front during rehearsals and the performance. He is also responsible for the morale of the people in the production and must help them work together for the success of the play.

The director has the additional task of being the nominal head of the "house" (that part of a theater which is the domain of the audience). He keeps in close touch with ticket selling, advertising, seating, and other business procedures. In school productions, his responsibility continues until the last bill is paid, all borrowed and rented articles and costumes are returned, and a final report to the school authorities is turned in.

### The Assistant Director

In the school theater, the position of assistant director is held by a capable student. He must be a person whom the director finds congenial and the students respect. He will serve as a liaison officer between the director, cast, and crew, taking charge of rehearsals in the absence of the director. This is a position you may aspire to at present if you are interested in all phases of the theater.

### The Prompter

This position should also be held by a dependable student who will attend every rehearsal. During rehearsals, under the supervision of the director, the prompter may hold the director's promptbook and make some of the penciled notes on moves and business, light and sound cues, and warning signals.

The numbering system is recommended for marking the *blocking*—the movements, positions, and crosses. Under this system, each movement on each page is given a number for easy reference by actors and director. Sound and light cues and other special effects are numbered in different colors. By using sketches in the promptbook, the prompter can clarify any questions concerning stage groupings, crosses, and changes.

The prompter marks special gestures and hurried directions at exciting moments so that such details will not be lost. He must mark every pause so he will not give an unnecessary prompt. During the performance the

Photo by Louise Phillips

A stage manager briefs his crew.

A property-girl visits secondhand stores in search of furniture and other props.

Photo by George E. Joseph

prompter can often save the show if emergencies arise. He can give the correct cues and lines; and, if the cast starts to skip passages, he can feed the vital lines to keep the meaning clear for the audience. If he fails at these crucial times, the entire production can be ruined. Audiences will often remember and laugh about one moment of confusion after they have forgotten all the fine points of a production.

Some directors do not use the prompter during the performance, preferring to have the actors know they are on their own. Others feel that a skilled prompter is essential. If your school does use a prompter, this is a position from which you may learn a great deal. It is a job that requires both reliability and intelligence.

## The Scenic Artist and the Technical Director

The *scenic artist*, or the designer, usually designs the settings and the costumes and plans the lighting. Though his designs may be simple or complex, they must always serve the function of giving the play visual dimensions in harmony with the aims of the director.

The work of the *technical director* is also vitally important. It is he who executes the designs of the scenic artist with the assistance of a crew for building sets, painting drops, creating costumes, and hanging lights. In some cases, the scenic artist and the technical director are the same person. Though their functions are different, they both aim at serving the director's intentions as effectively, simply, and beautifully as possible to achieve a unified production.

## The Stage Manager

Aided by his stage crew, the stage manager takes complete charge backstage during rehearsals and performances. In some cases he and his crew act both as the stage carpenters who build the set and as the "grips" who change the scenery. The stage manager also keeps a promptbook containing all cues and effects. He makes up cue sheets or charts containing the cues for lights, sound, and curtain. For the stage crew, he makes up a chart of set and prop changes to guide them through the play. During the performance the stage manager must handle any and all emergencies that may arise. A good stage manager is essential to a smooth production.

## The Backstage Assistants

The *property-man* and his assistants procure the furniture and props, in accordance with the designer's plans, store them backstage, arrange them, and give the hand props to the actors backstage just before entrances.

FUNDAMENTALS OF PLAY PRODUCTION          **295**

These hand props should be kept on tables on the appropriate side of the stage. They must be carefully replaced and never touched except when in use. The *wardrobe mistress, make-up people,* and *callboys* serve under the stage manager whose job it is to see that all backstage activities go smoothly, quietly, and rapidly in final rehearsals and all performances. The efficiency, ingenuity, and dependability of these assistants during long hours of hard labor are determining factors in a successful production. Without them, the play cannot go on.

## The Business Manager

The business manager is responsible for the financial arrangements of the production. In accordance with school policy, he may be in charge of all funds, pay all bills, and handle the printing and selling of tickets. He and the director should gauge probable receipts and achieve a reasonable profit by watching production and publicity expenses.

In the school theater, the business manager has the difficult task of issuing tickets to many salesmen and checking on sales. He should give out all passes to the show, with the permission of the director. He is also responsible for the "stage-door slips" which are issued to those working backstage. It is most important that people who do not have specific duties in the dressing rooms or backstage area not be admitted during performances. (If stage-door slips are not used, a program listing members of the staff may be substituted. A responsible person may use it to check entrances and exits at the stage door.)

The business manager also has charge of printing the programs, which should be designed by the scenic artist in harmony with the production. The cast is usually listed in the order of appearance. The business manager should be accurate in listing names of cast members, production staff, committee chairmen, and backstage crew. He should also see that acknowledgments are made for favors and assistance. Selling advertising to pay for the program is usually a matter determined by school authorities.

## The Advertising Man

The advertising man must promote the show in the school and in the community. Good publicity is vital to the financial success of the play. The public press, newspapers published at other schools, local radio stations, and church publications will give space and time to notices about public school productions if they are properly approached. In these days of broadcasting systems, tape recordings, and other devices in many high schools, there are almost limitless possibilities for promoting a play.

The advertising man and his assistants have a real opportunity to make original and artistic contributions to the success of a production. In their planning, the advertising staff would do well to consult the art department of the school. With serious dramas, advertising in keeping with the spirit of the play may include well-designed individual notices (wood cuts and black-and-white sketches) sent to all drama enthusiasts in the community. For comedies, cartoons of the cast and humorous items about the funniest situations can be featured, possibly with lively quotations from the play. The title of the play itself, the author, the skill or prominence of the performers, the past achievements of the director, and striking scenic effects can also furnish material for publicity.

If there is a good possibility of filling the house more than once, plans should be made for several consecutive performances before any advertising goes out. The repetition of a play several days or weeks after a single highly successful performance is seldom satisfactory because both cast and public lose interest rapidly. Also, the expense of renting costumes and furniture again takes what little money has been made. It is always better to have one packed house than several half-empty ones.

## The House Manager

The house manager is responsible for the seating and comfort of the audience, the competence and charm of the ushers, and the distribution of the programs. Uniformed ushers or girls in evening dress or appropriate costumes can add much to the pleasure of the audience.

## Other Personnel

School productions frequently involve still more people. Firemen and policemen are on hand if they are notified when a production is scheduled. Sometimes members of the faculty are required to be in attendance in the dressing rooms and backstage areas and they often take or sell tickets out front.

The school orchestra may furnish music for the overture or intermissions. If so, the program should be selected far in advance and properly rehearsed. Music should also be in keeping with the production and subordinate to it, not added as a special feature. Announcements or stunts between acts should be avoided.

### Discussion

1. Name the positions and duties of the various members of the production staff. Which interest you the most? Why?

**2.** In your school, what are some of the special problems connected with putting on a play? Are they being solved? Is the entire student body interested in them? Are the people in the community interested?

**3.** Discuss the school plays you have attended or assisted with and note the part the backstage people had in their success or failure.

**4.** For what purpose are the proceeds of your dramatic productions used? Are they used exclusively for improving the stage and its equipment, as a means of raising money for other school activities, or for charity? How do you think they ought to be used?

**5.** Which should be the paramount factor in planning a school production: the amount of money to be cleared, or the beauty and perfection of the staging?

**6.** Which departments assist in play productions in your school? Discuss their contributions.

**7.** Discuss possible difficulties which might arise during a performance. Show how the prompter and/or the stage manager might circumvent or overcome them.

*Applications*

**1.** Select a play you would like to see produced and plan an advertising campaign for its production. Bring in a design for a notice to be mailed and handed out, plan a design for the program and posters, list scenes to be photographed for local newspaper use, and select quotations for publicity.

**2.** Make a chart showing all of the people on a production staff and their relationships to each other.

**3.** Plan an advertising campaign for a production of *Poor Maddalena* by Louise Sanders.

**4.** Make a sample program for *Poor Maddalena*.

## PRE-REHEARSAL ACTIVITIES

### Choosing a Play

After the director and the executive committee have set up the special committees and after individual production staff members have been selected, the next step is to choose a play. This is usually done by the reading committee and the director.

Choosing a play is a crucial problem. Before a choice can be made, many plays must be read. A poor choice can ruin the reputation of the producing group; a good one can establish it. The producing group must know the purpose of the proposed production. Is it primarily a school project, recognized as an important artistic group activity? Or is it to raise funds for a specific purpose or organization? A play must be found which will fulfill its designated purpose, appeal to its particular audience, and be adaptable to the ability of the actors, the size and equipment of the stage, and the limits of the budget.

In the desire to reduce the royalty charge and to entertain the public, inexperienced groups sometimes choose silly farces which do not warrant an expenditure of time and energy. Rather than compromise on the quality of the script, it is better to present classics (most of which require no royalty) or cut production expenses sufficiently to pay the royalty on a contemporary play by a first-class writer. Remember that there are many classics which the other students and parents will thoroughly enjoy. There are also many plays of the last century now released from royalty charges that are really delightful. Try to avoid plays which a large portion of your audience may have seen recently and try to provide variety in the annual program of your school.

The size of the cast requires attention in the choice of a play. When the cast is large, more students receive the benefits of training and experience. However, large casts make for difficult rehearsals and staging. Ability to create the necessary stage settings and the possibility of adequate interpretation by available actors must be considered.

**A director and her reading committee consider the merits of several plays before making their final decision.**

Photo by Louise Phillips

## Securing Production Rights

Before a play is finally selected, the director or some authorized person should write to the author or company controlling the acting rights of the play. He should state the time and number of performances planned and request authorization to present the play. There are many regulations restricting the presentation of plays by amateurs, especially in the larger cities where stock and road companies appear. Therefore, full permission should be obtained for a public performance before preparations start.

## Planning the Production

The director must first study the play from every angle to determine the style and atmosphere he wishes carried out in the sets and costumes. He must understand the theme and decide how best to express it. He must decide how to emphasize the conflict, suspense, and climax of the plot. Most important of all, he must analyze the characters and their relationships to each other. For a period play he must study the historical background, social conditions, and attitudes of the people represented, as well as the costumes, furnishings, etiquette, and manner of speech and movement.

Early in his work on a play, he must make out a tentative budget. He must estimate the probable size of the audience and take into account sets and props which may be obtained without expense.

After studying the play, the director makes his *floor plan*. This is his diagram of the physical set and the action which will take place on it. During this early period, the director should have frequent conferences with his scenic artist and stage manager concerning many aspects of the production. Problems of handling the show backstage must be discussed. The director must also carefully adapt his plans for action to the stage design.

The entrances and exits must be practical and logical. The main entrance is often the center of interest in the design, as the stairway and balcony in Kaufman and Ferber's *The Royal Family*, the French window in Ferris and Cassella's *Death Takes a Holiday*, and the staircase in Kaufman and Ferber's *Stage Door*. The location and size of the furniture should be planned to create helpful, meaningful units for definite bits of action and to form attractive and balanced stage pictures. The light sources must be considered and marked on the floor plan. Windows provide daytime light; lamps, fireplaces, and perhaps chandeliers give light at night. Sufficient backing for windows and doors must be considered in planning the action and the director must make his needs clear to his scenic artist. The backstage storage areas for furniture, props, and sets must be diagramed. After the director, the scenic artist, and the stage manager have made over-all plans, the director will visualize important scenes carefully and plan for effective grouping. Unimportant characters can be momentarily emphasized by being placed upstage or apart from the others.

## Making the Promptbook

The promptbook, started by the director during the planning period and containing the entire play script, is the backbone of a production. Into this book go the director's plans as well as the telephone numbers and addresses of all the people involved in the production. The easiest way to make a promptbook is to paste the pages of the play in a large loose leaf notebook. This system requires two copies of the play. If there is only one copy available for this purpose, page-size windows can be cut in the sheets of the notebook and each page of the script can be fastened with scotch tape or glue into these windows.

Large margins around the script are essential for the sketches, cues, and notes, first made by the director in his preliminary planning and then added to and changed during rehearsals. The marginal notes show script cuttings, stage directions, and markings of difficult passages for pauses, phrasing, and emphasis. The sketches or diagrams of floor plans and sets show positions of furniture and actors in every scene. Stage groupings of actors can be drawn with the initials of the characters' names marked in little circles. Most directors like to sketch important crosses and counter-crosses in the promptbook and mark actors' movements with symbols. For example, "XR from C" means that the actor moves to his right from a position in stage center. "Enter UL, exit DR" means that the actor comes in from the farthest upstage entrance on his left and crosses the stage diagonally, going out nearest the footlights on his right.

Cues marked in the margin are for lights, curtains, and other effects both on and off the stage. As rehearsals progress, individual cue sheets are made from the book by the stage manager. These sheets are given to the electrician, the wardrobe people, the prop committee, the sound technician, and others whose tasks require written directions. In marking the promptbook, pencil rather than pen should be used. It is advisable to use different colors for particular types of cues and warning signals, such as red for lights, blue for curtain, and green for entrances and exits.

When a play is finished, the promptbook should be completed with a copy of the program and photographs of the production. Frequently a school play is repeated in five or six years without much duplication in the audience. Although every production has a new promptbook, the original can be most useful for reference purposes.

## Casting the Play

Few phases of production are more important to the ultimate success or failure of a play than the choice of the cast. No school activity demands greater tact, sincerity, fairness, and judgment than casting. It is usually helpful to have a student casting committee assist the director in conducting tryouts by taking names and addresses and recording the applicants' past experience. Final decisions on casting are made by the director, based on his estimates of which candidates can best capture the spirit of the play. A successful production demands that actors be equipped physically, mentally, and temperamentally to give convincing interpretations of the roles assigned to them.

**Eligibility to try out.** In some public schools, tryouts are limited to drama or speech students. In others, they are open to all students. This is a matter to be decided by the director or by the individual school. Perhaps the director will want to use a point system of stage experience and service to help determine eligibility for an important role. In some schools, scholastic standing in other departments and good citizenship are considered before an applicant is allowed to try out. In any case, eligible applicants must be made to understand that casting is usually probationary until the director has been able to determine the actor's ability to take direction, his willingness to work, and his understanding of his task.

**Publicizing tryouts.** Every possible means of publicizing the roles to be filled should be used prior to the tryouts. Posters, articles in the school paper, and posted mimeographed descriptions of the characters are all good ways of circulating the information. If possible, the director will place a copy of the play on reserve in the school library for all applicants to read or make the play available in some other way.

**Conducting tryouts.** The tryout arrangements must be determined by the number of people who wish to read for the play, the length of time which can be devoted to casting, and the kind of play to be presented. It is always preferable to hold tryouts in the auditorium or theater in which the play is to be performed. Sometimes, however, this is not possible.

When the applicants have assembled, the director can explain all details of the tryouts, discuss the play briefly, and describe the characters. Applicants should be asked to fill out cards giving names, addresses, phone numbers, height, weight, past experience in school plays, and any previous commitments which might interfere with attendance at rehearsals. The casting committee can take charge of getting this information.

Careful organization is essential to keep the tryouts moving rapidly and effectively. Here again the casting committee can assist the director.

A publicity committee appraises finished casting notices before posting them around the school.

Scenes for the tryouts are carefully selected by the director. They are chosen to challenge the applicants' acting ability and to show the appearance of the various applicants with each other. These scenes should include some climactic situations. If practicable, it is also a good idea to permit the candidates to select short speeches or scenes from the play in advance and present them singly or in groups.

The director should sit a good distance away from the stage or tryout area to check voice quality and projection and physical appearance.

Perhaps the most important aspect of tryouts is that they be conducted in a friendly and relaxed atmosphere. Each student who tries out must know that he is being given a fair chance. Good tryouts can set morale at a high level for the rest of the production.

**Second tryouts.** After the director has chosen certain candidates as possibilities for roles, he will probably want to call them back for a second reading. Some directors use improvised pantomimes late in the casting procedure to test the flexibility, imagination, and response of the candidates. No student should ever feel that he has been discarded if he is not cast, but only that the best choices have been made for the play.

FUNDAMENTALS OF PLAY PRODUCTION 303

**Students wait to try out.**

**Double casting.** The procedure of having two casts for the same play and letting each cast play alternate performances is called *double casting*. The obvious advantages are, of course, that more students have the opportunity to participate and there is no danger of a canceled performance due to illness or emergency. The disadvantage is that the busy director can hardly give everyone careful individual direction because he has to divide his time between two casts. Many school directors prefer to give more than one play a year rather than struggle with a double cast.

**Announcing the cast.** A means of encouraging full cooperation of the school paper is to hold the final announcement of the cast for publication in the paper rather than to post it. If the director is sure in his own mind that the leads in the tentative cast will work out satisfactorily, a photograph of them reading tryout sheets makes good publicity for the play. Early publicity should not, of course, encourage any member of the cast or backstage crew to consider himself indispensable.

*Discussion*

1. In your school, what are the special problems involved in selecting a play for public performance? What qualities would you look for in a play?
2. What is type-casting?
3. What plays have you seen which were really well selected and cast? Which were badly chosen or poorly cast, or both? In the poor plays, where do you think the fault lay?
4. What do you think of using two casts for alternate performances of the same play?
5. Discuss your personal experiences in selecting or casting plays.

*Applications*

1. Make a character description sheet of a play of your own choice for the use of candidates at tryouts.
2. Prepare a model actor-information card for use in casting.
3. Make a list of the characteristics you would hope to have if you were to be the director of a school production.
4. Work out a promptbook for a production of *Poor Maddalena* or any other play your school could produce.

## REHEARSING

Rehearsing is the creative and cooperative process which brings the play to the stage. If the director, cast, and backstage staff work together harmoniously and effectively, rehearsals afford a keen satisfaction found in few activities. They should begin as soon as the tentative cast and the understudies (if they are to be used) have been selected.

When properly conducted, rehearsals are absorbing and exciting because in each one a definite advance can be made. The members of the cast and crew should so enjoy their parts in the artistic enterprise that promptness, orderly conduct, and regular attendance become a matter of course. Today audiences expect smooth-running performances by amateurs as well as professionals. Such productions depend upon good rehearsals and the devoted cooperation of the cast, crew, and house staff.

### Reading Rehearsals

The first rehearsal is usually a *reading rehearsal* with the entire company seated around a discussion table. It should be attended by every person involved in the production. At this time, the director discusses the meaning of the play and the manner in which it is to be interpreted and acted. He describes just what is expected of everyone. He probably says that a fine performance coordinates acting, scenery, lighting, and properties into a stirring, meaningful presentation. The director reminds his company that the pleasure of play production lies in efficient, happy, conscientious teamwork. The common objective is to put on the best possible production of this particular play under the existing circumstances.

The director himself or members of the cast read the play aloud at this first rehearsal. Important details in characterization, diction, and tempo are pointed out. Actors make penciled notations of these details on their scripts. In the first hours of work on the play, the director can sense the actors' ability to understand lines and project personality. He can also judge their willingness to respond to direction. He watches to see how much attention is paid by everyone present. If there is ample time, a number of reading rehearsals can "set" the characters and the lines. More reading rehearsals are necessary when dialects or excellent stage diction are imperative. In any case, a number of reading rehearsals makes actors feel more secure about interpretation when rehearsing on the stage.

A time schedule for the entire rehearsal period should be worked out and copies made for participants to give their parents. This procedure helps parents understand how much time will be involved in the production. In making this *rehearsal schedule*, the director considers the time allotted for preparing the production, the length and difficulty of the play, and the availability of the cast. For instance, if the rehearsal period has been set at six weeks, after-school rehearsals should probably be planned for three

**Cast and crew go over the rehearsal schedule and make note of the sessions they must attend.**

Photo by Louise Phillips

hours a day, five days a week. (If the rehearsal period is to be eight, ten, or twelve weeks, rehearsals can be scheduled for alternate days. The individual director can readjust the schedule to fit his own situation.)

In a six-week schedule, the first week should complete the reading rehearsals and include "blocking" and "business" rehearsals for the first act. The second week should complete blocking and business rehearsals for the second and third acts, with a review of the first act. The third and fourth weeks constitute working and reworking rehearsals of the entire play. If the auditorium has not been available previously, a long Saturday rehearsal should be held at the end of the fourth week. At this time, whatever is technically difficult should be rehearsed. Sound, lights, props, scenery, furniture, and costumes should be used. The fifth week is for further polishing, stage-crew rehearsals, and run-throughs, culminating in a long rehearsal on Saturday. Sometimes this is the first dress rehearsal with full stage crew. In a school theater, the performance is usually on Friday night or on Friday and Saturday nights of the sixth week. On Monday of this last week, the staff should hold its last rehearsal in which interruptions can be made, problems discussed, final costumes and props checked, and all details settled.

If there is only one dress rehearsal, it should come on the Wednesday night before the Friday night performance. Tuesday may be spent in getting everything in final shape. If there are two dress rehearsals, they should be held on Tuesday and Wednesday. It is wise to invite a few people to a dress rehearsal to accustom the cast to playing before an audience. It is also wise to leave the night before the performance free for final adjustments.

Students involved in a production should be urged not to be absent from school because of their participation in a play. Much discrediting of school dramatics results from unnecessary cutting of classes and upsetting of routine when a play is being produced. With wise management and administrative cooperation, a big production can be put on without complicating the daily schedule. The auditorium should be closed to all other activities during the last week, and ample opportunity must be given the technical director and crew to put the set onstage, or "hang the set."

## Blocking Rehearsals

Blocking the movement and planning stage business follow the reading rehearsals. Work on the interpretation of lines should be delayed while attention is focused on movement and stage groupings. Most directors will have already worked out plans for using the stage area, emphasizing im-

In an early rehearsal, students block out the action for a scene from Thornton Wilder's *Our Town*.

portant groupings, and keeping effective stage pictures. However, in the early rehearsals they should be willing to discuss possible changes and incorporate spontaneous reactions of the actors. When the fundamental blocking of the first act has been set, that of the second should follow. The two acts can then be put together at one rehearsal. Following this, the third act should be set, and the first and second reviewed. As soon as the business of the first act is clarified, the lines may be memorized. It is better not to begin memorizing until the words and action have been correlated and can be absorbed simultaneously.

In planning stage business, the director must be sure that all gestures and movements are meaningful. In order to avoid later delay he should try to eliminate tendencies of the actors to fidget, shift weight, and gesticulate ineffectively. If the actors have studied dramatics, they should understand that every gesture and cross must be motivated and definite and that the center of interest should be accentuated at all times. The director must adhere to fundamental directions when dealing with inexperienced people to avoid confusing them with too much detail.

If blocking rehearsals cannot be held in the auditorium, the assistant director should arrange a rehearsal area which has exactly the same propor-

A close-up of tape and chalk markings used to indicate the positions of sets and furniture in a rehearsal area other than the actual stage.

tions as the stage. He should indicate the entrances and exits with chalk or tape and obtain furniture which resembles the pieces which will eventually be used.

## Working Rehearsals

After all of the action has been blocked out, the most creative part of rehearsing begins. Interpretation is developed, and words and action are put together. All the acting techniques previously discussed are brought into play and are coordinated with the director's carefully thought out plans. Some directors use the terms *essential* and *accessory* to describe action. The former is set by the director; the latter is worked out as a means of character delineation by the actor. Both are set during this period.

In working rehearsals, actors note and mark the key lines which must be projected to the audience if the meaning of the play is to be made clear. Exact positions and motivated movements are repeated until they become automatic.

Some directors sit downstage by the prompter, asking relevant questions and giving directions throughout these rehearsals. Others place the prompter in the wings and seat themselves halfway back in the auditorium.

Here they watch an entire scene and give instructions only at the end. Both methods have advantages. If the director is near the stage, he can use the intimate question-and-answer method to help an actor "think through" his lines and understand his role. If he is away from the stage, the director can better view the whole stage picture and the unity of the action. Also, he may note the blending and projection of the voices. Usually, a combination of methods is advisable. A good procedure for a director is to work intimately with a scene, bring out details of stage business, polish the inflections and pauses, and then retire to the back of the auditorium and watch the uninterrupted action from various vantage points.

During this period, a feeling of comradeship should develop. Both the actors and crew members should come to the director with their problems and suggestions and receive his considerate attention and advice. If the director remains poised and pleasant, many of the complications that attend school dramatics may be avoided. He is largely responsible for establishing morale because his methods will be copied unconsciously.

As early as possible in the working rehearsal period, the lines should be memorized. It is often wise to set a definite date after which no scripts can be used onstage. Only then can real characterizations be developed. At this point the actors should be left relatively free to move and speak, for spontaneous physical and vocal responses frequently improve a scene. When difficulties arise, it is often advisable for the director to "give the actor the stage," or let him move as he wishes. If the actor is really in character, his reaction will be the correct one. Actors must discover motivation for such mechanical changes as clearing the stage for the entrance of a dominant character or breaking up a situation to make way for a new one of contrasted feeling and tempo. Short units involving the same characters can be repeated until the small bits of business become effective and aimless action is eliminated. Ultimately, every movement, gesture, and facial expression must have an apparent reason and seem the natural reaction of the character.

The actors should be left as free as possible in their interpretation of lines, but they must not be permitted to fix a false inflection or swallow important words and phrases. Having the actor rewrite a passage in his own words often will make him appreciate the exact meaning of the lines. It is sometimes helpful if the director stops the actor suddenly and says, "Wait a minute. What are you saying? What is happening to your character in this scene?" As a last resort, the director may read the lines himself.

Speeding up or slowing down words and action to attain a certain mood or meaning is often difficult for amateurs. It is during the working rehearsals that the actors must develop tempo—learn to pick up cues rapidly, listen effectively, hold for a laugh or a pause, point lines, break up long speeches with action, and use appropriate body movement.

As soon as possible, mock costumes and props should be used, especially in period and stylized plays. Usually the assistant director is responsible for obtaining long skirts, proper shoes, coats, swords, hats, cups and saucers, cigarette cases—whatever the play requires—and storing them after rehearsals.

In addition to the general rehearsal schedule, a second, specialized schedule should be worked out for actors who are together in a, number of scenes. These scenes or fragments of scenes can be rehearsed separately by the assistant director or stage manager. This schedule of simultaneous rehearsals avoids long waits and consequent boredom and restlessness. Important roles can often be rehearsed separately. Love scenes and other intensely emotional scenes should always be directed privately until the action is crystallized and the responses are natural and convincing.

## Polishing Rehearsals

In the polishing rehearsals the units which have been rehearsed separately are fitted together. With lines completely memorized and stage action set, the real joy of rehearsing begins.

Everything possible should be done to enable the actors to become completely identified with their roles. Approximate costumes and accessories such as wigs and body padding should be worn. The essential elements of the production should be in place. Exits and entrances, windows, staircases, fireplaces, and basic furniture should be onstage. Telephones and lamps should be in position, and sound effects necessary for speaking cues should be set. Only then can the actors find themselves in the environment of the play and become a part of it. Once the mechanics of fitting themselves into the sets have been mastered, the actors can develop the nuances of vocal inflection and pantomime.

The director's job at polishing rehearsals is to establish the tempo of the whole production. The rhythm of the play should be developed and maintained. Sound and light cues must be carefully timed. Telephones, lamps, fireplaces, and sound effects should function smoothly. A single extraneous sound, a slight motion, an unmotivated gesture, or a poorly timed sound cue can destroy the effect of a scene. The director must scrutinize every stage picture from all parts of the auditorium. Having worked with the cast onstage, he should then move back into the auditorium and observe larger, uninterrupted units of the play. He must be sure that all dialogue is clear and that the action is logical. All jarring notes, inharmonious bits of business, however clever, must be ruthlessly cut.

About ten days before the first performance, the complete play must be put together in rehearsal. When the actors make their proper entrances and exits, wear costumes, and use props, the director can see exactly what is still needed to make the play a success. From this time on, the rehearsals must be by acts, played through without interruption. Separate rehearsals for difficult scenes can be held as needed, however.

In the polishing process, some scenes are built by having the lines "top" preceding ones, some are speeded up by rapid picking up of cues, and some are slowed down by effective pauses. It is possible to err in any of these directions. It is said that George M. Cohan's acting in his younger days was known for its overly brisk pace and rapid timing. However, once he discovered the effectiveness of the pause, he used it so often that it added eighteen minutes of playing time to *Ah, Wilderness*.

Members of the prop committee should have all props ready, and the wardrobe committee should have all costumes and accessories finished and on hand during polishing rehearsals. Curtain calls must be rehearsed, intermission time checked, and time allowances made for changes of costume.

## Crew Rehearsals

During the weeks of rehearsal, the scenic artist and technical director design and construct the scenery and arrange the lighting. The set should be onstage as soon as it is completed so that it may be changed if necessary. Two weeks before the first performance, the exits, entrances, stairways, and windows should be ready for the actors. Lamps and doorbells essential to the action should be usable. The property committee and the stage crew must practice swift, efficient, and silent scene changes. Nothing should be left to last-minute chance.

The stage manager must have a chart for each scene and know the exact position of every flat, prop, and piece of furniture. Each piece should be numbered and certain crew members assigned to it. The stage manager must see that everything is accurately placed onstage and stacked backstage. He acts as a "traffic director" and signals the crew at the appointed times for changes. Once the sequence has been established, it must be rehearsed until the changes take seconds rather than minutes to complete. The same members of the crew should always handle the curtain, lighting, and properties. Timing is important in every phase of their work. For example, the speed or slowness of the curtain must be determined by the mood of the scene or act.

**Special lighting rehearsals.** These rehearsals are imperative. Experimentation is necessary to obtain the exact effect desired. Any effect can be achieved, but often it takes hours of adjustment before shadows are removed, special areas are highlighted, artificial light sources appear natural, and the mood of each scene is established. Light must not be allowed to leak through the flats or be reflected from mirrors onstage.

Only a stand-by cast need be called to help in the experimentation. Usually the crew can act as stand-ins for lighting placement and adjustment. School lighting equipment is often inflexible and the regulations concerning its use are quite stringent. If there is any question of overloading the circuits, it should be settled before a lighting rehearsal begins.

**Dressing the stage.** This procedure is too often neglected in the later rehearsals when it should be done. It is often difficult to obtain the correct pictures, hangings, props, and household effects and to arrange them so that the stage looks "lived in" but not cluttered. It may take a week or more to locate just one article.

Securing curtains of the right color and texture is always a problem, but a good stage design demands that they be well chosen and properly draped. Backing for windows and doorways must be carefully planned. Often shrubbery, garden walls, and skylines seen through the stage windows must

A technician adjusts the lights during a special rehearsal for lighting effects.

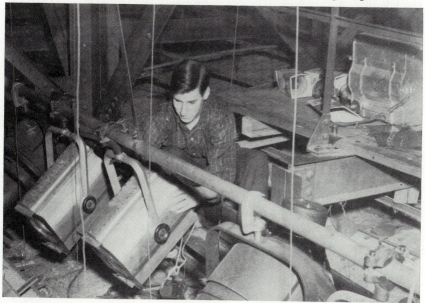

be properly lighted to show the time of day and to create the mood. It also may be necessary to have backstage floodlights kill any shadows which would precede the actors onstage. Ample space must be allowed for the cast to get on and off the stage in character. The cast must learn a safe means of using any stage stairways and balconies, even in the dark.

These matters must be settled before the dress rehearsals. However, the planning is worth the effort if it avoids hectic dress rehearsals and a slipshod performance. "Eventually, why not now?" is an excellent motto for everyone connected with a play to keep in mind, for it is easier to attend to the inevitable details beforehand than on the day of performance.

**Technical rehearsals.** These are the first rehearsals on the stage with complete stage equipment. They are not always possible to arrange and the group sometimes has to go directly from the polishing to the dress rehearsals. Far too often the auditorium is not available until the final week before the first performance.

Ideally, the last two weeks should be on the stage with the cast and stage crew working together. In this way, costumes, make-up, scenery, properties, and furniture can be considered simultaneously, from the standpoint of color, light, and form. A sense of proportion must be maintained at all times, with the dominant element made to stand out by its position or lighting.

The first time the cast and technical crew work together with the set there is likely to be chaos. There will probably be confusion and delays in getting lamps to work, doors to open, curtains to come down exactly on time, and props in the right place at the right time. During these technical rehearsals wardrobe people, callboys, and property people must get their performance duties clearly in mind and their materials organized. Actors should be trained to return props to the appointed tables backstage.

A long technical rehearsal on Saturday of the week before the performance is invaluable. All details of setting, costume, and make-up will not be ready but the essentials should be. A run-through of the whole play with changing of costumes, coordination of all effects, and curtain calls should begin fairly early in the forenoon. The assistant director, stage manager, and prompter work together to keep things going smoothly onstage. The director moves through the auditorium checking sight lines, acoustics, and total effects. The notes he takes should be read to the cast after the final curtain. Every person involved will write down his suggestions.

In the afternoon, weak scenes can be redone, important scenes restaged, and all loose ends and details settled. If possible, photographs should be taken for the press at this time with the leads in costume and make-up.

Crew members secure the pinrail ropes after making a scenery change.

### Dress Rehearsals

If possible, three dress rehearsals should be held, the last with an in-vited audience so that the cast can learn to point lines and hold the action if there is unexpected laughter or applause. An audience at the last dress rehearsal provides an occasion, too, for the house manager and ushers to learn their duties and familiarize themselves with the seating arrangement.

Usually photographs of the cast in various scenes are taken at a dress rehearsal. The picture-taking should be done either before or after the rehearsal so that the timing of the production and the establishment of moods are not interrupted. Every person involved in the dress rehearsals should have an instruction sheet listing the time actors are due for make-up, responsibilities for props, costumes, and stage equipment, and backstage regulations about outsiders who may wish to call or deliver flowers.

The final dress rehearsal should begin on time and go straight to the end without interruption. The cast and crew should be instructed not to correct mistakes obviously, but to go right along adjusting whatever is seriously wrong as best they can while the action continues. The main consideration is to avoid awkward pauses and the repetition of lines or action.

FUNDAMENTALS OF PLAY PRODUCTION     315

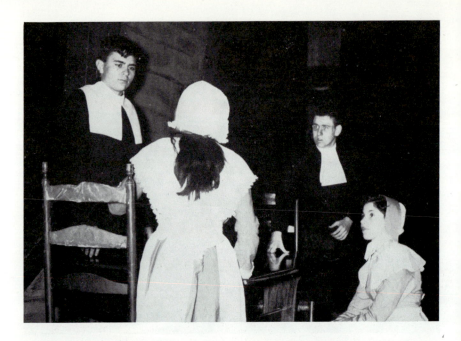

At the final dress rehearsal for a high school production of *The Crucible* everything functions smoothly. Onstage the actors go through the complete play, and
backstage the light crew receives and carries out its instructions.

Backstage organization must be efficient. There must be a chain of command from the director down so that everyone knows what his responsibility is. The director is the final authority. He will usually check the make-up, costumes, props, lights, and stage before he goes out front. Then the assistant director acts in his place, receiving suggestions from or sending questions to the director concerning the lights, furniture, and other matters. Next in command is the stage manager, who has full responsibility for the backstage area. He checks the lights and stage before the curtain goes up, sees that the cast is ready, gets the crew members in their places, and gives the signals for lights, curtain, and sound effects.

The callboy must be sure that the actors are posted on curtains. He should notify them ahead of time and then check to see that they are at entrance points ready for their cues.

The prompter should not be interrupted once the curtain is up. He should have the pauses and lines clearly marked so that he will not be tempted to prompt during a dramatic moment of silence. He must be alert every instant that the play is in progress. Any prompting should be for the actors, not for the audience. The prompter should be not only inaudible but also invisible to the spectators.

When the final dress rehearsal is finished, the actors should leave the dressing rooms in perfect order, put away their make-up, and hang their costumes neatly. The wardrobe mistress can then check to see if any pressing or mending is needed.

After the curtain calls have been rehearsed, the cast should wait for the director backstage. During final rehearsals some directors sit at the back of the house and dictate notes which are written on separate sheets of paper for each performer. As these are given out, the director explains the correction and may ask the actor to run through the line or business. Other directors prefer that the cast write down the comments and remember them. Both cast and crew should feel encouraged and confident after a dress rehearsal. If there is continued cooperation, a good dress rehearsal should insure a satisfactory performance.

*Discussion*

1. Discuss the director as an artist. What similarities exist between painting a picture and putting on a play? Between producing a play and conducting a symphony?

2. What aesthetic principles exist in all the arts? Apply them to the theater.

3. Explain the following terms: giving the actor the stage, topping lines, feeding cues, building a scene, contrasting tempos, holding for laughs, random movement.

4. Why is the actual handling of props, wearing of costumes, and application of make-up at rehearsals of such value? Tell about some unfortunate incidents that have occurred during performances due to lack of this kind of rehearsal.

5. What are the advantages and disadvantages of your school stage with regard to the production of a play?

6. Do you have sufficient backstage room for prop tables, scenery, and dressing rooms? How do you think this area might be used most efficiently?

7. Do you have a stagecraft class? Who conducts it? How is it taught—by the workshop or the lecture method, or a combination of both?

*Applications*

1. Rehearse and discuss *Poor Maddalena* according to the following:
   a. Divide the play into short units or scenes: the opening pantomime, the scene before the entrance of Bumbu, the unlocking of the door, the entrance of Paolo in Scene 2, the love scene, the telling of the news about the American lady, the departure of Paolo, and the final scene.
   b. Have different members of the class direct these scenes, with their own casts. All the principles of directing discussed in this chapter should be applied with special emphasis on the spirit of the scene, the center of interest, effective stage pictures, and—most important of all—consistent, correct, and appealing characterization.
   c. Present the rehearsed scenes and then discuss the following points:
      1) Which actors were the most satisfying as you watched them? Why?
      2) Where do the greatest difficulties lie? Did anything interfere with empathy? If so, what?
      3) In the interpretation of the part of Pierrot, was the character appealing as well as selfish and weak?
      4) In which scene was the best interpretation of Pierrette given? Explain your reasons for feeling it was the best. Were the emotional scenes overacted, underacted, or wisely handled? How did the different directors handle the characterization? Was a distinct difference made in the characterization of Pierrette and Maddalena?
      5) What were your emotional reactions to the various scenes? Were any passages effective enough to remain in your mind after the play was over? Do you like the play better or less than when you read it the first time? Why?
      6) What is your reaction to it as a suitable play for public presentation? In what do you think its chief appeal would lie? What might be some of the dangers and difficulties in staging it successfully?

2. Read Maxwell Anderson's *Joan of Lorraine* and write a report on any similar moments of inspiration you have experienced in your dramatic work.

*Chapter 12*

# Stage Setting
# and Lighting

An appreciation of the significance and beauty of stage settings and the magic of modern lighting is one of the rewards of your dramatic work. With the arrival of color television and the profusion of striking color and lighting effects in the latest motion pictures, you undoubtedly have developed a feeling for the importance of scenic art today.

## SCENIC DESIGN

The class in drama is concerned more with the principles of stage design and scenery than with actual set construction and the operation of lighting equipment. The latter are usually taught in a stagecraft class or are learned by practical experience. There are a number of excellent books listed in Appendix C at the back of this book which will give you the necessary details on designing and constructing scenic backgrounds.

In bringing a play to life, the scenic artist is next to the director in importance. The aim of both is to create a world of make-believe which will be accepted and appreciated by theatergoers. The scenic artist works with mass, line, and color to create an atmosphere. He does not build real rooms, houses, or mountain tops. He does not even create pictures of great beauty in themselves. He uses his painted canvas, magic lights, and artificial effects to stir imaginations so that the audience is transported to the realm where the playwright's dream seems to become a reality.

## Stage Terminology

To help you understand the various phases of scenic design and the kinds of stage equipment which have been developed in the last 350 years, you should be familiar with the following terms:

**acting area**   The portion of the stage used by the actors during the play.

**act curtain**   The curtain, hung just upstage of the footlights, which opens or closes each act or scene.

**apron**   The section of the stage in front of the curtain.

**asbestos curtain**   A fireproof curtain closing off the stage from the auditorium.

**backing**   Flats or drops behind scenery openings to mask the backstage area.

**backdrop**   A large piece of cloth hung at the back of the stage setting.

**backstage**   That part of the stage—left, right, and rear—which is not seen by the audience; also the dressing rooms, prop room, and waiting areas.

**batten**   A long piece of wood or pipe from which scenery and lights are suspended, also used for bracing a flat or weighting a curtain or drop.

**border**   A width of material hung across the stage above the acting area to mask the loft from the audience.

**box set**   A two- or three-wall set composed of canvas flats representing an interior of a room, usually covered by a ceiling.

**brace**   A jointed, adjustable, pole-like support for flats.

**curtain line**   The imaginary floor line the curtain touches when closed.

**cyclorama** or **cyc**   A background curtain hung around the three sides of the stage, either smooth or in folds.

**door stop**   A molding on the door jamb to keep door from swinging.

**drop**   Canvas cloth, fastened at top and bottom to battens, and hung from the grid.

**false proscenium**   A frame built inside the proscenium arch to reduce the width of the stage opening and designed to be in harmony with the atmosphere of the play.

**flat**   A piece of rigid upright scenery, a wooden frame covered with canvas.

**flies** or **loft**   The area above the stage in which scenery is hung so that the audience cannot see it.

**floor plan**   A drawing showing exactly how the scenery will be placed.

**fly**   To raise or lower scenery.

**gauze**   A large net curtain, which seems almost opaque when lit from the front and semi-transparent when lit from behind.

**grand drapery**   A border at the top of the proscenium used to lower the height of the stage.

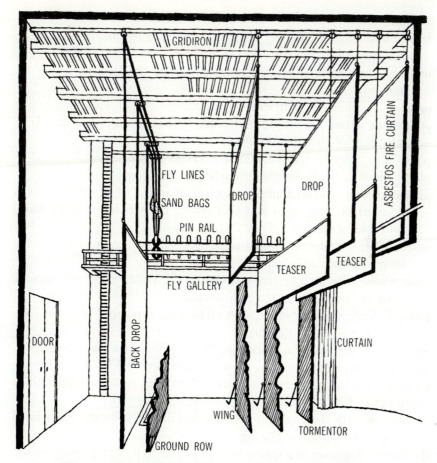

GRIDIRON

FLY LINES

SAND BAGS

PIN RAIL

FLY GALLERY

DROP

DROP

TEASER

TEASER

ASBESTOS FIRE CURTAIN

DOOR

BACK DROP

CURTAIN

WING

TORMENTOR

GROUND ROW

Diagram showing the positions of standard stage equipment

**greenroom**   A backstage lounge used as a reception or waiting room for the actors.

**gridiron** or **grid**   A series of heavy beams just under the roof of the stage, to which are attached the sheaves or blocks through which lines pass to raise or lower scenery.

**grip**   A stagehand.

**ground cloth** or **floor cloth**   A canvas covering the floor of the acting area.

**ground row**   A low profile of scenery which can stand by itself, used to mask the bottom of the cyc or backdrop.

**jog**   A narrow flat, usually less than two feet in width, used to form such things as alcoves and bay windows.

**lash line**  Sash cord used for lashing flats together.

**legs**  Pieces of cloth, usually hung in pairs, stage left and stage right, to mask the backstage area.

**masking**  Any piece of scenery used to conceal the backstage from the audience.

**parallel**  A collapsible platform.

**permanent setting**  A setting that remains the same throughout a play, regardless of change of locale.

**places**  An order for actors and crew to get to their positions.

**plastic piece**  A three-dimensional article or structure.

**practical-usable**  Terms applied to such parts of the set as doors and windows which must open and shut during the action and stairs which must bear a person's weight.

**profile**  The irregular edge of any piece of scenery such as branches of trees, shapes of rocks and skylines.

**proscenium**  The arch or frame enclosing the visible stage, the opening between the stage and the auditorium.

**rake**  To slant or set at an angle. A raked stage is inclined from the footlights to the rear of the stage.

**ramp**  A sloping platform connecting the stage floor to a higher level.

**returns**  Two pieces of scenery set downstage right and left to mask.

**set piece**  Individual pieces of scenery such as trees, rocks, and walls which stand by themselves.

**sky cyc**  Smooth cloth hung at the back and sides of the stage and painted to give the illusion of the sky.

**sky dome**  A quarter of a sphere built in plaster to make a permanent sky.

**stagecraft**  The art and craft of putting on a production.

**strike**  The stage manager's order to remove an object or objects from the stage or to store the set.

**teaser**  A short drop hung behind the act curtain, regulating the height of the stage opening and masking the front batten of onstage lights.

**tormentors**  Side pieces—flats or drapes—just back of the proscenium.

**traveler**  A stage curtain which opens at the middle of the stage and moves to the right and left, rather than one which moves up and down.

**wagons**  Low platforms, on casters.

**wings**  The offstage areas to the right and left of the set; also, one or more flats, usually hinged at an angle but sometimes parallel to the footlights, used as entrances onstage and to conceal backstage areas.

**wing setting**  A setting made with pairs of wings on both sides of the stage, used with a matching backdrop.

# The Evolution of Scenic Design

Throughout the history of the theater, technicians, inventors, and designers have devoted themselves to developing practical means of visualizing plays. Their improvement of both scenery and lighting has been of immeasurable service to all playgoers, playwrights, directors, and actors.

**Early history.** Stage design as we know it came into being in Italy in 1508 at the royal court of the Duke of Ferrara. The stage there was modeled on the ancient Roman theaters, solidly built and heavily decorated with elaborate niches, columns, and statues. One such Renaissance stage, the famous Teatro Olimpico, is perfectly preserved in Vicenza. It was the theater of the Olympian Academy and is sometimes known as The Palladian, after the architect Andrea Palladio, who made the initial designs. In 1585 Palladio's pupil Vincenzo Scamozzi placed perspective paintings of streets behind the entrances. The streets were lined with buildings covered with statues of diminishing size. The amazing effect is that of a city stretching into the distance. Because there is no backstage lighting, the perspectives are illuminated in daytime by the light from the theater's windows. The whole auditorium looks like an ancient Roman theater roofed over and surrounded by immense columns and lifesize

The interior of the Teatro Olimpico, in which the illusion of depth was created by placing perspective paintings of streets behind the entrances.

STAGE SETTING AND LIGHTING    323

statues. The space for the audience is in a crescent shape which joins the stage at the extreme left and right. The acting area is in front of the columned entrances.

In his fascinating book *The Theatre*, Sheldon Cheney traces the development of the proscenium arch from the large central entrance of The Palladian. He says that the arch, as we know it, was initially used in "the first modern theatre," the Farnese Theatre of Parma, erected in 1618. Here, an elaborate architectural structure surrounded a frame with a curtain. Behind this frame, the actors performed against painted scenes. The circular audience area was later replaced by chairs arranged in a horseshoe around a flat space like our arena stages of today. Still later, tiered seats filled in this space, the stage was raised, and our modern theater was established.

Painted scenes, often with buildings in perspective, had been used in ballrooms as backgrounds for court plays. Gradually artists supplanted the heavy wood and plaster sets with painted canvas ones, and scenic painters came into their own.

**Later developments.** During the seventeenth and eighteenth centuries, designers continued to build theaters with formalized, architectural, permanent settings. Painters followed their own inclinations in painting pictures for the sets. There was no effort made to create an artistic scenic unit for any given play. It was up to the actors and director to produce the proper atmosphere. The stages were very large in comparison with modern ones and the use of vanishing perspectives continued, with street scenes and forests fading off into the distance. Wing settings, which could be extended indefinitely in number, were widely used.

In the nineteenth century an effort was made to suit the scenery to the play. However, typical interior sets were still made of canvas drops and wings painted to represent walls, windows, curtains, furniture, potted palms, mirrors, and all the other details of a conservatory or parlor. Exterior scenes were also painted. For example, the conventional gardens and forests were replete with painted trees, shrubs, fountains, gates, and pathways. Street scenes had painted buildings, store windows, signs, and street lamps. Entrances were made through wings parallel to the back wall. These were often painted like the backdrop with furniture and draperies for interiors or cut-out greenery for exteriors. Some of these sets are still used in isolated "opery" houses, and imitations are made for revivals of the old-fashioned melodramas.

Things changed with the coming of realistic drama in the latter part of the nineteenth century. The flapping canvas wings and backdrops, painted with doors and windows and illogical shadows, were no longer serviceable. In addition, the director was becoming a power in the theater, responsible for the unity of the entire production. He needed a scenic artist to help interpret the spirit of a play. André Antoine in France and David Belasco in the United States are the two men most often associated with the realistic style, which became known as *naturalism*. Although photographically accurate, the mass of detail Belasco used in his plays distracted the attention of the audience from the situations. The spectator sometimes found himself poring over the contents of a what-not shelf and ignoring the activities of the actors. However, the solid walls, furniture, and practical windows and doors made interiors entirely livable. In the exterior settings, three-dimensional rocks, trees, and even buildings all worked toward making the realistic drama ring true. With the creation of an interior-exterior set, a building with removable walls, it even became possible to see action going on in several rooms at the same time.

## Contemporary Scenic Design

Today most of the plays you will see use *selective realism* in stage design. This modified form of realism developed because the many naturalistic details of the earlier method were confusing and distracting. Most designers now choose certain details to give the impression of actuality and discard others which may tend to over-emphasize realism.

**This set for the Rollins College production of *Pygmalion* is an example of realism in scenic design.**

*Courtesy of ANTA*

For interiors, all essential entrances, balconies, stairways, doors, and windows are built into a three-sided room, usually set at an angle rather than squarely on the stage in the old-fashioned manner. The fourth wall between the actors and audience is, of course, imaginary. Its presence is suggested by placing the furniture about centers of interest, sometimes with chairs and settees turned with their backs to the footlights. The onlooker sees a real room or house as it would look if one wall had been removed. An artistic color scheme is maintained in background, furnishings, and costumes. Natural sources of light are made apparent by the effective use of the fine lighting equipment available today. The stage set becomes an ideal background for the author's theme and a pleasing picture for the audience to enjoy. At the same time, it represents the actual living quarters of people and discloses their taste, financial status, cultural level, and habits of living.

Exterior sets are usually best suggested by practical and cut-out pieces against a sky cyc or back wall painted to simulate the sky. A "cut-out" tree trunk has only the thickness of its material. A "practical" tree is built

A scene from *Death of a Salesman*. In designing this set, Jo Mielziner selected details that would create the atmosphere of the Loman home but would not distract attention from the play itself.

Graphic House, Inc.

in the round and actually is used in some way. Other exterior pieces include rocks, walls, trellises, and house fronts. The illusion of a distant horizon or skyline is achieved by a *ground row* which masks the floor line of the sky drop. It is usually painted in natural colors. The tendency today is to avoid the use of the old-fashioned wings. Irregularly grouped trees are usually substituted.

You should be familiar not only with selective realism but also with some of the other types of contemporary stage design. The twentieth-century theater has profited from wide experimentation in scenic design. Some of the results are to be seen in the remarkably fine sets used in university and community productions.

The first decade of this century saw the rise of Adolph Appia in Germany and of Gordon Craig in England and Italy. These two men protested against realism by working with simple lines, mass, and color under luminous light. Their aim was to create symbolic sets which would interpret the essential message of the drama. Craig went so far as to suggest the use of super-marionettes in preference to living actors. Had his ideas been accepted, the actor, playwright, and stage director might ultimately have been eliminated, leaving a scenic artist the god of all things theatrical.

Appia and Craig's revolutionary ideas were carried out in this country in a modified form, especially in productions of the plays of the great American dramatist Eugene O'Neill. Flexible sets were made of screens, platforms, columns, and stairs. Psychologically meaningful lighting and color schemes expressed the spirit and mood of the plays. The staging was in direct contrast to the lifelike physical detail of the realistic style.

In twentieth-century Europe and America, the new ideas developed gradually into several major styles. You will want to know something about the distinctive qualities of these.

*Symbolism*, in scenic design, is the visualization of a play's idea or atmosphere through special scenic treatment. For instance, a lone, twisted tree might represent a wasteland and also suggest barrenness in the hearts of central characters. Effective lighting can also be used in symbolism. For example, a lowering shadow can represent an approaching disaster—emotional or real. A shaft of light through a colored window can indicate a great cathedral.

*Expressionism* is exaggerated symbolism which strives to intensify the emotional impact of a play by distorting a scenic element. For instance, in *The Adding Machine* one of the scenic pieces is a gigantic adding machine. Its size emphasizes the fact that it dominates the lives of the central characters.

Photo by Vandamm

**In the Mielziner set for W***interset,* **the height of the buildings and the hugeness of the bridge support have a symbolic relationship to the overpowering and tragic situation the central character faces.**

*Impressionism* seeks to make the audience react and see as a character does when he is stirred by such intense feelings as anger, horror, and fear. Unusual rhythms, exaggeration of minor details, and violent contrasts of light and design are used. They enable the theatergoer to see through the character's eyes and actually realize the impressions he is receiving.

All three of these methods—symbolism, expressionism, and impressionism—demand great artistry, for the designer must put intangible responses into concrete form by means of canvas, lumber, light, and paint.

*Constructivism* is a technique which uses an architectural or mechanical skeleton as a background for plays which deal with economic and social problems. The set often consists of a number of platforms connected by stairs, ladders, ramps, and arches, allowing the action to take place upon different levels.

Originated by Vsevolod Meyerhold in Russia, constructivism is one of the most interesting of the modern methods. Meyerhold dressed all of his actors in a nondescript cover-all type of costume and trained them to move with precise movement. He used the various levels of the sets to

A scene from *The Adding Machine,* showing Mr. Zero on the keys of the machine which has taken over his position. The exaggerated size of the machine is an example of expressionism in scenic design.

represent different states of mind and society. His technique has been used in other theaters in a modified form, for this method can help to create a background for any play a director may wish to produce. Lee Simonson's set for O'Neill's play *Dynamo* most nearly approximated this form of design. *Dynamo* presents the tragedy of a modern soul lost in a mechanical civilization. The set actually was a necessary background for the action of the play which ended in the death of the hero caught in the machine. For a complete explanation of constructivist techniques, you might read Norris Houghton's *Moscow Rehearsals.*

**Designers.** In the first half of this century, America has produced some of the most sensitive and brilliant scenic artists in the theatrical world—such men as Robert Edmond Jones, Lee Simonson, Norman Bel Geddes, Jo Mielziner, Donald Oenslager, Howard Bay, Mordecai Gorelik, and Peter Larkin. Their chief aim has been to reflect the mood of a play by nonrealistic backgrounds of great simplicity which are thoroughly in keeping with the message of the play. You can see photographs of their sets in such books as *Stage Design Around the World Since 1935,* published by the In-

The Cleveland Play House used this constructivist setting in its production of *The Field God*.

ternational Theatre Institute, and in old and new copies of *Theatre Arts* magazine.

Today most designers avoid both extreme realism and obscure abstraction. Instead, they try to create an atmosphere which will touch the imagination of actor and spectator and enable them to enter the emotional life of the character. Many effective staging methods are being used today. The space stage does not employ realistic scenery but uses sharply defined light to create locales, often against a black background. In the *unit setting*, a structural piece such as a wall, column, platform, or stairway is used in different positions to create new locales (see page 332). The *skeleton setting* is still another method. Here a frame of scenery is used with different doors or openings or pieces to change locales.

**Theater buildings.** You will probably see an entirely new form of theater building during your lifetime. The theaters in the cities, with shallow stages and cramped backstage areas, are almost all outmoded. Because real estate in urban areas is so expensive, it is impossible to erect the kind of building envisioned by modern architects. It is on the university and college campuses and in many of the newest high schools that you will find the finest theaters. More and more schools are being equipped with small classroom stages, small auditoriums (connected with the backstage area of the large auditorium or having their own backstage areas), and large, perfectly equipped auditoriums and stages. There is frequently an outdoor theater in addition, together with rehearsal halls, work and storage areas, and the latest equipment for moving and storing sets and costumes. Approximately two thousand of these campus theaters are in operation, and there are hundreds of smaller-scale community theaters which are almost as well planned. With new theaters will come new forms of plays written especially for their stages (many without the proscenium arch), and the directors and designers will find new forms of scenic art, perhaps carried out in plastics, metals, and glass rather than canvas and wood.

## Discussion

1. As you have watched television, how have the settings interested you?

2. Have you seen any stage plays in which the sets have been outstanding? If so, describe them.

3. Refer to the types of drama discussed in Chapter 5 and decide what style of scenic design would be most appropriate for each.

4. What new terms have you come to know in this section? Give brief definitions for each of them.

5. In what ways does a scenic artist help to bring a play to life?

6. Movie musicals usually have elaborate dance sequences. Describe the types of scenic design used in several of them.

7. Have you seen any television shows or films using types of stage design other than realistic? If so, describe them.

## Applications

1. As a class arrange a visit to the best equipped theater in your community and make a study of both front and backstage areas.

2. As a class prepare individual reports on the various styles of stage design from the books on play production in Appendix C.

3. Read a play and then select the style of design you would apply to it. In a written report, describe this style and explain your reasons for choosing it.

Henry Kurth designed this setting for an off-Broadway production of James Forsyth's *Heloise*. His clever use of the unit setting made it possible to have five effective changes of locale in a very tiny stage area. As you look at Mr. Kurth's drawings, notice how he has employed a single flat to create changes of scene.

# PROCEDURES IN SCENIC DESIGN

The basic principle of scenic design is that the designer must reproduce and enhance the playwright's and director's intentions and create a background for the action which does not intrude on that action. A set can be beautiful, clever, or startling, but if it disregards this principle, it no longer fulfills its function.

Before making any plan, the designer discusses the play and its style of production with the director. He then makes a pencil sketch which scenically expresses the meaning and spirit of the play. After considering available equipment and material and the budget, he enlarges this sketch into a stage drawing to scale. Next he works out a detailed floor plan—an exact diagram showing the position and size of entrances, windows, fireplaces, stairways, the backing for all doors and windows, and any pieces of plastic scenery or ground rows to be used. The furniture may be included in the original floor plan or in one made after rehearsals have started. Sets should be planned so that they may be set up and struck rapidly, carried easily, and packed away efficiently. Naturally, they should be built firmly enough to stand steadily. They also should allow the actors to move easily and safely and to be seen effectively.

## Basic Principles

Unity and emphasis are the two most important design principles to keep in mind. *Unity* demands that all elements of the design unite to form a perfect whole centering about the main idea of the play. Everything which is not essential to the meaning of the play or its production should be eliminated. All furniture and properties must be in keeping with the background and, if possible, be a part of the stage design in period and composition. Overstuffed, ponderous pieces covered with dull plush give a sense of stodgy smugness. Delicate gilt and gay brocade suggest frivolous enjoyment. Severe, straight patterns in neutral tones show puritanical repression. Futuristic shapes and extreme colors create a feeling of restlessness.

*Emphasis* demands that the object by which the audience is to be impressed should attract attention. The center of interest—a chair, table, throne, balcony—can be emphasized by placing it in a prominent position, making it the focus of all lines of interest, and by playing light on it. Everything else on the stage should be subordinated to the center of interest.

Proportion and balance must also be considered, for the empathic response to a setting is strongly affected by the correct use of these elements.

*Proportion* demands that the human being be taken as the unit of measurement. In realistic plays line and mass are scaled to man's actual size. In symbolic sets, however, line and mass must demonstrate the relationship between man and outside forces. For example, characters may seem to be dwarfed by rocks, huge columns, or towering buildings. The use of lines alters the sense of proportion and affects the observer psychologically. Curves and angles, usually combined with strongly contrasted colors, give a sense of intense excitement. Long vertical lines in draperies, columns, or costumes suggest dignity; they may be used for cathedrals, temples, and solemn places. Horizontal lines have the opposite effect.

Except in stylized settings, asymmetrical or informal balance is preferable to symmetrical. In any case, the center line must not be forgotten, and the two halves of the stage picture must *balance*, or attract equal interest. The director and scenic artist must work closely together because the position, number, and importance of the people on stage form an intrinsic part of the scenic pattern. For example, a strong character, who is to exemplify spiritual leadership and be the center of interest in a scene, can be placed on a height to one side against tall columns, a high arched doorway, or long drapes, with the other characters, perhaps a large crowd, below him. The importance of the strong character's influence in the minds of the audience will offset the numbers of the crowd, and the stage picture will balance.

## Model Settings

Most scenic artists make scale models for each scene. In your class you should have the experience of making and working with at least one such stage setting.

If your classroom is not already equipped with an electrically wired model stage, one should be made. Plan your stage to scale—1 inch to 1 foot is an excellent size, neither too small nor too large for practical settings. If possible, the model should be made in the school shops. The wiring should be properly checked, the curtain should function, and details should be worked out so that they are technically correct. Small strings of colored lights may be used. If possible, arrange to have three circuits of lights, one for green, one for red, and one for blue, so you can try out the effects of light on pigments and materials and gain some understanding of lighting problems.

In constructing your setting, first analyze the theme and moods of your play and settle upon the most suitable style of design. Then make your floor plan to scale, working out the necessary entrances, windows, and such structures as fireplaces and stairs. If you want to make figures to represent your characters, plan them in proportion to the set and furniture to be used.

You can make your setting out of cardboard, plastic wood, or actual wood or plaster. It should contain every detail of design and color, as well as the furniture, lamps, and props. Be especially careful to make the doors, windows, fireplaces, wall designs, and other such details to scale. Also be sure light can enter from backstage and overhead.

## The Use of Color

Color is one of the most important elements of staging, for the various colors and their combinations produce very different emotional effects. The relationship between characters or scenes and colors used may be determining factors in a play's success. On the stage, color effects are achieved by playing colored lights on the pigments used in sets, costumes, and stage furnishings. Because colored light makes very definite and often surprising changes in the appearance of pigment, it is necessary to experiment with both to get the result you want. Though this may be a long and involved process, you will find it fascinating to see what happens to fabrics and painted surfaces under different lighting.

In all of your work with color, remember that you are seeking to arouse an emotional response by using a color scheme which interprets the spirit and mood of each scene. However, before you begin you should have some knowledge of the nature of color and the ways in which it can be used to best advantage. In the following paragraphs only a brief introduction to the subject is given. This introduction can and should be supplemented by reading in the color and lighting sections of the books on play production listed in Appendix C.

In pigment, the *primary colors* are yellow, blue, and red. The *secondary colors* are orange, the combination of red and yellow; green, of yellow and blue; and purple, of blue and red. When dealing with light, the primaries are green, blue, and red. The secondaries are yellow, blue-green, and purple.

Colors differ from each other in hue, value, and intensity. *Hues* are the various colors seen in the spectrum of a beam of light which passes through a prism. Black is the absence of color; white is the fusion of colors. In daylight many colors are present. As light falls on different surfaces, the colors are absorbed or reflected. A surface that absorbs all the colors and reflects none is black. A surface that absorbs all the hues but green appears to be green because it reflects only that color.

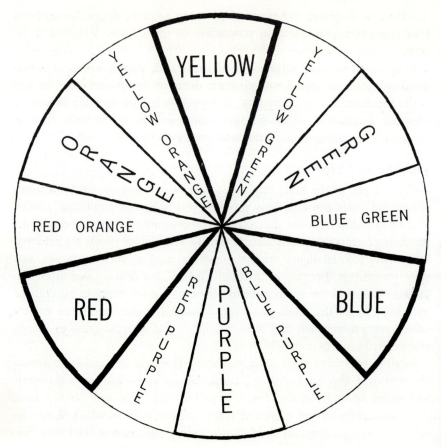

Diagram of a color wheel for pigment

The *value* of a color is determined by the amount of black or white mixed with it. Light or pastel colors contain a good deal of white. Dark or deep colors contain more black. The light colors are generally expressive of youth, gaiety, and informality. Dark colors suggest dignity, seriousness, and repose. Each color is said to have a *value scale*, running from white at one end to black at the other. Hues near the white end of a value scale stand out against a black background, while hues near the black end of a scale are most strongly contrasted against white. If a costume or prop is to be emphasized, it should be placed against a background of different value or hue. If it is to be made inconspicuous, it should be shown against a background of its own value or hue so that it, in effect, disappears.

*Intensity* is the brightness or dullness of a color. You can usually intensify a color by casting on it a light of the same color. Intensity will be lessened if you use a light of its complementary color. The *complementary color* for any one of the primary colors is achieved by mixing together the other two primaries. Thus purple is the complement of yellow; orange, of blue; and green, of red.

A color wheel is an invaluable aid in designing, for it shows the relationships of the various hues. The colors next to each other on the wheel are said to be *analogous*. For example, yellow, yellow-orange, and orange are analogous since they all contain yellow. The same principle applies to each color of the wheel. The colors directly opposite each other on the wheel are said to be *complementary*.

Since neither pigments nor materials for coloring lights are apt to have pure color, endless experiments are required to get a desired effect. You can experiment with the effect of light on pigment on your model stage and settings. Run through the color cycle of night to day—black, pale gray, light yellow, light red, deep red, orange, and full daylight. Then reverse this cycle and run from daylight to darkness through the sunset hues, ending with the green conventionally used to simulate moonlight on the stage.

Colors are referred to as "warm" or "cool." Yellow, red, and orange are the warm colors. You see them in sunlight and fire. Blue, blue-green, and purple are the cool colors. You see them in deep pools and leafy shadows. Warm hues are said to advance, or move forward in space, because they attract attention quickly. Cool colors recede because they are less noticeable. A stage background painted in warm colors appears smaller because it seems nearer, while one painted in cool colors looks larger. A warm-colored costume or object generally catches the eye at once and looks important. Objects or persons dressed in cool colors are generally less noticeable to the audience. The warm colors are stimulating and exciting, appropriate for emotional scenes. Cool colors give a sense of tranquility. Too much of the former can be very irritating and too much of the latter depressing.

The psychological effect of color has been made the subject of interesting experimentation. It is an accepted fact that different hues of various intensity exert definite influence and produce emotional responses. However, authorities do not agree on the exact nature of the effects on different people. On the stage certain traditions are accepted, based on known reactions to color. Their use is an important means of getting satisfactory empathic responses in play production.

The following emotional values have been traditionally assigned to colors, and these color meanings are useful in stage design:

> Blue—calm, cold, formal, spiritual, pure, depressing
> Orange—exhilarating, cheerful
> Scarlet—aggressive, passionate
> Yellow—cheerful, happy
> Pale pink—fanciful, romantic
> Soft green—restful, soothing, cool
> Purple—mournful, mystic, regal
> Gray—neutral, depressing, negative, somber
> Brown—earthy
> Black—melancholic, tragic, gloomy

In any stage set there should be a controlling color scheme which carries out the predominant mood and atmosphere of the production. The most effective schemes are those which give a single impression, although other colors are often used for contrast. For example, the over-all feeling may be one of warmth but there may be an accent of coolness. When the design features analogous hues, a dash of a complementary color will give emphasis to the stage picture. "Color clashes" are often used deliberately to achieve a particular effect.

Frequently paintings or other works of art will be the inspiration for the composition or color scheme of a stage picture. The influence may be detected in the costumes, lighting, settings, and properties. Most designers keep voluminous scrapbooks with colored illustrations to suggest effective use of color, subordination, harmony, contrast, and other details of design.

A brief description of an experimental color scheme which was highly effective will illustrate how color can be used in planning a stage picture. Whimsicality against a background of intense hate and suspicion was to be suggested by the setting for *Shall We Join the Ladies?* by James M. Barrie. The color scheme was composed of analogous hues running from pale yellow to vivid scarlet. The youngest woman was dressed in light yellow organdy, the most sophisticated one in brilliant scarlet chiffon with crystal jewelry, the oldest in golden-brown velvet, the most hysterical in orange silk, the most placid in dull gold lace, the others in prints which held the various hues together. One military costume had white trousers and a brilliant scarlet coat trimmed with gold. The black of the men's dinner suits set off the brilliance of the women's gowns. A large bowl of fruit on the sideboard repeated the yellow, orange, and red of the costumes. The furniture was carved and heavy. The walls were a neutral gray. The amber light, which remained unchanged, was focused from a gilded bronze chandelier upon the circular table where the thirteen characters were seated. The color contrast was provided by a cool green light in a moonlit sky seen through a French window. The window was hung with rich, gold velour curtains draped to carry attention toward the head of the table. Here the leading character, an elderly little man in a high carved chair, formed the center of attention. All lines of interest centered on him except when some other characters momentarily held the attention.

## Set Backgrounds

The *set backgrounds* in most school productions are of three types: painted box sets, draperies, and screens. Only general information concerning them is of value to a class in drama. If you are interested in set construction, join the stage crew or attend any classes in which the carpentry work for theatrical productions is done. The planning, building, sizing, and painting of scenery and its rapid and efficient handling in productions is one of the school theater's most challenging activities. Any experience you can gain in creating workable and artistic settings will prove very worthwhile. Printed directions and information on stagecraft are included in several of the books in the Play Production section of Appendix C.

An adjustable *box set* is the most practical form of painted scenery because it is suitable for the average modern play, the type most often presented. In fact, for interiors it is indispensable. It can be varied in shape by interchanging flats and using different curtains and furniture. It will give long service if it is properly constructed of good materials.

For a box set, it is advisable to have the flats vary in width—4-foot, 3-foot, and 2-foot—to permit changing the shape and appearance of the room. There should be at least two window flats to carry either the window or bookcase units, two door flats, and two flats hinged into a French door. The detachable units to go with these pieces include two window frames, two window sashes, two bookcases, two doors and door frames, one set of French doors and frames, and a fireplace. Stairways, platforms, and a ceiling, if possible, should also be constructed.

*Draperies* or curtains have been exceedingly popular as backgrounds in school auditoriums. They are adaptable for many stage settings and also furnish an excellent background for lectures and ordinary programs. However, they are a poor substitute for box sets in most contemporary plays. They are more effective for fantasies, experimental dramas, and pageants. They should be made of a dull cloth with a heavy finish so that they will drape well, be opaque, and reflect no light. Cotton, velvet, bur-

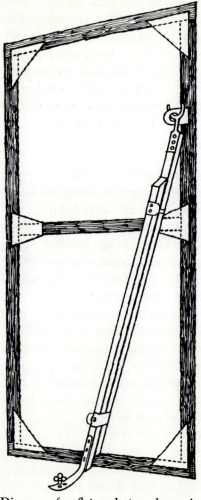

lap, rep, velour, flannel, and lined monk's cloth are commonly used for this purpose. Light tan, gray, and blue are useful, but black is often the most effective. These curtains should be made in separate strips from 4 to 6 feet in width, webbed at the top and weighted at the bottom so they will not move easily.

They may be hung in a multitude of ways. With each piece overlapped, they can be used as a solid curtain for a stage of any size. They can be used in a semicircle or in irregular patterns. They can be combined with scenery. They can be draped up to form exits and entrances.

A most satisfactory reversible cyclorama can be made of pieces of natural-colored monk's cloth lined with black sateen with two sets of borders and four half-pieces to use above doors and windows. This furnishes two sets of drapes, one of a neutral color and one of black. These can be combined to give many different effects in many different types of settings. This type

Diagram of a flat and stage brace in use.

of cyclorama adapts itself very well to a skeleton set of arches, platforms, screens, and steps.

A set for *Death Takes a Holiday* utilized sections of a beige cyclorama. The center of interest was an immense window towering out of sight. Arched doorways on either side framed the stairway and entrance hall. This simple set, furnished with authentic pieces of fine Italian furniture, created the illusion of the Villa Happiness better than a more realistic one.

*Screens*, the third type of background, are always helpful in the classroom. They can be arranged in any number of ways to give the impression of walls, houses, and doorways. They may be realistic, stylized, or expressionistic in design, but they must be interesting in shape, size, and color.

The *space stage* is often an appropriate background for plays which do not have to be given realistic treatment. It is planned to give the impression of an absolute void. A plaster dome or black cyclorama often serves as the only backing and the acting areas are defined by light. Step units, ramps, and platforms are used. Upon them the action moves in an uninterrupted flow from one lighted area to another.

The *formal stage* is one which has a permanent neutral background that remains the same throughout the action of the entire play. This background can be a platform, a step unit, or a draped cyclorama. It is similar to the backgrounds used in staging Shakespearean and Greek dramas.

Thornton Wilder's *Our Town* and Orson Welles' production of *Julius Caesar* eliminated all scenery and used bare stages. The success of these productions proved that the meaning of a fine play can be presented by first-class actors under a good director whatever background is employed.

## Scene Shifting

Scenic designers of multiple-set plays must include arrangements for scene changing in their plans. There are many ways to change sets effectively and rapidly on the legitimate stage. Revolving stages have triangular sections which permit a change of set while a scene is being viewed. Elevators bring up different sets from beneath the stage. Space stages have small sets on different levels which can be illuminated separately or simultaneously. Wagon stages are also used to transport sets.

## Summary of Procedures

Whatever style of scenic art is employed, the modern director and his scenic artist must work together in accord with principles that govern all forms of art. Unity must be observed in the settings, costumes, and acting so that all elements combine to present the main idea of the play. Balance and proportion must be kept at all times. One side of the stage must not be made to look heavier than the other by a concentration of large pieces of furniture, masses of scenery, or groups of people. This is not always a matter of physical balance or symmetry. Sometimes the importance of a single character can balance an entire mob. Size, color, movement, and brilliance of illumination also affect the balance of the stage picture. Emphasis must be kept constantly in mind. A character or object may be made to stand out by means of contrasting color, by holding the center of the stage, or by being the focus of all lines of direction.

*Discussion*

1. Explain the use of color on the stage. Are you conscious of the emotional effect of color? Give examples of your response to color on the stage and tell whether or not the response was satisfying and why.

2. Explain the characteristic differences between hue, value, and intensity in color.

3. Study the color wheel on page 336 and explain its value in scenic design. What is meant by analogous colors? By complementary colors?

4. Do you think a familiarity with the problems of scenic design will add to or detract from your pleasure as a theatergoer? Why?

5. Explain the importance of the scenic artist in a production.

*Applications*

1. Reread *Poor Maddalena* and plan the two stage settings. Carefully read the suggestions of the author, and then plan how you would carry them out if you were the scenic artist for the production. Consider the following points:

    a. How would you design the background for the land of fantasy against which Pierrot and Pierrette are posed when the curtains open? Why is this an important consideration?

    b. How would you represent the moon? Where would it be? How would it be made? The trapdoor? The key?

    c. Would you have the rose be a single blossom, or would you use rose-bushes as a part of your scenic design? Design some stylized rosebushes, not in the least realistic, which might be an intrinsic part of your stage design.

    d. What colors would you use in the setting for the first and third scenes? Why? How would you utilize them?

    e. The second scene must be strictly realistic. Plan the exact background and furniture you would use. In making your plans look at photographs depicting an average Italian home.

    f. What props would you use to give an Italian atmosphere?

    g. What colors would you use in the second scene? Why?

    h. How might you design the scenery so that a complete change of set between scenes would not be necessary?

2. Try to arrange a class theater party for a stage production, either amateur or professional. Focus your attention and later class discussion on the scenic design in all its phases.

3. Draw up plans for three permanent set backings for your high school stage. Explain the advantages and disadvantages of each.

4. As a class, construct a model stage rigged with individual electrical circuits for red, green, and blue lights. Have every member of the class make a floor plan to scale and design a stage setting for a particular scene in a play. Show each set under the lights from daylight through sunset to night.

**5.** Have an exhibit of all the sets made in the class. Long tables can be set up and a roll of white corrugated paper cut with proscenium openings to fit each set arranged on them.

**6.** From the books in Appendix C prepare and deliver reports on the following:

> How to Make Flats
> Methods of Painting Scenery
> How to Use Drapes for Plastic Effects
> The Use of Platforms in Stage Design
> Styles in Modern Scenic Design

**7.** Plan a symbolic, expressionistic, or realistic design for any one scene from a Shakespearean play.

## STAGE LIGHTING

Stage lighting is a modern development in the history of the theater. Until the sixteenth century, all dramatic performances were held outdoors and in daylight. Torches and candles were introduced to indicate the night. In the early part of the seventeenth century, after the construction of indoor theaters, lamps with reflectors were used for stage illumination. In 1803 the introduction of gaslights was an important step in the use of light for dramatic effect, but the fire hazard was a great disadvantage.

**From the crude lamps used in the theater 300 years ago, lighting equipment has developed into the complicated array of lights, battens, and ropes pictured here.**

Photo by George E. Joseph

Electricity made its debut toward the end of the nineteenth century and revolutionized stage lighting. At the turn of the century, Adolph Appia used electric light as a means of interpreting moods and a method of scenic design to arouse emotional responses. Since then, progress has been rapid. Today stage lighting does more than any other element to create the proper atmosphere and set the shifting moods of a play.

## Lighting Terminology

You should be familiar with the lighting equipment in your school, and, if you ever do any backstage work, you will need to know some of the terms used by lighting technicians.

**amperage**  The strength of an electric current flowing through a wire.

**border lights** or **borders**  Rows of lamps in long, compartmentalized troughs which are hung by chains from pipe battens above the stage.

**cable**  Heavily insulated wire for joining instruments to electrical outlets or a switchboard.

**circuit**  The complete path of an electric current.

**color frames**  Metal holders which fit into a lighting instrument to keep a color filter in place.

**connectors**  Devices for joining cables to each other, or cables to instruments.

**dimmer**  An electrical device which controls the amount of current flowing into a lighting instrument, thus increasing or decreasing the intensity of the light.

**ellipsoidal reflector spotlight**  A highly effective lighting instrument with a reflector shaped like an ellipsoid.

**floodlight** or **flood**  A lighting instrument in a metal box, open at one side, whose inner surface is painted a flat white to diffuse the light. Lamps used vary from 500 to 1,500 watts. They can be hung from battens overhead, placed on the floor, or supported on a standard.

**footlights** or **foots**  Trough lights along the front of the apron to throw light up and back toward the acting area.

**fresnel**  A highly efficient spotlight, featuring a lens designed in a series of concentric circles, which projects a clear, strong light with a soft edge.

**fuse**  A protective device set in an electric current and destroyed by the passage of excessive current.

**gelatin** and **glass roundels**  Transparent color media placed on lighting instruments to produce different colors.

**kill light**  Command to turn a light off.

**light plot**  Diagram showing the placing of the instruments and plugging system, and where the beams from all the instruments fall.

**light cue sheet**  The lighting technician's guide for all dimmer readings and settings at act or scene openings and all lighting changes.

**linnebach projector**  A lantern for projecting images from a slide onto a backdrop from the rear of the backdrop.

**load**  The wattage of lights and electrical pieces of equipment supplied by one circuit; an overload will burn out a fuse.

**spotlight** or **spot**  A metal-encased lighting instrument which gives out a concentrated light and can be directed specifically. It is used to light acting areas. In wattage, it varies from 250–400 (baby spot) to 1,500–2,000.

**strip lights** or **strips**  Lamps arranged in metal troughs, mainly used for lighting cycs or backings.

**switchboard**  The panel which holds the dimmers, switches, and fuses. Ideally all stage circuits are united in this one board so that they may be switched on and off by one operator. A board may have any number of circuits and/or dimmers. A portable switchboard is often the most satisfactory type for the school theater.

**throw**  The distance from a lighting instrument to the area to be lit.

**voltage**  The force with which electric current goes through a wire.

**wattage**  The measurement of electric power; all lighting instruments, lamps, dimmers, and fuses are given wattage ratings to denote their electrical capacities.

## Necessary Equipment

Flexibility is the chief aim in choosing lighting equipment. This requires equipment which is not permanently mounted and can be utilized in different ways for different purposes. If you ever have the responsibility of purchasing lights for a church, school, or club stage, put your money first in good spots and cables. Don't purchase anything without consulting the latest catalogues of electrical and lighting companies.

The size of the stage, the availability and location of pipe battens and other mountings, and the theater's budget will influence how much any given theater will invest in lighting equipment. However, every school stage should try to have the following:

1. Six ellipsoidal reflector spotlights of 500 to 750 watts each (higher wattage for large auditoriums) for lighting downstage acting areas from mountings concealed in the house ceiling, from ceiling beams, from the balcony rail, or from stands on the house floor

2. Six spotlights of 500 watts each (fresnels are recommended) for lighting upstage acting areas from a pipe batten behind the first teaser

3. Two floodlights for special effects, such as sunlight or moonlight

4. Several border light units hanging from pipe battens for toning and blending together the areas of illumination cast by the spotlights—thus avoiding sharp divisions or pools of light. (Similar units can be placed on the floor and used as striplights for lighting backings or cycs.)

5. Portable or permanent footlight units for toning the illumination of the acting areas

6. A switchboard

In addition, of course, stage cables, cable connectors, clamps for hanging or mounting, color frames to fit the instruments, and color mediums will be needed. The two color mediums most often used in school theaters are roundels, which are made in six different colors, and gelatin, which is made in over seventy different colors. The most valuable colors in gelatins are the more delicate tones, such as pinks, straws, ambers, light blues, and greens. Gelatin booklets are available on request from lighting companies.

## Special Equipment

The use of the scioptican projector to simulate drifting clouds, rain, flame, and other moving effects can add a good deal to stage atmosphere. Great care must be taken to have the correct angle of light so that the actors do not cast shadows on the sky or backdrop. These effects should not be overdone or they will call attention to themselves. Slides of scenes for the Linnebach projector can be purchased or rented from lighting concerns. Both of these projectors involve considerable expense.

## Planning the Lighting

The lighting for every play must be worked out with painstaking experimentation by the director, scenic artist, and lighting technician. The lighting technician makes his light plot showing the areas to be lit and the location of the instrument which will light them. At all times he is concerned with the script itself and how lighting can complement its values and the director's intentions. By the time the location of the furniture is definite and the acting areas set, the electrician's light plot and cue sheet should be made. The light plot shows the exact position of every lighting unit during every scene. At the dress rehearsal and the performance, the cue sheet enables the technician to synchronize the lighting with the action and dialogue.

1

2

## STANDARD LIGHTING INSTRUMENTS:

1. Ellipsoidal reflector spotlight.

2. Spotlight with a Fresnel lens.

3. Floodlight.

4. Hanging borderlight unit.

5. Footlight unit.

3

4

5

**Purposes.** The primary purpose of stage lighting is to enable the audience to see the actors and the action. Lighting can also establish the time of day and state of the weather. This light should appear to come from such sources as the sun, moon, windows, fireplace, lamps, and open doors. In realistic settings, the chief problem is to arrange the lighting so that such natural sources are apparently furnishing the light and throwing shadows. In reality, of course, the foots, borders, spots, and floods are doing it. A third purpose of light is to accent objects and give them plasticity or roundness.

In addition, lighting has an aesthetic purpose—the creation of mood and atmosphere and the heightening of the audience's emotional reaction.

**Location of lights.** Spotlights placed in the auditorium on ceiling beams give the most effective downstage lighting. There should be three lights placed together on the far left and three on the far right. Spotlights hung behind the front teaser, two on the right, two in the middle, and two on the left are used for upstage lighting. Both upstage and downstage areas are usually lit by two instruments to an area. Their beams cross each other diagonally (see diagram on page 349). Cross-spotting can highlight faces or emphasize the center of interest. The front stage, especially, can be made the focal area in this way. Also shadows can be wiped out or interesting ones created. Foots and borders can be used to insure visibility but should be kept dimmed as low as possible most of the time. It must be emphasized that this is a minimal plan and can be adjusted or added to according to the individual theater's demands.

## Regulating the Lights

All the lighting equipment can be regulated from the switchboard, which is the nerve center of the whole system. Stage cables, joined by stage connectors or plugs, are the only safe and satisfactory means of carrying the current to the lamps. Ordinary electric wire and plugs must not be used onstage because of the fire hazard. Twist-lock connectors are safest since they minimize accidental breaks in the circuit often caused by actors stepping on ordinary ones and forcing them apart.

The lighting technician at the switchboard must follow the script and cue sheet for all cues to dim up or down in accord with action onstage. The turning on and off of lamps on the stage or in adjacent hallways, the closing of window curtains, the stirring up of a fire in the fireplace—all are actions calling for a change in light. These cues should have a warning signal far enough in advance to prevent any slip in timing. Every cue for lights must be worked out in rehearsals, and the lighting technician must have a

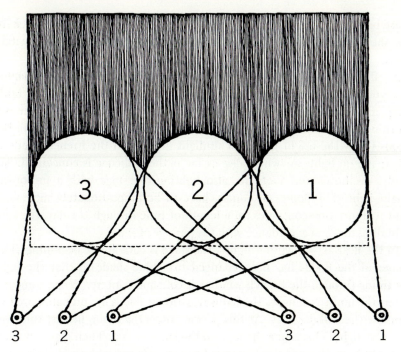

Diagram of lighting plan for downstage acting areas

Diagram of lighting plan for upstage areas

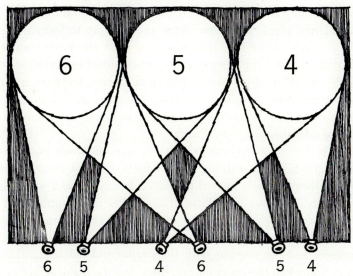

place backstage where he can watch the action, get directions, and check his cue sheet. Exact lighting cues must be pasted in large type on the switchboard.

To illustrate some of the lighting problems in a realistic play, imagine that your setting is a room lighted by a fireplace, a French window, a table lamp, and a door leading into a hallway. The scene changes from a summer morning in one act to a winter night in another act. In the former, amber floods throw the bright beams of sunlight in through the French window. There are no lights anywhere else as far as the audience is concerned. Actually, overheads and foots are also lighting the stage with a uniformly bright light. The floods, of course, have to be proportionately more brilliant. If the action continues for a length of time through the day, the sunlight dims down in accordance with the passage of time.

In the next act—a winter night—the stage is dark at the beginning. The amber in the floods has been changed to a blue shade so that the light streaming through the French window is cold and wintery. When someone enters the house and lights the hallway, strips or floods are probably used to illumine the hall doorway. As this person enters the room, he first turns on the table light. This is just the light in the lamp at first. Then gradually, imperceptibly to the audience, an overhead spot is brought up, lighting the area around the table. Then he stirs up the fire. A red light is lit in the fireplace and a section of the red foots near the fireplace is brought up. When the actor presses the overhead light button onstage, the technician simultaneously throws on the overheads and foots. The moonlight, the glow from the table lamp and the fireplace then appear to be diminished.

In nonrealistic plays, the scenic artist and lighting technician can use their imaginations to the full. However, they must always remember that the composition of a stage design can be either ruined or perfected by the use of light. Shadows of persons and three-dimensional objects and structures can be confusing as well as effective. The artist and technician must continually experiment when they are seeking to emphasize a pattern with highlights or subordinate it with shadow.

A gauze curtain is a valuable adjunct in stage lighting, especially for nonrealistic effects. With a strong light in front of it, the curtain is nearly opaque. A setting properly lighted behind it, however, has a soft radiance of great beauty. The fine play *Tiger at the Gates* was stunningly opened with a gauze curtain painted with a formalized Trojan-horse design. Behind it were shadowed the exquisite figures of Helen, Cassandra, and the other women, and the warriors with their capes and helmets and armor. All became real when the gauze curtain lifted and the dialogue began.

**Lighting effects.** Trying out stage lights is a time-consuming process, for they do strange things to scenery, costumes, and make-up. This is because lights and pigments do not mix in the same way. The only way to determine exactly what will happen is to test costumes, make-up, and scenery under lights. Only a few of the most common combinations of color in pigment and lights can be mentioned here. However, several of the books listed in Appendix C give detailed discussions of this intriguing and complex problem.

A safe general rule is that warm pigment colors—red, orange, and yellow—are intensified by warm colors in the lights and are dulled by cool colors—blue, green, and purple—and vice versa. Blue or green light turns red pigment black or a dark purple. This is why heavy rouge in moonlit scenes appears to be very dark. Blue is a dangerous color for costumes. It becomes purple under red light, greenish-orange under amber, green under green, purple under purple, and blue-green under yellow. Kings and queens wearing purple robes must be carefully lighted, as purple becomes red under red and amber lights, brown under yellow, and blue under blue. Green retains its own color only under green or yellow light. All colors change their intensity under different lights, taking on tints that may clash onstage although they blend in daylight. Any color of light thrown on a white surface or material will retain its pure hue.

Materials also are affected by lights. Smooth textures, like satin and rich silk, reveal lights and shadows. Rough weaves, like cotton flannel, absorb them. No matter how cheap the fabric, brilliantly colored materials are effective under stage lights, but the same fabric in a neutral color is harder to make effective. There are a number of dangers in using printed and striped materials in costumes. Many colors on the same dress cause a serious problem under stage lights. In period plays, the lighting is often complicated by long, curled, or heavily powdered wigs, and such contrasting textures as velvet, silk, lace, and lawn, which are usually combined in the costumes.

A typical lighting problem arose in a production of *St. Simeon Stylites* by F. Sladen-Smith. The costuming was modeled on Byzantine mosaics, and the symbolism of color was used. The lady offering love to the saint wore rose silks, stenciled in blue, with a plum-colored velvet cloak and high jewelled headdress. Purple sateen with long, brightly stenciled bands was chosen for the king. Yellow sateen cut in sharp angles and decorated with black spots and stripes was the costume for the king's jester. The devil wore scarlet velvet and silk, and his blackamoor friend was dressed in orange and green silk. Gunnysack with brown strips and a long brown cloak were chosen for the saint. All of these worked nicely together, but the lady's maid had been dressed in brilliant green to show her vivacity and youth. Unfortunately, the big scene of the play was at sunset. When the red light fell on the green dress, the maid, who should have been at her most vivacious moment, was clothed in funereal black! The problem was solved by bringing up a yellow flood on the maid as the red floods and overheads were brought up, and a strip of white overheads was added. The yellow and white lights were kept up full with the reds during the maid's scene and her costume retained its color.

**Lighting rehearsals.** Artistic ideals can only be realized by long, practical rehearsals in which all kinds of lighting experiments are made, for one never knows what beauty of highlight or shadow may result from a shifting of light. Lighting rehearsals are especially necessary after the scenery is onstage and the furniture and props are in place. Every aspect of stage, backstage, and house lighting can then be worked out thoroughly.

No light from the stage should shine directly into the eyes of anyone in the audience. All mirrors and shiny furniture surfaces onstage should be checked to be sure that they do not reflect too much light. Stage lamps need not carry a bulb brighter than 10 watts; for the actual light, of course, comes from the spots and other equipment.

**With the scenery and props onstage and the actors in costume, technicians experiment with different lighting combinations.**

Avoid blowing fuses by making sure that circuits are not overloaded. During rehearsals every stage light should have its wattage noted. An exact record should be kept of the number of lights and electrical effects called for on each circuit. If necessary, some adjustment can then be made before the actual performance. However, to be on the safe side, a supply of fuses should always be kept on hand. Only the lighting people should be allowed to touch the switchboard or other lighting equipment. All stage cables should be securely connected and placed out of the way so that no one will stumble over them. Several thorough lighting rehearsals can eliminate most of the delay caused by experimentation during dress rehearsals and will improve the lighting of the entire production.

*Discussion*

1. Discuss the purposes of stage lighting. Give examples of effective lighting on the stage, in the movies, or on television.
2. Explain how lighting would change the colors in this situation: a girl is wearing a bright yellow dress and heavily rouged make-up, and the lights change from daylight to sunset to moonlight.
3. Explain the color changes if the girl wore the same make-up, a light blonde wig, and a white satin dress.
4. Attend a play and watch especially for the lighting effects. Try to figure out exactly how they are achieved and discuss them in class.
5. Name some of the differences between a floodlight and a spotlight.
6. Why are spotlights so important in stage lighting?

*Applications*

1. Write or present a report on one of the following topics:
   The History of Stage Lighting
   The Function of the Lighting Technician
   The Uses of Special Lighting

2. Prepare a list of flexible units needed for properly lighting your auditorium. With what improvements would you start? Find the probable cost of each item.
3. Prepare a lighting plot and lighting cue sheet for the following:
   *Dear Brutus* by J. M. Barrie, Act II
   *Cock Robin* by Rice and Barry, both sets
   *Joan of Lorraine* by Maxwell Anderson, any scene
   *Death Takes a Holiday* by Casella and Ferris, Act II

4. From experimentation and your reading in books in Appendix C, report on the ways in which light affects pigments.
5. Work out the lighting cues for *Poor Maddalena*.

STAGE SETTING AND LIGHTING      **353**

*Chapter 13*

# Costume and Make-up

Studying the principles of costuming and make-up may give you valuable ideas about your own wardrobe and appearance, for the same basic principles govern costuming and make-up both on and off the stage. However, the rules are more specialized and more rigidly enforced behind the footlights. In this chapter, only the basic principles will be considered. The creation and carrying out of designs may be done outside of class.

## COSTUME

A stage costume expresses the personality of the character, revealing his social position, taste, and idiosyncrasies. As a part of the stage design, costumes should help to communicate the meaning, period, and spirit of the play. A costume must also be comfortable, easy to put on and take off quickly, and strong enough to stand the strain of vigorous movement.

### Effective Costuming

In style, material, and cut, a costume must be appropriate to the social background and period of the play. It should be in harmony with others on the stage or in strong contrast to them, in accordance with the particular characters and situations. Character parts can often use exaggeration for humorous or emotional effects. National costumes should be authentic.

In modern plays, real-life standards of good taste and suitability to the occasion and season apply. The best-dressed men and women wear simple appropriate clothes of good material, cut along conservative, flattering lines.

354

You will have little to do with the design of your costumes in a period or stylized play. Nevertheless, you should understand the theories of costuming in order to cooperate intelligently in wearing whatever is designed for you in your role. You should always do justice to costumes by wearing them properly, moving in the manner of the times, and handling trains, swords, hoops, wigs, and hats in accordance with the customs of the age to which they belong. It is more important that such clothing be distinctive in form and outline than in trifling detail. The cut and color of the costume should clearly individualize each character all of the time.

Fantasies, allegories, and mystic dramas make strong demands upon the originality and artistry of the designer. However, extreme costuming may threaten the intelligibility of the ideas and even cause laughter in the audience. Milton Smith in his book *Play Production* suggests that analogous colors can be used to advantage in the costumes of associated groups of characters. Complementary colors can be used for the opposition groups. This suggestion applies to any production, of course.

## Costume Design

Each historic period has its own distinctive line and form in dress. This is the *costume silhouette*. Look carefully at the silhouettes in this chapter and notice how each period has its own characteristics. If a costume does not re-create the basic silhouette of the period it is not effective, no matter how beautiful or ingenious it may be.

After a costume conference with the director, the designer usually makes a sketch of every costume and attaches samples of the fabrics desired. Materials can then be bought, dyed, assembled, and tested under lights. If the costumes are purchased, they should conform as closely as possible to the artist's design. It is often difficult for amateurs to realize that one inharmonious costume, no matter how lovely or how becoming, can ruin an atmospheric effect. The director or designer, or both, should always be present if costumes are being rented. Shoes, hats, purses, wraps must be obtained early; neglect of these details can ruin the harmony of the design and mood.

**Appropriateness.** On the stage, certain problems of dress are intensified. Actors and actresses should study their full-length reflections at a distance to get the proper perspective on themselves in costume. The director should observe every costume from various parts of the auditorium.

Small details become important onstage. For example, long skirts are more graceful than short ones, especially when the actress is seated. Draped scarfs and stoles are very effective if they are skillfully handled. Trimming,

**Ancient Greek Dress.** Costumes like these would be appropriate for any Greek play, dramatizations of Greek myths, and William Shakespeare's *A Midsummer Night's Dream.*

to be noticed, must be somewhat conspicuous, but if it is overly so, it should be discarded. Stockings receive the direct rays of the footlights and often change color. Light stockings may make the legs seem larger. Boys must also remember that their socks show on the stage! Once an expensive dress outfit of tails and white tie was rented for an actor who played an English lord. The effect was almost spoiled on the night of performance when he forgot to change his brilliant striped socks to black ones. In a social comedy depicting people of breeding, such errors are serious, for good taste in dressing and manners are intrinsic to effective characterization.

Costuming can cause more temperamental upheavals than any other

**Medieval Dress.** Appropriate for any play or pageant set in late medieval times, George Bernard Shaw's *Saint Joan*, and Anatole France's *The Man Who Married a Dumb Wife*.

phase of amateur production. Costume designers must never forget that the psychological reaction of being comfortably clad in becoming and suitable clothes greatly assists an actor's work. Most people want to look their best when appearing in public, so costumes should fit well and bring out the best physical characteristics of the actor—unless a particular role dictates otherwise. The color is important but good lighting and make-up can make almost any combination attractive. In real life, clothes may not make the man, but on the stage they do. Fortunate indeed is the actor who has the knack of wearing clothes well and making them a part of the role he creates.

**Elizabethan Dress. Appropriate for any Shakespearean play, George Bernard Shaw's** *Dark Lady of the Sonnets,* **and Maxwell Anderson's** *Elizabeth the Queen.*

**Color and material.** In realistic plays, any material which will create garments suitable for the character and for the stage picture can be used. Symbolic plays require a careful choice of fabric, texture, and color.

Lines in garments should harmonize with those of the human body without constriction or exaggeration. Vertical lines and solid colors make a stout person look slimmer and taller. Horizontal lines broaden the figure and cut height. Glaring colors and large prints, striking decorative effects, and strong contrasts must always be used with discretion. Satin is a glossy, lustrous material; in light colors it can make a person look much larger. Velvet, on the other hand, absorbs light, and dark velvet takes off pounds. Prints are often unsuitable for the stage since lights often obliterate or overemphasize part of the pattern and create a grotesque effect.

Restoration Dress. Appropriate for plays by William Wycherley, William Congreve, George Farquhar, and Molière.

The texture of the materials determines the outline of the costume. Knitted and woven goods drape in clinging lines, organdy and tarlatan have flare, velvet and dyed flannel hang in heavy folds.

Expensive and cheap materials should not be combined because the highlights show up cheap cloth. However, rich color will often make a poor fabric look more luxurious.

Oilcloth, cardboard, plastics, rubber sheeting, felt, cellophane, and other similar materials can be used to make striking headpieces and shoulder lines. All sorts of familiar textiles can be utilized in creating bizarre or unusual outfits. By an expenditure of ingenuity and time the creative designer can produce costumes at very little cost. He should get his creations ready as soon as possible in order to see them in actual use under stage lights.

Eighteenth-century Dress. Appropriate for plays and pageants about the American Revolution, Richard Brinsley Sheridan's *The Rivals* and *A School for Scandal*, and Oliver Goldsmith's *She Stoops to Conquer*.

Whatever the material, it must be used with discretion so that the costume is comfortable as well as appropriate to the spirit and period of the play. One unfortunate Candida in Shaw's play was so weighted by a voluminous Victorian gown (made of an awning-like material) that she could not rise from the floor after she had dropped gracefully beside her husband's chair.

## Obtaining the Costumes

Any concrete plan by which the designer organizes his ideas and presents exact information to the director and cast simplifies costuming. It is always helpful if the costume designer makes work sheets or costume charts. These

**Mid-nineteenth-century Dress. Appropriate for plays about the War Between the States, Rudolf Besier's** *The Barretts of Wimpole Street*, **Robert Sherwood's** *Abe Lincoln in Illinois*, **and Ruth and Augustus Goetz's** *The Heiress.*

work sheets or charts may be put together in a number of different ways. Regardless of form, they should show the essential costume items for each actor in each scene. They should also describe the colors, fabrics, and designs of these items. Ruled columns, placed next to the costume descriptions, are of great value. As each listed task is completed, a check mark may be placed beside it. In this way, anyone can quickly see just what has been finished and what still must be done. Such charts can facilitate matters so that the costumes are ready before dress rehearsals start.

One of the first problems to be settled is whether the costumes are to be made, rented, or borrowed. This decision must be made in ample time for the costumes to be collected with a minimum of effort and expense.

**Late Nineteenth- and Early Twentieth-century Dress. Appropriate for George Bernard Shaw's *Candida*, Henrik Ibsen's *Hedda Gabler*, and Oscar Wilde's *The Importance of Being Earnest*.**

Making the costumes serves several purposes. Those students who design and make them gain valuable experience, and a more uniform pattern for the play in both color and line is possible. In addition, much expense is avoided, and the school wardrobe receives permanent additions. If the costumes are to be made, a well-stocked wardrobe room is essential. If your school does not already maintain a department where costumes can be properly stored and cared for, you and your classmates should get one started. Prepare cupboards with generous hanging space for costumes and many drawers to hold such accessories as artificial flowers, feathers, materials, laces, and shoes. You will find that the stock grows quickly when your

Dress in the 1920's. Appropriate for Edna Ferber and George S. Kaufman's *The Royal Family*, Booth Tarkington's *Seventeen*, and Sandy Wilson's musical *The Boy Friend*.

need for costumes becomes known in the community. Friends will contribute by giving you old clothes, many of which can be adapted or altered for use in your school plays. Also, every class and school play will add more costumes to the wardrobe.

When you are ready to make the costumes, individual sketches and costume charts and sheets should include notes on the kind, amount, and cost of materials. Then there is the question of whether you will buy colored fabrics or dye your materials. Dyeing makes possible a more satisfactory and unified costume scheme, but it requires skill in a complex activity, a place for the dyeing, and people willing to work until the job is completed. Before the dyeing is done, patterns should be cut to the exact measurements of the actors and be approved by the director, scenic artist, and actors. When all material has been dyed and checked under the stage lights, it may be cut from the patterns and sewed together. The complete garments must be strong and firm enough to stand the strain of rehearsals and performance, but they do not need to have elaborate, ornamental sewing. The main emphasis in costume planning should be on the total effect as seen from the auditorium. The perfection of a costume cannot be judged by the design alone; it must be observed in action on the stage with the correct scenery and lighting. Costume design and construction are complex processes, but effort is rewarded by the achievement of an original and artistic production.

If you decide to rent costumes, be careful. Rented costumes can be both expensive and ineffectual. There are other arguments against renting. After selecting, fitting, and returning costumes, you have nothing to show for your effort but a large bill. Rented costumes are often available for only one dress rehearsal and the performance and must be rerented if additional performances are desired. At a crucial moment it may be difficult to get publicity photographs of the cast in complete costume. On the other hand, men's evening clothes, uniforms, unusual national costumes, wigs, and special properties are often unobtainable in any other way. If you do decide to rent costumes, the cast, designer, and committee should go to a reputable concern and select what they want, within the financial limits previously set.

Having the members of the cast and committee buy or borrow their own costumes may seem to be the simplest method of costuming a show—but it seldom is! It is very difficult to obtain garments which will achieve the planned and desired effect—even those which at first seem easy to get. In period plays, suitable costumes loaned by generous friends are apt to be valuable and fragile, and no assurance can be offered that they will not be soiled or torn. Some young people have a rather careless attitude toward expensive articles of apparel, even though they have been borrowed and are often irreplaceable.

Costumes and properties must be ready whenever the director demands them. This should be at least a week before the first dress rehearsal. Then they may be worn by the cast and seen by the whole company. Never should the slightest detail be postponed until the first performance! Only under extraordinary circumstances should anything be left until the last dress rehearsal, when shoes, coiffures, hose, gloves, cigarette cases, everything, must be exactly as they will be on the opening night. All make-up and costume changes must be made and timed accurately during a rehearsal. Only in this way can the actors appear at their best during the performance—poised, natural, and effective.

## Care of Costumes

After the costumes have been obtained they must be cared for during rehearsals and performances. A competent wardrobe mistress should be chosen. She should have responsible assistants in all the dressing rooms. The assistants help the actors with their changes, hang up clothes, keep all accessories close at hand, and see that everything is returned in good condition after the performance. In addition, the actors themselves should feel responsible for their costumes and properties. They should remember that grease paint, powder, spirit gum, and nail polish are almost impossible to remove and that torn fabrics can seldom be mended satisfactorily. They must personally see that their every costume, accessory, and property can be returned to the school, costumer, or friend exactly as it was received. All borrowed clothing should be dry cleaned or washed before it is returned to the owner.

Dressing-room floors should be covered with paper if long trains of fine materials are worn. The stage floor also should be kept clean; it should be vacuumed before dress rehearsals and performances. Protruding nails, unexpected steps, low ceilings, and other backstage hazards should be reduced to a minimum.

After almost every production, some things need to be replaced or repaired. The decision as to whether or not such expenses are to come out of the proceeds should be made at the beginning of rehearsals.

*Discussion*

1. Explain in detail the important considerations in planning a costume.
2. Name some plays in which correct local customs and dress were important. Have you seen instances which violated your personal knowledge of a locale? What were they?
3. Cite some unfortunate instances where cast members did not know how to use swords, carry canes or handbags, wear trains and coronets, or carry out other special costume tasks. What was the result?
4. Why does the effect, not great cost, count in stage costuming?
5. Why are valuable heirlooms and expensive fabrics and jewelry of comparatively little use in a production?
6. How may a costume affect the success or failure of an actor in a part?
7. What are some sources from which designers and actors can get ideas for the correct costuming of a play or part?

**8.** Discuss the characteristics of dress illustrated in the costume silhouettes in this chapter.

**9.** Study your own physique. Note especially the lines of your figure and the color of your eyes, skin, and hair. What style of dress do you think is most appropriate for you? Why?

**10.** In a modern play featuring well-dressed men and women, what would be the problems of the designer? Of the actors?

**11.** Why are styles of hairdressing so important on the stage? The height of heels? The color of shoes and stockings? The size and shape of hats and sleeves? The length of skirts?

**12.** Discuss the three methods of getting costumes for plays. Decide which is the best one for your particular school and community.

**13.** In modern movies and plays, how do the costumes help in characterizations and bring contrast and interest into the stage design?

**14.** Analyze the costumes you have seen in period plays or movies with regard to their authenticity, their beauty, and their appropriateness to individual characters. Was there any symbolism in the use of color, line, and proportion?

*Applications*

**1.** Give reports in class on the history of dress. Bring examples of costumes, either actual or pictured, typical of the various periods.

**2.** Describe in detail the costumes suitable for the following characters and scenes: Portia at the trial, Petruchio in the wedding scene, Romeo and Juliet at the ball and during their final scene in the tomb, Death in his first entrance in Casella and Ferris' *Death Takes a Holiday,* the butterflies and ants in scenes from Čapek's *The Insect Comedy,* Sabina in the last act of Wilder's *The Skin of Our Teeth,* the wedding dress in Barrie's *Quality Street;* the costumes for Act III, Scene 1, of Ferber and Kaufman's *Stage Door,* and the dream sequence in Rodgers and Hammerstein's *Oklahoma!*

**3.** Select any one character from a play and, after consulting library references, plan all the costumes he or she should wear in the play. Use authentic material. Bring a list of your sources of information with your report.

**4.** Make a costume chart for the characters in any play you think you would like to stage. Have each costume fit your plan for the stage setting. Show the relationship of each costume to all the others. Symbolize the characters by the use of color.

**5.** Select practical and pleasing fabrics for the costumes in exercise 4 above. If a member of the class is studying dressmaking, have her explain how to purchase the materials and make the costumes.

**6.** As a class project, dress a set of small dolls for a play of your own choice.

**7.** Experiment with costumed figures in a model theater. Bring in samples of various kinds of materials in many colors and test them under different lights.

8. Read the chapter on costuming in one of the books listed in Appendix C and give a report on it in class.

9. Get as many pictures of Pierrot and Pierrette costumes as you can find. Which ones would you prefer for *Poor Maddalena?* What materials would you use? Which would be practical and inexpensive? How would you dress Bumbu—in what colors, style, and materials? Where would you get ideas for the Paolo and Maddalena scene? What colors would you use and why? How would you plan the costumes for the quick changes of scene?

10. The class might find it profitable to devote several days to demonstrations on the techniques of costume-making. These might be given by a teacher in the home economics department, a guest, or one of the members of the class. Some possible subjects include the following:

Types of materials appropriate to certain historical periods
How a costume pattern is first cut from paper and then duplicated with cloth
Methods for cutting material to make a gored circular skirt
Methods of dyeing costume materials, types of commercial and aniline dye, the use of a "setting agent"
Painting materials to give the effect of brocade, lace, or armor

11. Arrange an exhibit of the costume sections of your notebooks. Combine the costume sections with those on settings and color if you wish.

## MAKE-UP

Make-up has several functions. It accentuates normal features so that they can be clearly projected to the audience, and it helps to create a character. It also counteracts the undesirable effects of artificial illumination. There is an additional reason for the use of make-up in school productions. Amateurs often are more comfortable onstage if they can lose their own identity under grease paint.

You have probably been looking forward with keen anticipation to learning make-up techniques.

To understand the fundamental principles of make-up, you should read the books suggested in Appendix C, listen carefully to instructions given in class, and watch demonstrations of make-up application. However, you cannot hope to become proficient without continual practice and experimentation. Make-up techniques cannot be mastered by watching a demonstration or reading instructions. To help yourself acquire the skill, you should study faces to see how they show the effects of age and emotion. Observe portraits, cartoons, magazine covers, and advertisements. As suggested in Chapter 10, you should devote a section in your notebook to a collection of pictures in color, photographs, and sketches, showing what people of various types look like at different ages and under the stress of changing emotions. Using these as models, you can practice make-up techniques until you are able to create a wide variety of effects. A small make-up kit may be ordered from any one of the big companies for your own use. It is a good idea to serve on the make-up committee for a production as soon as you have sufficient background. Watch the experienced people who make up the leading characters in school plays. From them you will be able to learn some of the most efficient ways of obtaining artistic results.

On the school stage, make-up must be handled with special care. Youthful faces do not always adapt themselves readily to older roles, and heavy make-up, inexpertly applied, looks "tacked on." Only the slightest amount of grease paint should be used. It is much better to err by using too little than to use too much. For classwork, a mere touching up of the face and appropriate dressing of the hair can suggest age and nationality effectively. However, every student of the drama should study and practice elaborate as well as simple make-up.

**A make-up apprentice practices her technique on a brave actor.**

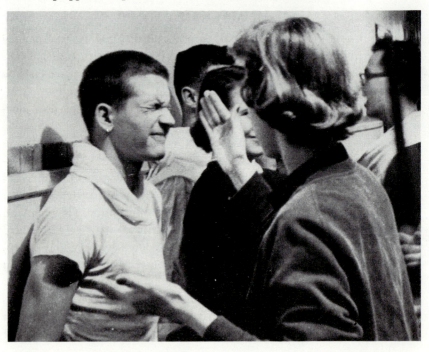

## The Make-up Kit

If your school does not already own a well-stocked make-up box, you should arrange to purchase one through your class or club. If separate kits must be provided for the boys' and girls' dressing rooms, buy two. Metal tool chests convert into excellent make-up kits, and regulation boxes can be purchased from any theatrical supply house.

In many schools a special committee, headed by someone experienced in make-up techniques, is responsible for the make-up used during a production. This committee should obtain the following essentials:

Grease paints—These come in tubes or sticks and are used for foundations. Shades ranging from light pink to dark sunburn are necessary for straight parts. For character parts such as sallow or florid old age, there are various mixed tones. For different nationalities, there are appropriate shades.

Face powders—In shades to harmonize with the foundation.

Moist rouge—Light, medium, and dark.

Liners—Grease paints in colors such as blue, brown, yellow, red, and white.

Before a performance, actors wait to be made up by the busy make-up crew.

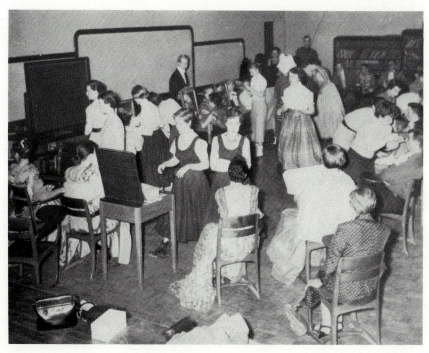

Lipsticks—Girls should use their own unless their make-up and costumes demand a change. Buy the natural shades from brilliant to dark.

Dermatograph pencils—Blue, brown, red, and black eyebrow pencils.

Dry rouge—Light, medium, and dark.

Mascara—Black and white.

Cold Cream—Large jars for cleansing and protecting the skin.

Powder puffs—Large and small.

Roll of absorbent cotton.

Baby brush for removing excess powder.

Hair whitener—Aluminum powder or cornstarch, with toothbrushes for applying to hair.

Liquid body make-up—Light and dark.

Paper liners, orange sticks, and camel's hair brushes for making wrinkles, painting lips and eyebrows.

Crepe hair—Gray, light brown, medium brown, black.

Spirit gum and alcohol or acetone.

Burnt cork, nose putty, and black-tooth enamel.

Clown white.

Large mirrors.

Paper toweling to protect the dressing tables.

Cleansing tissues.

Hand mirror, comb, brush, scissors, penknife, matches, toothpicks, needles, black and white thread, straight pins, hairpins, bobby pins, and safety pins of all sizes.

Make-up manufacturers will send you catalogues listing supplies and prices. Also available from these firms are excellent pamphlets on the choice and application of particular make-ups.

The make-up committee is responsible for setting out the materials, keeping them neat during rehearsals and performances, putting them away, and cleaning up the make-up rooms. Members of the cast should handle the school's make-up supplies as carefully as they do their own, for they are expensive and should not be used extravagantly or promiscuously.

Before a performance or rehearsal, the make-up chairman should spread out paper towels at the tables to be used for making up. Upon the towels he places the make-up needed for the show, including plenty of cold cream, cleansing tissues, and powder puffs. Though not on the tables, the complete make-up supply should be available for emergencies.

Large scrap baskets will help the actors keep the make-up room clean and neat. Everyone should be warned against spilling powder (especially aluminum powder), spirit gum, and paints. At the close of a performance or rehearsal, every article should be carefully checked and put in its proper place in the make-up kit or drawer. Messiness and carelessness in class or performance are an unpardonable waste of expensive materials.

## Make-up Principles and Procedures

The style of make-up is determined by the particular play to be given. Actors should rehearse with make-up on early enough for the director and his assistants to make suggestions and work out the necessary changes.

In general it may be said that making up is like painting a portrait. First the face is made as blank as possible with the foundation grease paint. Then a new countenance is produced by the use of colors, liners, crepe hair, and nose putty. Changes in facial contours can be achieved only by the use of light and shadow. A pigment lighter than the foundation tone highlights an area and makes it appear to come forward. A tone darker than the foundation shadows an area and makes it seem to recede.

Before beginning to make up, put on a smock or apron, bind back your hair, and spread out the materials you will need. Allow ample time for the make-up—at least half an hour for a straight role and an hour or more for a character part.

The first step in the application of stage make-up is to cleanse the face thoroughly, removing all dirt and any cosmetics. If there are any skin irritations, apply a very light covering of fresh cold cream to fill all pores. Then moisten the fingertips with cold water and cool the surface of the face.

The second step is the application of the correct color base. Foundation grease paints should be put on very lightly; the color depends upon the character being depicted. For straight parts, use your most becoming shade; for character parts, the most appropriate one. Men and boys use a darker foundation than girls do. Apply the grease paint in small dabs or streaks on the forehead, cheeks, and exposed portions of the neck. Blend the grease paint from the center out, until a very thin but perfectly smooth coating covers all the exposed area. Many beginners make the mistake of using large gobs of grease paint. This creates an unnecessarily heavy mask and wastes materials. Heavy grease paint also causes a sticky hairline and makes the skin perspire so that lines cannot be carefully drawn. Therefore, use as little grease paint as possible. Be sure to reach down into the collar line and around the hairlines of forehead and neck.

The third step is the application of shadow and highlight. If your chin, nose, or brows are too prominent, blend a darker foundation or rouge delicately over the outstanding feature which would attract highlights. If, on the other hand, your nose or chin is not prominent enough, apply a lighter foundation or even white. In character make-up, you can emphasize the natural hollows of your face and neck with carefully blended gray liner and bring out the bony structure with white or yellow. Shadows and highlights are intensified in the make-up of the very aged. Double chins can be made less conspicuous by shadowing their highlights. If exaggeration is desired, hold the chin very low on the throat and highlight the folds of flesh.

The fourth step is the application of moist rouge. For a feminine straight part choose a color to blend with your costume. Put a crescent on the cheek bones where it will help the shape of your face. If you want to shorten your face, blend the rouge horizontally, high under the lower eyelids and out toward the temples. If you want to narrow your face, blend toward the center and down. Be sure to keep the rouge high on the cheekbones and to blend it carefully. Never leave a definite line of cheek rouge for it will stand out under stage lights. Remember that red turns dark brown under green or blue lights. If you are to be in a moonlit scene, use very little rouge. Men and boys blend just enough rouge over the entire cheek areas to create a healthy glow over the face. In character parts rouge is used over the jowls to make them look heavy.

The fifth step is making up the eyes and brows. In straight make-up the eyes must be large and expressive. Women blend eye shadow from the upper lids, beginning with a heavy line and fading out before reaching the eyebrow. Brown is the most flattering color, although some actresses use green, blue, or purple. Never apply it too heavily. Be sure to have someone check to see that the shadow does not kill any highlight below the eyebrow. Men use eye shadow to deaden disfiguring highlights and to suggest age.

The eyes are enlarged by penciling. This is a difficult step, for the eyes must be alike. They must enhance the characterization, not attract attention to themselves. In real life, the eye is framed by the upper and lower lashes. At a distance, the lashes appear to be two lines. In a straight make-up, the lines of the lashes are accented by brown pencil. The line on the upper lid is extended like a long eyelash. The line on the lower lid is drawn low enough so that there is a space between the edge of the lid and the penciled line. This device has the effect of enlarging the eye. The two lines meet beyond the outer corner of the eye.

In straight parts the eyebrows should frame the eyes rather than attract attention to themselves. Again, use the brown pencil to arch the eyebrow. Taper off beyond the eye with a line parallel to the curve of the eye. Most natural eyebrows do not have identical arches. By matching the eyebrows make-up can greatly improve their appearance. In character make-ups, all sorts of effects can be achieved by changing the eyebrows. Close, heavily drawn brows make an actor look villainous. Lifted into a round, thin arch, eyebrows give a stupid or amazed expression. Twisted or drooped at contrasting angles, eyebrows make a face seem plaintive, menacing, or leering.

The sixth step is putting in wrinkles, if your role requires them. Raise your eyebrows or frown until the natural lines of your future wrinkles appear. Then relax and immediately draw the lines with a brown liner. Wrinkles must be made with a continuous rather than a dotted line.

If you have already developed wrinkles on your forehead and around your eyes, you may use another method. First spread brown liner over the upper part of your face. Then elevate your eyebrows and squint your eyes. Wipe off the liner very carefully before relaxing. When you relax, the natural wrinkles will be accentuated. Again form the wrinkles, holding them while you put on powder and brush it off. Then apply the foundation grease paint (made almost liquid by putting it on the palm of the left hand and kneading it with the right). Add face powder and brush it off—still without relaxing. Your natural wrinkles should then be well accented.

One of your most difficult problems will be making up for attractive, middle-aged characters. A few definite wrinkles in the frown lines on the forehead and about the nose may be all that is needed. For old age you can have as many wrinkles as the character requires. Be careful in drawing crow's feet about the eyes. If they are messy, they appear only as a smudge.

The seventh step is painting the lips. Girls can usually do this best for themselves. Boys should use a little lip rouge and then wipe it off carefully with a tissue, leaving only an impression of color. A camel's hair brush is used by most professionals for painting the lips, for it can achieve the exact effect desired. Be sure to get the lipstick or rouge well inside the lips. If your mouth is too large, carry your foundation color over your lips and paint whatever new mouth you wish. If your mouth is too small, you can enlarge it enough to avoid distorting your features. The line of the mouth can create many subtle expressions to heighten your characterization. For example, a full, sensuous mouth can be made puritanical by blocking out the curves and using light, straight lines in their place. Avoid making your mouth the center of interest in your face, however, unless the part you are playing demands it.

The eighth step is putting on the powder and finishing touches. Always use a powder lighter than the foundation, but avoid white except for eccentric effects. The powder holds the make-up in place and prevents its running under hot lights, so it must be pressed in thoroughly and carefully. Be sure to cover the entire exposed area. Brush off the excess powder very lightly with the baby brush. Do not disturb the lines of the make-up or leave streaks and powder spots. If the powder deadens the cheeks, use dry rouge to brighten them but leave no lines or spots.

Mascara is a finishing touch. Apply mascara or melted cosmetic with great care! Put it on the upper lashes only, unless your eyes are very large. Use brown instead of black unless you are a real brunette. False eyelashes, put on with liquid adhesive and carefully trimmed to suit the character and stage lighting, are often very effective and highly practical.

After the play is over, remove the make-up completely. Wearing stage make-up outside the theater marks you as an amateur and exhibitionist. Use cold cream, then wipe it off with cleansing tissues or soft towels. Long strokes and circular motions will avoid rubbing the make-up into the skin. To close the pores, wash your face in cold water.

## Special Make-up Problems

For make-ups requiring beards you should use the professional methods so far as possible. Cold cream or grease paint should not be put on the area where a beard is to be. The woolly crepe hair should be dampened, straightened out, dried, and then applied bit by bit over a light coat of spirit gum and pressed in. Put on more hair than is needed; it can then be trimmed to any shape desired. An unshaven effect can be created by stippling the proper lining color on the grease paint foundation with a rubber sponge before powdering, or by stippling with an eyebrow pencil. You can also use pipe tobacco for a realistic effect, pressing it into spirit gum. In putting on mustaches, be sure to press the small pieces of crepe hair very firmly into the spirit gum to avoid their loosening during speech. Then trim them with great care. Be sure to keep a balanced appearance.

If you use nose putty, remember that it must be kneaded into a pliable mass in your hands and carefully shaped before being applied to a spirit-gummed area. After it has been applied and the edges blended smoothly, the putty can be covered with the same foundation as the rest of the face. New substances with greater similarity to flesh are coming on the market all the time. Keep in touch with catalogues if you want to experiment with this kind of make-up. When you remove beards, mustaches, or putty, use alcohol or acetone to dissolve the spirit gum.

Hair is an integral part of both make-up and costume. Well-planned and carefully dressed coiffures can help to transform high school girls into sophisticated middle-aged women, glamour girls, or exotic adventuresses. The use of easily removed hair tints can change a girl's stage personality. The use of ordinary white powder on hair is never recommended. Aluminum powder is much more satisfactory, for it gives a natural, iron-gray gleam which is beautiful under stage lights. Unfortunately it is difficult to apply and may be injurious to the scalp or eyes. Aluminum powder is brushed into the hair in small quantities with a toothbrush or hairbrush and then is blended carefully. Cornstarch is also used for turning hair gray. In small quantities it is rather satisfactory, but it has a tendency to deaden the highlights of the hair and a cloud of white powder arises if anyone touches it. Costume changes over whitened hair are not difficult, particularly if the hair is covered with a protective scarf.

Only expensive wigs appear natural and effective. They should be individually fitted, if the budget permits, and they should be adjusted and handled with great care. Wigs are put on from the front and fitted back over the head. The real hair, if it shows, must be tinted to match the wig. A "bald wig" must fit perfectly, and the places where it meets the forehead and neck must be cleverly concealed by make-up. For men, eccentric haircuts and hairdoes are often more realistic than wigs.

Boys' hair problems are important, for a perfect make-up and an impeccable adult costume can be ruined by a boyish cut. To avoid the "skinned rabbit" appearance, boys should let their hair grow, regardless of the comments of unsympathetic schoolmates. Two weeks before the performance, a good barber may cut the hair to suit the characterization. As a general rule the hair should not be cut after that time. Boys can easily change the color of their hair with mascara. White mascara is excellent for middle-aged parts. The hair should be freshly washed so that there is no grease on it. The mascara may then be applied with a wet toothbrush, brushing it back from the forehead. This same method can also be used for girls with short haircuts.

To make up your hands for old age use a foundation and emphasize the depressions with gray or brown and the knuckles and other bones with yellow or white. Girls must remember that highly colored fingernails are appropriate for only certain types of women and can often ruin an otherwise excellent make-up.

Liquid make-up in keeping with the costume, period, and type of character is used for arms and legs and backs and chests, when they are visible. Since footlights are apt to lighten colors, the darker tones are safest.

Remember that in both class and school plays it is the actor, not grease paint and costume, who creates the real illusion. However, care expended upon a first-class ensemble of correct costume, make-up, hairdress, and accessories will give you an assurance which will help you create a convincing characterization. Make-up is an integral part of the actor's whole appearance. It is to be used and enjoyed as another tool in his craft.

Hal Holbrook prepares for his one-man show, *Mark Twain Tonight*

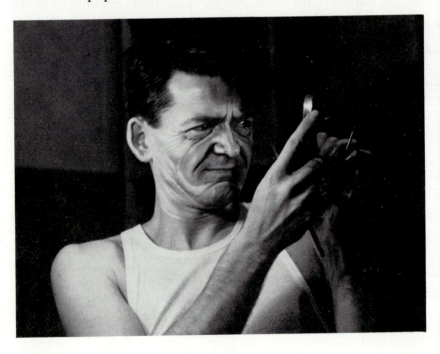

Make-up art transforms Holbrook, thirty-four, into Mark Twain at seventy.

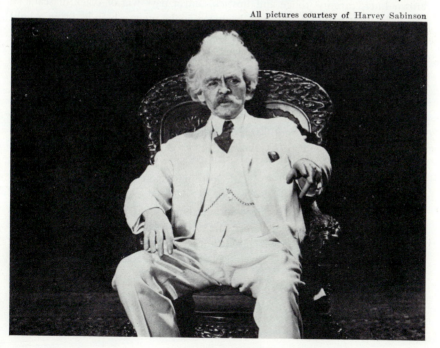

*Discussion*

1. Tell the class about the most successful make-ups you have seen on the stage. Explain your reasons for feeling that they were particularly good.

2. Discuss the make-up of the last play you attended as a class.

3. What do you consider the most serious faults in the make-up used in high school plays?

4. Discuss the relationship between empathy and make-up.

*Applications*

1. Divide the class into couples. Practice make-up on each other in accordance with the suggestions in this chapter and the books listed in Appendix C. First learn how to apply a "straight" make-up. Then try character types, racial and national make-ups, and finally turn to Shakespeare. Plan the make-ups for such intriguing characters as Caliban, Othello, King Lear, Falstaff, the nurse in *Romeo and Juliet*, Cleopatra, Benedick, Grumio, Malvolio, and Bottom. Also create make-ups for a group of characters from one play, such as Le Beau, Adam, Audre, Touchstone, and William in *As You Like It*.

2. Make up several students as Pierrot, Pierrette, and Bumbu from *Poor Maddalena*, using bizarre effects against a dead white. Could these make-ups be used in an actual production of the play? Why? Why not?

3. If you have blonde hair, make up as a brunette, using a dark foundation, brown liner, carmine rouge and lipstick, and a dark wig or black mascara (if you have short hair). If you are a brunette, make up as a blonde, using a light foundation, blue liner, bright rouge, and a light wig.

4. Bring in reports on the following topics:

   The History of Make-up

   The New Materials for Street Make-up (Write for information from three big companies or consult a local authority.)

   How to Use Crepe Hair and Nose Putty Effectively

   How to Create Some Bizarre Characters

   How the Colors of Make-up Can Produce Contrast in Characterizations in a Cast

   How Lights on Make-up and Costumes Can Create Complete Changes in Color Schemes

5. If you are a girl, study your coloring, skin texture, and general type. Then work out a correct street make-up, remembering that refined women are never artificial but always well groomed. Make the most of your good looks by using the right colors in your make-up and in the cut and styling of your hair.

*Chapter 14*

# The Performance

# and Its Evaluation

From every angle, the presentation of a play—whether a class play produced as a student project or an artistic public performance —is the climax of hours of labor by the author, director, scenic artist, actors, and stage crew. It is, therefore, worthy of the best effort of everyone involved and should be approached as a serious and important occasion. No detail is too small for conscientious consideration, and no regulation for backstage deportment is too unimportant to be followed strictly.

## PERFORMANCE NIGHT

Too often amateurs look upon performance night as an adventure from which every thrill, both on and off the stage, must be extracted. Instead, they should be straining every nerve to see that the performance begins on time and moves swiftly, without delays or mistakes, to an impressive end. Whenever you are in a play, you must be mentally and physically alert, in order to do your best.

### The Director

The director usually calls his cast together immediately before the curtain rises to check on costumes, make-up, and personal props. It is important for him to be poised and relaxed, for his state of mind will be reflected

**Families, friends, and neighbors line up at the school box office on opening night.**

in the actors and crew. He may warn them about interpolating new words and action and end his talk with words of encouragement and optimism. Most directors will then leave the backstage area and go out front to see the performance. The director's work is done, and the show belongs to the actors, the stage manager, and the crew.

## The Assistant Director

If you are assistant director, your work, like the director's, is usually over before the performance begins. However, you may be assigned backstage duties by the director. On the other hand, he may ask you to be out front to take his notes for after-the-show criticisms. In any case, you will come early in the evening to check the stage area with the director and stage manager. You will probably see that all the cast is assembled just before curtain time wherever the director designates, to be seen by him and to hear any final instructions he may wish to give them.

## The Stage Manager

On performance night, running the show is the province of the stage manager. If you have this position, you will be responsible for everything

Ushers distribute the programs and escort the audience to their seats.

backstage—settings, properties, furniture, lights, and sound effects. See that every member of your crew is on the job and knows exactly what to do. Check the prop tables. Make sure that lights are in place and that furniture is on the marked locations onstage. Be sure the electrician is on the job with some extra fuses and cues posted. A crew member should also be ready with any sound effects for the first act. If there is to be a recording made during the performance, see that the person in charge is on hand with all equipment ready. Be sure that the prompter is in place, the opening scene actors onstage, incidental lights on or off as they should be (and working), and the backstage area in order. Then you may give the signal for house-lights off and curtain up. From then on you watch every cue until the end of the show. A slow curtain, failure in offstage noises, lighting errors, and lost properties will be blamed on you!

After the show have the stage cleared unless there is to be another performance. In that case, the stage must be reset in every detail for the opening of Act I. Reset your stage at once rather than just before the next performance. Within one day after the final performance the settings must be dismantled, all equipment taken down, and props and costumes stored or returned.

THE PERFORMANCE AND ITS EVALUATION     381

## The Prompter

If you are the prompter, arrive in time to take one final look through the book to be sure all cues are clearly marked, especially the ones that have proved tricky in rehearsals. Take your place early and stay there quietly in case members of the cast and crew want information. After the curtain goes up, you will follow every word and action on the stage. Do not allow yourself to be distracted by anything or anyone. Your business is to keep your head and be on the job every instant. The minute you become inattentive and lose your place, someone is sure to need a cue. You will not get excited if there is a sudden silence, for you will know whether a pause is called for. If none is, you will give the cue. If important lines are skipped you will, if possible, feed the lost lines. Skip the ones that have been spoken, and give the next ones. Don't do anything at all if unimportant words and phrases are missed, as they certainly will be, for the audience won't know the difference. If there are to be other performances, show any serious mistakes to the actors who made them so they may restudy the scene, but don't make them feel they have spoiled the show. If there is only one performance, say nothing at all, for post-mortems only make hurt feelings when the show is over. When your work is finished, return the promptbook to the director or put it safely away.

## The House and Business Managers

If you are the house manager, you will make sure the lobby and auditorium are in good shape. You will check with the business manager to see that the box office is set up and change on hand. You will see that well-trained ushers come as early as necessary. You yourself should arrive first, to put on the lights and unlock the doors. Judge the time when the people of your community are likely to appear and make your plans accordingly. You will have the programs sorted for each performance and ready for distribution at each aisle. Since you are the official host for the producing group, you must look your best and see that the audience is served courteously and efficiently. Keep some ushers at the door throughout the show for latecomers or emergencies. If policemen and firemen are in attendance, see that they are placed where they can watch the play and help you silence any group that creates a disturbance. After the final curtain, have the ushers pick up any lost articles and rescue extra programs. Be sure the auditorium is ready for cleaning the next morning before you turn out the lights and lock the doors. You also should check with the business manager to see that money and tickets have been put safely away, in accordance with school policy.

Within one day after the last performance, the business manager will see that bills and tickets are turned in. Under the supervision of the director, he will then be responsible for paying all bills and giving a report to the school administration.

## The Stage Crew

If you are on the stage crew or working with props, you know exactly what to do. Stay in your assigned position, work quickly and quietly in changing sets and moving furniture. Leave the actors and prompter strictly alone. At the end of the final performance, strike the set, clear the stage, and sort the furniture and props. Put away all equipment that belongs to the school and give the rest to the proper persons for return to their owners. Between performances see that the furniture is covered and all perishable articles in a safe place.

## The Wardrobe and Make-up Staffs

If you are on the wardrobe staff, go over every costume and its accessories on the day of the performance. Have the clothes pressed and hung

**The wardrobe staff completes its work on the costumes.**

Photo by Louise Phillips

properly. Come early to help the first actors who appear. Do everything you can to hurry changes during acts and intermissions and to get the players onstage. After each costume has been worn, hang it up carefully. At the end of the show, have everything in order and ready for the next performance. You may have to do some pressing so that the costumes which have been used will look fresh and neat for the next performance.

If you are on the make-up staff, come early, get into your smock or large apron, place paper or towels over the dressing tables, and lay out the materials in the way you have found most convenient during the dress rehearsals. If the cast is large and if the make-up staff applies the make-up, you will work at long tables, putting on the foundations, rouge, eye shadow, and lipstick in that order. The most experienced make-up person should do the character parts, which take the most time. If hair is to be whitened, especially with aluminum powder, have one person handle the whole job in an isolated area. Make sure that floor and furniture are covered by newspapers.

**In the make-up room before the performance, actors and staff apply the finishing touches.**

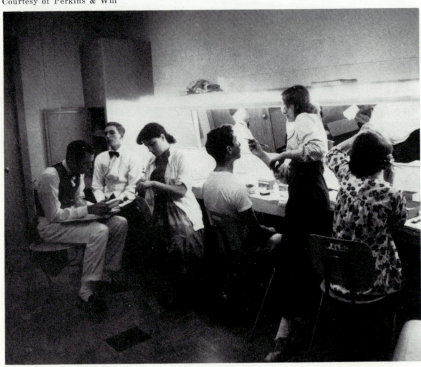

Try to keep spirit gum and other liquids far back from the edges of tables. Be sure you have plenty of supplies like paper tissues, scissors, crepe hair, and cotton. When the whole cast has been made up, put away the grease paints and other things which will not be needed again. Lay out the dry rouge, eye shadow, pencils, and powder for freshening make-ups during the show. Try to keep tissues and cotton off the floor to avoid a mess later. Place large containers conveniently near the tables and try to get the actors to throw trash into them. Before you leave, get everything in shape for the next performance.

## The Actor

If you are an actor, arrive early and sign in on the board posted by the stage manager. Check all your costumes. Get dressed at once and hang your street clothes away from the costume area. Leave no valuables around. Cover your costume with an apron or large towel and go to the make-up room as soon as possible. If you make yourself up, use the supplies sparingly, work slowly and carefully, and keep the materials where they belong. If you have changes in costume during the show, get help to prevent spoiling both your make-up and clothing. When you are ready, stay in the dressing room or go to the waiting room. Keep quiet and poised. Do not study your lines. Try to get into character instead of being boisterous, funny, and temperamental.

When you are called, get to your place onstage immediately. While you are waiting to go on, never crowd over the prompter to see your lines, or peer into the wings or through a peephole at the audience. Enter and leave the stage in character without undue excitement and go straight to the dressing or waiting room. Get your own props from the table on entrances and return them to the table on your exits, if they are to be used again during the performance. After the final curtain call, wait for the director to dismiss you. He may have important directions or wish you to hear the recording of the play immediately. Under no circumstances should you leave the backstage area until you have taken off your make-up and put on your street clothes. Be sure you turn in your book or "sides" after the last show.

## The Final Result

By the time the overture starts, all the stage crew and actors should be in their places. If the cast is large, it is usually better to have the actors remain in the dressing rooms until five minutes before their entrances. Care should be taken to prevent actors from throwing their shadows on the wings or background, or projecting whispered voices over the footlights.

The most effective device to assure an appreciative audience is to begin promptly at the advertised time. It is better to forget last-minute details than to risk facing an audience disgruntled by a long wait. If the play has been so adequately rehearsed that lines, cues, and actions are semi-automatic, the actors will be free to respond to the inspiration of playing before a responsive audience. During the performance the actors should forget technique and participate in the creative joy of being an integral part of a living drama.

Fine performances which reflect credit on both the school and the community are produced on school stages. Here a sincere love of the theater is shared by the actors, production staff, and director. Young people have idealism, enthusiasm, and unspoiled talent which can surmount the handicap of inexperience. Under the creative guidance of a fine teacher-director, the high school production can achieve a reality and sincerity which make it a spiritual and aesthetic experience for the actors, crew, and audience. Every school with high standards, good management, and good direction can reach this ideal.

## Discussion

1. In the plays in which you have taken part, have you had sufficient sleep and rest before the performance? Did you plan your costumes and props well enough to avoid the nervous excitement of last-minute demands upon yourself and your family?

2. Explain in detail the importance and duties of the prompter.

3. Discuss the responsibilities of an audience at a performance. Why should members of a class in drama carefully consider the etiquette of going to plays as well as the technique of being in them?

4. In a successful production, which do you think would give you the greatest satisfaction: being an actor, the director, or the stage manager? Why?

5. In the last play that you saw, what, specifically, do you think accounted for its success or failure?

6. What are the things you would have to check on before a performance if you were the director, the stage manager, the prompter, or the house manager? What would be your duties during the performance itself?

## Applications

1. As a class project, plan a production of a Shakespearean play. Make a promptbook, model sets for the scenes, a chart or set of dolls to show the costumes, a set of cues for the lighting effects, and a list of props. Work out the action with dolls or with pegs in the model sets, and write down all the movements and stage pictures.

**2.** Let each member of the class present his ideas regarding the staging of a one-act play read by the class.

**3.** Divide the class into groups and have each produce a one-act play in class (see pages 269 to 273). Apply the suggestions in Part Four in so far as the classroom equipment will permit.

   **a.** After the play has been produced and you have had the experience of either serving as director or assisting him, write a paper on the subject "The Problems of Play Production."

   **b.** Write a criticism of each production in this series, discussing particularly the technical aspects.

**4.** *Poor Maddalena* adapts itself splendidly to high school production, but remember that no public performance is allowed without permission of the publishers and payment of a royalty. Work out the production as a class project, selecting the cast from among your classmates. Apply everything you have discussed concerning the interpretation and production of this play. The following considerations are only a few of the many to keep in mind:

   **a.** Apply the principles in the chapters on stage settings and lighting, costuming and make-up to show the marked difference between the lands of fantasy and reality. Decide what types of costumes are appropriate and see that the make-up is in keeping with the different costumes.

   **b.** Check on the stage pictures throughout the action, seeing that the characters and furniture are properly balanced.

   **c.** Plan and rehearse the action (without dialogue) throughout the entire play. Very carefully establish the difference between the stylized actions of Pierrot and Pierrette and the natural responses of Paolo and Maddalena. Work out the exits and entrances with special care, especially those to and from the land of reality.

   **d.** The director must check the tempo of the various bits of action while keeping a marked contrast between the second scene and the first and third. He must see that Scene 2 builds up to the dramatic conclusion without permitting the emotional intensity of the strong early bits of action to top it. The following particularly difficult bits of action should be carefully rehearsed: the opening pantomime, the entrance of Bumbu, looking into the world of reality and making the audience see what the characters see, the action accompanying the love scene beginning "There is something in your singing which tears a girl's heart in two," the end of Scene 2, the repetition of "Poor Maddalena!" in Scene 3, and the end of the play.

   **e.** Decide what the most effective bits of action in the whole production should be and determine where the audience should react with smiles, tears, and applause. See if those situations get such reactions.

**5.** Put on a public performance of a long play. There are many listed in Appendix C that have proved successful for high school production.

# DRAMATIC CRITICISM

The ability to appreciate and enjoy a play because you know the criteria for judging its merits is undoubtedly one of the chief benefits to be derived from the study of dramatics. You may be surprised to hear some people say that they are glad they know nothing about the theater because they can enjoy a play so much more than does a student of the drama—in other words, they cling to the outworn adage "ignorance is bliss." Though this adage may not be quite true, it does have a certain point. Now that you know something about plays and their production you must not become so critical that you cannot fully enjoy the thrill of theatergoing. You must approach it as an adventure, in a receptive mood, ready to laugh or cry or applaud, and willing to lose yourself in the life of the characters before you on the stage.

You may now feel, as most theater lovers do, that no matter what degree of mechanical perfection the theaters of the screen and air may attain, they can never take the place of the legitimate stage. They can never create that intangible, magnetic quality which passes across the footlights from actor to audience. They can never become the coalescence of light and color, voice and movement, mass and perspective, imagination and reality which is the living theater. That is why some producers are still willing to risk the road, why summer stock continues to attract audiences, why community theater is a vigorous movement, and productions of the educational theater in high schools and colleges throughout the country are steadily improving.

Dramatic criticism has been a popular form of literature and journalism for almost a hundred years. You yourself may well consider it a profitable and satisfying career to pursue. Go to the public library and browse through the drama section. Familiarize yourself with the works of such famous critics as George Bernard Shaw, Norman Hapgood, Walter Prichard Eaton, Brander Matthews, Clayton Hamilton, Heywood Broun, Montrose J. Moses, George Jean Nathan, Alexander Woollcott, Stark Young, Joseph Wood Krutch, Burns Mantle, James Agate, and Percy Hammond. There is no better way to gain a perspective on the theater and actors than by reading dramatic criticism. Through your local public library you should also keep up with current reviews in such periodicals as *The New York Times*, *The New York Herald Tribune*, *The New Yorker*, *The San Francisco Chronicle*, *The Philadelphia Bulletin*, *The Chicago Tribune*, *The Christian Science Monitor*, and the *Saturday Review*. *Theatre Arts* magazine will keep you in touch with plays across the country and abroad, as well as those on Broadway.

At his desk after an opening-night performance, Brooks Atkinson, drama critic for *The New York Times*, writes his review for the morning paper.

## The Drama Student as Theater Critic

You will remember that there are four considerations to keep in mind as you form your estimate of a play: the play itself, its interpretation by the actors, its staging by the director, and its reception by the audience. Your judgment is naturally colored by your personal preferences, immediate state of mind, experience, and technical knowledge of the theater. Often the person with you can make or mar your enjoyment of a performance.

**The play.** Naturally the type of a play and its fundamental purpose will influence your attitude toward it. A frothy satire cannot move you to the same emotional depths as a great tragedy, but it can give you a delightful evening's entertainment. The theme of the play will be of great interest to you. Keen discussions of successful first nights often center around the playwright's choice of theme. Determine for yourself what you think the playwright is saying and be prepared to justify your belief. Without spending too much time in speculation, you might ask: "What did the author try to do? Did he do it? Was it worth doing?"

The playwright's style in writing dialogue and developing characters will interest you more than it does the average theatergoer. You should catch clever dialogue and appreciate a beautiful turn of phrase. Gradually, you can analyze the distinguishing characteristics of the author's genius. The characters should become real people. As the play progresses, you should feel that you are making new acquaintances and accepting or rejecting them. During the intermissions you can discuss these new acquaintances and speculate upon their ultimate actions. You can also take time to consider the playwright's skill in giving the actors meaningful lines to say and exciting things to do.

**The acting.** Your chief interest may be in the acting itself. Now you can make a fair appraisal of the artists in the cast. If an actor creates a living person by using the best of his physical and spiritual equipment and technical training, he deserves your applause. The star system has led many people to condemn the work of an actor because of prejudice or to acclaim any performance of a favorite star, no matter how good or bad his interpretation of a particular role is. You can help to create a better American theater by refusing to accept press-agent glorification and by judging for yourself whether or not an actor has given a sincere interpretation of his part. Your experience should enable you to admire the power of a beautiful and flexible voice, the beauty of a graceful and effective body, and the appeal of a fine characterization.

**The production.** You can now appreciate the part played by the director, scenic artist, and stage manager in the production of the play. The average theatergoer never thinks of the setting or realizes the existence of a scenic artist and backstage crew. As a student of drama, however, you will be able to notice and enjoy the staging, especially if the wheels run smoothly and the scenic background and offstage effects are properly created.

**The audience response.** The reaction of the audience may or may not be a fair criterion in judging a play. However, the average audience is eager to be pleased, and if a play does not hold their attention, something must be wrong with the play or its production. Of course, not all plays are suitable for presentation before all audiences. Often a play which succeeds on Broadway fails on the road, or vice versa. Local reactions may be affected by religious views or business interests. The degree of culture and sophistication of the audience may also influence the reception of a play. Nevertheless, a good play usually pleases most people. Listen to comments between acts and at the end of performances. This will add spice to your theatergoing and help you to analyze audiences as well as plays.

Unfortunately, the term *criticism* is often mistaken for a negative attitude. Carping on faults is a deplorable tendency either in the theater or out of it. Essentially you go to a play to enjoy yourself, to lose yourself in the activities before you. However, if you are discriminating, you save your tears and smiles until you are really stirred emotionally and then give them whole-heartedly. True enjoyment in the theater is a fifty-fifty proposition —if the audience is appreciative, the actors will give their best and the play can be judged fairly. A cold, unenthusiastic audience "sitting on its hands" can kill the fervor of even great stars and ruin the essential spirit of a play. There is no greater artistic pleasure than witnessing a good play well produced before an excited audience; but don't be carried away if the work does not prove worthy of your enthusiasm.

## Evaluating a Play

The real theater enthusiast frees his imagination and emotions while watching a play. At the same time, he uses his intelligence and discrimination to heighten his appreciation of what he is seeing. The following questions may help you to evaluate the plays you attend, the television dramas you watch, and the movies you see.

### Theme

1. Is the fundamental idea underlying the play true or false in its concept of life?
2. Is the theme warped by a distorted or limited life experience on the part of the author?
3. Does seeing the play add something positive to your understanding and experience?
4. Is the theme consistent with the setting, plot, and characters presented in the play?
5. Do you agree with the author's philosophy?
6. In your opinion, should the general public be encouraged to see the play?

### Plot

1. Does it have a clear-cut sequence of events?
2. Does it rise to a strong climax?
3. Does the suspense hold until the end?
4. Was it emotionally stirring?
5. Are you satisfied by the final outcome?
6. If not, what outcome would you consider more satisfactory?
7. Which are more interesting: the events or the people?

## Characterization

1. Are the characters true to life?
2. Do the characters seem to fit into the social and geographical background of the play?
3. Do they definitely arouse such feelings as sympathy, affection, amusement, disgust, admiration, or hatred on the part of the audience?
4. Are their actions in keeping with their motives?
5. Are the situations at the climax and conclusion the result of their inherent natures?

## Style

1. Is the dialogue brilliant and entertaining in itself?
2. Is the dialogue consistent with the characters and setting?
3. Is the dialogue an end in itself or an adequate means of plot advancement and characterization?
4. Does the dialogue make you think about the playwright or the characters themselves?
5. Do you remember lines after seeing the play because of their significance or beauty?
6. Would people of the social class represented talk in real life as they do in the play?
7. Is the power of expression worthy of the ideas expressed?

## Acting

1. Is the interpretation of any given role correct from the standpoint of the play itself?
2. Does the actor make his character a living individual?
3. Is he artificial or natural in his technique?
4. Are you conscious of his methods of getting effects?
5. Does he grip you emotionally? Do you weep, laugh, suffer, and exult with him?
6. Is his voice pleasing and his charm magnetic?
7. Is his use of dialect correct in every detail?
8. Does he keep in character every moment?
9. Do you think of him as the character he is depicting or as himself?
10. Does he use the play as a means of self-glorification, or is he an intrinsic part of the action at all times?
11. Does he apparently cooperate with the other actors, the director, and the author in interpreting the play by knowing his lines, helping to focus the attention on the center of interest, and losing himself in his part?

## Staging

1. Is the setting in keeping with the play itself?
2. Is it appropriate in its design to the locality and social strata represented?
3. Is it beautiful and artistic in itself?
4. Is it conducive to the proper emotional reaction to the play?
5. Are the costumes and properties in harmony with the background?
6. Does the setting add to or detract from enjoyment of the play?
7. Is the interest centered in the total effect or in the details?
8. Has the expenditure of money in the production been justified by the total value of the effects obtained?

## Audience Reaction

1. Is the audience attentive or restless during the performance?
2. Is there a definite response of tears, laughter, or applause?
3. Is there an immediate appreciation of clever lines, dramatic situations, and skillful acting?
4. Is the applause spontaneous and whole-hearted, or politely perfunctory?
5. After the performance are people hurrying away, or do they linger to discuss the play?
6. Is the audience apathetic or animated, bored or buoyant, serious or scoffing?
7. To what types of people does the play seem to appeal?

## Discussion

1. Give some concrete examples to prove that the most highly trained theatergoer is the most enthusiastic one.
2. In what do you think the real enjoyment of any art lies? Do you see any similarity between the enjoyment an athlete gets from a football game and that which a student of the theater derives from a play?
3. Do you often laugh or cry at a movie or a play? Give some examples of scenes which have stirred you emotionally.
4. Why is it fun to see a good play well produced before an enthusiastic audience?
5. Why is consideration of the four divisions—the play, the acting, the production, and the audience reaction—essential in appraising a play?

## Applications

1. Read *The Art of Playgoing* by John Mason Brown and then discuss it in class, especially Chapters 3, 4, 5, 8, 10, and 11.

# HILLTOP BEACON

Vol. IV, No. 9     ROSLYN HIGH SCHOOL     Wednesday, May 6, 19??

## Audiences Praise 'Carousel' Production

In what may become a school tradition, the spring thespian production this year was again a musical. On the nights of April 17th and 18th, Rodgers and Hammerstein's operetta "Carousel" was presented in the Roslyn High School auditorium. Reactions were, in general, favorable.

In what was really a mammoth effort, over one hundred students and no less than six faculty members combined to effect the production of the very difficult operetta.

There were two sets of lead actors, one for each of the nights. Only one lead actor, Richard Haback, who portrayed Billy Bigelow, performed both nights. Barbara Addison and Judy Gaines alternated as Julie, Elaine Simon and Marla Maes took turns playing Carrie, and Steve Peck switched off with Carmine Copabianco, playing Mr. Snow.

Mr. Wandmacher, technical director of the production, was responsible for the radical difference between the stage sets for the Broadway production and the Roslyn production. The latter were simpler and more "suggestion" props than actual scenery so that the net effect was that of a stylized musical comedy. In places, it tended to look a little like a Dali painting or as if the set were waiting for the addition of a gypsy, a guitar, and a Rousseau lion with big eyes. The overall effect was good, however, and in many places refreshingly original.

The production was supervised by Dr. Rafael Grossman, while the student music director was Joseph Madeline Minns. Choreography was well handled by Mrs. Galetti, and it was nice to see that someone was trying to add this touch to a production like "Carousel."

Mrs. Grossman was the program accompanist and the student co-directors were Gary Blowers and Bette Goldberg.

The play itself was faithfully followed throughout the Roslyn production, which produced an unusually long show (about two hours and forty minutes). It is difficult for any group of high school actors and singers to engross an average audience for that length of time.

Summing up: an excellent show overall, handled in a successfully experimental manner. It is a fine thing somebody in Roslyn is willing to try a production such as this.

### STUDENT PRINTS STAFF CHOSEN

The Editorial Council for the 1959 issue of the Student Prints was chosen on April 16th from a group of Juniors. The tradition has always been to elect the Editorial staff from the Junior Class, although all classes are asked and urged to contribute. The jobs of Editor-in-Chief, Publicity Editor, Business Editor and Typing Editors, were voted upon by the eight junior classmen present. The officers are as follows: Editor-in-Chief, Mike Crichton; Publicity Editor, Dana Kruschel; Business Editor, Eugene Meyer and Typing Editors, Pam Solias, Susan Berman and Joan Radam. The Art Editor has not yet been chosen because all the available talent was not present at the meeting. Other juniors on the staff are: Heloise Console, Roy Furman, Carol Arber, Elizabeth Blum, Roberca Friedlander and June Goldstein.

It is estimated that the book will sell for .35 cents as it did two years ago, and will not be incorporated in the last issue of the Beacon, but rather in its own booklet form, thus providing more space for more work. The main problem in producing the book is, for a change, money. Therefore, subscriptions will be taken early to pay for costs, and only a certain number will be printed, so it is advised that they be bought and paid for as early as possible.

Manuscripts are to be handed Mrs. Ramee, at which point they will lose all identifying marks and be voted on impartially by the Editorial Council. Many entries which are worthy of recognition will, of need, be turned down because of space, but every one is urged to enter as many manuscripts as they want and all will receive careful consideration.

### School Introduces Language Lab

Room 118, better known to foreign language students as the "lab," is the setting for a new experience in language study. Each period of the day and after school, the six soundproof booths are occupied by French and Spanish students intent on perfecting their pronunciation and increasing their comprehension of the spoken word. Others are listening to taped passages of literature or music.

Each booth is equipped with a set of earphones, a microphone and two turntables, one of which plays the Master Disc to be heard or imitated and the other on which is placed a blank disc. A master console equipped with a tape recorder can also relay ma-

### ROSLYN SUCCESSFUL AT SCIENCE CONGRESS

In the Second Annual North Nassau Science Congress, the students of the Roslyn Public Schools were dominant, and about fifty awards were taken by students of the High School, Junior High and Elementary Schools.

High School students were judged among themselves, and seven Roslynites placed with projects in all phases of science. Four won First Prize in their respective divisions.

Ojars Lasmanis won Fire Place in Physics (Mechanical) and Bob Rosenfield won First Place in Physics (Heat, Light and Sound). Lester Lefkowitz copped a First in Animal Biology. Lawrence Shaper took an Honorable Mention in Physics, and Douglas Ross, the only student to win two awards, claimed a Second Place in Earth Science and a Third in Human Biology.

In the Freshman division, winners included William Kaplan, First Place in Physics, and John Lecosta, Honorable Mention in Earth Science.

### Sklarew Honored by N.N.S.C. Award

The North Nassau Science Congress has announced that its choice for the Junior Scientist of the Month of April is Robert Sklarew. Bob, a senior this year at Roslyn, has received a number of awards in his seventeen years.

Our school is among the first on Long Island to install laboratory equipment.

Each aide supervises the laboratory one period per week; some two, and even three periods. *(Continued on Page Two)*

### Tri-School Concert Held at Westbury

On February 11th, Saturday night, the bands of Roslyn, Westbury and Mineola combined to perform at the Tri-School Concert, which was held at the new Westbury High School. Additionally, the choruses of Roslyn, Westbury and West Hempstead participated in the program.

The massed bands and choruses combined to form a large band of about 110 pieces and a chorus of an approximately equal number of singers.

#### Zobian Receives $1,000 Award

Mr. James Zobian, Chemistry teacher at Roslyn, has just been announced as the recipient of an award of one thousand dollars made by the Nichols Foundation through the American Chemical Society.

Mr. Zobian has also been awarded grants from the Fund for the Advancement of Education, specifically, the National Committee on High School Teacher Fellowships. He is presently the president of the New York State Science Teacher's Association and this year became the head of the Roslyn High School Science Department. He is a graduate of St. Lawrence University.

Student Prints, the annual Roslyn High School literary magazine, is now considering manuscripts. Because of a lack of time, students are urged by the Board of Editors to submit manuscripts as soon as possible. Manuscripts should be given to your English teacher or Mrs. Ramee in Room 206.

### FUN-D FAIR
*By Roy Furman*

In keeping with its glorious tradition of huge extravaganzas, Roslyn High School will present its Ninth Annual Fund Fair on May 23rd. Under the extremely capable guidance of Mr. Benson and student directors Marcia Goldstein and Linda Teran, the Fair will be staged on the Roslyn High Athletic field as an all day affair.

As in previous years, the proceeds will be turned over to the scholarship fund, which is reserved for students in need of pecuniary assistance for their later schooling.

Presiding over the Fun-d Fair will be a queen, supposedly the most beautiful creature in Roslyn High School. The contestants for this coveted position are: Sandra Gaudy (Freshman), Marie Dell'Olio, (Sophomore); Susan Einghoff, (Junior); and Karen Smith, (Senior). A unique method of electing the queen has been devised. Four huge jars will soon be situated in the Student Lounge during the fourth, fifth and sixth periods. Each jar will "belong" to a candidate. The students will then deposit money in the jar of their choice. In this manner, the "richest" girl will be the queen with the other candidates acting as her court.

As in the previous fairs, each homeroom will be in charge of a booth, as will several school clubs, along with the Parent's Council. Everything under the sun will be for sale at these booths, including a real, "live" Nike missile (quite expensive though!).

So, come one, come all to the greatest little Fun-d Fair in the world on May 23rd and support your school scholarship fund.

A tense moment in the High School production of "Carousel." Supine is Richard Haback, and clustered around him are Alan Braveman, Judy Gaines, Everett Jacobs and Laurie Sills.—Photo by Spector.

Photo inset by August K. Spector.

A high school reviews its production of *Carousel* in the school paper.

2. Read some examples of current dramatic criticism in such publications as *The New York Times, The New York Herald-Tribune, The San Francisco Chronicle, The Philadelphia Bulletin, Time, The New Yorker, The Christian Science Monitor,* and the syndicated articles on the theater in your local papers. Discuss them in class, noting the style of the writer, his point of view, his apparent background, and his ability to criticize fairly.

3. Go to the best movies and plays available. Discuss and analyze them in class, answering the questions listed in this chapter on pages 391 to 393.

4. Form the habit of reading current theatrical magazines at your school or public library. Ask for bound copies of those now out of print. The librarians will be glad to help you find reviews of the plays you read in class. *Theatre Arts, The Billboard, Variety, Life,* and back copies of *Theatre Arts, Stage,* and *Theatre* will be of great interest to you.

5. Listen to programs on radio and television presented by dramatic critics and discuss them in class.

6. Arrange a class theater party for a stage play. Afterwards write individual criticisms, using the questions on pages 391 to 393 as a guide. Read your reviews aloud in class, comparing notes and discussing the various reactions. Note which members of the group are most discriminating, most negative, most enthusiastic, or best able to express their ideas entertainingly and forcefully.

7. Keep a section of your notebook or a separate scrapbook for criticisms of current plays. You may some day have the opportunity to see these plays or movies based on them, and it will be interesting to compare your reactions with those of the best critics. You will also become familiar with the names of the best actors, playwrights, designers, and directors and their achievements. Read the plays when they appear in printed form, and whenever possible, compare your imagined sets with photographs of the production.

## Appraisal of School Productions

After each class and school play, some appraisal should be made by the students before and behind the footlights. With class plays, your discussion, probably led by the teacher of dramatics, should center about the theme and its interpretation by the author and the cast. A written criticism of the play should be turned in the next day by each member of the class who watched it. Those taking part in any capacity should write an essay entitled "What I Gained in This Production" or some similar title.

The written criticism can well take the form of the play reviews you have been following in the press. Make sure it includes some mention of the four considerations in judging a play. The comments about the acting should be helpful and not discouraging. They should emphasize the best phases of the actors' work and give suggestions for improvement. Opportunity should be given for all the members of the cast to read the reviews.

Students again, two of the previous night's actresses compare views on the performance with their teacher-director.

Do not let yourself be upset if you are adversely criticized for your acting, which you may have thought was pretty good. Accept suggestions for improvement, think them over carefully, and see how they work in your next role. Do not let your head be turned by exorbitant praise or your enthusiasm dampened by lack of appreciation. Just go on developing your abilities and gaining by experience.

At the close of a big school production, all the people involved usually celebrate with a cast party, where all the thrills and disasters are relived and various opinions are expressed. Then there is the excitement of seeing what the school paper has to say about the production. The comments, both pro and con, of members of the audience will go on for months. Profit by them if you can, but do not let them get you down.

There should be a meeting of all students who worked on the show soon after the last performance. Each one should be given the opportunity of reading his comments on what the total experience has meant to him, as well as his evaluation of the play. If such a meeting cannot be held, first consult the director, whose judgment is worth your careful consideration, and then analyze your growth by yourself. If possible, a tape recording should be made of each performance. The group should listen to it carefully. Each participant should take notes, especially on his own part, checking voice, pauses, diction, and general effectiveness.

It is to be hoped that you will have at least two performances—three or more are preferable—so that you can experience the reactions of different audiences and feel the effect on your acting. One of the joys of interpreting a role several times is your deeper grasp of its subtleties each time you play it. Of course, you must never change any business which has been rehearsed, no matter what the audience does. Whether you are asked to or not, you will find it valuable to write out your reactions to the entire experience and put the comments into your notebook for future reference.

*Discussion*

1. Does your feeling about the success of a recent school play coincide with the reaction of the audience?
2. What phase of the experience gave you the greatest pleasure? What worried you the most?
3. Do you want to act in any more plays or help on the production staff? Give your reasons.
4. What were the best elements of the production? The weakest?
5. Were there any serious faults? How might they have been avoided?
6. What changes in the production would you suggest if there could be another run of the show?
7. Do you feel that your share in the production has helped you physically, mentally, and spiritually? If so, how?
8. What phase of the theater do you think will interest you most in the future? Do you feel any urge to enter upon a theatrical career? If so, what type of work do you now feel you would like to pursue?
9. What would be the advantage of following the theater as an avocation in college and community productions rather than taking it up professionally?
10. Do you think you will major in dramatics in college? If so, where would you like to study? Why? (*Lovejoy's College Guide*, published by Simon and Schuster, gives brief descriptions of over two thousand colleges and universities. After consulting it, you should write for catalogues from several schools. At the same time, you may request detailed information on dramatic facilities and courses.)

# Part Five

# Motion Pictures,

# Radio, and

# Television

⟨₹ Today the drama is an important part of your daily life. Television is bringing live and taped dramatic films into your home, and the movie industry is offering products of increasingly high caliber. If you choose your fare wisely, either at home or in the moving-picture houses, you can enjoy good theater as it is being presented to the largest audiences in the history of entertainment. On the other hand, if you are not discriminating, you can easily waste valuable hours watching worthless shows. Perhaps the greatest service your study of dramatics offers you is the opportunity to develop good taste in choosing plays, motion pictures, and television programs for your entertainment. As your critical abilities become more practiced, you will no longer be satisfied with the mediocre but will select the best from the mediums available to you.

Apparently the crucial days are over when most movie theaters seemed to be closing their doors before the lure of television. Today both entertainment mediums are reaching their particular audiences and are flourishing.

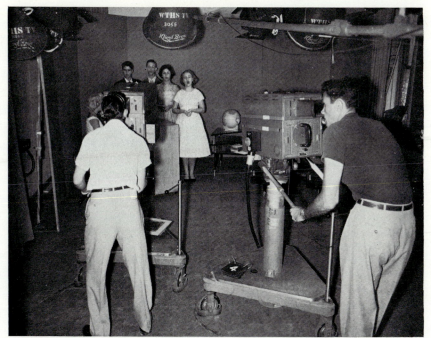

Revolutionary changes are taking place in the television and movie industries. In television, the most important advances are the introduction and growing use of video tape and the improvement of color programs. The movies also are refining their use of color and are employing the relatively new wide-screen processes. There is an increasing tendency to shift production from the huge movie companies into ones controlled by actors who employ freelance directors and dramatists from the fields of both film and the legitimate theater.

In addition, the film industry is being internationalized. American producers are doing more pictures in foreign lands and are going to great expense to transport actors and equipment to these locales to obtain realistic backgrounds. We are seeing more foreign film stars in American pictures, as well as in those produced in their native lands. This internationalization of the movies and its resulting familiarity with foreign places, ideas, and people may prove to be one of our most practical means of increasing world understanding.

*Chapter 15*

# Motion Pictures

The universal appeal of the motion picture, its technical perfection, the comparatively low cost of admission, and the ease of attendance all combine to make it the most widespread form of popular theater the world has ever seen. You are one of some 250 million film viewers from all over the world.

The story of motion pictures goes all the way back to Leonardo da Vinci and includes the names of creative thinkers from many countries. Some knowledge of the history of motion-picture development and the industry will increase your appreciation of the remarkable progress made in the last fifty years. Students interested in this history will be rewarded in their research by finding a fascinating story of technical ingenuity and artistic achievement. (Several challenging and worthwhile research topics are suggested on page 407.)

## RECENT DEVELOPMENTS IN MOTION PICTURES

### The Wide Screen

Screens heightened, widened, and curved are the latest developments of the industry. Introduced in 1951, wide screens have been installed in more than a third of the world's theaters. Most authorities feel that the wide screen will become universal in a few years because of the greater clarity, depth, and realism possible with its use. By 1955, half of Hollywood's films were being turned out by means of these new processes. You can get detailed information on them from a recent edition of an encyclopedia or by writing to the Association of Motion Picture Producers, 8480 Beverly Boulevard, Hollywood 48, California. The following brief discussion of wide-screen systems may give you an added interest as you see the films which use them.

*Cinerama,* one of the first popular wide-screen processes, created a sensation when it was introduced in New York on September 30, 1952. The picture shown was the thrilling *This Is Cinerama,* produced by the late Michael Todd, Lowell Thomas, and their associates. Viewers had the illusion of being "catapulted" from their seats into the action of the film.

In Cinerama, the picture that the audience sees is actually a composite of pictures taken by three separate cameras. The pictures taken by the three cameras are projected simultaneously on an immense curved screen. Magnetic stereophonic sound is used. Seven channels—five behind the screen and two at the sides—give the audience the feeling of being surrounded by sound.

*CinemaScope* is probably the most familiar wide-screen process because it was one of the first to be used extensively. The first full-length picture using this process was *The Robe,* directed by Henry Koster and released in 1953. CinemaScope utilizes a lens which compresses a picture covering a wide angle into the space on standard-size film. Another lens widens and enlarges the picture in projection. CinemaScope also uses stereophonic sound.

*VistaVision* has the important feature of permitting the size of its image to be adjusted to all theater screens.

*Todd-AO,* developed by Michael Todd and Brian O'Brien, uses one camera and one projector. The picture is thrown onto a large, curved screen with a high reflectance surface. The process uses a six-channel stereophonic sound system. Perhaps you saw the first great Todd-AO picture, *Oklahoma!* This was followed by *Around the World in 80 Days,* which won an Academy Award.

Wide-screen systems are being developed and improved, and it is generally believed that they will dominate the motion-picture productions of the future. However, as you watch old films on television and new ones on the wide screens of the movie theaters, you will soon realize that it is the screenplay, its direction and interpretation, and the skill of the motion picture cameramen in bringing to life the director's ideas that make a good movie.

A scene from Vittorio de Sica's award-winning film *The Bicycle Thief*, produced in Rome with an all-Italian cast of inexperienced but natural actors.

## Internationalization

The motion-picture industry is working closely with UNESCO to encourage (on a nonprofit basis) the exchange of documentary films which present an accurate, artistic, and instructive picture of various nations.

Co-production is the most practical of the international movements in the film industry. Producers of different countries pool their resources—talent, money, technical and directorial skills—in making a picture. Then all share in the returns from the world-wide distribution. Thus feature films are being made all over the world, and the actual backgrounds of foreign lands are coming alive for the millions who see them.

As far as you are concerned, it is actually seeing the foreign stars—Anna Magnani, Alec Guinness, Cantinflas, Vittorio de Sica, Miyoshi Umeki, Claire Bloom, Laurence Olivier, and Fernandel, to name only a few—that will give you the greatest thrill. Among the foreign films you should not miss are the prize-winning Indian documentary *Pather Panchali*, the French comedy *The Sheep Has Five Legs*, the exquisite Italian-Japanese *Madame Butterfly*, and any Shakespearean films featuring players from the Old Vic and Stratford Memorial Theatre companies.

## Movies on Television

Television programming often features the showing of movies made originally for exhibition in movie theaters. Some of the films shown are fine ones of the past such as *Conquest*, a story of Napoleon; *The Yearling*, concerning a small boy's affection for a tame deer; *What Every Woman Knows*, with Helen Hayes and Brian Aherne in James M. Barrie's popular play; the original *Ruggles of Red Gap*, with an all-star cast headed by Charles Laughton in the title role; *Anna Karenina*, the Russian classic with Greta Garbo and Fredric March; *Pygmalion*, with Wendy Hiller and Leslie Howard; and the Dickens' tales *David Copperfield*, *Great Expectations*, *A Tale of Two Cities*, and *Oliver Twist*. It must be admitted that some of the films shown on television are inferior. As in all television viewing, you must learn to be selective. However, if you choose wisely, you will have the unique theatrical experience of comparing the work of stars in their youth and later years. You will also be able to see the work of some of the great actors who are no longer living.

## Special Categories of Films

**Feature films.** Cecil B. De Mille's *The Ten Commandments* holds the present record as the most supercolossal of all feature films. Produced in VistaVision at a cost of over 8 million dollars, it will probably be one of the last pictures made under the studio setup with all sixty-four departments working full blast. It was the seventieth picture made by De Mille, who, in 1913, produced Hollywood's first feature-length film, *The Squaw Man*. The greatest number of extras ever used in a motion picture were hired for the Egyptian scenes in *The Ten Commandments*. The crowds, together with their animals and other possessions, appeared on the largest set ever constructed for a motion picture.

**Animated cartoons.** Walt Disney has probably contributed more than any one man to the sheer delight of film entertainment with his animated cartoons, culminating in the first feature-length cartoon, *Snow White and the Seven Dwarfs*. His *The Lady and the Tramp* was the first wide-screen cartoon.

**Documentaries.** *Documentary films* are those which feature the effective and natural presentation of factual material in dramatic form. They are often produced for special purposes and are aimed at particular groups. The United Nations, the State Department, the United States Army Signal Corps, several news bureaus, and business firms sponsor such factual pictures. Two of the early American documentaries were *The River* and *The Plow That Broke the Plains* by Pare Lorentz. These films proved of such economic and social significance that they were shown widely and were followed by other pictures in the same style. Robert and Frances Flaherty were among the first to document on film the lives of real people in their native environments. Their *Nanook of the North, Man of Aran*, and *Moana* are classics in the documentary field as is *Louisiana Story*, winner of an International Film Award.

**Other categories.** Other categories of films are *newsreels*; *educational films* produced for schools, colleges, universities, and adult education groups; and *industrial films* produced by and for specific industries to teach their employees or trainees and to inform the public about their products.

### Organizations Representing the Film Industry

A number of necessary steps have been taken to organize the huge industry which involves so many human and mechanical elements.

The Motion Picture Association of America, Inc., handles the intricate problems of public relations and other matters of national and international importance. (The organization is located at 28 West 44th Street, New York City 18.) One of its aims is to enlist public support for the improvement of film standards, both moral and artistic. In addition, the organization works to improve advertising, community service, foreign markets, public information, motion-picture theater service, and title registration.

A Disney artist completes a series of sketches for *Fantasia*.

Robert Flaherty relaxes during the filming of his documentary *Moana*.

Since 1930 a production code for ethics and an advertising code have been developed. These have helped to establish general and specific principles to govern the policies of companies belonging to the association.

The Academy of Motion Picture Arts and Sciences helps encourage high artistic achievement by giving awards—the famous Oscars—for the best work in all branches of film production each year. These awards are for the best performances of an actor and an actress, the best direction of a film, the best-written screen play, the best sound recording, the best photography, and so on. The announcement of awards is one of the most exciting annual Hollywood events.

The Motion Picture Research Council, Inc., is a nonprofit organization which works with motion-picture production groups to encourage the development and interchange of technical inventions within the whole industry.

The Motion Picture Export Association of America handles all of the complicated problems dealing with the export of our films to the countries of the world. The organization works out the negotiations with foreign governments but does not actually rent or sell films. It handles the participation of the United States in the many international film festivals and arranges for distinguished visitors from abroad to see the studios in Hollywood. Both activities are aimed at enhancing mutual good will. It maintains a fact book, which provides its members with concise information on trading conditions in over sixty countries. It works closely with the International Federation of Film Producers. Overseas offices, to handle important matters at first hand, are in London, Paris, Rome, Frankfurt, Stockholm, Tokyo, Rio de Janeiro, Bombay, and Jakarta. In conformity with the Production Code, the association sifts out the films going abroad and determines whether a picture "in any way distorts, exaggerates, or misleads in its portrayal of Americans or the American way of life." The Foreign Film Advisory Unit assists foreign producers in marketing their films in this country.

*Discussion*

1. How far do you think the influence of motion pictures can go toward establishing better relations between nations? Why?

2. Have you seen any of the silent movies? Did you like them? How did they differ from films of today?

3. Do you feel color has helped the artistry of films? How?

4. Have you ever seen a picture produced in the Far East? How did it differ from those produced in the United States?

**5.** Describe any Shakespearean pictures you have seen.

**6.** Are you interested in the problems and techniques of the movie industry or only in the films as good entertainment? Why?

**7.** Which of the foreign stars have you liked the best? The least? Give reasons for your reactions.

**8.** Do you enjoy seeing the old films on television or in reruns? Which pictures have you enjoyed the most? Do you think the wide screens, color, and improved sound would give them a greater appeal or are they sufficient in themselves?

**9.** Do you think the Lincoln Center for the Performing Arts in New York City should include a motion-picture theater? If so, what type of pictures do you think should be shown there?

*Applications*

**1.** Research reports on the history of the motion picture may include any of the suggestions listed below. You may want to refer to several sources of information such as encyclopedias, card catalogues and bibliographies in your school or community library, or the *Readers' Guide to Periodical Literature*. For specialized questions you might write to the sources mentioned on pages 404 and 406.

    **a.** Give reports on the lives and contributions to the development of motion pictures of:

| | | |
|---|---|---|
| Peter Mark Roget | Thomas A. Edison | Adolph Zukor |
| Eadweard Muybridge and John D. Isaacs | George Eastman | Lewis J. Selznick |
| | C. Francis Jenkins | Carl Laemmle |
| Dr. Joseph Plateau | Edwin S. Porter | D. W. Griffith |
| Dr. Coleman Sellers | George Méliès | Cecil B. De Mille |

    **b.** Give reports on the following topics:

The First American Film Stars
The First Talkies and Their Impact on the Industry
The Development of Color Films
Scientific Principles of the Motion-picture Camera
The Production Code and/or the Advertising Code of the MPAA
The New Wide-screen Processes
Some Problems Facing the Motion-picture Industry Today
The Relationship between Television and the Movies at Present

**2.** Look up the principle of "the persistence of vision" upon which the creation of motion in pictures is based. Some early forerunners of the movies were manually operated machines such as the *phenakistoscope*, the *zoetrope*, the *praxinoscope*, the *kinetoscope*. All of them used this principle. If you can find pictures and descriptions of these machines, perhaps you can make one to show to the class.

3. Make as complete a list as you can of pictures which have won Academy Awards as best picture of the year during the past ten years. Check the ones you have seen, and explain why they have won awards.

4. Bring in as many examples of clever advertising and promotion for recent films as you can find.

5. Formulate a debatable proposition on the comparative merits of American and foreign films. Choose a proposition from those submitted by the entire class and debate it in class.

6. Make your own list of the ten best movies of last year.

7. As a class attend a foreign film. Write a report on its technique, story, acting, and the audience response.

8. Talk to a leading motion-picture exhibitor in your community about the possibility of showing a Shakespearean film as a civic project.

## MAKING A FILM

The second half of this century sees motion-picture production moving into a new era. Films are being made in actual settings the world over. Stars are making deals with the great studios to work for a percentage of profits per picture or are leasing the facilities of the studios and producing their own films. Independent directors and screen writers are making their own terms instead of working under contracts of long duration. The development of the wide screen and other new processes is increasing the cost of production and exhibition. In turn, the admission charge is affected. The studios are making many more films for television and are selling their old pictures in huge blocks for television showings. Today there is a very definite demand from the public for superior pictures. Movies must meet this demand in order to win back the audience they lost to television and to hold the audience they have.

### The Key People

The general process of making a picture remains fundamentally the same. The key people are the producer, director, cinematographer, film editor, and actors. All are supported by the technical men who work behind the scenes.

**The producer.** He is the production chief who selects the screenplay, hires the director (unless he chooses to direct a production himself), and supervises and coordinates the many elements of making a movie. He works closely with the director in selecting the cast, approving the sets, and checking the final cutting. In addition, he makes the financial decisions and arranges for the release and exhibition of the picture in this country and abroad.

**The director.** He is the person responsible for combining the acting, photography, action, sound, and musical score into an effective interpretation of the screenplay. You will probably sense the difference in taste and technique between the leading directors as you watch pictures more analytically. You may already have your favorites, as do movie fans the world over. Carol Reed, John Huston, Henry Koster, William Wyler, George Stevens, Joshua Logan, John Ford, Stanley Kramer, Leo McCarey, and Alfred Hitchcock are only a few of the names that draw at the box office almost as well as those of the stars they direct.

**Director Mark Robson gives a few pointers to Ingrid Bergman on the set of** *Inn of the Sixth Happiness.*

Before the shooting starts, the director works out every scene, visualizing each one as a part in the culminating action of the picture. However the actual shooting of scenes does not follow in sequence. Matters of technique and location determine the order of taking scenes—not the emotional and logical building of the plot. The director works with the actors for the proper interpretation of each scene. Before the shooting, he settles with the cinematographer the position of the cameras and the number and types of shots. During the filming, he controls the shooting and reshooting of each scene. Later he checks the "rushes," the shots made each day, and selects those to be used. At the end, he supervises the cutting and editing of the film. Holding down the overhead costs, keeping to the working schedule, and handling the actors and technicians successfully are all a part of his job.

**The cinematographer.** Often called the director of photography, he is responsible for putting the screenplay on film. Through the mediums of light, shadow, and frequently color, he creates the atmosphere and beauty of each shot. He does not handle a camera himself but works on composition and lighting while directing his assistants, who make sure that the lenses are functioning and focused properly. The American Society of Cinematographers and other national societies are made up of distinguished camera artists from all over the world. Today they are being appreciated and awarded special notice everywhere. You should form the habit of watching the credit lists at the beginning or end of each movie for the names of such men as James Wong Howe, Claude Renoir, Joseph Valentine, Rudolph Mate, Kohei Sugiyama, Jack Cardiff, and Hal Mohr. Look for the fine points of photography in their films.

**The film editor.** During the filming of a picture, perhaps three times more film is shot than will ever be used. The film editor must assist the director in viewing all the film and cutting out scenes or parts of scenes that are not necessary to the story. He must arrange scenes shot out of sequence into their logical sequence. The film editor's work demands great skill and artistry.

**The actors.** The work of film actors is discussed in the section beginning on page 421.

### Work Behind the Scenes

Surrounded by towering walls, some Hollywood studios are still worlds in themselves. Mazelike streets, leading to the immense sound stages, are filled with people in every imaginable garb. The miles of outdoor sets are extremely interesting. There are villages of all nations and periods, ancient ruins, city tenements, western towns, artificial lakes, oriental bazaars, railway stations of many countries, the exteriors of famous buildings—all standing as shallow, empty fronts waiting to be brought to life and teeming activity. Within the great studios are countless sound stages in varied degrees of preparedness for production. When a scene is being shot, the sound stage becomes a focal point of human and mechanical preparation.

**A section of MGM's 187-acre studio in Culver City, California.**

With space at a premium in the property department, the ceiling as well as the floor is used for storage.

In a section of the men's wardrobe department, uniforms of all sizes and kinds are stored neatly away for future use.

Each movie that you see is a product of the efforts of the key people and also the many departments which perform special functions. Several thousand men and women carry out instructions from the department heads. On studio staffs there are research specialists, librarians, dialogue coaches, make-up artists, engineers, carpenters, mechanics, script girls, clerks, chefs, nurses, teachers for the child actors, gardeners, policemen, pages, painters, engravers, and many others.

**Research.** One of the most fascinating of all the production units is the research department. Scores of librarians deal with millions of facts, photographs, and printed materials, and they check the authenticity of every detail of settings, costumes, customs, and idioms. Catalogued materials, ranging from works in the oldest art galleries and museums to the latest articles on all conceivable subjects, are on file and can be located on request.

**Props.** All movable articles are stored in the props department. Immense space is required to stow away the accumulations on every studio lot. There is a collection of furniture of every period, lamps, mirrors, bric-a-brac, utensils, firearms, typewriters, rugs, newspapers of every kind, and many other objects. The files must be kept up to the minute, for the property-man is expected to produce anything of any period for anyone at any time. He must have it intact, correct, and in the right spot at the exact moment it is needed.

**Costuming.** The wardrobe department is in charge of all costuming. Extensive research, artistry, ingenuity, skill, patience, and sensitivity go into the costuming for every picture, not to mention the thousands of dollars and the yards of material used. Sketches are first made by the head designer, and the amount, color, and cost of material estimated. It may be necessary to make or rent thousands of outfits for the numerous extras, who must be correctly attired. Exact colors and fabrics must be carefully selected for color photography. The relationships of the lines and colors to the scenic background must be considered also. "How far ahead of current styles should the film be?"—this is a real problem to the dress designer. The picture may be released one or two years after it is made, and styles do change. The costume accessories in period films—such little things as handkerchiefs, belts, hair ornaments, and jewelry, not to mention shoes, hats, and furs—must be considered and carefully made. In a picture like *War and Peace*, costumes which supposedly have been worn for long periods of stress and strain must be aged convincingly, or a series of costumes and accessories showing the various stages of disintegration must be made up.

**Make-up.** The work done by the make-up department must be uniform in style and very natural, particularly for close-ups and color shots. In many scenes each actor must have exactly the same make-up, even when there is a long interval between "takes." Wigs and hairdressing are also an important part of costuming and make-up. Very difficult and elaborate character changes and exceptional types must be done by trained and experienced people.

**Sets.** The art, construction, and electrical departments work in close cooperation. The art director designs and plans the sets, the set-construction people build them, and the electrical specialists light them to bring out their full beauty and effectiveness. All must concur on the style of design; the shape, size, safety, practicability, and availability of the sets; and the best construction materials to convey the time, mood, locale, and atmosphere of the scene. These departments must also work together on location, often using artificial effects to accent the natural beauty of the scenic backgrounds. For example, the citizens of Hawaii were amazed at the arrival of many plastic coconut palms for the sets of *South Pacific* when hundreds of real palms were available. Plastic constructions are taking the place of painted scenery, and many sets are being created with the new materials that are constantly coming on the market. In most instances, blueprints and models are made to exact scale by the art department so that the director, cameraman, and sound technician can work out all details of action in advance and thus avoid wasting time and money.

**Special effects.** The special effects department creates the amazing illusions that make the motion picture a distinct art. Nothing seems impossible to them. Hurricanes, explosions, and other major disasters are often created with the help of miniature ships, airplanes, locomotives, and buildings. Sometimes, on location, great areas are converted into tropical forests, deserts, and fantastic worlds. Cloud effects, snowstorms, transformation scenes, earthquakes, air battles, and all the other wonders in motion pictures are worked out in this department.

**Sound.** The sound department today is so basic to studio organization that it is hard to remember the days when silent pictures were made. Carefully tested microphones pick up the sounds on the set and they are checked by the "mixer," who regulates the volume. The dialogue, sound effects, and music are ultimately combined on the same sound track and synchronized with the picture frames.

**Music.** The music department provides the musical score or background music for a film. Musical directors work with world-renowned composers and performers. Large staffs in each studio include conductors, arrangers, lyric writers, score writers, and all the various music specialists. Musical background is usually composed and arranged after the film is completed. First, the musical director studies the scenario and the film. Next, the action is timed scene by scene and speech by speech. Then the music is correlated with spoken words. Detailed cue sheets are made and the music is rehearsed until the synchronization is perfect. When the director feels the score is right, it is recorded on the sound track.

The set for the movie *The Diary of Anne Frank* is very similar to the actual warehouse and factory in Amsterdam where the Franks and their friends hid from the Nazis. The room at the top left is the Secret Annexe where they lived for two years until their capture.

## The Film Itself

**The story.** As in all theatrical enterprises, the first step is to find a story. Popular novels, successful short stories, and plays are used, but Hollywood has never been restricted to published material alone. Scouts and agents throughout the world transmit story outlines and critical analyses. Each of these is turned over to a reader who writes a criticism and synopsis. The reader may also supply information on film trends, the suitability of certain actors for the roles, a probable purchase cost, and a comparison with popular pictures already showing. The head of the story department then presents the report to the executive staff in a conference, and usually tells the story orally to give the staff time to visualize and discuss its possibilities.

When a story is accepted, it is turned over to screen writers who prepare a *screen treatment*, a scene-by-scene description without detailed dialogue or action. This is submitted to the censorship office. Then it goes to the production manager, director, artist, and photographer. Tentative budgets determine the approximate time and money allotted to the picture.

Finally writers are assigned to work on the *scenario*, a detailed treatment of each scene, showing plot development. Screen writers include many of the most brilliant playwrights in the world. Some of them are hired at a weekly salary, others are maintained on a contract basis. Today authors are often employed by independent producers for a single picture.

When the scenario is completed, a shooting script is made. Copies are sent to the head of every department for a detailed breakdown of the sets, props, cast, and all specific needs. The final shooting schedule utilizes the efforts of all the departments for weeks, months, or sometimes years.

**Shooting the film.** On stage the actual filming is started by the ringing of a bell. The director then calls, "Quiet please. Roll 'em over." When the camera and sound are synchronized, he calls, "Camera!" At the end of the "take" he says, "Cut!" If he wants the "take" saved, he says, "Print it"; if not, he declares it "N.G." (no good), and a "retake" is made.

Shooting a scene is the culmination of the infinite labor of hundreds of people for many weeks, and it involves tremendous expenditure of money and emotional and physical energy. After rehearsals on the set have fixed the business and lines, scenes are usually taken of only three or four minutes of action. They are shot from all angles, sometimes by several cameras at the same time, but usually by one camera in a number of different positions. This is done in order to secure the very best effect and to cover any mistakes later evident on the film. All the scenes using the same set are shot one after the other, regardless of the continuity of the story. As a visitor you see only these seemingly disconnected bits of action.

The script girl plays an important part in the shooting. She must check every detail of costume, make-up, and action in order to be sure that no change is made between one scene and others which are taken much later on another set—even though these latter scenes, in the film itself, may merely involve the passing of action from one room to another.

While the picture is being shot, the dialogue is recorded on the sound film and the action on the picture film. After shooting is completed, prints are made from the picture and sound negatives, and both are rewound together in order that the daily rushes may have both sound and picture.

**The director, on a movable platform, oversees the shooting of a scene on one of the studio's sound stages.**

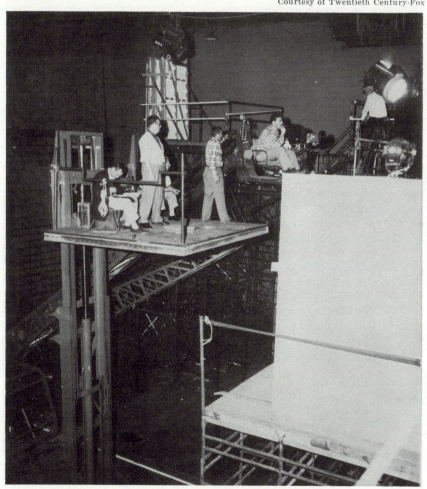

**Cutting.** The cutting of the film is almost as important as the shooting because the footage of the film taken is many times that of the final picture. Every scene is numbered and marked on both the picture and sound film in order that the cutter may keep the continuity intact. An accurate report of the number of the scene and the exact kind and number of shots taken of it is kept by the script girl and turned in to the cutter. Every day the sound and picture reels taken that day are viewed by the director. He decides which takes he wishes to use and whether retakes are needed.

The film editor then cuts the film, assembling the scenes in continuity, taking account of the center of interest, purpose of the shot, and tempo of the action. He determines whether to use a montage, a dissolve, or other special effects. The trims are the pieces cut away, and they are kept to be used later if needed. In some cases, whole documentary films and short subjects have been edited from the scraps on the cutting room floor. The selected shots are clipped together and later spliced with cement. This rough cut is then reviewed on the screen and possibly reedited. In the last stage, the fade-outs, dissolves, and wipes, which denote the passage of time or distinct change of scene, are put in.

**Film editor Barbara McLean views the day's rushes, deciding which to cut and which to retain.**

**Sound synchronization.** After the editing has been done, the picture is scored. The musical score is usually written especially for the picture, in harmony with the mood and atmosphere of the individual scenes. The music is recorded before a screen on which the picture is thrown, and the orchestra leader and mixer synchronize the music with the action. The sound effects are also introduced after the editing. Many of the effects are already on hand, made from records. Others are created especially for the picture. The music and sound effects are all recorded on different sound tracks which are then re-recorded on a new track. At last this new track is synchronized with the film, and the print of the picture and sound track are run off to permit further editing. In the case of dubbing in another language so that the film may be used in foreign countries, the re-recording includes synchronizing the dialogue in the same way.

**Previews.** After the film has been re-recorded with sound effects and music, all the tracks are recorded on the master track and the first preview print is made. It is much longer than the final film will be. The film is then previewed, usually in an obscure neighborhood theater before a typical audience, with the producer, director, and important members of the staff in attendance. The audience reaction is noted in detail, especially with regard to the actors, theme, and total effect of the picture. It is after this preview that the final decisions are made about which actors are to be featured, played down, or eliminated, what scenes are to be shortened or cut out entirely, and what effects are to be strengthened. The picture is then re-edited and perhaps repreviewed.

## Summary of Production Procedures

The production of a motion picture might be summarized in this way. The producer is appointed and the story chosen. The director, the production manager, and their staffs are selected. The story treatment is made and passed by the censorship office. After this, the shooting script is written and broken down in the various departments. Budgets for all departments are worked out and passed on by the production manager. Shooting schedules are made. Blueprints, models, and effects are created; electrical and sound equipment is installed; sets are made, dressed, and lighted. Stars are acquired by the producer and the entire cast is selected by the director and casting department. Costumes are designed, made, and fitted. At last the scenes are shot, checked in the daily rushes, edited, cut, and spliced. All music and sound effects are dubbed in, and the film and sound synchronized. The completed film is previewed. Then it is re-edited, advertised, distributed, and shown to you at movie theaters.

*Discussion*

1. Which phases of motion-picture production interest you the most? Give your reasons.

2. Would you be interested in earning your living by working in any of the departments discussed here?

3. What pictures have you seen recently which seemed particularly well produced? In what respects?

4. What very expensive films have been box-office failures? Give reasons for your choices.

5. Can you name any simply produced pictures which were so well directed that they became box-office successes?

6. Analyze the work of the six directors you consider the finest now working in Hollywood.

7. What is your reaction to the new wide-screen processes?

8. Who are some of your favorite producers, directors, and cinematographers? Why does their work appeal to you?

9. In what directions do you think motion-picture production will develop in the future? Will there be more movies made, or fewer? Will the major studios concentrate their efforts on making films for television? Give your reasons.


*Applications*

1. Look up the following film terms and define them: blimp, boom, mixer, screen treatment, underscoring, dubbing, sound track, trims, grips, dolly, rushes, montage.

2. Describe the following shots: pan, angle, close-up, cut-back, double exposure, flash, wipe, process, cut-in, dissolve, flash.

3. Read Christopher Isherwood's humorous novel *Prater Violet*, Jane Allen's *I Lost My Girlish Laughter*, Kaufman's *Once in a Lifetime*, or Jessamyn West's *To See the Dream*. Report on what you learn about motion-picture production.

4. As a class attend the best picture being shown in your community at the present time. Divide the class into groups, each one to watch some particular phase of production—the photography, sound effects, use of music, montage, make-up, costuming, use of crowds, appropriateness of furniture and props, and the work of the director and other movie personnel discussed in this chapter.

5. Using the books listed in Appendix C and articles in current magazines, give reports on such topics as sound recording, going on location, editing a film, the "master minds" on a studio lot, a day in a studio, the art of cinematography, the work of the various departments, and the importance of independent producing companies.

# MOTION-PICTURE ACTING

Although few of you may ever appear in a Hollywood movie, many of you think of the films when you think about acting. Actually there are a number of differences between acting on the stage and acting in a movie.

## Technical Limitations

Acting on the screen is controlled by mechanical devices and technical considerations which are entirely apart from the actor, although he is the focus. Scenes are seldom played in sequence but always in accordance with the demands of the stage set, location, convenience, casting, and production problems. Scenes of three or four minutes in length are shot at a time, usually accepted after from three to fifty retakes. These retakes are often due to faulty mechanical details rather than poor acting. The actor must, therefore, create the proper emotional response instantly, without building up to it or growing into it as he can on the stage. There can be no continuity of response in developing a character.

The film actor must constantly adjust himself to the restrictions of stage space, light angles, and camera positions, as well as to the response of his fellow actors. He cannot depend on the audience, which is the barometer a stage actor follows. He must also suffer the discomforts of bright, hot lights, close, stuffy sets, lengthy waits between scenes, and long hard hours of work—usually beginning at seven in the morning and continuing until five or six o'clock in the evening.

Many actors aspire to Hollywood careers. The salaries are very high, and, if an actor can attain a popular standing with movie audiences, the resultant financial security is far greater than that in the theater. If an actor achieves stardom, he receives a type of audience worship that is probably unique in the entertainment world. The rewards of security and popularity are hard to resist.

## General Acting Procedures

The whole procedure of screen acting differs from that of the stage. Scripts are rewritten and revised so rapidly that actors have little time to learn their lines. Usually, the actor is given the script two or three days in advance of a shooting so that he may memorize the lines for the short scene scheduled. Rehearsals are not held until the day of the shooting. On that day the actor arrives at the studio at about six o'clock in the morning and spends long hours in being made up. A reading rehearsal is then held on the set, and the scene is worked out in detail. Rehearsals without scripts continue as long as the director or the rigid shooting schedule allows.

As the Gestapo approaches the Secret Annexe in *The Diary of Anne Frank*, the actors must show their intense fear of capture. To heighten the terror, director George Stevens fires blank rounds from a pistol.

In the finished scene the tense and anxious faces of the actors, as they listen to the footsteps of the Nazis below their attic, prove the wisdom of director Stevens's method.

The actors are then dismissed while the technicians adjust the lighting and sound equipment. The stand-ins take the place of the actors during this phase. Then a complete rehearsal with the cast is held under the lights, and minor changes are made. At long last, the scene is shot from many angles until the director, cameraman, and sound engineer are convinced that sufficient shots have been taken and the best possible recordings have been made. If some mistake is discovered in the day's rushes, then the whole process must be repeated.

Until the première, the actor usually does not know how much of his role remains in the picture. One capable actress went to Hollywood and, after a successful interview, was given expensive screen tests which led to her being cast in an important film with a leading star. The film was one of the hits of the year, but her role had been cut by the editing to one of minor importance. She has never had another chance, although her work was entirely satisfactory. Such can be the life of a screen actor in Hollywood!

*Discussion*

1. Whom do you consider the best actors and actresses on the screen today? Analyze their ability and appeal.
2. What advantages does the screen actor have over the stage actor?
3. Can you differentiate between the work of an actor who has appeared on both the stage and screen and one who has worked only in the movies? What differences do you see?
4. Would you rather act on the stage or screen?
5. Name as many film actors as you can who have been popular with the public for more than ten years. Explain their steady success.
6. Who are some of the actors now producing their own pictures?
7. Which stars are also excellent dancers, singers, or directors?
8. Why is naturalness of characterization so important in screen acting?

## THE SCREEN AND THE SCHOOL

A new enthusiasm for the study of motion pictures has come with television's use of movies. Perhaps your work in class will be the impetus for your study of the movies as an artistic medium. At the university level, excellent departments of cinematography are functioning all over the United States and in many European countries. In addition to teaching the theory of motion pictures, very fine films are actually written and produced by the students under expert direction. One such film is *Anywhere —In Our Time* which was made by Dr. Hedwig Traub's students at the University of Munich.

University students in Munich, Germany, film *Anywhere—In Our Time,* a
movie for which they wrote their own script.

## Sources of Information about Movies

The services of the MPAA will be of special interest to you. The Children's Film Library makes available the finest pictures for young people. The Community Relations Committee appraises new films in a publication entitled *The Joint Estimates of Current Entertainment Films,* referred to as "the Green Sheets." Every week the members of the committee preview a new picture and write out their individual reactions—judging entertainment values, artistic and technical excellence, and ethical and social values. These reviews are pooled and a composite paragraph is written for the publication. Starred films are those of special merit. All are checked as being suitable for family, young people, adults, or children. By writing to the Director of Community Relations, Motion Picture Association of America, 28 West 44th Street, New York City, you can arrange to have "the Green Sheets" sent to your school. Perhaps you will want to post copies on the bulletin board. You and your schoolmates can save yourselves time and money by being selective in choosing your film fare.

Another publication from which you can obtain specialized information on any field of motion-picture activity is the *International Newsletter.* This bulletin is issued by the International Committee of the MPAA, 8480 Beverly Boulevard, Hollywood 48, California.

The cinema collection at the Museum of Modern Art in New York City contains a film library where the finest of motion pictures are preserved. In its beautiful auditorium, you can see the films of Méliès and the other pioneers, the best silent films, and the outstanding features of today. You can also browse through one of the most complete collections of cinema books and magazines in the country. In addition to its film section, the library has comprehensive references on dance, theater, design, and photography. Your local museum may feature its displays, which range from photo-panel exhibitions to large collections of original works. Your school can arrange to rent and exhibit many of the famous films individually or in historical series. Films may be ordered from the museum's catalogue, which will be sent to you upon request from the Museum of Modern Art, 11 West 53rd Street, New York City.

Dr. William Lewin has for years been a leader in the field of film appreciation with his Educational and Recreational Guides, Inc., 10 Brainerd Road, Summit, New Jersey. In 1957, in collaboration with Alexander Frazier, he put out the book *Standards of Photoplay Appreciation,* which you should examine. It covers all phases of the subject with excellent rating sheets which will help you in evaluating pictures.

Pictures from all over the world compete for prizes at the many film festivals now held annually in Europe. Information concerning them can be obtained from the International Committee of the MPAA. Mrs. Flavia Paulson, Executive Director of the International Exhibition of Cinematographic Art in Venice, one of the oldest of the festivals, has issued an illustrated report of all of the films presented there. This report is a study of the entire history of motion-picture drama.

Winning films from all of the various European festivals usually are shown in the United States. You should make a point of seeing them, if possible, for they are among the best motion pictures being produced today.

## Seeing Films in School

In the United States, sixteen millimeter film is now the standard for educational pictures, which are being released by the thousands for use in our schools. You have probably seen many travelogues, episodes from history, and documentaries issued for educational use.

Today feature films and the best documentaries from the big studios are also being made available for use during school hours. Excerpts from fine films based on great literary works have been edited by specialists for classroom use. Such films as *The Story of Louis Pasteur, The Howards of Virginia, The Crusades, Treasure Island, Jane Eyre,* and *Great Expectations* have brought history and fiction to life for many classes.

Actually seeing and discussing films as a class project is probably one of the most satisfactory means of developing an appreciation for the distinct qualities of the art of motion pictures. However, you can also extend your appreciation by viewing old films on television as a part of your homework.

You and your classmates are the logical student group to order films for your school. You can get help, as well as films, from The Film Council of America, which sponsors educational films and has its offices at 6 West Ontario Street, Chicago 10, Illinois. It is an important organization made up of seven national groups, including the National Education Association.

## Objectives of Movie Study

As a result of your classroom study you should know what constitutes a good film, and you should become a discerning as well as enthusiastic movie fan.

A good movie must be entertaining, though not necessarily humorous. By means of visual effects, dialogue, sound, and music, the film must reveal a fluid, plausible, interesting story which builds through exciting climaxes to a logical conclusion. The scenic backgrounds should present the story accurately, effectively, and correctly, forming an appropriate background for the action without attracting undue attention or arousing curiosity.

The actors should be effectively made up and costumed in keeping with the period, social background, and atmosphere of the play. They should speak clearly and fluently, using speech appropriate to the characters they are portraying. Above all, they should be so spontaneous and natural that you forget completely that they are not real people experiencing the events taking place. Through the magic of the camera mental processes can be made visual, the worlds of reality and fantasy can be depicted, and almost any action can be presented without interference of time, place, or human limitations. You should be taken into the minds of the characters to understand what they are thinking and into their hearts to feel what they are feeling. The characters' past, present, and future should be revealed with emotional rather than with realistic coherence.

In short, a good film combines many elements into a unified whole and lifts people out of themselves into the magic world of the imagination. At the same time, it leaves the audience with a wider understanding of humanity, a more realistic outlook on life, and higher ideals of conduct.

To be a good movie fan you must carefully select the pictures you see. Base your choices on intelligent reviews in the best magazines and on the reputations of the authors, actors, producers, and directors. Do not let criticism of unimportant details spoil a good picture for you. Instead, develop an appreciation of fine acting, beautiful scenes, and lovely music. Do not accept sentimentalism, false standards, and unethical conduct just because they are presented effectively. Keep your own ideals intact, profiting by the experiences depicted on the screen.

As a student of the movies, you should follow the work of the best producers, directors, playwrights, scenario writers, and actors. You should compare and analyze their methods and encourage their work by contributing to the box-office returns of only the best pictures. The world's finest producers, directors, and technicians are developing an art unique in history. Your enthusiastic appreciation or dull acceptance of their efforts will determine just how far they can and will go.

*Applications*

1. Bring to class reviews of some recent pictures, written by the best critics. Recheck them after you have seen the films yourselves and decide whether you agree or disagree with the critics' judgments.

2. Make a simple chart by which you and your classmates can judge a picture fairly. As a group, go to see a movie and mark its qualifications on your individual charts. Then, in the classroom, discuss the film on the basis of your charts.

3. Prepare reports on the lives of movie personalities who have caught your interest.

4. Make your own list of five candidates for the Best Picture Award this year. Give reasons for your choices.

5. Gather all the material and information you can on the influence of television on the motion-picture industry.

6. Work out an attractive poster on which you can keep a starred list of the best films playing in your local theaters, especially those in the neighborhood of your school. Appoint a committee to act as judges and another to keep the chart up to date. Give many members of the class a chance to work on this evaluation of current films.

7. Visit the manager of your most important local theater. Discuss with him the distribution, publicizing, censoring, and box-office returns of pictures in your community. Find out whether the best pictures bring in the biggest returns. Find out how a daily movie program is made up and how much choice the manager himself has in regard to the movie fare he offers the public. Write up your findings for publication in your school magazine.

8. See the sponsor of your school paper and arrange to have a motion-picture section which your class will prepare.

9. Make a collection of catalogues of all the documentary and educational film companies you can contact. Then arrange a showing of their best films. This may be done either as a school service program or to make money for carrying on motion-picture appreciation work in your school and community.

## *Chapter 16*

# Radio and Television

The invention and development of television is the greatest step in communications the world has ever seen. Television's unique power is its ability to bring the world into your home to inform and entertain you. In so doing television brings the peoples of all nations closer together. The day will come when television will make it possible for you to observe major events all over the world *as they are happening.*

Television is more than a medium of entertainment. However, in this chapter, you will be concerned mainly with its entertainment values and, in particular, its dramatic productions. Before considering television, it may be helpful to take a brief look at its immediate predecessor and closest relative, radio.

## RADIO

The phenomenal growth of television has greatly altered the once powerful role of radio in the entertainment world. When radio was at its peak of popularity, programming included broadcasts by fine comedians such as Fred Allen and Jack Benny; dramatic programs such as the "Lux Radio Theatre," one of the few hour-long shows in radio; plays by writers such as Arch Oboler and Norman Corwin; documentaries such as "You Are There"; panel discussions such as "Town Meeting of the Air" and "The Author Meets the Critics"; informative programs such as "Information, Please" and "Invitation to Learning"; amusing situation comedy series such as "The Halls of Ivy"; long-running serials such as "Dr. Christian" and "One Man's Family"; excellent news coverage; and programs of music. These shows are representative of some of the good programming that was available on radio.

430

Today radio is predominantly a medium for news, news analysis, programs of general discussion, and music—the "disk jockey" type of show and the programs of serious music. Lately radio broadcasters have been experimenting with stereophonic sound with happy results for music lovers. Radio also has other important uses: it serves as a means of communication for people in remote or isolated areas, and it is used in navigation, in national defense, and in many areas of public service. The writing and producing of radio plays to popularize local projects and raise money for worthy causes continues to be a valuable community activity.

In spite of the impact of television, radio drama still has a place in the world of the theater. There are many theater enthusiasts who prefer the imaginative appeal of a radio play because they can visualize the characters and backgrounds as they wish them to be.

Many public schools have well-equipped stations, and radio training is a regular part of the curriculum. Broadcasting over the public address system in the big high schools is a vital part of modern education. The ability to use a microphone effectively is almost necessary for leadership in student affairs. As an individual and as a member of a class in dramatics, you may well be called upon to participate in some form of broadcasting. Therefore, a brief summary of radio techniques should be of use to you.

**Edward R. Murrow comments on the news.**

Courtesy of CBS Radio

## Radio Techniques

The ideal radio voice is pleasant, vital, and flexible, with interesting variations in pitch, rate, and emphasis, but without sudden changes in volume. When you speak in your own person or act a straight part, you should create in the listener's imagination a picture of a sincere, friendly, and attractive individual. Of course, when you are playing a character part, the quality, tempo, and pitch of your voice must be altered to create an auditory impression consistent with your role.

The chief faults to be avoided are monotony, breathiness, high pitch, and sudden loudness. Provincialisms in speech, unvarying pitch patterns, and set inflections are fatal. Let the meaning and feeling of your lines be your paramount consideration so that your voice may be colorful and interesting. Careful grouping of words and breathing between phrases will keep your thought clear. Analyze your character carefully but think in aural terms: how have age, culture, mood, and situation affected his voice?

When "on the air," you must be in complete control of yourself. You must read your lines as if speaking them for the first time, but you must also watch the director and respond to his signals without spoiling the smoothness of your delivery.

In writing a radio play, your chief consideration is to fit your script to the time allotment while making your main idea clear. Decide at once how you will tie your incidents together—by a narrator who is a character in the play, an impersonal announcer, or musical curtains. In a simple radio play, one plot is all you need. It should center around a single dramatic incident with a clear-cut problem to be solved by your hero and/or heroine. Use as few characters as possible and have them vocally distinctive. When you have finished your first draft, record it on tape or stand behind a curtain and read it to a listener. Note his reactions. Then rewrite the script and time it exactly. Put in your sound effects and time it again. If it is your responsibility, write out the opening and closing announcements, trying to keep them original and to the point. Final copies of the script should be typed with double spaces and wide margins. Stage directions and the names of characters should be underscored in red so that the scripts will be easy to read under the stress of rehearsing and broadcasting.

Casting should be done on the basis of the voice alone—its distinctive characteristics and its contrast with the other voices. Rehearsing is also centered on the aural effects produced by the voice alone. Studio rehearsals are preceded by painstaking ones in which the polishing and timing are carefully worked out. Usually one microphone rehearsal of lines alone is held and checked. Then the sound effects and music are introduced. A

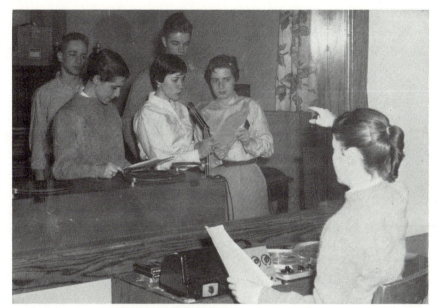
High school students produce their own radio show.

final "dry run" of the whole continuity is all the studio preparation you will have.

In performance, follow the markings on your script carefully, talk simply and naturally in character, speak directly into the microphone, keep your throat relaxed, and get your breath between thought groups. Don't correct any mistakes you make. Follow directions instantly, keeping your voice an integral part of the aural pattern the director is creating.

If the writing and rehearsing of your play have gone well, the broadcast should be a smooth-running production with distinct and interesting characters. The main point of the program should be effectively put over by a single emotional appeal.

*Applications*

1. As a class, listen to a radio play and analyze it from the standpoint of its production and the aural appeal of the whole program.

2. Present some of the scenes given earlier in this text as radio broadcasts and tape record them. Play these recordings back and criticize them in detail.

3. Have the entire class select a community project it wishes to support. Write and produce a radio play to arouse public enthusiasm. If it is good enough, your local station may permit you to put it on the air.

## History of Radio

The history of radio and the development of networks and independent stations form an engrossing story. Many people, inventions, and events are involved. The student who is interested in this history—whether it be from a technical, legal, or biographical point of view—will undoubtedly find it interesting to do research in this field. In the Applications which follow, suggestions are made for several research projects.

*Applications*

1. Give reports on the contributions to radio of the following inventors and scientists:

| | |
|---|---|
| Michael Faraday | Guglielmo Marconi |
| James Clerk Maxwell | Reginald A. Fessenden |
| Heinrich Hertz | John Ambrose Fleming |
| Edouard Branly | Lee De Forest |

2. Learn why the federal government found it necessary to require licensing of stations and other regulating controls of radio. Find out how this was done by the Radio Act of 1912, by the establishment of the Federal Radio Commission in 1927 and the Federal Communications Commission in 1934.

3. Report on the formation of the four major radio networks and on the services that a network and its affiliated stations offer each other.

4. Write a report on some of the entertainers who became nationally famous on radio and tell which ones made the transition to television successfully.

## THE DEVELOPMENT OF TELEVISION

## Technical Background

A television camera picks up light rays from a scene being played. These light rays are converted into electrical impulses which become electromagnetic waves. The electomagnetic waves are sent through the air to receiving sets. Here they are changed back into electrical impulses which re-create the original light rays and form a visible light pattern. This is the picture on your screen. At the same time, the microphones pick up sound waves and convert them to an electric signal which is transmitted to your receiver. Here the signal is reconverted to sound.

As early as 1884, the German scientist Paul Nipkow worked on a method of building a practical television system. Other scientists were able to use Nipkow's findings in continued efforts to make television transmission possible.

In 1923 Vladimir Zworykin introduced the *iconoscope*, an electron tube, the electric eye of the television camera. The tube developed for the reception of images was called the *kinescope*. Additional contributions were made by François Henroteau, John L. Baird, and others.

Experimental demonstrations of television were made during the late 1920's. In the early thirties, experimentation stations were established by the major networks. Other developments of the thirties included the use of six- and ten-foot screens, field tests, and the institution of daily telecasts. The first of these in the United States was the telecast of the opening of the New York World's Fair on April 30, 1939. President Roosevelt spoke at the opening and thus became the first United States president to be televised.

The *image orthicon tube*, introduced in 1939, was an important step in the advance of television engineering. The advantage of this tube was that it was so highly sensitive that it needed little light and thereby reduced heat and glare within television studios.

The Federal Communications Commission established in 1934 to regulate broadcasting and assign stations to localities, held its first meeting dealing with television control on June 23, 1936. However, it was not until July 1, 1941, that the FCC authorized commercial television broadcasting.

**General David Sarnoff presides at the opening of the New York World's Fair in 1939, an event marking the introduction of television as a service to the American public.**

World War II put a stop to television production, but television was used as a valuable means of civil defense in New York City. During this period, research and experimentation in the laboratories continued. After the war, television became a boom industry. Advances were rapid as the public was captured by the new miracle. Images were often fuzzy, and programming was sometimes uneven, but television had caught on. The FCC approved commercial color television in 1953. Color City in Burbank, California, was dedicated on March 27, 1955, and was the first large television area to be built exclusively for colorcasts.

In less than ten years, television came out of the laboratory and grew into one of our nation's most important industries. Progress in technical skills has been extraordinary. Live international hookups have already been made and will undoubtedly become more frequent. Today the number of television homes in the United States is nearly 45 million.

### Programming

Television productions today fall into three basic categories—live, filmed, and taped. Previously they were either live or filmed. A *live* show is what the term implies. It is "alive" and is actually taking place as you see it, whether the show be a studio performance or an on-the-spot telecast of a news or sporting event. Films on television are of three types: films made specifically for television, film clips used as insertions in live shows, or films made originally for use in motion-picture theaters. References made here to filmed shows are to those made for television, not to the other two types listed above.

The live show has the advantage of immediacy and spontaneity. It has an exciting quality of freshness because it is happening before your eyes. However, the live show has the disadvantage of being a "once only" experience. It cannot be recaptured. If mistakes are made on the air by the actors or the technical crew, there is no chance to go back and correct them. The live show must carry on to the show's end without stopping. On the other hand, the filmed show, which may be produced in short scenes, can avoid technical flaws. If an actor blows up in his lines, the cameras can stop and the sequence can be refilmed. A filmed show is more economical in the long run because the film can be shown and then released again for a highly profitable repeat.

In the early days of television, programming was live, for the most part. Programs consisted of experiments with dramatic sketches and material based on vaudeville. One of the most important of the early dramatic events on television was Gertrude Lawrence's appearance in scenes from

*Susan and God* on June 7, 1938. The "Philco Television Playhouse" presented *Dinner at Eight* on October 3, 1948. This was the first in a series of television productions of Broadway plays. Vaudeville was also a "natural" for television. On August 10, 1948, a network opened its New York station with a vaudeville show from the stage of the Palace Theatre, the famous old vaudeville house. Milton Berle's phenomenal success with the "Texaco Star Theatre" in the late forties demonstrated the suitability of vaudeville for television.

An examination of television programming today presents one with a rather baffling problem. Shows seem to run in trends. A certain type of program becomes popular and is followed by a veritable battery of shows of the same type. For instance, several years ago, comedies such as "Your Show of Shows" with Sid Caesar and Imogene Coca and the "Red Buttons' Show" were the most popular programs on television. Suddenly the public apparently tired of comedies and most of them went off the air. A new trend started when the "$64,000 Question" landed on the scene like a bombshell. This program was quickly joined by numerous other quiz shows. All of them consistently garnered high ratings from the services which measure audience viewing habits. The next trend was the Western. Dramas such as "Gunsmoke" and "Have Gun, Will Travel" and others like them were in great demand.

**Richard Boone as Paladin in "Have Gun, Will Travel."**

Due to the constant race and stiff competition for audience acceptance, the life expectancy of any one series is very short. For instance, the once highly popular quiz shows came in for trouble in the fall of 1958 when charges of fraud were made against some of them. Many of the quiz programs left the air almost immediately. As a general rule, specific types of programs come and go rapidly in television.

However, certain shows have been able to maintain their popularity through the years. Among these are the variety programs such as those conducted by Ed Sullivan, Steve Allen, Perry Como, and Dinah Shore; panel shows such as "I've Got a Secret" and "What's My Line?"; drama-comedy series such as "The Loretta Young Show" and "The Millionaire"; and comedy shows such as "The Jack Benny Show."

Live drama on television has had a somewhat irregular history. Only a few seasons ago there were quite a number of weekly, live dramas on television. Among these were "Robert Montgomery Presents," "The Philco Television Playhouse," "The Kraft Theatre," "The Goodyear Theatre," "Studio One," "Climax," and "Playhouse 90." Though many of these shows are not on the schedule today, new ones have come along to take their place. In recent years, good dramatic programs have included the "United States

**Helen Hayes stars in the "Omnibus" production of** *Mrs. McThing.*

Steel Hour," "Armstrong Circle Theatre," "DuPont Show of the Month," and "Omnibus." This last program is often, but not always, a dramatic show. Other dramatic programs are the "spectaculars," which are not regularly scheduled and are usually 90 to 120 minutes in length.

Television programming also includes news broadcasts, news commentaries, documentaries, discussion forums, religious programs, detective and mystery series, children's programs, women's programs on home management, and coverage of sports events. Perhaps you can identify still other types of programs.

## Discussion

1. What effects do you think television is having on the home life of America?

2. In which type of television program are you most interested? Why?

3. Describe the best live television play you have ever seen performed. Give your reasons for thinking it the best.

4. Which of the plays that you have read or seen would you like to see televised?

5. Compare a play you have seen on television with a play you have seen on the stage or in a movie theater. Which did you like best? Why?

6. Choose one of the shows which has been on television for several seasons. Try to give reasons for its continuing popularity.

7. Have you seen color television? Compare it with black-and-white television.

## Applications

1. Look up and report on the lives and scientific contributions to television of the following men:

| | |
|---|---|
| Lee De Forest | John Logie Baird |
| Paul Nipkow | Allen B. Dumont |
| Vladimir Zworykin | David Sarnoff |

If you wish, you may report on any other personalities in the television industry who interest you and have helped to develop the medium.

2. List the following terms and explain their importance in television:

| | | |
|---|---|---|
| iconoscope | stereoscopy | mosaic |
| kinescope | monitor | electron gun |
| image orthicon tube | shading | key light |
| coaxial cable | mobile unit | |

3. Work up a section in your notebook devoted to the development of television and its programming.

# TELEVISION DRAMA

## Acting on Television

Television is a difficult medium for the actor because he performs under the constant pressures of time, limited space, and mechanical restrictions. Studios are continuously in use. Therefore, television productions are usually rehearsed and put together elsewhere, so that the actor often does not have enough rehearsal time in the studio under the actual performance situation.

Television acting demands the smoothness of film acting, the spontaneity and physical awareness of stage acting, and the vocal color of radio acting. Timing and finish are essential. Any hesitancy, feeling for words, or fumbling action, appears exaggerated to the home audience. An actor on television has to remember that rapid shifts in position distort the image on the screen. With the heat of the studio lights, the tangle of wires and cords, and the camera looming up for a close shot, the television actor must really concentrate if he is to keep his wits about him.

The lines and business rehearsals are similar to those for stage productions. The tension mounts with the final camera and lighting rehearsals. The actor must move from one set to another as quickly as possible and, at the same time, must keep the action and movement fluid. There is no time for detailed polishing rehearsals in which the actor has the satisfaction of working out each detail in the environment of the set in which he will appear.

The director is too busy to coach actors. He expects them to respond effectively without delay. Their characters must be worked out completely, with movements and gestures set, before the final adjustment to the technical equipment of the studio.

A television actor must learn to make an easy transition from one emotion to another, as television dramas are more condensed than other dramatic scripts. He must call forth all his technical skill in creation and in interpretation.

Once in the studio, actors sometimes have the feeling that they no longer matter much. During long hours of technical rehearsals, attention is focused on cameras, lighting, sound, and all the other elements that make up a television production.

Studios vary in the use of teleprompters and cue cards to assist the actor. However, these aids are often used in the daily "soap operas." Many of these programs are live and actors cannot always memorize their lines because they are on every day.

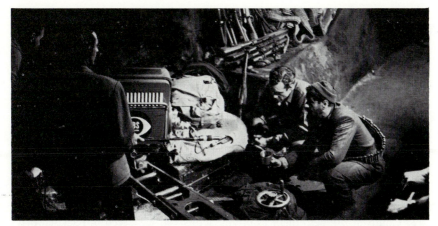

Actors and cameramen rehearse a scene for "Playhouse 90's" television version of Ernest Hemingway's *For Whom the Bell Tolls.*

A close-up of a teleprompter.

Success in television does not come easily. As in the movies, an actor must photograph well, and he must have warmth and directness because of the intimacy of television. He must be able to assume his role fully under the pressures of studio conditions.

Many books on television are coming out all the time, but there are two especially for the actor. You may want to study and work with these books. They are *The Television Actor's Guide* by William Hodapp and *Radio and Television Acting* by Edwin Duerr.

*Discussion*

1. Describe several of the best acting performances you have seen on television.

2. Compare the performances of any actors you have seen in televised plays and on the stage or screen.

3. As television actors develop, watch their careers and see if public adulation grows for them as it does for actors in the other mediums. Do you think the home atmosphere will influence the public's feeling toward these performers? If so, in what way?

4. Do you think television will increase or lessen the appreciation of great acting as an art? Why?

5. Explain the disappearance from television of some of its most popular players. Do you prefer seeing familiar faces or new ones? Why?

6. Do you think television drama will develop its own lasting stars? Explain.


## Producing a Television Play

A brief summary of the process of producing a television play can give you only a vague idea of the hours of intensive effort which lie behind every show you see. The technical skill and artistic talent of dozens of people working under terrific tension are involved. Watching both studio rehearsals and performances gives an appreciation of the peculiar problems of television. One such problem is the necessity to indicate lapses of time and many shifts in locale. These changes take place within minutes during the actual playing time. Still, they may involve complicated changes in make-up, costume, and background details. In spite of this and many other intricate problems, a television play must move rhythmically and without any abrupt changes or breaks in tempo. The camera, which is one of the most vital elements, should unobtrusively explain the story in attractive, easily followed, arresting shots.

**The story.** Television plays are written with the home screen continually in mind. In writing or reading a play to be televised, the author and di-

**Technicians, cameramen, and crew hurriedly adjust sets and equipment during a change of scene in the color spectacular *Naughty Marietta*.**

rector imagine the sets and action and hear the lines as they will sound to people relaxed in a home atmosphere. Since eye appeal is greater than ear appeal in this medium, material is considered first from the visual and then from the aural standpoint.

Dialogue must be well written and must advance the action. Something must be happening all the time. The plot should center on a few strong characters who have definite dramatic appeal. The basic ideas of the story must be of universal interest, stimulating but not too sophisticated. Holding the attention of every member of the household (and perhaps their friends) is a serious problem and one with which television staffs contend constantly.

Many of the 90- and 120-minute dramas which you see are adapted from plays, novels, and short stories. However, producers like Fred Coe have helped to develop writers of original television stories. Paddy Chayefsky, Tad Mosel, David Shaw, Horton Foote, and Rod Serling are only a few of them. These and other writers like them have created plays specifically designed for the television medium.

5

THE BULLY:

*T# 1 - Wide 2 Shot for X lamp post* Put 'em up!

LITTLE CLARENCE:

(HESITANTLY)

Well ... O.K.

*#1 #3 get Tite 2 shots*
*@ lamp post*

(CLARENCE PUTS UP HIS FISTS. THEY
START TO BOX. AFTER A LITTLE SPARRING,
CLARENCE MIRACULOUSLY CONNECTS TO THE
BULLY'S JAW, KNOCKING HIM TO THE GROUND.
CAMERA MOVES IN FOR A CLOSE-UP OF
CLARENCE, WHO GAPES IN ASTONISHMENT AT
WHAT HE HAS DONE.)

*Hit ET*
*T#3 Luke @ lamp post for X to Bully on Floor*

BROOME:  (NARRATING)

I could hardly believe my eyes. Could
it be that I had actually beaten a boy

*Pan down to Bully* nearly twice my size? How was this

possible?

*Pan back to Luke*

(LITTLE CLARENCE LOOKS UP INTO THE
CAMERA)

And then, the revelation came ...
(SNEAK IN SOUND OF CHOIR SINGING A HYMN
LITTLE CLARENCE SMILES)

As clear as the spire on top of our

*he X R pick up* church. It was simply this: the fact
*book* that I had gone to choir practice

brought me good luck!

(MORE)

jcw

Courtesy of CBS Television

A page from a television script. The dialogue is on the right, and the directions for cameras, lights, sound effects, and stage business are on the left. The numbers 1 and 3 refer to the cameras to be used for a particular shot.

Every television show should have at least three separate scripts. The first is the brief scenario which tells the story in a brief and interesting fashion. The second is the play script which is written in two columns. The visual directions for the camera, lights, and stage business are given on the left; the dialogue is on the right. The third is the director's final production script which includes all of the technical instructions developed during rehearsals. Most directors want a number of copies of the final script to give the various assistants.

**444**     MOTION PICTURES, RADIO, AND TELEVISION

**Production procedures.** In general, getting a play on the screen follows a pattern. First the producer selects the script, appoints the director, and then supervises all phases of the production. The unit manager is the producer's personal representative. He handles all the details in the staging, financing, and organizing of activities involved in getting the play on the screen. The director is personally responsible for the casting and rehearsing of the play and the planning of camera shots and sets. Working with many assistants, he controls the dress rehearsal and performance. In a short space of time he must correlate all the elements—actors, camera, lights, and sound—into a smooth-flowing production. He must know exactly what he wishes the camera to do and how effects may be obtained.

About ten days before the performance, the director calls a conference of his staff—the unit manager, stage designer, assistant director, technical

**Art Carney, playing the part of a television writer, supervises the production of one of his plays from the control room.**

Courtesy of CBS Television

director, costume designer, and others. With them he discusses the general plans. He explains how he hopes to create the atmosphere and develop the characters. Copies of the script are given out and all apparent problems are taken up. The director then selects his cast and, outside the studio, goes into dry rehearsals which are conducted much like those of any other play.

In the meantime, the unit manager has made an outline, most appropriately called "The Monster." This outline lists the names of everyone involved in the technical side of the show and gives their schedules for the production period. It also includes the exact time of the vital studio rehearsals on the day of the telecast. It is the unit manager's responsibility to have all details checked and everyone on hand at scheduled rehearsal times.

The technical director and the scenic artist make their plans for getting the sets and all technical equipment into shape. The latter designs the sets and collects the drapes, properties, furnishings, or artificial outdoor settings. Some exteriors are made in miniature. Exquisite little houses, churches, trees, and doorways can be easily photographed with cloud, snow, and rain effects. Slides and films are also used on rear-projection screens to provide backgrounds for the more expensive telecasts. Interiors are usually corners of rooms or localized centers of interest around a few pieces of furniture, planned in proportion to the shallow stage. Even in black-and-white television, colors give the impression of depth and contrast.

The lighting of television stages is constantly being improved. Some form of key lighting is necessary to illuminate the center of interest. Other spots and lamps at strategic points provide fill-in light to kill the shadows and general lighting to add depth to the small stages.

The costume designer plans and, if necessary, designs the costumes. He arranges to provide them for the dress rehearsal or he has the cast bring their own costumes, which must meet his specifications.

**Rehearsals.** The director handles the rehearsals and the performance from the studio control room. Usually he is seated at his control console with his talk-back microphone. The script girl is at his right, and the technical director is at his left. Each of the director's assistants works from a console in the control room. The technical director directs the engineers by microphone. The video engineer communicates with the cameraman as he handles the camera angles. The audio engineer controls and blends all the sounds—voices, music, and sound effects—and directs the boom microphones which are suspended on extension rods and moved around the set over the actors' heads. Sometimes the actual sound effects are near his console and at other times are in another area entirely but connected by telephone. The floor manager is on the stage floor. He receives directions over the talk-back microphone while he cues and, if necessary, directs the actors. In the control room a number of monitors or receivers pick up what each camera is photographing. During rehearsals the director watches these monitors and makes his choice of the shots he wants used. During the performance itself, he watches the show over these same monitors.

The camera rehearsals are the vital ones because they determine the success of a telecast. A television camera has a three-lens turret which can be rapidly rotated to change the field of view. A signal light tells the operator when his camera is on the air. This light also tells the actors which camera is "hot," or sending a picture to the home screen. Formerly the dolly moved the camera back and forth and sideways. Now the "zoom" lens is replacing the dolly, eliminating the necessity of changing camera positions.

Since mobility of the camera is important, no carpets are used on the floor of the studio, which is painted to resemble tiles, wood, or rugs for each set.

**Director John Frankenheimer, in white shirt and hip boots, wades into the water to work with his staff on the camera angles for a dramatic scene in "Playhouse 90's"** *Old Man.*

Courtesy of CBS Television

Particular camera images are chosen to achieve desired psychological effects, for the emotional response of the audience depends entirely upon the pictures that are seen. The director must know the key picture situations in his play and use the camera and lights to make them live for the spectators. By his manipulation of line, mass, and form, he can make the pictorial composition of every bit of action effective.

During the blocking rehearsals, most of the lighting, sound, and camera problems are worked out. The scenic designer is always on hand to rearrange his properties, for weird and unexpected effects frequently appear in shots. For example, pictures, statues, and wallpaper may suddenly seem to rise from the heads of the actors. The sound engineers check the placement and effectiveness of their equipment. Sometimes the boom microphones cannot catch the lowered voices used in intimate scenes, and small microphones must be concealed behind vases and books.

When a complete run-through of the entire play is held, all the effects are used. The actors time their crosses from set to set and adjust themselves to the lighting areas. These lighting areas have become especially important since the introduction of the rear-projection screen. Either stills from slides or moving-picture films may be projected in this method of "set painting," which demands very careful lighting. The actors must get in exact positions. These run-through rehearsals are very expensive and more than one per show, though greatly to be desired, is seldom possible.

After a complete run-through a conference of the director, staff, and cast is held. All problems are ironed out, and there is a break until the dress rehearsal. At this last rehearsal the orchestra, cast, technicians, cameramen, and lighting engineers bring the play to life on the screen. The video engineer shades the picture by controlling the light content, and the audio engineer controls the sound. The producer is usually present at the dress rehearsal and attends the final conference when last-minute changes are made in sets, lights, costumes, make-up, and sometimes in camera angles.

**The performance.** At the performance the director literally conducts a drama as a symphony conductor directs his orchestra. Unlike a stage director whose work is done when the curtain rises on opening night, the television director is responsible for the running of his show. From his place in the control room he watches the action on several monitor sets and selects the best picture to be sent out at any specific moment to the home sets. He gives all cues for sound and cutting to film. With a carefully rehearsed cast, and with an alert crew of cameramen and assistants at his command, the director can be reasonably certain that his show will be seen as he planned it.

**Director, cast, and crew assemble for a final conference before the dress rehearsal of** *For Whom the Bell Tolls.*

## Discussion

1. Explain the statement, "Eye appeal is greater than ear appeal."

2. As a viewer express your opinions about whether the live dramatic show or the filmed dramatic show is better.

3. Have you ever seen any mistakes such as cameras or microphones coming into view on a live show? How has this affected the illusion?

4. Give some examples of live shows which used filmed inserts for certain sequences? Why do you think the film was used?

5. What do you think is the future of live television dramas in competition with filmed dramas for television? Give reasons to support your opinion.

## Applications

1. Through your local bookstore or library, look up some of the latest books on television. Try to arrange for the purchase of one of them for the school library.

2. Arrange with the manager of a nearby television station for a class visit. Ask to watch a local show in rehearsal and in performance. Take notes on the television terms used, the signals for cues, and the duties of the station personnel involved in the program.

3. Based on what you learned at the television station, write a report on the job in television that appeals to you most and give the reasons for your choice.

4. Using Appendix C and your library, give an oral report on the opportunities in television for young people today.

# THE FUTURE OF TELEVISION

## New Developments

Every year miraculous devices appear in television. One such device is video taping. By this process, a television signal is put on a magnetic tape which records both the sound and the picture of a given program. Do not confuse this process with filming. Tapes which resemble those used on school or home tape recorders are used, but the process is far more complex since both picture and sound are being recorded. When a show is video taped, it can be played back immediately, for it does not require developing as films do. The quality of these recordings is so good that taped programs are practically indistinguishable from live shows. Therefore, high quality rebroadcasting is possible. This is most useful on occasions when time differences have made it impossible for everyone in the country to see the same program at the same time. Many programs today are on tape.

Perhaps you have heard something of the lively controversy in television today over "fee" versus "free" television. The supporters of "fee" television propose to broadcast shows which would be unavailable to those who did not "buy" programs. In order to receive a "fee" program, the viewer would drop a coin in a box attached to his set. This would not in any way affect the "free" program. Proponents of the "fee" system say that it will improve the quality of programming. Opponents say that pay television is unfair to the viewer in that it denies him free entertainment.

There is no doubt at all that television drama will be greatly changed by technical improvements. Color television recorded on magnetic tape and transmitted on commercial network facilities is a reality. The possibilities ahead are vast. Television screens as large as murals may be developed. Portable sets with very small screens will be on the market. Video tape recorders with playback units may allow you to make recordings of televised plays at home, borrow such recordings from the public library, or buy them for a permanent collection of your own.

## Training Opportunities

More and more opportunities for specialized training in television are being offered today. Many universities and colleges now have television departments. This is especially true in New York City and Los Angeles where practicing directors and technicians from the studios give courses, and the best critics lecture on all phases of the subject. The American Theatre Wing in New York City offers training in acting for television. Its classes are held right in the studios, the mechanics are handled by professional technicians, and the subject matter is taught by outstanding directors. Live dramatic shows are produced at the University of Southern California in Los Angeles and the southern branch of the University of California in Westwood, a suburb of Los Angeles.

Since 1949 the School of Radio Technique (SRT) in New York City has provided thorough training in the technical phases of television and in 1955 full color equipment was installed. A studio control room functions as in the studios and actual directing experience is possible. The cameras are handled by the students themselves. The major networks use the facilities of this studio to give special training to executives and other personnel. Only television professionals are on the faculty. Though not assured, positions for graduates are usually found.

## Educational Television

Only a mention of educational television can be given here, but you are probably already familiar with the trend toward teaching by television. Closed-circuit systems have been used for instruction in medical schools and industry, and you may possibly live in a community where classes are telecast over a closed-circuit television system managed by the public schools. The next twenty-five years may see a revolution in public education in which the present problems of teacher shortages, crowded classrooms, and the need for new schools may be partially relieved by television.

A guest professor illustrates his physics lecture on the network educational program "Continental Classroom."

Courtesy of NBC Television

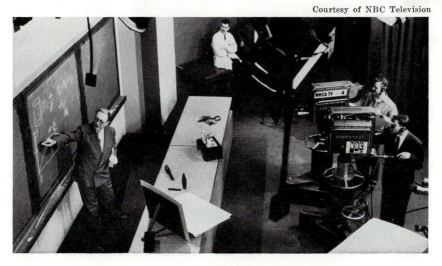

## Television's Future Influence

All sorts of guesses are being made by commentators, magazine writers, and interested people everywhere regarding the future influence of television on the daily lives of human beings the world over. They are asking, and trying to answer, questions such as these: Will the next generation be better or worse for having spent so many hours indoors before a screen rather than in physical activities outdoors? Will the average man and woman stop reading, writing letters, conversing, and pursuing hobbies and remain glued to the television screen? Will dramatic productions and grand opera be available in our homes on either "fee" or "free" television?

Important for the future of humanity and civilization in general are the probing questions: How will television influence world thinking? Will seeing the world on television take the place of travel or encourage it? How will world relationships be affected as we watch events as they happen and as world personalities become almost a part of the home circle?

Such queries and considerations are provocative and will have some bearing upon the future of television.

**Chet Huntley visits Israel in preparation for a special program on that nation.**
Courtesy of NBC Television

## Discussion

**1.** Explain the phenomenal growth of the television industry in the last few years. What does this development indicate to you about its potential effect on the public and on the industry's future progress in techniques and programming?

**2.** How do you feel about "fee" television as opposed to "free" television? What are the advantages and disadvantages of each?

**3.** What do you think television drama will be like in the future?

**4.** Do you think television will continue as a big industry? What financial elements are, and will be, an intrinsic part of its future?

**5.** How effective do you think educational television is? Cite some examples and explain your reasons for believing that it is either a good or a poor way of instructing people.

## Applications

**1.** Write a paper on "The Place of Television in the Theater of the Future."

**2.** Follow reviews and articles about television in magazines and newspapers at home. At the library read the television sections of such papers as *The New York Times* and *The New York Herald Tribune* as well as of such magazines as *Variety, Theatre Arts, Saturday Review,* and *Billboard.* Also consult the specialized television periodicals. On the basis of your reading, write a report on important trends you see developing in the television industry.

**3.** Give an oral report on the opportunities in television for young people today.

**4.** Make a list of the private schools, universities, and other organizations offering good training in the field of television.

**5.** Prepare a written report on the part that television may be able to play in the development of international understanding.

# Appendix A

## *Poor Maddalena**

by Louise Saunders

### Characters

PIERROT   PIERRETTE   BUMBU

*Scene I. The Land of Fantasy*
*Scene II. The House of Maddalena*
*Scene III. The Land of Fantasy*

### SCENE I

*The land of fantasy, best shown by plain black curtains on which one can throw the colored pictures of one's mind. The curtains stretch, on either side, to a painted sky of deep blue. Against the sky, suspended by a silk cord, hangs a round, yellow moon. There is a pink door flat on the ground.*

*When the curtain rises on the land of fantasy* PIERROT *and* PIERRETTE *are going through their eternal pantomime. He tells her that he loves her passionately, and points to his heart to prove it. She shows, with pretty, appropriate gestures, that she scorns his love.* PIERROT *sinks to his knees in despair. She takes pity on him and throws him a rose. He seizes it joyfully and pursues her. Just as he is about to catch her she stops suddenly, stretches out her arms, and yawns.*

PIERRETTE. Do you know, Pierrot, forgive me, but this love of yours is becoming rather tiresome.
PIERROT (*With a sigh*). I must confess that it bores me a little too.
PIERRETTE. You see, we have done this so many times—the same rose, the same pursuit—but it never leads to anything. We just go through it again.
PIERROT. What else is there to do?

* For all presentations of any kind, other than study use in the classroom, permission must be obtained from and royalty paid to Longmans, Green & Co., Inc., 119 W. 40th Street, New York 18, N.Y.

PIERRETTE (*Her chin in her hands*). I don't know—but I feel that there must be something.

PIERROT. If we hadn't gone over it often we wouldn't be able to perform it so beautifully. Your technique, Pierrette, is wonderful, and, if I may say so (*With pride*), mine—

PIERRETTE. Oh, of course. That's just it. We know how to show our love so prettily, so faultlessly, that sometimes I wonder whether we really love each other at all!

PIERROT (*Pointing*). I swear, by the round moon—

PIERRETTE (*Contemptuously*). Oh, the moon—(*In a whisper*) Pierrot, I have heard that in the world of men the moon is not always round!

PIERROT. Not round? Can it be square then? (*He laughs.*) That might be amusing.

PIERRETTE. I have heard that in the great world, down there (*She points to the pink door.*) it grows smaller and smaller, and sometimes only half of it is there, as if it had been broken, and sometimes it goes away entirely and the sky is empty!

PIERROT. That would be awkward. How could I bring my lute and sing beneath your window if there were no moon? How could I shiver with cold if—

PIERRETTE. Oh, Pierrot, you don't know what cold is. You have never been really cold, and neither have I.

PIERROT. Pierrette, what a thing to say! I have but to shiver like this (*He shivers.*)—now, see, I am cold. Brrr! It is one of my best effects.

PIERRETTE. You are only cold because you shiver, but men, I think, shiver because they are cold. That's the great, great difference, Pierrot. It's all make-believe with us.

PIERROT. My dear Pierrette, it is more artistic to feel cold because one shivers than to shiver merely because one happens to be cold. That way has a certain crudity about it that is far from attractive. Really, I don't understand you tonight. Every gesture with which I show my adoration for you has been thought out to the smallest detail. I give you perfection. What more can you want?

PIERRETTE. I want to feel things, Pierrot. You and I show just the reflection of love, like a misshapen image in the water. I long to see it in reality, to hold it close. I want it to touch my heart and make it glad!

PIERROT. I've noticed that there was something, a subtle something, lacking in you lately. It is spoiling your art, this idea of yours.

PIERRETTE. Perhaps, but if we could feel love, just once, I think it might enrich our art. (*She kneels on the ground by the pink door.*) When I look at this door, this door to the great world that has always been shut to us, I so long to open it. (*She tries to lift the door.*) Pierrot (*Eagerly*), don't you think that we could get the key from Bumbu and go down there, you and I, for a little while?

PIERROT. Why should we do anything so unpleasant? Still—(*He hesitates.*) If, as you say, such an experience might help our art—

PIERRETTE. It would! It would!

(*There is the loud sound of a bass-drum.*)

Shsh! Here he comes, Bumbu! You *will* ask him for the key? You will?

PIERROT. Perhaps.

(BUMBU, *a big clown in yellow, carrying a bass-drum, appears at the back, against the sky.*)

BUMBU. Behold Bumbu, my children, spirit of grotesque! Bumbu! (*He beats the drum.*) Hear my drum. It shouts not of mediocrity but of exaggeration—not of comedy, but the comic—the comic! (*He beats the drum.*) A red grin on the face of a painted buffoon, gargoyles that leer beneath the solemn spires of a church, the draggled finery of the very poor—natural things distorted! When the corners of men's mouths are twisted down in pain, my drum and I can jerk them up again to laughter—red and yellow laughter, splashed upon the gray monotony of life! I am Bumbu, spirit of grotesque, spirit of laughter. Without me the world would go mad. (*He beats the drum.*)

PIERROT. Oh, do be quiet, Bumbu. We know quite well who you are.

BUMBU (*Putting down his drum*). True, my children, but that is only because I have told you so often. If I did not, you might forget and think me the spirit of tragedy—for many do.

PIERRETTE. Bumbu, dear Bumbu, we want you to do something for us, don't we, Pierrot?

PIERROT. Pierrette has been begging me to ask you for the key to the door of the world.

BUMBU. What made you think of that, my children? Are you tired of your little game of love?

PIERRETTE. Oh, yes, we are so weary of it, aren't we, Pierrot, for it's always the same; you know that. Please, please open the door. Let us go down.

BUMBU. You are better here, my children, in the land of fantasy, for here there is no sorrow and no joy. Here the lights are dim and shadows have lost their terror. Down there in the mad world you would be jostled and pushed about. The air is thick with flying stones of misfortune. You might be hit by them, crushed, frightened. You couldn't be happy as you are here, dreaming with Pierrot, among the roses, under a painted moon.

PIERROT. Stay here, Pierrette. I don't want to go down.

PIERRETTE. And joy—is there no joy there, Bumbu, where love is real?

BUMBU. There is great joy, but it comes too close, sometimes, and burns.

PIERROT. Stay here, Pierrette.

PIERRETTE. I want to go. Let me go.

PIERROT. Pierrette, stay here. (*He strikes a chord on his lute.*) Come, dance with me.

PIERRETTE. No, no. (*She sinks to the ground and buries her face in her knees. Then she holds out her hand.*) Look, Bumbu, what is this? It fell from my eyes!

PIERROT. Show it to me. How wonderful! See what Pierrette has found, Bumbu, this sparkling thing, like a diamond. What can it be?

BUMBU. That, my children, is a tear.

PIERROT. A tear! I've never seen a tear before.

BUMBU. There are many in the great world, but in the land of fantasy, Pierrette, there should be no tears.

PIERRETTE. I love my tear. It's so beautiful! Lovely colors are trembling in it, all the colors of light.

BUMBU. That light, reflected from the tears of men, you and Pierrot have been using to weave into dance or song.

PIERROT. The key! Give me the key, Bumbu. I, too, would go down into the world of tears, for tears are exquisite!

(BUMBU *produces a huge key from his belt and hands it to* PIERROT.)

BUMBU. Here it is, my children. Open the door if you must. I shall be waiting for you here, I, Bumbu, spirit of mockery.

PIERRETTE. Quick, Pierrot, open it!

PIERROT (*Struggling with the lock*). It doesn't fit.

PIERRETTE (*Eagerly*). Oh, yes; it fits. It must, doesn't it, Bumbu? Here, let me try. (*She takes the key.*) Oh, I can't turn it.

PIERROT. Give it to me. It works hard.

BUMBU. So does everything that has to do with the great world.

(PIERROT *struggles with the lock.*)

PIERRETTE. You have given us the wrong key.

BUMBU. No, that is the key. You will open it after a while.

PIERROT (*Excitedly*). It's turning!

PIERRETTE. Let me help.

PIERROT. No, I can do it. There! (*He turns the key and lifts the door. A strong light shines through the opening.* PIERROT *kneels beside it and looks down.*)

PIERRETTE (*Her hands over her eyes*). Oh, it's blinding, that white light!

BUMBU. You will get used to it.

PIERRETTE. What do you see, Pierrot?

PIERROT. I see a great heap of gold, mountain-high. Men are crawling over it, clutching it, and slipping down. At its base there is a dark crowd of people, scrambling, fighting one another, but near the top there are not so many. They climb more easily. I see a temple with shadowy columns reaching to the sky, but it is empty—no, not quite. Just then I saw a man leave the temple and join the others at the mountain of gold. And look—there goes another. He is running—and another! Yes, but there are still men left in the temple. I can see them now. Listen, they are singing. Oh, what music! Do you hear?

PIERRETTE. Why, Pierrot, I don't see that at all. There are lights and flowers and girls dancing. They seem to have little wings on their feet, but the feathers keep dropping from the wings all the time. The air is white with them. When the feathers have gone, they don't dance any more. See, there is one who is trying to gather the feathers and put them back on her wings, but she can't do it. She is crying. And that girl took hers off and threw them away. Why did she do it? What a pity!

PIERROT. Pierrette, how absurd you are. I see only a mountain of gold and a shadowy temple, and music. Surely you hear the music.

PIERRETTE (*Slowly*). Yes, I hear singing, too. It streams out like a silver banner in the wind—but—listen—it stops too soon and changes to something quite different.

PIERROT. Let us go down. I'll take my lute.

PIERRETTE. And I my tear. Good-by, Bumbu, good-by foolish painted land of fantasy.

PIERROT. Good-by, round pasteboard moon.

PIERRETTE. Pierrot and I are going to find life; we are going to find love where things are real!

(*They disappear.* BUMBU *sits beside the open door and watches them. He beats his drum once softly and laughs.*)

BUMBU. Bumbu, spirit of grotesque, Bumbu! (*Then he leans his head on his drum and stays there, waiting.*)


## SCENE II

A *man's voice is heard singing* "O Sole Mio." *The curtains part, showing a bare little room in Italy, opening on a small balcony. There are a few chairs in the room, and a table on which are a loaf of bread and a bottle of wine.* PIER-RETTE, *now* MADDALENA, *an Italian peasant girl, stands leaning against the balcony, listening to the voice, still singing in the street. She listens in a sort of ecstasy, dancing a little by herself until the song breaks off abruptly. A girl's laugh rings out from below.* MADDALENA *leans over the balcony and calls happily,* "Paolo." *She starts back again in sudden anger and runs to the door. She calls again, in quite a different way,* "Paolo."

PAOLO *enters lazily, still humming, with his guitar, and lounges against the door. He is* PIERROT, *in the corduroy trousers and red sash worn by the peasants of Italy.*

MADDALENA (*Hotly*). I saw you kiss her, when you had finished your song— that girl down there leaning against the wall—I saw you!

PAOLO (*Tightening the strings of his guitar*). Why not? Her lips were soft.

MADDALENA. And are my lips not enough for you? (*She beats her mouth with her hand.*) Mine?

PAOLO. Enough? Yes. Still I don't mind taking a little extra when it comes my way. She thanked me for the song. (*He laughs.*) Come, let me try yours now to see which are the sweeter.

MADDALENA (*Fiercely*). No. (*She stamps her foot.*) You were singing to me.

PAOLO. To you and to all girls who are slim and have fire in them like you.

MADDALENA. Do you think *I* would do that—let other men—Oh!

PAOLO. And Pasquale—has he never succeeded in buying even a kiss with all his money? "Marry me, Maddalena," I've heard him whine at you, "I'll make you rich." (*He laughs.*) Old Pasquale.

MADDALENA (*Passionately*). When I have had the gold of your love, could I value the other kind that can be put in bags and thrown on the table?

PAOLO (*Shrugging his shoulders*). Let that be as you please. But I can tell you, the kind that comes in bags is not to be despised. (*He takes the handkerchief from around his neck and wipes his forehead.*) Whew! It was hot, down there in the sun.

MADDALENA. I hate you sometimes!

PAOLO (*Taking up his guitar*). Very well. I'll go then. Good-by. (*She runs to him.*)

MADDALENA. No, no, please don't go, Paolo. Please, please don't go. (*She holds him by the arm.*) Forgive me. I'm sorry. I didn't mean it. You know I didn't mean it!

PAOLO. Oh, well—

MADDALENA. It's because I love you so, Paolo. (*She covers her heart with her hands.*) I love you, I love you!

PAOLO (*Patting her shoulder*). Funny little Maddalena.

MADDALENA. You'll stay?

PAOLO. Of course. I came to see you. Pour me a glass of wine.

MADDALENA (*Bringing the wine and sitting at his feet*). There is something in your singing that tears a girl's heart in two. How can I blame them if they—if they—but *me*, Paolo, you must do more than kiss—me you must *love*. You do love me?

PAOLO. I've told you so many times.

MADDALENA. Tell me again.

PAOLO (*Holding her by the chin and looking into her eyes*). I love you, Maddalena. There, will that do? (*He hands her his empty wine-glass.*)

MADDALENA. Your voice, it's so wonderful! It makes me think of the light shining through the blue glass in the church. It always makes me want something, oh, so badly.

PAOLO. What, Maddalena? Tell me?

MADDALENA. I don't know, but I think it's—I think I long to kill myself for you, to sacrifice myself, to pour myself out at your feet! (*He laughs and plays with her scarf.*) I didn't want to love you like this. I felt afraid. But my heart was like a tight little bud of a flower at the first touch of the hot sun. Its petals all relaxed and fell apart. Now they are open and dropping, and you may crush me, if you like. You may crush me!

PAOLO (*Half laughing, and seizing her by the shoulders*). Perhaps I will.

MADDALENA. I want you to.

PAOLO. And leave nothing for Pasquale?

MADDALENA. Pasquale! Don't speak to me of him! (*A pause*) Do you remember that day among the olive-trees, you and I, all the hot afternoon, and that night on the hill, under the stars, when you—cried for joy of me? I could see the tears on your cheeks. Oh, Maria, I thought I should die then of happiness!

PAOLO. Maddalena, that was beautiful, my Maddalena.

MADDALENA (*Opening a locket that hangs about her neck*). And my jewel, how it shone that night. It seemed to shoot a thousand colors, like fire.

PAOLO. Let me see it again. (*He looks at it.*) It's so strange, your having this, a poor girl like you. I wonder where it came from.

MADDALENA. I don't know. I've always had it. I wish I knew.

PAOLO. It must be worth a great deal of money.

MADDALENA (*Taking it back quickly*). I shall never sell it; I couldn't.

PAOLO. No, I suppose not.

MADDALENA (*Eagerly*). Paolo, listen. Let's go to the house of the Padre and arrange to have him—to have him marry us soon. He's there; I know he's there. I saw him go down the hill an hour ago on his donkey, with a basket of grapes. Paolo, please.

PAOLO (*Pushing her hands*). Maddalena, I came to talk to you sensibly.

MADDALENA (*Chilled*). Sensibly?

PAOLO. Yes, sensibly. Christo mio, must we always be love-making? Maddalena, I have had a great piece of good luck.

MADDALENA. Good luck?

PAOLO. Yes, for me. (*Excitedly*) Maddalena, there is an American lady staying at the hotel. She heard me sing one night in the gardens there by the gate. She knows, yes, she *knows* what I have here. (*He points to his throat.*) It's not always to be wasted on these simpletons, these know-nothings who hang about this village. It's for the world!

MADDALENA (*In sudden terror*). Paolo, what do you mean?

PAOLO. She called me into the hotel. There were other people there, rich people all in grand clothes. Psh, what did I care for that? I'll be the equal of them all soon and more, for I have a fortune in my throat. That's what she said—a fortune in my throat! (*He speaks quickly, in intense excitement.*) Maddalena, she's going to send me to Milano—oh, she needn't fear, I'll give her back the money—I'll study there—I don't need much study, it's true—and in a few years you'll see, posted in big head-lines, "Rubini, Paolo Rubini, the greatest tenor in Italy, the greatest in the world." (*He laughs exultantly.*)

(MADDALENA *is silent, her face in her hands.*)

Well, what is the matter?

MADDALENA (*In a low voice*). Paolo, don't go. Stay here with me.

PAOLO. Stay here, wasting myself among a lot of fools who don't know an artist from a mountebank? You're mad!

MADDALENA. I know—what you are—I know.

PAOLO. And this is the way you take it—you who have said that you loved me!

MADDALENA. But you'd be happy, Paolo. Think what it would mean. You and I—to be together, to love each other always—here, where life is beautiful and simple and quiet. Oh, what can you want more than happiness?

PAOLO. Yes, I'd be happy, there is no doubt of that, as a pig is happy—but what does that matter. (*Fiercely*) Don't you understand? I have something in me that must come out or die. Do you think I'm going to throw it away, waste it, for the sake of happiness?

MADDALENA. No, that was foolish of me. I do understand, I do; of course you must go; only—(*Her voice chokes with tears.*) take me with you. I'll help you so much. Indeed I will. I'll do anything. Take me, too.

PAOLO. Maddalena, that's impossible. I'd like to have you, of course, but what could I do with you? You would be in the way. I mustn't let anything hold me back, don't you see? I'm going to rise like the sun! There's a good girl. You stay here and marry Pasquale.

MADDALENA (*Frantically*). Oh, you don't know what you are saying to me. I shall die. I can't live without you. No, no, no, no, no! You can't leave me like this. You can't!

PAOLO. Don't you see how absurd you are? Tomorrow, when I have gone, you will be sorry that you behaved in this way. I can't do anything that would spoil my chance of success. You have no right to ask me that.

MADDALENA. I wouldn't spoil it. You needn't pay any attention to me. It wouldn't matter. Listen—I could cook things for you, the things you like.

PAOLO. There will be plenty of people to do that.

MADDALENA. Oh, you are killing me! You are sticking knives into my heart! (*She sinks to her knees and clutches his feet.*) Don't leave me behind. Don't make everything black and hopeless like this. Don't, don't, don't! (*He tries to free himself from her.*)

PAOLO (*Impatiently*). Maddalena, let me go—you little idiot! (*He wrenches himself from her grasp.*)

(*She lies motionless, sobbing wildly.*)

PAOLO (*At the door*). I'm sorry. (*He hesitates.*) Good-by.

MADDALENA. No, no—wait. (*She sits up.*) I must say something to you.

PAOLO. Well, what is it?

MADDALENA (*Trying to control herself*). In a minute—

PAOLO. Maddalena, I haven't much time. There is much to do.

MADDALENA. I'm trying not to cry. I know you don't like to see me cry. Paolo, you are quite right. You couldn't take me. I'd be—ridiculous among the people who are going to be your friends when you are a great singer. I know it now.

(*He kneels beside her and pats her shoulder.*)

PAOLO. Indeed you wouldn't. You are better than all the rest of them put together. Huh, they're not much.

MADDALENA. And the American lady—she wouldn't like it if I went too.

PAOLO. Well, no, she wouldn't, Maddalena. You see—

MADDALENA. Yes, I see.

PAOLO. It isn't as if I loved her as much as I love you. I could never care for any one else like that.

MADDALENA. You will love her more because she will give you more—fame, wealth—your opportunity, while I could only give you love. All that there is, all that there ever was in love I gave you, but love could never satisfy you, Paolo. It isn't enough. Paolo (*She gives him the locket from about her neck.*), take this. I want to give it to you, and sometimes it will make you think of all the beauty we have seen together.

PAOLO. No, Maddalena.

MADDALENA. Yes, please, you must.

(*He takes it.*)

PAOLO (*Looking at her*). What are you going to do?

MADDALENA (*Slowly*). What am I going to do? I don't know. Marry Pasquale, perhaps, after a while. One gets pushed into things and there is no use in trying to resist. And now, good-by. When you go, when you are down there in the street, will you sing to me?

PAOLO. Yes, Maddalena, you've been so wonderful. I won't forget you.

MADDALENA. Forget me? (*She laughs a little.*) Oh, yes, you might as well.

(*He goes out. She doesn't move. Presently* PAOLO's *voice can be heard singing "O Sole Mio." She listens a moment with closed eyes, then flings herself down, sobbing over and over again, "Paolo, Paolo!"*)

## SCENE III

*The curtain rises again on the land of fantasy.* PIERROT *is just climbing out of the door on the ground.* BUMBU *helps him.*

PIERROT. That was very interesting. (*He glances around.*) Where is Pierrette?

BUMBU (*Looking down*). She is coming.

(PIERRETTE's *voice calls, "Help me, Bumbu." She appears. They lift her up.*)

PIERRETTE. What a climb! It's quite exhausting. Oh, Bumbu, I'm so glad to see you again. (*She stretches out her hands.*) And Pierrot!

PIERROT. Pierrette! I treated you very badly, you know. How could I have treated you like that?

PIERRETTE (*Shrugging her shoulders*). Oh, well, it's the way of men. How lovely it is here, how peaceful. And the roses! Bumbu, I had forgotten that in the land of fantasy the roses have no thorns.

PIERROT. And no perfume!

PIERRETTE. What does that matter! Bumbu, how long have we been away?

BUMBU. It's impossible to tell, for here, where we are, there is no time.

PIERRETTE. I think it has been many years. Years, do you know what they are? They are the spokes of a great relentless wheel that carries one up, up, up, up, up—then, just as slowly, just as surely, it brings one down, down to the mud again. Time stole all the treasures of my soul. It sucked dry the wine of my body. I grew old and wrinkled. My hair was thin, and I shuffled when I walked! Oh! (*She shudders.*) And yet, somehow, I never knew or realized what it had done to me. A warm fire, a sugared cake could, at the end, make me whimper with delight. (*She turns suddenly and points to* BUMBU, *fiercely.*) It's you, Bumbu, spirit of grotesque, who feed the old those little petty joys to make them forget what they have lost!

BUMBU. Yes, it's I, Bumbu! My little penny whistles amuse them for a time when the shouts and tumult of the world sound far away.

PIERROT. Maddalena! She was always young in Paolo's memory! Sometimes he thought that he would go back to her—but he never did. (*He sighs.*) Poor Maddalena!

BUMBU. Poor Maddalena!

PIERRETTE. Poor Maddalena! (*She shrugs her shoulders.*) Oh, well, she had her memories.

PIERROT. Some of them were bitter.

PIERRETTE. Yes. But when she married Pasquale, do you think she could have been content with him, if she hadn't known love—before? That's what saved her and (*She laughs.*) that's what saved Pasquale as well. Tell me, what did Paolo do with Maddalena's jewel, the tear—for that's what it was?

PIERROT. He kept it for a long while, then it seemed beautiful no longer. Its brilliance faded and—somewhere—he lost it.

PIERRETTE. It's just as well.

BUMBU. Was he happy—Paolo?

PIERROT. Happy? No, only at first. His great triumphs were never enough. He wanted more, and after a time he ruined himself, and, what is worse—he ruined his voice.

BUMBU. And now, my children, I'll shut the door again. (*He pauses.*) Will you have one last look?

PIERRETTE. No, no!

PIERROT. Never.

(BUMBU *locks the door.*)

PIERRETTE. Poor things, down there—little half beings all of them, searching for completeness, for one glimpse of perfection.

PIERROT. Love brings that to them—to a few.

PIERRETTE. Yes, it does. That's why they crave it, but down in the great world love hurts! Oh, how can it hurt them like that, fill them like that, so overpoweringly, then pass so quickly away?

PIERROT. Because it's of no importance, I assure you.

PIERRETTE (*With conviction*). Oh, yes, indeed it is.

PIERROT. When it's born in the imagination and is as unreal as a dream?

PIERRETTE. That's true, but it can be the only thing that matters—while it lasts.

PIERROT. Paolo loved fifty times.

PIERRETTE. Maddalena loved only once.

PIERROT. Poor Maddalena!

PIERRETTE. She had quite enough of it, thank you. To love once, Pierrot, is fifty times better than loving fifty times. That must have been a great nuisance!

PIERROT. It was, when it interfered with his art. Still, I can't deny that at times it seemed well worth even that.

BUMBU. Only at times, I'll warrant you, and never for long. Those foolish mortals who spend their time chasing bright bubbles, sure to burst. Only art, my children, accomplishment, can lead them to discover riches that may be stored away, one by one, until they grow to treasure indestructible. If they but knew.

PIERROT (*Gaily*). Still, the pantomime of love, you'll admit, is enchanting. (*He points to his heart, then to* PIERRETTE.)

PIERRETTE. And that of disdain. (*She shows her scorn of* PIERROT *by pantomime.*)

PIERROT (*While dancing, as in the beginning*). All reflections, all images of things are lovelier than the things themselves. Do you agree with me, Pierrette?

PIERRETTE (*Also dancing*). Far more exquisite, more delicate. I quite agree, Pierrot.

PIERROT. You are adorable, Pierrette.

PIERRETTE. Pierrot, you are charming. Do you love me?

(PIERROT *runs and pulls down the moon, on its silken cord, from the sky.*)

PIERRETTE. Our delightful moon, that never shrinks, that always remains so beautifully round! (*She tosses it to him.*)

(*He throws it back.* BUMBU *beats his drum.*)

BUMBU. Play, my children, play. Mortals cry for the moon, but we, in the land of fantasy, need only laugh. The moon is ours!

THE CURTAIN FALLS

*Questions for Study*

Scene I

1. What is accomplished by the opening pantomime? What effect does the unexpected yawn have on you?
2. What is accomplished by the opening sentence?
3. What is the significance of the discussion about shivering with cold in relation to the art of acting?
4. Do you think Pierrette is wise in wanting more than perfection? Note the simile she uses when she refers to their love. Do you think it is an effective way of expressing her idea?
5. Do you agree with her when she suggests that if they could really feel they would enrich their art?
6. What is accomplished with the first mention of the door to the world?
7. Analyze Bumbu's opening speech. What does he mean when he calls himself "the spirit of grotesque"? Why does his drum shout of exaggeration rather than mediocrity, and of the comic rather than of comedy? What is the difference between comedy and the comic? What examples does he give of the way in which humanity has expressed the spirit of the grotesque? Explain the metaphor about red and yellow laughter splashed on the gray monotony of life. Do you think the world would go mad without the spirit of the grotesque to make people laugh in the midst of their sufferings? Can you give examples from your own life when something grotesque has made you forget your unhappiness?
8. Why does Bumbu say that he is often taken for the spirit of tragedy?
9. Is he right when he says they are better off in the land of fantasy than in the world of reality? Why? Can you give any examples of some flying stones of misfortune which might crush and frighten them?
10. Can you give any examples of joy coming so close that it burns?
11. Why are all the colors of light trembling in Pierrette's tear? Do you agree with Pierrot that tears are exquisite? Why does he call them that?
12. What do you think makes the white light of the world, and why is the land of fantasy in shadows and dim light?
13. Why don't Pierrot and Pierrette see the same things when they look through the door to the world? Explain the significance of what each one sees, especially of the mountain of gold and the dancing girls and dropping feathers.
14. Can you imagine what they will find out about love? Are you interested in seeing their adventures in the world of reality?

Scene II

1. What has happened to Pierrot and Pierrette in the world of reality?
2. What is going on outside Maddalena's balcony? Are you surprised at Paolo's actions, when you remember that he is Pierrot?

3. Why are the figures of speech Maddalena uses to describe her love so effective?

4. Has Pierrot found real love in the land of reality? Has Pierrette?

5. What is the difference between an artist and a mounteba.?k?

6. Do you think that Maddalena's idea of happiness would be ideal for mankind in general?

7. Do you sympathize with Paolo and his ambition?

8. Do you think he should accept Maddalena's offer to go with him? Why or why not?

9. Why wouldn't the American lady like to have Maddalena go with Paolo? Do you think Paolo will love her more than he does Maddalena?

10. Do you think Paolo will forget Maddalena?

11. What do you think will become of them? Imagine some of the experiences each will have in his later life.

12. Compare the first and second scenes in terms of the relationship of the characters to each other and in terms of the two backgrounds.


Scene III

1. Have Pierrot and Pierrette been affected by their experiences in the world of reality? If so, how?

2. Why are roses in the land of fantasy without thorns or perfume?

3. Why is there no time in the land of fantasy? What did time do to Maddalena? Do you think it does that to all of us? What is Bumbu's mission in the world of reality? Describe the ideal old age.

4. What really happened to Paolo and Maddalena? Are you surprised, pleased, or disappointed with their complete experience in the land of reality? What will be the result of the experience for them?

5. How had Maddalena's experience with Paolo saved her and Pasquale?

6. Analyze Pierrot and Pierrette's descriptions of love. With which one do you agree? Just what did each of them find out about love and life? Which do you think lived the more complete life? Do you want to love once or fifty times?

7. Is Bumbu right about art? What are some of the riches which artistic accomplishment brings to us? Why should everyone have a creative vocation or avocation? What are some creative hobbies?

8. Do you agree with Pierrot that all images of things are lovelier than the things themselves?

9. What is the meaning and significance of the closing line of the play? Is it a fitting end to the play?

10. Do you think that Pierrot and Pierrette are glad or sorry that they went to the land of reality? Will they want to go back again? Would you like to live in the land of fantasy? Why?

*The Play as a Whole*

1. Answer the following questions on the play's structure after you have read the entire play.

    **a.** What are the time, place, and preliminary situation of the play? Where is the initial incident? The climax?

    **b.** Summarize the plot in two or three sentences.

    **c.** What is the problem presented? How is it met? Is it solved?

    **d.** State the theme in one sentence. Is it a fundamental truth of life? Does it present any definite ideas regarding the relationships of human beings to each other? Do you agree with it?

    **e.** What are the most dramatic situations in the play?

    **f.** Analyze the characters of Pierrot and Pierrette, giving their strong and weak points. Describe their appearances.

    **g.** Discuss the dialogue of the play. Do the characters talk as they should? What is the difference between the ideas and the expression of them in the two settings presented?

    **h.** Pick out all of the figures of speech, and show their value in the play.

2. Explain the symbolism of the play. For example, what does the tear represent, and how does it carry out its meaning throughout the play? What do Bumbu and his drum represent? Why does the author use Bumbu as the means by which Pierrot and Pierrette are introduced to the world of reality?

3. Can you explain the difference between realistic and romantic drama as illustrated in this play? Do you prefer the scenes in the land of fantasy or the one in the world of reality? Do you think the second scene would make a complete play in itself? Why? If it had been the play, do you think any other elements should have been added?

4. Have you gained any new ideas about life and love from this play? If so, what are they? Do you agree with the author's ideas as expressed in this play? Do you think any of them will mean anything to you later?

5. Do you think there are any passages worth memorizing? If so, what are they and what ideas expressed in them have particular value?

6. Are there any touches of humor in the play? Of pathos? Of tragedy? Where do they occur?

7. Did you like the play? Why?

8. Write up the play in your notebook, according to the outline given on page 83.

9. Write character sketches of Pierrot and Pierrette, bringing out the beauty, weakness, pathos, and power of each of them; illustrate your points by quotations from the play and comments on their actions.

10. Assign the parts in the play to different members of the class in turn. Read the play aloud, setting the stage, and performing the action as far as possible with books in hand.

# Appendix B

## PLAYS FOR STUDENT PRODUCTION*

The following play lists have been compiled in an effort to meet the contrasting needs of all types of schools. The plays vary in appeal and value but all are suggested as possible material for play production, play reading, and additions to class and school libraries.

Individual publishers of each play are not given. However, information on availability, script purchases, amateur performance rights, and royalties may be obtained by writing to Walter H. Baker Company, Boston, Massachusetts, Dramatists Play Service, Inc., New York, or Samuel French, Inc., New York. These companies stock and distribute plays of other play publishers as well as their own.

### LONG PLAYS—ROYALTY†

| TITLE | AUTHOR | SETS I | SETS E | CHARACTERS M | CHARACTERS W | TYPE |
|---|---|---|---|---|---|---|
| Abie's Irish Rose | Nichols | 2 | | 6 | 2 | C |
| Adam and Eva | Bolton | 1 | 1 | 6 | 4 | C |
| Admirable Crichton, The | Barrie | 2 | 1 | 13 | 12 | C |
| Adorable Spendthrift, The | Briant | | 1 | 8 | 7 | C |
| Adventures of Tom Sawyer | Braun | 1 | | 6 | 7 | P |
| Alice Sit-by-the-Fire | Barrie | 2 | | 3 | 6 | C |
| All-of-a-Sudden-Peggy | Denny | 2 | | 6 | 5 | C |
| All Roads Lead to Hollywood | Reach | 1 | | 4 | 10 | C |
| Almost Eighteen | Thomas | 1 | | 5 | 7 | C |
| Applesauce | Conners | 2 | | 4 | 3 | C |
| Arms and the Man | Shaw | 2 | 1 | 6 | 3 | C |
| Arrival of Kitty | Swartout | 1 | | 5 | 4 | C |

* Under "Sets," *I* stands for Interior, *E* for Exterior, and *cyc* for Cyclorama; under "Characters," *M* stands for Men and *W* for Women; under "Type," *C* stands for Comedy, *S* for Serious, *M* for Mystery, *P* for Period play, and *F* for Fantasy.

† Royalty charges for these plays vary from $10 to $50 and depend upon the number of performances.

| Title | Author | Sets | | Characters | | Type |
|---|---|---|---|---|---|---|
| | | I | E | M | W | |
| Belvedere | Davenport | 1 | | 5 | 4 | C |
| Best Foot Forward | Halm | 1 | | 10 | 7 | C |
| Big Hearted Herbert | Kerr and Richardson | 1 | | 7 | 6 | C |
| Big Pond, The | Middleton and Thomas | 2 | | 7 | 2 | C |
| Bishop Misbehaves, The | Jackson | 2 | | 7 | 3 | M |
| Black Flamingo, The | Janney | 1 | | 9 | 4 | P |
| Boomerang, The | Smith and Mapes | 2 | | 6 | 5 | C |
| Brat, The | Fulton | 1 | | 4 | 7 | C |
| Broken Dishes | Flavin | 1 | | 6 | 4 | C |
| But Not Good-bye | Seaton | 1 | | 8 | 2 | C |
| Caine Mutiny Court Martial | Wouk | 1 | | 19 | | S |
| Call of the Banshee, The | Hepenstall and Kullinan | 1 | | 8 | 7 | M |
| Cappy Ricks | Rose | 1 | 1 | 6 | 3 | C |
| Captain Applejack | Hackett | 2 | | 6 | 5 | C |
| Cat and Canary, The | Willard | 2 | | 6 | 4 | M |
| Ceiling Zero | Wead | 1 | | 18 | 4 | S |
| Charm School, The | Miller and Milton | 2 | | 6 | 10 | C |
| Cheaper by the Dozen | Clark | 1 | | 9 | 7 | C |
| Chicken Feed | Bolton | 1 | | 7 | 4 | C |
| Cinderella Man, The | Carpenter | 2 | | 8 | 3 | C |
| Clarence | Tarkington | 2 | | 5 | 5 | C |
| Clutching Claw, The | Kettering | 1 | | 6 | 7 | M |
| Cock Robin | Rice and Barry | 2 | | 8 | 4 | M |
| College Widow, The | Ade | 2 | 1 | 15 | 10 | C |
| Come Out of the Kitchen | Thomas | 3 | | 6 | 5 | C |
| Copperhead, The | Thomas | 2 | 2 | 9 | 6 | P |
| Country Cousin, The | Tarkington and Street | 2 | 1 | 7 | 6 | C |
| Curious Savage, The | Patrick | | 1 | 5 | 6 | C |
| Cyrano de Bergerac | Rostand (Kruckemeyer adaptation) | 2 | 3 | 30 | 16 | P |
| Danger—Girls Working! | Winthrop | 1 | | | 11 | M |
| Date with Judy, A | Leslie | 1 | | 5 | 9 | C |
| Dear Ruth | Krasna | 1 | | 5 | 5 | C |
| Death Takes a Holiday | Cassella and Ferris | 1 | | 7 | 6 | S |
| Devil in the Cheese, The | Cushing | cyc | | 7 | 2 | F |
| Divine Flora, The | Ryerson and Clements | 1 | 1 | 12 | 14 | C |

| Title | Author | Sets I | Sets E | Characters M | Characters W | Type |
|---|---|---|---|---|---|---|
| Don't Ever Grow Up | Reach | 1 | | 7 | 10 | C |
| Dulcy | Kaufman and Connelly | 1 | | 8 | 3 | C |
| Enchanted April, The | Campbell | 2 | | 5 | 5 | C |
| Enchanted Cottage, The | Pinero | 1 | 1 | 5 | 4 | F |
| Enemy, The | Pollock | 1 | | 7 | 3 | S |
| Ever Since Eve | Ryerson and Clements | 1 | | 6 | 5 | C |
| Excursion | Wolfson | 1 | | 18 | 10 | S |
| Expressing Willie | Crothers | 2 | | 6 | 5 | S |
| Family Upstairs, The | Delf | 1 | | 4 | 5 | C |
| Fanny and the Servant Problem | Jerome | 1 | | 5 | 17 | C |
| Far Off Hills, The | Robinson | 2 | | 5 | 5 | C |
| Father of the Bride | Francke | | 1 | 11 | 7 | C |
| Fighting Littles, The | Francke | 1 | | 5 | 10 | C |
| First Lady | Dayton and Kaufman | 2 | | 14 | 11 | C |
| First Year, The | Craven | 2 | | 5 | 4 | C |
| Fly Away Home | Bennett and White | 1 | | 7 | 6 | C |
| Fool, The | Pollock | 2 | | 13 | 8 | S |
| Four Daughters | Hurst | 1 | | 5 | 5 | C |
| Four-Flusher, The | Dunn | 2 | | 8 | 5 | C |
| Fresh Fields | Novello | 1 | | 3 | 6 | C |
| Galahad Jones | Loving | 1 | | 7 | 7 | C |
| Ghost of Rhodes Manor, The | Latham | 1 | | | 10 | M |
| Ghost Train, The | Ridley | 1 | | 7 | 4 | M |
| Glee Plays the Game | Gerstenberg | 1 | | | 14 | C |
| Going on Seventeen | Manning | 1 | | 6 | 8 | C |
| Goose Hangs High, The | Beach | 1 | | 7 | 6 | C |
| Great Expectations | Dickens (Chadwicke adaptation) | 1 | | 7 | 8 | S |
| Growing Pains | Rouverol | 1 | | 8 | 10 | C |
| Gypsy Trail, The | Housum | 1 | | 5 | 4 | C |
| Headed for Eden | Duval | 1 | | 7 | 10 | S |
| Henrietta the Eighth | Gordon | 1 | | 6 | 9 | C |
| Heroes Just Happen | Finch and Smith | 1 | | 11 | 13 | C |
| He Who Gets Slapped | Andreyev | 1 | | 20 | 13 | F |
| Holiday | Barry | 2 | | 7 | 5 | C |
| Hooray for Youth | Manning | 1 | | 7 | 10 | C |
| Hoosier School Master | Spence | 1 | | 17 | 10 | C |

| Title | Author | Sets | | Characters | | Type |
|---|---|---|---|---|---|---|
| | | I | E | M | W | |
| Ice Bound | Davis | 1 | | 6 | 6 | S |
| If I Were King | McCarthy | 3 | 1 | 20 | 9 | P |
| I Killed the Count | Coppel | 1 | | 10 | 3 | M |
| I'll Leave It to You | Coward | 1 | | 4 | 6 | C |
| In the Next Room | Robson and Ford | 2 | | 8 | 3 | M |
| Intimate Strangers, The | Tarkington | 2 | | 4 | 4 | C |
| I Remember Mama | Van Druten | 1 unit | | 9 | 13 | S |
| It Can't Happen Here | Moffitt and Lewis | 3 | | 10 | 3 | S |
| Ivory Door, The | Milne | 1 | 1 | 11 | 4 | F |
| Janice Meredith | Rose and Ford | 3 | | 21 | 4 | P |
| January Thaw | Roos | 1 | | 7 | 6 | C |
| Jenny Kissed Me | Kerr | 1 | | 4 | 10 | C |
| Joan of Lorraine | Anderson | 1 | | 18 | 5 | S |
| Journey's End | Sherriff | 1 | | 10 | | S |
| Judy Drops In | Swan | 1 | | 6 | 3 | C |
| June Mad | Ryerson and Clements | 1 | | 7 | 6 | C |
| Junior Miss | Chodorov and Fields | 1 | | 11 | 6 | C |
| Kempy | Nugent | 1 | | 4 | 4 | C |
| King of Hearts, The | Kerr and Brooke | 1 | | 6 | 2 | C |
| Kiss for Cinderella, A | Barrie | 4 | 1 | 11 | 10 | F |
| Ladies in Waiting | Campion | 2 | | | 9 | M |
| Ladies of Cranford | Horne | 1 | | | 13 | C |
| Laff That Off | Mullally | 1 | | 4 | 3 | C |
| Leave It to Psmith | Wodehouse | 3 | 1 | 10 | 8 | M |
| Letters to Lucerne | Rotter and Vincent | 2 | | 4 | 9 | S |
| Life Begins at Sixteen | Manning | 1 | | 6 | 9 | C |
| Life With Father | Lindsay and Crouse | 1 | | 8 | 8 | P |
| Little Geraldine | Loving | 1 | | 4 | 8 | C |
| Little Minister, The | Barrie (Fernand adaptation) | 1 | | 5 | 6 | C |
| Little Miss Fortune | George | 1 | | 4 | 7 | C |
| Little Old New York | Young | 2 | 1 | 12 | 4 | P |
| Little Princess, The | Burnett | 3 | | 6 | 15 | P |
| Little Women | Alcott (Ravold adaptation) | 1 | | 4 | 6 | P |
| Loose Ankles | Janney | 1 | | 6 | 7 | C |
| Mad Hatters, The | Gordon | 1 | | 4 | 8 | C |

| Title | Author | Sets | | Characters | | Type |
|---|---|---|---|---|---|---|
| | | I | E | M | W | |
| Magnificent Obsession | Douglas | 1 | | 5 | 5 | S |
| Martha-by-the-Day | Lippman | 3 | | 5 | 5 | C |
| Mary the Third | Crothers | 2 | | 5 | 5 | S |
| Meet Me in St. Louis | Benson | 1 | | 7 | 9 | C |
| Merely Mary Ann | Zangwill | 3 | | 8 | 10 | C |
| Merton of the Movies | Kaufman and Connelly | 5 | | 7 | 4 | C |
| Mirandolina | Goldoni and Gregory | 3 | | 5 | 1 | P |
| Miss Lulu Bett | Gale | 2 | | 4 | 5 | S |
| Mister Pim Passes By | Milne | 1 | | 3 | 4 | C |
| Monsieur Beaucaire | Tarkington | | 1 | 14 | 7 | P |
| Moon Makes Three, The | Harris | 1 | | 7 | 8 | C |
| Mrs. Bumpstead-Leigh | Smith | 1 | | 6 | 6 | C |
| Mrs. McThing | Chase | 2 | | 9 | 10 | F |
| | | | | 2 children | | |
| Mrs. Moonlight | Levy | 1 | | 4 | 4 | F |
| Mrs. Partridge Presents | Kennedy and Hawthorne | 1 | | 6 | 6 | C |
| Mrs. Wiggs of the Cabbage Patch | Flexner | 1 | 1 | 15 | 11 | C |
| My Man Godfrey | Hatch | 1 | | 6 | 6 | C |
| Mystery at Greenfingers | Priestly | 1 | | 4 | 6 | M |
| My Three Angels | Spewack | 1 | | 7 | 3 | C |
| Nervous Wreck, The | Davis | 1 | | 9 | 2 | C |
| New Fires | Burdette | 1 | | 6 | 9 | C |
| New Poor | Hamilton | 1 | | 6 | 6 | C |
| Ninth Guest, The | Davis | 1 | | 7 | 3 | M |
| Noah | Obey (Wilmurt adaptation) | | 3 | 5 | 4 | S |
| Nothing But the Truth | Montgomery | 2 | | 5 | 6 | C |
| Nut Farm, The | Brownell | 1 | | 6 | 4 | C |
| Officer 666 | MacHugh | 1 | | 9 | 3 | C |
| One Foot in Heaven | Spence | 1 | | 8 | 9 | C |
| One of the Family | Webb | 2 | | 4 | 6 | C |
| Our Hearts Were Young and Gay | Kerr and Skinner | 1 | | 8 | 9 | C |
| Outward Bound | Vane | 1 | | 6 | 3 | S |
| Pair of Sixes, A | Peple | 2 | | 8 | 4 | C |
| Passing of the Third Floor Back, The | Jerome | 1 | | 6 | 6 | S |
| Patsy, The | Connors | 1 | | 5 | 4 | C |
| Peg O' My Heart | Manners | 1 | | 5 | 4 | C |

| Title | Author | Sets I | E | Characters M | W | Type |
|---|---|---|---|---|---|---|
| Polly of the Circus | Mayo | 2 | 1 | 8 | 6 | C |
| Polly with a Past | Middleton and Bolton | 2 | | 7 | 5 | C |
| Pomander Walk | Parker | | 1 | 10 | 8 | P |
| Poor Little Rich Girl, The | Gates | 2 | 4 | 9 | 10 | F |
| Poor Nut, The | Nugent | 3 | 1 | 11 | 5 | C |
| Pride and Prejudice | Jerome | 3 | | 10 | 16 | P |
| Prince There Was, A | Cohan | 3 | | 7 | 6 | C |
| Private Secretary, The | Hawtrey | 2 | | 9 | 4 | C |
| Prologue to Glory | Conkle | 1 | 5 | 14 | 7 | P |
| Prunella | Housman and Barker | | 1 | 12 | 10 | S |
| Purple Mask, The | Lang | 5 | | 15 | 9 | P |
| Quality Street | Barrie | 2 | 1 | 6 | 7 | P |
| Queen's Husband, The | Sherwood | 1 | | 11 | 4 | C |
| Rainmaker, The | Nash | 1 unit | | 6 | 1 | S |
| Ramshackle Inn | Batson | 1 | | 9 | 6 | M |
| Reflected Glory | Kelly | 3 | | 7 | 5 | S |
| Rejuvenation of Aunt Mary, The | Warner | 3 | | 7 | 6 | C |
| Remember the Day | Higley and Dunning | cyc | | 13 | 12 | S |
| Ring Around Elizabeth | Armstrong | 1 | | 5 | 7 | C |
| Road to Yesterday, The | Dix and Sutherland | 3 | | 8 | 6 | P |
| Rollo's Wild Oat | Kummer | 4 | | 7 | 5 | C |
| Romantic Age, The | Milne | 1 | 1 | 5 | 4 | C |
| Romantic Young Lady, The | Sierra | 1 | | 5 | 6 | P |
| Royal Family, The | Ferber and Kaufman | 1 | | 11 | 6 | C |
| R.U.R. | Čapek | 2 | | 13 | 4 | F |
| Sabrina Fair | Taylor | | 1 | 4 | 4 | M |
| Seven Days | Rinehart and Hopwood | 2 | | 6 | 4 | C |
| Seven Keys to Baldpate | Cohan | 1 | | 9 | 4 | M |
| Seven Sisters | Ellis and Herzeg | 1 | | 6 | 8 | C |
| Seventeen | Tarkington | 2 | 1 | 8 | 6 | C |
| Shannons of Broadway, The | Gleason | 1 | | 18 | 6 | C |
| Shooting High | Metcalf and Spence | 1 | | 10 | 9 | C |
| Show-off, The | Kelly | 1 | | 6 | 3 | C |
| Skidding | Rouverol | 1 | | 5 | 5 | C |
| Skinner's Dress Suit | Dodge, Marsten, and Paulton | 2 | | 6 | 5 | C |

| TITLE | AUTHOR | SETS | | CHAR-ACTERS | | TYPE |
|---|---|---|---|---|---|---|
| | | I | E | M | W | |
| Smiling Through | Martin | 2 | | 5 | 5 | S |
| So This Is London! | Goodrich | 3 | | 7 | 4 | C |
| Spring Dance | Barry | 2 | | 6 | 7 | C |
| Spring Fever | Hughes | 1 | | 6 | 6 | C |
| Spring Green | Ryerson and | | | | | |
| | Clements | 1 | | 8 | 7 | C |
| Stardust | Kerr | 1 | | 7 | 11 | C |
| Stephen Foster | Smith | | 1 | 7 | 5 | P |
| Strange Boarders | Batson | 1 | | 8 | 7 | M |
| Strawhatters' Case, The | Foster and Noble | 1 | | 8 | 6 | M |
| Strongheart | DeMille | 3 | | 17 | 5 | C |
| Successful Calamity, A | Kummer | 1 | | 9 | 3 | C |
| Sunkissed | Van Sycle | 1 | | 8 | 8 | C |
| Sun-up | Vollmer | 1 | | 7 | 2 | S |
| Swan, The | Molnar | 1 | | 12 | 8 | S |
| Thirteenth Chair, The | Veiller | 1 | | 10 | 7 | M |
| Three Live Ghosts | Isham and | | | | | |
| | Marcim | 1 | | 6 | 4 | C |
| Thunder Rock | Ardrey | 1 | | 8 | 3 | S |
| Tiger House | St. Clair | 1 | | 5 | 5 | M |
| Tight Wad, The | Keith | 1 | | 6 | 5 | C |
| Time Out for Ginger | Alexander | 1 | | 5 | 5 | C |
| Tin Hero, The | George | 1 | | 4 | 8 | C |
| Tish | Rinehart | 1 | | 5 | 8 | C |
| Tommy | Lindsay and | | | | | |
| | Robinson | 1 | | 5 | 3 | C |
| Torchbearers, The | Kelly | 2 | | 6 | 6 | C |
| Truth About Blayds, The | Milne | 1 | | 4 | 4 | C |
| Turn to the Right | Hazzard and | | | | | |
| | Smith | 2 | 1 | 9 | 5 | C |
| Tweedles | Tarkington and | | | | | |
| | Wilson | 1 | | 5 | 4 | C |
| Uncle Fred Flits By | Wodehouse | 1 | | 7 | 7 | C |
| Valiant One, The | Crothers | 1 | | 3 | 5 | S |
| Wappin' Wharf | Brooks | 1 | | 8 | 3 | P |
| We Shook the Family Tree | Clark | 1 | | 5 | 7 | C |
| What a Life! | Goldsmith | 1 | | 10 | 12 | C |
| White Collars | Ellis | 3 | | 5 | 4 | S |
| Whiteheaded Boy, The | Robinson | 1 | | 5 | 7 | C |
| Whole Town's Talking, The | Loos | 1 | | 5 | 7 | C |
| Wind and the Rain, The | Hodge | 1 | | 6 | 3 | C |
| Winslow Boy, The | Rattigan | 1 | | 7 | 4 | S |
| Wren, The | Tarkington | 1 | | 4 | 3 | C |
| Years Ago | Gordon | 1 | | 4 | 5 | P |

| | | SETS | | CHAR-ACTERS | | |
| TITLE | AUTHOR | I | E | M | W | TYPE |
|---|---|---|---|---|---|---|
| Yellow Jacket, The | Hazleton and Benrimo | 1 | | 17 | 12 | P |
| Yes and No | Horne | 1 | | 3 | 4 | C |
| You and I | Barry | 2 | | 4 | 3 | S |
| You Can't Take It with You | Hart and Kaufman | 1 | | 9 | 7 | C |
| Young April | Rouverol | 1 | | 7 | 9 | C |
| Youngest, The | Barry | 1 | 1 | 4 | 5 | C |
| Young Idea, The | Coward | 2 | | 7 | 7 | C |
| Young Lincoln | Braun | 1 | | 7 | 9 | S |
| Young Man's Fancy, A | Thurschwell and Golden | 1 | | 10 | 9 | C |
| Youth Takes Over | Smith and Finch | 1 | | 10 | 17 | C |

## LONG PLAYS—NON-ROYALTY*

| | | SETS | | CHAR-ACTERS | | |
| TITLE | AUTHOR | I | E | M | W | TYPE |
|---|---|---|---|---|---|---|
| Aaron Slick from Punkin Crick | Cormack | 2 | | 3 | 4 | C |
| Alice in Wonderland | Carroll | 2 | 1 | 16 | 14 | F |
| Black Gold | Short and Phelps | 1 | | 5 | 5 | S |
| Contrast, The | Tyler | cyc | | 5 | 4 | P |
| Cricket on the Hearth | Dickens (Brown adaptation) | 2 | | 7 | 8 | P |
| Doctor in Spite of Himself | Molière | 1 | 1 | 6 | 3 | P |
| Fan, The | Goldoni | | 1 | 10 | 4 | P |
| Fashion | Mowatt | 1 | | 8 | 5 | P |
| Gammer Gurton's Needle | Clements | cyc | | 6 | 4 | P |
| High School Mystery, The | St. Clair | 1 | | 6 | 6 | M |
| Imaginary Invalid, The | Molière (Stone adaptation) | 1 | | 8 | 4 | P |
| Importance of Being Earnest, The | Wilde | 2 | 1 | 5 | 4 | C |
| It's a Long Lane | Hershey | 1 | | 4 | 5 | S |
| Knight of the Burning Pestle | Beaumont and Fletcher | cyc | | 19 | 5 | P |
| Lena Rivers | Holmes and Albert | 1 | | 6 | 7 | S |
| Master Patelin, Solicitor | Anonymous | 1 | 1 | 7 | 2 | P |

* Some of these plays are non-royalty only if a definite number of script copies are purchased for the use of the cast. Be sure to check with one of the publishers given on page 468 to see whether such a requirement exists for the play you wish to produce.

| Title | Author | Sets I E | Characters M W | Type |
|---|---|---|---|---|
| M'Liss | Mitchel and Harte | 1 | 5 5 | C |
| Moonstone, The | Collins and Spence | 1 | 9 7 | M |
| Our American Cousin | Taylor | 1 | 10 7 | C |
| Pulling the Curtain | Taggart | 1 | 7 8 | C |
| Pillars of Society | Ibsen (Leverton adaptation) | 1 | 10 9 | S |
| Ready Made Family, A | Tobias | 1 | 4 6 | C |
| Rivals, The | Sheridan | cyc | 8 4 | P |
| Romancers, The | Rostand | 1 | 5 1 | C |
| School for Scandal | Sheridan | cyc | 13 4 | P |
| She Stoops to Conquer | Goldsmith | cyc | 13 4 | P |
| Tomboy | Loving | 1 | 5 9 | C |
| Uncle Tom's Cabin | Stowe and Aiken | cyc | 15 6 | P |
| Young and Lively | George | 1 | 6 6 | C |

## SHORT PLAYS—ROYALTY*

| Title | Author | Sets I E | Characters M W | Type |
|---|---|---|---|---|
| Ah, Sweet Mystery | Kirkpatrick | 1 | 3 5 | C |
| Andante | Coutts | 1 | 3 2 | S |
| Angels Don't Marry | Ryerson and Clements | 1 | 1 2 | C |
| Aria da Capo | Millay | 1 | 4 1 | F |
| Artist, The | Milne | 1 | 1 1 | C |
| Barbara's Wedding | Barrie | 1 | 4 2 | S |
| Bard at Bakersville High | Kirkpatrick | 1 | 3 5 | F |
| Behind a Watteau Picture | Rogers | 1 | 6 2 | F |
| Birthday of the Infanta, The | Wilde | 1 | 4 1 | S |
| Bishop's Candlesticks, The | McKinnel | 1 | 3 2 | S |
| Bound for Mexico | Hughes | 1 | 4 1 | S |
| Boy Comes Home, The | Milne | 1 | 2 3 | S |
| Boy Meets Family | Reiser | 1 | 3 4 | C |
| Bread | Eastman | 1 | 2 4 | S |
| Bridges | Kummer | 1 | 2 1 | C |
| Cabbages | Staadt | 1 | 3 4 | C |
| Caleb Stone's Death Watch | Flavin | 1 | 6 4 | S |
| Camberley Triangle, The | Milne | 1 | 2 1 | C |
| Chinese Love | Kummer | 1 | 4 2 | S |
| Cinderella Married | Field | 1 | 2 4 | C |

* Royalty charges for these plays vary from $5 to $10.

| Title | Author | Sets | | Char-acters | | Type |
|---|---|---|---|---|---|---|
| | | I | E | M | W | |
| Cleaned and Pressed | Hove | 1 | | 2 | 3 | C |
| Clod, The | Beach | 1 | | 4 | 1 | S |
| Confessional, The | Wilde | 1 | | 3 | 2 | S |
| Crabbed Youth and Age | Robinson | 1 | | 3 | 4 | C |
| Cross-stitch Heart | Field | 1 | | 2 | 3 | F |
| Curtain | Clements | 1 | | 1 | 2 | C |
| Curtain, The | Flannagan | 1 | | 4 | 2 | S |
| Dark Lady of the Sonnets, The | Shaw | | 1 | 2 | 2 | C |
| Dear Departed, The | Houghton | 1 | | 3 | 3 | C |
| Devil and Daniel Webster | Benét | 1 | | 6 | 1 | F |
| Drums of Oude, The | Strong | 1 | | 7 | 1 | S |
| Early Victorian | Hughes | 1 | | 2 | 1 | C |
| El Cristo | Larkin | 1 | | 4 | 2 | S |
| Enter the Hero | Helburn | 1 | | 1 | 3 | C |
| Evening Dress Indispensable | Pertwee | 1 | | 2 | 2 | C |
| Farewell to Love | Ryerson and Clements | 1 | | 1 | 1 | C |
| Feast of Ortolans | Anderson | 1 | | 18 | 2 | S |
| Fifteenth Candle, The | Field | 1 | | 2 | 3 | S |
| Finger of God, The | Wilde | 1 | | 2 | 1 | S |
| First Dress Suit, The | Medcraft | 1 | | 2 | 2 | C |
| Fixins | Green | 1 | | 2 | 1 | S |
| Flattering Word, The | Kelly | 1 | | 2 | 3 | C |
| Florist Shop, The | Hawkbridge | 1 | | 3 | 2 | C |
| Flower of Yeddo, A | Mapes | 1 | | 1 | 3 | C |
| Food | de Mille | 1 | | 2 | 1 | S |
| Funny Business | Hughes | 1 | | 7 | 4 | C |
| Ghost Story, The | Tarkington | 1 | | 5 | 5 | C |
| Glamour | Wilde | 1 | | 2 | 1 | C |
| Gloria Mundi | Brown | 1 | | 2 | 4 | S |
| Good Medicine | Arnold and Burke | 1 | | 1 | 2 | C |
| Grandma Pulls the String | Delano and Garb | 1 | | 1 | 5 | C |
| Happy Journey from Camden to Trenton | Wilder | 1 | | 3 | 3 | C |
| Harlequinade in Green and Orange | Hughes | | 1 | 2 children 3 | 3 | F |
| Her First Party Dress | Manning | 1 | | 3 | 4 | C |
| Hero of Santa Maria | Goodman and Hecht | 1 | | 3 | 2 | C |
| Hints to Brides | Nicholson | 1 | | 2 | 2 | C |
| House with the Twisty Windows, The | Pakington | 1 | | 4 | 3 | F |
| How Do You Do, Sir? | Kreymborg | 1 | | 1 | 1 | S |

| Title | Author | Sets | | Characters | | Type |
|---|---|---|---|---|---|---|
| | | I | E | M | W | |
| How He Lied to Her Husband | Shaw | 1 | | 2 | 1 | C |
| Hyacinth Halvey | Lady Gregory | 1 | | 4 | 2 | C |
| If the Light Be Darkness | Beardley | 1 | | 3 | 1 | S |
| In 1999 | de Mille | 1 | | 1 | 2 | C |
| Jazz and Minuet | Groiloff | 1 | | 3 | 5 | F |
| Joan the Maid | Ould | | 1 | 3 | 3 | S |
| Judge Lynch | Rogers | | 1 | 2 | 2 | S |
| Just Neighborly | Dean | 1 | | 2 | 2 | C |
| Knave of Hearts, The | Saunders | 1 | | 15 parts | | C |
| Land of Heart's Desire, The | Yeats | 1 | | 3 | 3 | F |
| Let's Make Up | Olson | 1 | | 3 | 3 | C |
| Lima Beans | Kreymborg | 1 | | 1 | 1 | C |
| Londonderry Air | Field | 1 | | 2 | 2 | C |
| Lonesome-like | Brighouse | 1 | | 2 | 2 | C |
| Lost Princess, The | Totheroh | 1 | | 10 | 4 | F |
| Make Room for Rodney | Holbrook | 1 | | 3 | 3 | C |
| Maker of Dreams, The | Down | 1 | | 2 | 1 | F |
| Manikin and Minikin | Kreymborg | 1 | | 1 | 1 | F |
| Man in the Bowler Hat, The | Milne | | 1 | 4 | 2 | C |
| Man on the Curb | Sutro | 1 | | 1 | 1 | S |
| Man Who Married a Dumb Wife | France | 1 | | 7 | 3 | C |
| Man Who Thought of Everything | Taylor | 1 | | 1 | 2 | C |
| Marriage Has Been Arranged, A | Sutro | 1 | | 1 | 1 | C |
| Mayor and the Manicure, The | Ade | 1 | | 2 | 2 | C |
| Men, Women and Goats | Kennedy | 1 | | 3 | 2 | C |
| Minuet, A | Parker | 1 | | 2 | 1 | C |
| Monkey's Paw, The | Jacobs | 1 | | 4 | 1 | S |
| Monsignor's House | Lavery | 1 | | 12 | 2 | S |
| Mouse, The | Armstrong | 1 | | 4 | 1 | C |
| My Lady's Lace | Knoblock | | 1 | 2 | 2 | C |
| Neighbours | Gale | | 1 | 2 | 6 | C |
| | | | | 2 children | | |
| Nevertheless | Walker | | | 1 | | C |
| New School for Wives | Kirkpatrick | 1 | | 2 | 6 | C |
| Nine Lives of Emily, The | Kirkpatrick | 1 | | 3 | 4 | C |
| Noble Lord, The | Wilde | | 1 | 2 | 1 | C |
| Now Is the Time | Kirkpatrick | 1 | | 2 | 5 | C |
| Now That April's Here | Reach | 1 | | 2 | 4 | C |
| Old Lady Shows Her Medals | Barrie | 1 | | 2 | 4 | S |

| Title | Author | Sets I | E | Characters M | W | Type |
|---|---|---|---|---|---|---|
| Old Peabody Pew, The | Wiggin | 1 | | 1 | 8 | C |
| One Egg | Hughes | 1 | | 2 | 1 | C |
| One of Us | Emery | 1 | | 2 | 4 | S |
| 'Op O' Me Thumb | Fenn and Pryce | 1 | | 1 | 5 | C |
| Patchwork Quilt | Field | 1 | | 2 | 4 | C |
| Pearls | Totheroh | 1 | | 2 | 2 | S |
| Pink and Patches | Bland | | 1 | 1 | 3 | C |
| Playgoers | Pinero | 1 | | 2 | 6 | C |
| Portrait of a Gentleman in Slippers, A | Milne | 1 | | 3 | 1 | F |
| Present-day Courtship | Bottomley | 1 | | 1 | 1 | C |
| Princess Marries the Page, The | Millay | 1 | | 6 | 1 | S |
| "Q" | Leacock and Hastings | 1 | | 3 | 1 | C |
| Question of Figures, A | Olson | 1 | | | 6 | C |
| Red Carnations | Hughes | 1 | | 2 | 1 | C |
| Red Owl, The | Gillette | 1 | | 4 | 1 | S |
| Rich Man, Poor Man | Burrill | 1 | | 3 | 9 | C |
| Riders to the Sea | Synge | 1 | | 1 | 3 | S |
| Robbery, The | Kummer | 1 | | 3 | 2 | C |
| Shall We Join the Ladies? | Barrie | 1 | | 8 | 8 | S |
| Sham | Tompkins | 1 | | 3 | 1 | C |
| Six Queens of Henry | Price | 1 | | 2 | 6 | F |
| Slave With the Two Faces, The | Davies | | 1 | 3 | 4 | F |
| Soap Opera | Kirkpatrick | 1 | | 3 | 3 | C |
| Sparkin' | Conkle | 1 | | 1 | 3 | C |
| Spreading the News | Lady Gregory | | 1 | 7 | 3 | C |
| Such a Charming Young Man | Akins | 1 | | 6 | 3 | C |
| Sunny Morning, A | Quintero | | 1 | 6 | 3 | C |
| Suppressed Desires | Glaspell | 1 | | 1 | 2 | C |
| Table d'Hôtes and à la Cartes | Kirkpatrick | 1 | | 3 | 3 | C |
| Teapot On the Rocks | Kirkpatrick | 1 | | 3 | 3 | C |
| Thank You, Doctor | Emery | 1 | | 3 | 2 | C |
| That's Hollywood | Ryerson and Clements | 1 | | 2 | 4 | C |
| Thirty Minutes in a Street | Mayor | | 1 | 12 | 11 | C |
| Threshold, The | McCauley | 1 | | 2 | 2 1 child | | S |
| Travelling Man, The | Lady Gregory | 1 | | 1 | 1 | S |
| Trifles | Glaspell | 1 | | 3 | 2 | S |

| Title | Author | Sets | | Characters | | Type |
|-------|--------|------|---|-----------|---|------|
| | | I | E | M | W | |
| Trysting Place, The | Tarkington | 1 | | 4 | 3 | C |
| Twelve Pound Look, The | Barrie | 1 | | 2 | 2 | C |
| Two Crooks and a Lady | Pillot | 1 | | 3 | 3 | S |
| Two Slatterns and a King | Millay | 1 | | 2 | 2 | F |
| Ugly Duckling, The | Milne | 1 | | 2 | 2 | C |
| Valiant, The | Hall and Middlemass | 1 | | 5 | 1 | S |
| Vanishing Princess, The | Golden | 1 | | 3 | 1 | F |
| Wedding, A | Kirkpatrick | 1 | | 4 | 3 | C |
| Welsh Honeymoon | Marks | 1 | | 3 | 2 | C |
| Where But in America | Wolff | 1 | | 1 | 2 | C |
| Will, The | Barrie | 1 | | 5 | 1 | C |
| Winsome Winnie Clinton | Baddeley and Leacock | 1 | | 5 | 3 | C |
| Wisdom Teeth | Field | 1 | | 1 | 3 | C |
| Woman's Privilege, A | Hayes | 1 | | 2 | 2 | C |
| Women Folks, The | Kirkpatrick | 1 | | 1 | 6 | C |
| Workhouse Ward, The | Lady Gregory | 1 | | 2 | 1 | C |
| World Without End | Wilde | | 1 | 6 | 6 | F |
| Write Me a Love Scene | Ryerson and Clements | 1 | | 2 | 2 | C |
| Wurzel Flummery | Milne | 1 | | 3 | 2 | C |
| Yes Means No | Rogers | 1 | | 3 | 2 | C |
| Young Man's Fancy, A | Manning | 1 | | 3 | 3 | C |

## SHORT PLAYS—NON-ROYALTY*

| Title | Author | Sets | | Characters | | Type |
|-------|--------|------|---|-----------|---|------|
| | | I | E | M | W | |
| Advantages of Being Shy, The | Hoffman | 1 | | 1 | 5 | C |
| Advertising for a Husband | Bird | 1 | | 3 | 2 | C |
| Affected Young Ladies, The | Molière | 1 | | 6 | 3 | P |
| All-American Boy | Jones | 1 | | 3 | 3 | C |
| Billy's First Date | Olson | 1 | | 3 | 6 | C |
| Blue Beads | Martens | 1 | | 1 | 3 | S |
| Boor, The | Chekhov | 1 | | 2 | 1 | C |
| Box and Cox | Morton | 1 | | 2 | 1 | C |
| Brace of Sixes, A | Davitt | 1 | | 2 | 1 | C |
| Call It a Day | Graham | 1 | | 8 | 20 | C |
| Curse You, Jack Dalton | Braun | 1 | | 3 | 4 | C |
| Elmer | McNeil | 1 | | 3 | 6 | C |
| Enter Dora—Exit Dad | Tilden | 1 | | 4 | 1 | C |

* See note on non-royalty plays on bottom of page 475.

| TITLE | AUTHOR | SETS | | CHAR-ACTERS | | TYPE |
|---|---|---|---|---|---|---|
| | | I | E | M | W | |
| Ghost of a Show | Carriere | 1 | | 7 | 4 | C |
| Great Man | Crandall | 1 | | 2 | 1 | S |
| Green Coat, The | Augier and de | | | | | |
| | Musset | 1 | | 3 | 1 | C |
| Gringoire, the Ballad Monger | DeBanville | 1 | | 4 | 2 | P |
| Haunted Theatre, The | Randall | 1 | | 3 | 3 | M |
| He Ain't Done Right by | | | | | | |
| Nell | Braun | 1 | | 3 | 4 | C |
| His First Shave | Else | 1 | | 2 | 3 | C |
| Inevitable Hour, The | Byrnes | 1 | | 8 | 2 | S |
| Jealousy Plays a Part | George | 1 | | 2 | 5 | C |
| Jeweled Hand, The | George | 1 | | 3 | 4 | M |
| Man's Monument, A | Eastman | 1 | | 4 | 4 | F |
| Marriage Proposal, A | Chekhov | 1 | | 2 | 1 | C |
| Oh, Nono! | Kester | 1 | | 1 | 1 | C |
| Out of the Night | Smith | 1 | | 7 | 3 | M |
| Paul Splits the Atom | Sergel | 1 | | 3 | 4 | C |
| Rector, The | Crothers | 1 | | 1 | 6 | C |
| Red Lamp, The | Booth | 1 | | 3 | 3 | C |
| Sauce for the Goslings | Warren | 1 | | 3 | 4 | C |
| Sweet "16" | Thyson | 1 | | 10 | 8 | C |
| Taming of Sue, The | Clement | 1 | | 6 | 9 | C |
| They Put On a Play | Hosey | 1 | | 4 | 5 | C |
| Third Act, The | Angerman | 1 | | 6 | 3 | C |
| Two Cowards, The | Labiche | 1 | | 3 | 2 | C |
| Washington's First Defeat | Nirdlinger | 1 | | 1 | 2 | C |
| What Grandmothers Know | Brumm | 1 | | 1 | 4 | C |
| Who Gets the Car Tonight? | Sergel | 1 | | 3 | 2 | C |
| Who Wins the Bet? | Francis | 1 | | 2 | 1 | C |
| Woman's Might | Storm | 1 | | 3 | 5 | S |
| You and I and Joan | Kimball | 1 | 3 | 18 parts | | S |

## CLASSIFIED SHORT PLAYS

(Royalty and Non-royalty)*

### FOR BOYS

| | | | | | |
|---|---|---|---|---|---|
| Afraid of the Dark | Callahan | 1 | | 7 | S |
| Alas Poor Yorick | Hurd | 1 | | 8 | C |
| Attu! | O'Dea | 1 | | 12 | S |
| Bound East for Cardiff | O'Neill | 1 | | 11 | S |
| Crime Cure, The | Bruce | 1 | | 9 | C |

* These plays vary in fee from non-royalty to $25.

| Title | Author | Sets I | E | Characters M | W | Type |
|---|---|---|---|---|---|---|
| Dawn Will Come | Weinstock | cyc | | 3 | | S |
| Father Suliac's Cabbages | Johnson | | 1 | 3 | | C |
| First Cousins | Kaszner | 1 | | 6 | | S |
| Gamblers | Gogol | 1 | | 8 | | C |
| Game of Chess, The | Goodman | 1 | | 4 | | S |
| Gassed | Springer | 1 | | 5 | | C |
| Glittering Gate, The | Dunsany | | 1 | 2 | | S |
| In the Zone | O'Neill | 1 | | 9 | | M |
| Just Two Men | Pillot | | 1 | 2 | | S |
| Lost Silk Hat, The | Dunsany | | 1 | 5 | | C |
| Message from Khufu | Cottman and Shaw | 1 | | 4 | | S |
| Moonset | Clark | | 1 | 6 | | S |
| Moonshine | Hopkins | 1 | | 2 | | S |
| Name Is Johnston, The | Bowler | 1 | | 5 | | C |
| Night at an Inn, A | Dunsany | 1 | | 8 | | S |
| Night at Valley Forge, A | Andrews | 1 | | 4 | | S |
| Nor Long Remember | Hoffman | 1 | 1 | 7 | | S |
| Open Secret | Adler, Bellak, and Ridenour | 1 | | 7 | | S |
| Other Apostles, The | Callahan | 1 | | 7 | | S |
| Owl and Two Young Men, The | Conkle | | 1 | 2 | | C |
| Refund | Wilde | 1 | | 7 | | C |
| Rising of the Moon, The | Lady Gregory | | 1 | 4 | | S |
| Scruples | Barrett | 1 | | 4 | | C |
| Sky-fodder | Reynolds | | 1 | 3 | | S |
| Still Alarm | Kaufman | 1 | | 5 | | C |
| Submarine, The | Lowther | 1 | | 3 | | S |
| Submerged | Cottman and Shaw | 1 | | 6 | | S |
| Thirteenth Domino, The | Latham | 1 | | 6 | | C |
| When Men Reduce as Women Do | Kicks | 1 | | 5 | | C |
| Zone Police, The | Davis | 1 | | 4 | | S |

*FOR GIRLS*

| Title | Author | Sets I | E | Characters M | W | Type |
|---|---|---|---|---|---|---|
| All on a Summer's Day | Ryerson and Clements | | 1 | | 4 | F |
| Bad Penny, The | Field | 1 | | | 4 | S |
| Bridegroom Waits, The | Hayes | 1 | | | 8 | C |
| Buried Treasure | Watkins | 1 | | | 7 | C |
| Dress to Dance In, A | Price | 1 | | | 4 | S |

| TITLE | AUTHOR | SETS | | CHARACTERS | | TYPE |
|---|---|---|---|---|---|---|
| | | I | E | M | W | |
| Fine Feathers | Ryerson and Clements | 1 | | | 8 | C |
| Gay Ninety | Ryerson and Clements | 1 | | | 8 | C |
| If the Shoe Pinches | Hughes | 1 | | | 4 | C |
| If Women Worked as Men Do | Goodfellow | 1 | | | 4 | C |
| Joint Owners in Spain | Brown | 1 | | | 4 | C |
| Just Women | Clements | 1 | | | 7 | C |
| Kleptomaniac, The | Cameron | 1 | | | 7 | C |
| Ladies Alone | Ryerson and Clements | 1 | | | 3 | C |
| Lady Fingers | Hughes | 1 | | | 4 | C |
| Love Is Like That | Ryerson and Clements | 1 | | | 3 | C |
| Maid Goes Forth to War, A | McCune | | 1 | | 4 | S |
| Mrs. Harper's Bazaar | Hughes | 1 | | | 8 | C |
| My Lady Dreams | Pillot | 1 | | | 6 | F |
| Necklace Is Mine, The | Peterson | 1 | | | 5 | C |
| Overtones | Gerstenberg | 1 | | | 4 | F |
| Permanent | Reach | 1 | | | 8 | C |
| Purple Doorknob | Eaton | 1 | | | 3 | M |
| Rehearsal | Morley | 1 | | | 6 | C |
| Rocking Chairs | Kreymborg | | 1 | | 4 | C |
| Romance and Rummage | Eaton | 1 | | | 11 | C |
| Romance, Inc. | Hughes | 1 | | | 5 | C |
| Sacrifice in Brocade | Price | 1 | | | 5 | S |
| Sanctuary | Rees | 1 | | | 7 | S |
| Saved | Rogers | 1 | | | 6 | C |
| Silhouette and the Stars, The | Price | 1 | | | 8 | S |
| Slow Curtain | Box | 1 | | | 6 | S |
| Star-struck | Ryerson and Clements | 1 | | | 9 | C |
| Theories and Thumbs | Field | 1 | | | 6 | S |
| They're None of Them Perfect | Kerr | 1 | | | 6 | C |
| Three Cents a Day | Bosworth | 1 | | | 6 | C |
| Too Many Marys | Campion | 1 | | | 6 | C |
| Wallflowers | Reach | 1 | | | 5 | C |
| When Shakespeare's Ladies Meet | George | 1 | | | 6 | P |
| Will O' the Wisp | Halman | 1 | | | 4 | S |
| Xingu | Wharton and Seller | 1 | | | 8 | C |

| Title | Author | Sets I E | Characters M W | Type |
|---|---|---|---|---|

## CHRISTMAS

| Title | Author | I | E | M | W | Type |
|---|---|---|---|---|---|---|
| Among Those Presents | Fernway | 1 | | 7 | | C |
| And a Happy New Year | Manning | 1 | | | 7 | C |
| By-line for St. Luke | Lorensen | 1 | | 3 | 4 | S |
| Children of the Inn | Tull | | 1 | 8 | 4 | S |
| Christmas at the Old Folks' Home | Palmer | 1 | | 10 | | C |
| Christmas Awakening, A | Cutler | 1 | | 4 | 3 | C |
| Christmas, Inc. | Kerr | 1 | | | 7 | S |
| Christmas That Bounced, The | Johnson | 1 | | 2 | 5 | C |
| Dust of the Road, The | Goodman | 1 | | 3 | 1 | S |
| Fiat Lux | Vilas | 1 | | 3 | 1 | S |
| Light of the World | Smith | 1 | | 21 | 22 | S |
| Long Christmas Dinner, The | Wilder | 1 | | 5 | 7 | S |
| Mimi Lights the Candle | Coulter | 1 | | 1 | 8 | C |
| Nativity, The | Sanchez and Robinson | 1 | | 19 | 1 | S |
| One Night in Bethlehem | Brown and Temmers | 1 | 1 | 17 | 5 | S |
| Other Wise Man, The | Van Dyke | cyc | | 11 | 14 | S |
| Sounding Brass | Nichols | 1 | | 18 parts 2 children | | C |
| Star Eternal | Price | 1 | | 2 | 2 | S |
| Star Song | Ryerson | 1 | | 4 | 5 | S |
| Tree, The | McMartin | 1 | | 4 | 4 | S |
| Why the Chimes Rang | McFadden | cyc | | 3 | 1 and extras | |

## EASTER

| Title | Author | I | E | M | W | Type |
|---|---|---|---|---|---|---|
| Boy Who Discovered Easter, The | McFadden | 1 | | 2 | 2 | S |
| Cathedral, The | Lowther | 1 | | 2 | | S |
| El Cristo | Larkin | 1 | | 4 | 2 | S |
| Everyman | Anonymous | | 1 | 11 | 6 | S |
| Magda | Rockwell | 1 | | 4 | 2 | S |
| Mansions | Hildegarde | 1 | | 1 | 2 | S |
| Mary Magdalene | Maeterlinck | | 1 | 6 and mob | | S |
| Resurrection, The | Gilder | | 1 | 9 | 5 | S |
| Terrible Meek, The | Kennedy | | 1 | 2 | 1 | S |
| Two Thieves, The | Kennedy | | 1 | 2 and choir | | S |

# Appendix C

## CLASSIFIED BIBLIOGRAPHY FOR SUPPLEMENTARY READING AND CLASSROOM LIBRARIES

An asterisk (*) following the title of a book indicates that it is out of print; however, it may be available in your library.

### PLAY COLLECTIONS—LONG PLAYS

Barrie, James M., *Representative Plays*, Charles Scribner's Sons, New York, 1926.

Cerf, Bennett, and V. H. Cartmell, *Sixteen Famous American Plays*, Modern Library, Inc., New York, 1942.

————, *Sixteen Famous British Plays*, Random House, Inc., New York, 1942.

Chapman, John, *Theatre '53* (to current date—a series), Random House, Inc., New York.

Coffman, G. R., *Book of Modern Plays*, Scott, Foresman and Company, Chicago, 1925.

De Mille, A. B., *Three English Comedies: She Stoops to Conquer, The Rivals, A School for Scandal*, Allyn and Bacon, Inc., Englewood Cliffs, N.J., 1924.

Dickinson, Thomas H., and J. R. Crawford, *Contemporary Plays,** Houghton Mifflin Company, Boston, 1925.

Eastman, Fred, *Modern Religious Dramas,** Henry Holt and Company, Inc., New York, 1928.

————, *Plays of American Life*, Samuel French, Inc., New York, 1945.

Fitts, D., *Greek Plays in Modern Translation*, The Dial Press, Inc., New York, 1947.

Gassner, John, *Library of Best American Plays*, 1916 (to current date—a series), Crown Publishers, Inc., New York.

————, *Treasury of the Theatre*, Simon and Schuster, Inc., New York, 1951.

————, *Twenty Best European Plays on the American Stage*, Crown Publishers, Inc., New York, 1957.

————, *Twenty Best Plays of the Modern American Theatre*, Crown Publishers, Inc., New York, 1939.

Gilbert, W. S., and Arthur Sullivan, *Complete Plays*, Modern Library, Inc., New York, 1936.

Hamilton, Edith, *Three Greek Plays*, W. W. Norton & Company, Inc., New York, 1937.

Hubbell, Jay B., and John O. Beaty, *Introduction to Drama*, The Macmillan Company, New York, 1930.

Kronenberger, Louis, *Best Plays*, Dodd, Mead & Company, Inc., New York, published annually.

————, *Cavalcade of Comedy*,* Simon and Schuster, Inc., New York, 1953.

Law, Frederick H., *Modern Plays*,* Appleton-Century-Crofts, Inc., New York, 1924.

Le Gallienne, Eva, *Civic Repertory Plays*,* W. W. Norton & Company, Inc., New York, 1928.

Leonard, S. A., *Atlantic Book of Modern Plays*,* Little, Brown & Company, Boston, 1921.

Leverton, G. H., *Plays for the College Theatre*,* Samuel French, Inc., New York, 1932.

Lind, L. R., *Ten Greek Plays in Contemporary Translation*, Houghton Mifflin Company, Boston, 1958.

MacMillan, Dougald, and Howard M. Jones, *Plays of the Restoration and 18th Century*, Henry Holt and Company, Inc., New York, 1938.

Manly, John M., *Specimens of Pre-Shakespearean Drama*,* Ginn & Company, Boston, 1897.

Matthews, Brander, *Chief British Dramatists*,* Houghton Mifflin Company, Boston, 1924.

————, *Chief European Dramatists*, Houghton Mifflin Company, Boston, 1916.

Milne, A. A., *Four Plays*,* Penguin Books, Inc., Baltimore, 1939.

Moses, M. J., *Representative American Dramas*,* Little, Brown & Company, Boston, 1925.

————, *Representative British Dramas*,* Little, Brown & Company, Boston, 1918.

————, *Representative Continental Dramas*,* Little, Brown & Company, Boston, 1924.

————, *Representative Plays by American Dramatists*,* E. P. Dutton & Co., Inc., New York, 1926.

Neilson, William A., *Chief Elizabethan Dramatists*, Houghton Mifflin Company, Boston, 1911.

Quinn, Arthur H., *Representative American Plays*, Appleton-Century-Crofts, Inc., New York, 1953.

Rhys, Ernest, *Everyman with Other Interludes*,* E. P. Dutton & Co., Inc., New York, 1906.

Stauffer, Ruth, *Progress of the Drama Through the Centuries*,* The Macmillan Company, New York, 1930.

Tatlock, John S. P., and Robert G. Martin, *Representative English Plays*, Appleton-Century-Crofts, Inc., New York, 1938.

*Theatre Guild Anthology*,* Random House, Inc., New York, 1936.

Thomas, Russell, *Plays and the Theatre*,* Little, Brown & Company, Boston, 1937.

Tuckers, S. M., and A. S. Downer, *Twenty-five Modern Plays*, Harper & Brothers, New York, 1948.

Watson, E. Bradlee, and Benfield Pressey, *Contemporary Drama, Thirty-seven Plays*, Charles Scribner's Sons, New York, 1941.

Wilder, Thornton, *Three Plays*, Harper & Brothers, New York, 1957.

## PLAY COLLECTIONS—SHORT PLAYS

Baker, George P., *Harvard Plays, the 47 Workshop,** Vol. I, Brentano's, Inc., New York, 1918.

Barnum, M. D., *School Plays for All Occasions,** Grosset & Dunlap, Inc., New York, 1934.

Barrie, James M., *Echoes of the War,** Charles Scribner's Sons, New York, 1919.

————, *Half-hours,** Charles Scribner's Sons, New York, 1917.

Beck, Warren, *Six Little Theatre Plays,** Walter H. Baker Company, Boston, 1931.

Berman, Sadye, *Plays for the Schoolroom*, Samuel French, Inc., New York, 1937.

Brighouse, Harold, *Open Air Plays*, Samuel French, Inc., New York, 1926.

Brown, Albert H., *Six New Plays for Boys*, Samuel French, Inc., New York, 1937.

Busfield, Roger M., Jr., *The Playwright's Art—Stage, Radio-Television, Motion Pictures*, Harper & Brothers, New York, 1958.

Butler, Mildred A., *Literature Dramatized,** Harcourt, Brace and Company, Inc., New York, 1926.

Campion, Rose, *Ten Easy Acts for Women*, The Dramatic Publishing Co., Chicago, 1930.

Carroll, Paul Vincent, *Plays for My Children,** Julian Messner, Inc., Publishers, New York, 1939.

Carter, Jean, and Jesse Ogden, *The Play Book,** Harcourt, Brace and Company, Inc., New York, 1937.

Cerf, Bennett, *Thirty Famous One-act Plays*, Modern Library, Inc., New York, 1943.

————, *Twenty-four Favorite One-act Plays*, Barnes & Noble, Inc., New York, 1958.

Church, Virginia, *Curtain! A Book of Modern Plays,** Harper & Brothers, New York, 1932.

Clark, Barrett H., *Representative One-act Plays by British and Irish Authors,** Little, Brown & Company, Boston, 1921.

Clark, Barrett H., and Kenyon Nicholson, *The American Scene,** Appleton-Century-Crofts, Inc., New York, 1930.

Cohen, H. L., *Junior Play Book,** Harcourt, Brace and Company, Inc., New York, 1923.

————, *One-act Plays*, Harcourt, Brace and Company, Inc., New York, 1934.

Conkle, E. P., *Crick Bottom Plays*, Samuel French, Inc., New York, 1928.

Cook, George C., and Frank Shay, *Provincetown Plays,** Appleton-Century-Crofts, Inc., New York, 1921.

Dean, Alexander, *Seven to Seventeen,** Samuel French, Inc., New York, 1931.

Dunsany, Lord, *Five Plays,** Little, Brown & Company, Inc., Boston, 1914.
———, *Plays of Gods and Men,** G. P. Putnam's Sons, New York, 1923.
———, *Plays of Near and Far,** G. P. Putnam's Sons, New York, 1923.
Eastman, Fred, *Plays of American Life,** Samuel French, Inc., New York, 1937.
Eaton, Walter P., *Twelve One-act Plays,** Longmans, Green & Co., Inc., New York, 1926.
Eliot, S. A., *Little Theatre Classics,** Little, Brown & Company, Boston, 1918.
Field, Rachel Lyman, *Cross-stitch Heart,** Charles Scribner's Sons, New York, 1927.
———, *Six Plays,** Victor Gollancz, Ltd., London, 1930.
Findlay, Bruce and Esther, *Tell-a-Vision Plays,** Row, Peterson & Company, Evanston, Ill., 1938.
Finney, Stella B., *Plays Old and New,** Allyn and Bacon, Inc., Englewood Cliffs, N.J., 1928.
Firkins, Oscar, *Two Passengers for Chelsea,** Walter H. Baker Company, Boston, 1928.
Fisher, Aileen, *The Big Book of Christmas*, Row, Peterson & Company, Evanston, Ill., 1951.
Gerstenberg, Alice, *Comedies All,** Longmans, Green & Co., Inc., New York, 1930.
Gheòn, H., and H. Brochet, *St. Anne and the Gouty Rector and Other Plays*, translated by Marcus S. Goldman and Olive R. Goldman, Longmans, Green & Co., Inc., New York, 1950.
Green, Paul, *In the Valley and Other Carolina Plays*, Samuel French, Inc., New York, 1928.
Gregory, Lady A., *Seven Short Plays,** G. P. Putnam's Sons, New York, 1909.
Howells, William D., *Mousetrap and Other Farces,** Harper & Brothers, New York, 1894.
Jagendorf, M. A., *One-act Plays for Young Folks,** Samuel French, Inc., New York, 1934.
Johnson, Theodore, *Diminutive Comedies,** Walter H. Baker Company, Boston, 1936.
———, *Easy Plays for 'Teen Age Girls*, Walter H. Baker Company, Boston, 1938.
Kaser, Arthur L., *Ten Easy Acts for Men*, The Dramatic Publishing Company, Chicago, 1930.
Katzin, Winifred, *Short Plays from Twelve Countries,** George G. Harrap & Co., Ltd., London, 1936.
Kelly, George, *The Flattering Word and Other Plays,** Little, Brown & Company, Boston, 1925.
Knickerbocker, E. V., *Plays for Classroom Interpretation,** Henry Holt and Company, Inc., New York, 1921.
———, *Short Plays*, Henry Holt and Company, Inc., New York, 1949.
Koch, F. H., *Carolina Folk Plays,** Henry Holt and Company, Inc., New York, 1922.

Kozlenko, William, *Contemporary One-act Plays,** Charles Scribner's Sons, New York, 1938.

―――, *100 Non-royalty One-act Plays*, Grosset & Dunlap, Inc., New York, 1947.

Kreymborg, Alfred, *How Do You Do, Sir and Other Plays*, Samuel French, Inc., New York, 1940.

―――, *Puppet Plays,** Samuel French, Inc., New York, 1926.

Lewis, B., *Contemporary One-act Plays,** Charles Scribner's Sons, New York, 1922.

Locke, Alain, *Twenty Plays of the Contemporary Negro Theatre,** Samuel French, Inc., New York, 1931.

Mayorga, M. G., *Best Short Plays*, 20th Annual Edition, The Beacon Press, Boston, 1957 (available in cloth and paperback).

―――, *Plays of Democracy,** Dodd, Mead & Company, Inc., New York, 1944.

―――, *Representative One-act Plays by American Authors,** Little, Brown & Company, Boston, 1919.

―――, *Twenty Short Plays on a Royalty Holiday*, Samuel French, Inc., New York, 1937.

McCaslin, Nellie, *Legends in Action*, Row, Peterson & Company, Evanston, Ill., 1945.

―――, *More Legends in Action*, Row, Peterson & Company, Evanston, Ill., 1950.

Morley, Christopher, *One-act Plays,** Doubleday & Company, Inc., New York, 1924.

Moses, M. J., *One-act Plays for Stage and Study*, Vol. X, Samuel French, Inc., New York.

―――, *Representative One-act Plays,** Little, Brown & Company, Boston, 1922.

Reines, Bernard J., *For Country and Mankind*, Longmans, Green & Co., Inc., New York, 1944.

Ryerson, F., and C. C. Clements, *Angels Don't Marry and Other One-act Plays*, Samuel French, Inc., New York, 1938.

―――, *Ladies Alone*, Samuel French, Inc., New York, 1937.

Sams, Oscar E., Jr., *Tested One-act Plays** (non-royalty), Noble & Noble, Publishers, Inc., New York, 1939.

Saunders, Louise, *Magic Lanterns,** Charles Scribner's Sons, New York, 1923.

Smith, A. M., *Short Plays by Representative Authors,** The Macmillan Company, New York, 1926.

Tuckers, S. M., *Twelve One-act Plays for Study and Production,** Ginn & Company, Boston, 1929.

Vernon, V. and F., *Modern One-act Plays from the French*, Samuel French, Inc., New York.

Walker, Stuart, *Portmanteau Plays,** Appleton-Century-Crofts, Inc., New York, 1917.

Webb, Marie, *One-act Plays*, The Macmillan Company, New York, 1940.

Wilde, Percival, *Three Minute Plays*, Walter H. Baker Company, Boston, 1927.

# GENERAL REFERENCES ON THE THEATER

Adams, W. B., *The Irresistible Theatre*, The World Publishing Company, Cleveland, 1957.

Baker, Blanch, *Theatre and Allied Arts*, The H. W. Wilson Company, New York, 1952.

Bentley, Eric, *In Search of Theatre*, Alfred A. Knopf, Inc., New York, 1935.

———, *The Playwright as Thinker*, Reynal & Hitchcock, Inc., New York. Meridian Books, Inc., New York, 1958 (paperback).

Brooks, Cleanth, and Robert B. Heilman, *Understanding Drama*, Henry Holt and Company, Inc., New York, 1948.

Brown, John Mason, *Still Seeing Things*, McGraw-Hill Book Company, Inc., New York, 1950.

Burton, Richard, *How to See a Play*,* The Macmillan Company, New York, 1929.

Cheney, Sheldon, *The Theatre*, Longmans, Green & Co., Inc., New York, 1952.

Clark, Barrett, *World Drama*, Dover Publications, New York, 1955.

Clurman, Harold, *Lies Like Truth*, The Macmillan Company, New York, 1958.

Freedley, George, and John A. Reeves, *A History of the Theatre*, Crown Publishers, Inc., New York, 1955.

Gassner, John, *Form and Idea in Modern Theatre*, Henry Holt and Company, Inc., New York, 1956.

———, *Masters of the Drama*, Dover Publications, New York, 1953.

———, *Theatre in Our Times*, Crown Publishers, Inc., New York, 1954.

Gorelik, Mordecai, *New Theatres for Old*, Samuel French, Inc., New York, 1952.

Houghton, Norris, *Moscow Rehearsals*, Harcourt, Brace and Company, Inc., New York, 1936.

Hughes, Glenn, *Story of the Theatre*, Samuel French, Inc., New York, 1928.

Jones, Robert Edmond, *The Dramatic Imagination*, Theatre Arts Books, New York, 1941.

MacGowan, Kenneth, and W. Melnitz, *The Living Stage: A History of the World Theatre*, Prentice-Hall, Inc., Englewood Cliffs, N.J., 1955.

Nathan, George Jean, *The World's Great Plays*, The World Publishing Company, Cleveland, 1957.

Nicoll, Allardyce, *The Development of the Theatre*, Harcourt, Brace and Company, Inc., New York, 1949.

———, *World Drama*, Harcourt, Brace and Company, Inc., New York, 1950.

Simonson, Lee, *The Stage Is Set*,* Harcourt, Brace and Company, Inc., New York, 1950.

Sobel, Bernard, *New Theatre Handbook and Digest of Plays*, Crown Publishers, Inc., New York, 1948.

Wright, Edward A., *A Primer for Playgoers*, Prentice-Hall, Inc., Englewood Cliffs, N.J., 1958.

Young, Stark, *Immortal Shadows*, Charles Scribner's Sons, New York, 1958. Hill and Wang, Inc., New York, 1958 (paperback).

———, *The Theatre*, Hill and Wang, Inc., New York, 1958 (paperback).

Allen, J. T., *Stage Antiquities,** Longmans, Green & Co., Inc., New York, 1927.

Boas, Frederich, *Queen Elizabeth in Drama*, The Macmillan Company, New York, 1950.

Bowers, Faubion, *Japanese Theatre*, Hermitage House, Inc., New York, 1952.

Chambers, E. K., *The Medieval Stage*, Oxford University Press, New York, 1903.

Clark, Barrett, and George Freedley, *A History of Modern Drama*, Appleton-Century-Crofts, Inc., New York, 1947.

Craig, Hardin, *English Religious Drama of the Middle Ages*, Oxford University Press, New York, 1955.

Davis, William S., *Life in Elizabethan Days*, Harper & Brothers, New York, 1930.

Disher, Maurice W., *Clowns and Pantomimes,** Houghton Mifflin Company, Boston, 1925.

Ernst, Earle, *The Kabuki Theatre*, Oxford University Press, New York, 1956.

Kincaid, Zoe, *Kabuki, the Popular Stage of Japan,** The Macmillan Company, New York, 1925.

Murray, Gilbert, *Euripides and His Age*, Oxford University Press, New York, 1946.

Nathan, George Jean, *Theatre in the Fifties*, Alfred A. Knopf, Inc., New York, 1953.

Nicoll, Allardyce, *A History of Restoration Drama, 1660–1700,** The Macmillan Company, New York, 1923.

———, *British Drama*, Barnes & Noble, Inc., New York, 1957.

———, *Stuart Masques and the Renaissance Stage,** Harcourt, Brace and Company, Inc., New York, 1938.

Selden, Samuel, *International Folk Plays*, The University of North Carolina Press, Chapel Hill, N.C., 1949.

Shaw, George Bernard, *Quintessence of Ibsenism*, Hill and Wang, Inc., New York, 1957 (paperback).

Stevens, Thomas W., *The Theatre from Athens to Broadway,** Appleton-Century-Crofts, Inc., New York, 1932.

Summers, Montague, *Restoration Drama,** The Macmillan Company, New York, 1934.

Waley, Arthur, *The No Plays of Japan*, Grove Press, New York, 1957.

Wells, Henry W., and Roger S. Loomis, *Representative Medieval and Tudor Plays,** Sheed and Ward, Inc., New York, 1942.

Williams, Raymond, *Drama from Ibsen to Eliot*, Oxford University Press, New York, 1953.

Yanjnik, R. K., *The Indian Theatre,** George Allen & Unwin, Ltd., London, 1933.

Zoete, Beryl de, and Walter Spies, *Dance and Drama in Bali,** Harper & Brothers, New York, 1939.

Zucker, Adolph, *The Chinese Theatre,** Little, Brown & Company, Boston, 1925.

# SHAKESPEARE

Adams, Joseph Q., *The Life of William Shakespeare*, Houghton Mifflin Company, Boston, 1923.

Barker, F. G., *Forty-minute Plays from Shakespeare*, The Macmillan Company, New York, 1924.

Black, Anges, and J. Y. Freeman, *Introduction to Shakespeare*,* Ginn & Company, Boston, 1930.

Bradley, A. C., *Shakespearean Tragedy*, Meridian Books, Inc., New York, 1955 (paperback).

Chute, Marchette, *Shakespeare of London*, E. P. Dutton & Co., Inc., New York, 1949.

Clarke, M. C., *Girlhood of Shakespeare's Heroines*,* E. P. Dutton & Co., Inc., New York, 1907.

De Banke, C., *Shakespearean Stage Productions, Then and Now*, McGraw-Hill Book Company, Inc., New York, 1953.

de Chambrun, C., *Shakespeare: A Portrait Restored*, Appleton-Century-Crofts, Inc., New York, 1957.

Gray, H. D., *Short Scenes from Shakespeare and How to Act Them*,* The Macmillan Company, New York, 1929.

Harrison, G. B., *Elizabethan Plays and Players*, University of Michigan Press, Ann Arbor, Mich., 1956 (paperback).

———, *Introducing Shakespeare*, Penguin Books, Inc., Baltimore, 1939 (paperback).

Lamb, Charles and Mary, *Tales from Shakespeare*, many editions.

Lamborn, E. A. G., and G. B. Harrison, *Shakespeare: The Man and His Stage*, Oxford University Press, New York, 1924.

Masefield, John, *William Shakespeare*, The Macmillan Company, New York, 1954.

Neilson, W. A., and C. J. Hill, *The Complete Plays and Poems of William Shakespeare*, Houghton Mifflin Company, Boston, 1942.

Onions, C. T., *A Shakespeare Glossary*, Oxford University Press, New York, 1919.

Parrott, T. M., *William Shakespeare: A Handbook*, Charles Scribner's Sons, New York, 1955.

Quiller-Couch, A., *Shakespeare's Workmanship*, Cambridge University Press, New York, 1931.

Ryland, George, *The Ages of Man*, Wm. Heinemann, Ltd., London, 1950.

Scott, Walter, *Kenilworth*, many editions.

Shakespeare, William, *Complete Works*, many editions.

Sprague, A. C., *Shakespearian Players and Performances*, Harvard University Press, Cambridge, Mass., 1953.

Thorndike, A., *Shakespeare's Theatre*, The Macmillan Company, New York, 1954.

Webster, Margaret, *Shakespeare Without Tears*, The World Publishing Company, Cleveland, 1955. Premier Books, New York, 1957 (paperback).

## THE AMERICAN STAGE

Atkinson, Brooks, *Broadway Scrap Book,** Theatre Arts Books, New York, 1947.

Blum, Daniel, ed., *A Pictorial History of the American Theatre 1900–1956*, Greenberg: Publisher, Inc., New York, 1956.

Chorpening, Charlotte, *Twenty-one Years with Children's Theatre*, Children's Theatre Press, Anchorage, Ky., 1954.

Clurman, Harold, *The Fervent Years*, Hill and Wang, Inc., New York, 1957 (paperback).

Cosgrave, Luke, *Theatre Tonight*, House-Warren, Hollywood, Calif., 1955.

Downer, Alan S., *Fifty Years of American Drama, 1900–1950*, Henry Regnery Company, Chicago, 1951.

Harmon, Charlotte, *Broadway in a Barn,** Thomas Y. Crowell Company, New York, 1957.

Hughes, Glenn, *A History of the American Theatre, 1700–1950*, Samuel French, Inc., New York, 1951.

————, *The Penthouse Theatre*, Samuel French, Inc., New York, 1942.

Krutch, Joseph, *American Drama Since 1918*, George Braziller, Inc., New York, 1957.

Langner, Lawrence, *The Magic Curtain*, E. P. Dutton & Co., Inc., New York, 1951.

Maney, Richard, *Fanfare: The Confessions of a Press Agent*, Harper & Brothers, New York, 1957.

Moses, M. J., and J. M. Brown, eds., *The American Theatre: as Seen by Its Critics, 1752–1934,** W. W. Norton & Company, Inc., New York, 1934.

Young, John W., *The Community Theatre*, Harper & Brothers, New York, 1957.

Zolotow, M., *No People Like Show People,** Random House, Inc., New York, 1951.

## ACTING

Alberti, Eva, *A Handbook of Acting*, Samuel French, Inc., New York, 1932.

Albright, H. D., and others, *Principles of Theatre Art*, Houghton Mifflin Company, Boston, 1955.

Boleslavsky, R., *Acting: The First Six Lessons*, Theatre Arts Books, New York, 1937.

Chekhov, Michael, *To the Actor*, Harper & Brothers, New York, 1953.

Cobby, Maisie, *Calling All Playmakers!* Sir Isaac Pitman & Sons, Ltd., London, 1956.

Cole, Toby, and Helen Krich Chinoy, *Actors on Acting*, Crown Publishers, Inc., New York, 1954.

Dolman, J., *The Art of Acting*, Harper & Brothers, New York, 1949.

Franklin, Miriam, *Rehearsal: Principles and Practice of Acting for the Stage*, Prentice-Hall, Inc., Englewood Cliffs, N.J., 1950.

McGaw, C., *Acting Is Believing*, Rinehart & Company, Inc., New York, 1955.

Redgrave, Michael, *The Actor's Ways and Means*, Theatre Arts Books, New York, 1954.

Selden, Samuel, *First Steps in Acting*, Appleton-Century-Crofts, Inc., New York, 1947.

————, *The Stage in Action*, Appleton-Century-Crofts, Inc., New York, 1946.

Seligman, M., and S. Fogle, *Solo Readings for Radio and Classwork*, Dramatists Play Service, Inc., New York, 1941.

————, *More Solo Readings for Radio and Classwork*, Dramatists Play Service, Inc., New York, 1944.

————, *Still More Solo Readings for Radio and Classwork*, Dramatists Play Service, Inc., New York, 1947.

Seyler, Athene, and Stephen Haggard, *The Craft of Comedy*, Theatre Arts Books, New York, 1946.

Stanislavsky, C., *An Actor Prepares*, Theatre Arts Books, New York, 1936.

————, *Building a Character*, Theatre Arts Books, New York, 1949.

Strickland, F. C., *The Technique of Acting*, McGraw-Hill Book Company, Inc., New York, 1956.

## PLAY PRODUCTION

Bailey, H., *ABC's of Play Production*, David McKay Company, Inc., New York, 1955.

Boyle, W. P., *Central and Flexible Staging*, University of California Press, Berkeley, Calif., 1956.

Buerki, F. A., *Stagecraft for Non-professionals*, University of Wisconsin Press, Madison, Wis.

Burris-Meyer, H., and E. G. Cole, *Scenery for the Theatre*, Little, Brown & Company, Boston, 1938.

————, *Theatres and Auditoriums*, Reinhold Publishing Corporation, New York, 1949.

Cornberg, Sol, and Emanuel L. Gebauer, *A Stage Crew Handbook*, Harper & Brothers, New York, 1957.

Dietrich, J. E., *Play Direction*, Prentice-Hall, Inc., Englewood Cliffs, N.J., 1953.

Friederich, Willard J., and John H. Fraser, *Scenery Design for the Amateur Stage*, The Macmillan Company, New York, 1950.

Gassner, John, *Producing the Play*, (Dryden) Henry Holt and Company, Inc., New York, 1953.

Gross, Edwin and Nathalie, *Teen-Theatre*, McGraw-Hill Book Company, Inc., New York, 1953.

Gruver, Bert, *The Stage Manager's Handbook*, Harper & Brothers, New York, 1953.

Hake, Herbert V., *Here's How: A Guide to Economy in Stagecraft*, Row, Peterson & Company, Evanston, Ill., 1947.

Heffner, H. C., S. Selden, and H. D. Sellman, *Modern Theatre Practice: A Handbook for Non-professionals*, Appleton-Century-Crofts, Inc., New York, 1947.

Hewitt, Barnard, J. F. Foster, and M. S. Wolle, *Play Production: Theory and Practice*, J. B. Lippincott Company, Philadelphia, 1952.

Selden, Samuel, and Hutton D. Sellman, *Stage Scenery and Lighting,* Appleton-Century-Crofts, Inc., New York, 1936.
Smith, Milton, *Play Production,* Appleton-Century-Crofts, Inc., New York, 1948.
Southern, Richard, *Changeable Scenery,* Transatlantic Arts, Inc., Hollywood-by-the-Sea, Florida, 1952.
———, *Proscenium and Sight Lines,** Faber and Faber, Ltd., London, 1939.
Ward, Winifred, *Playmaking with Children,* Appleton-Century-Crofts, Inc., New York, 1957.
———, *Theatre for Children,* Children's Theatre Press, Anchorage, Ky., 1950.

## COSTUME AND MAKE-UP

Baird, J. F., *Make-up,* Samuel French, Inc., New York, 1941.
Barton, Lucy, *Historic Costume for the Stage,** Walter H. Baker Company, Boston, 1935.
Brooke, Iris, *History of English Costume,* British Book Centre, Inc., New York, 1952.
Corson, R., *Stage Make-up,* Appleton-Century-Crofts, Inc., New York, 1949.
Davenport, Millia, *Book of Costume,* Crown Publishers, Inc., New York, 1948.
Grimball, Elizabeth, and Rhea Wells, *Costuming a Play,* Appleton-Century-Crofts, Inc., 1925.
Melvill, Harald, *The Magic of Make-up,* The Citadel Press, New York, 1957.
Strenkovsky, S., *The Art of Make-up,* E. P. Dutton & Co., Inc., New York, 1937.
Walkup, F. P., *Dressing the Part,* Appleton-Century-Crofts, Inc., New York, 1950.

## SPEECH

Bender, J. F., *NBC Handbook of Pronunciation,* Thomas Y. Crowell Company, New York, 1951.
Borchers, G. L., *Living Speech,* Harcourt, Brace and Company, Inc., New York, 1949.
Fairbanks, G., *Practical Voice Practice,* Harper & Brothers, New York, 1944.
Jones, Daniel, *An English Pronouncing Dictionary,* E. P. Dutton & Co., Inc., New York, 1925.
Monroe, A., *Principles and Types of Speech,* Scott, Foresman and Company, Chicago, 1955.
Sarett, Lew, and others, *Basic Principles of Speech,* Houghton Mifflin Company, Boston, 1946.
Thonssen, L., and H. Gilkinson, *Basic Training in Speech,* D. C. Heath and Company, Boston, 1953.
Van Riper, C., *Speech Correction: Principles and Methods,* Prentice-Hall, Inc., Englewood Cliffs, N.J., 1954.
Wise, C. M., *Applied Phonetics,* Prentice-Hall, Inc., Englewood Cliffs, N.J., 1955.
Woolbert, C. H., and S. E. Nelson, *Art of Interpretative Speech,* Appleton-Century-Crofts, Inc., New York, 1947.

Bendick, Jeanne, *Making the Movies*,* Whittlesey House (McGraw-Hill Book Company, Inc.), New York, 1945.

Bendick, Jeanne and Robert, *Television Works Like This*, Whittlesey House (McGraw-Hill Book Company, Inc.), New York, 1959.

Bettinger, H., *Television Techniques*, Harper & Brothers, New York, 1955.

Bretz, Rudy, and Edward Stasheff, *Television Scripts for Staging and Study*, Hill and Wang, Inc., 1953.

Broderick, E. B., *Your Place in TV*, David McKay Company, Inc., New York, 1954.

Carlisle, J. S., *Production and Direction of Radio Programs*, Prentice-Hall, Inc., Englewood Cliffs, N.J., 1939.

Crews, A. R., *Radio Production Directing*, Houghton Mifflin Company, Boston, 1944.

Crowther, Bosley, *Lion's Share: The Story of an Entertainment Empire* (a history of the movies), E. P. Dutton & Co., Inc., New York, 1957.

Curran, Charles W., *Screen Writing and Production Techniques*, Hastings House, Publishers, Inc., New York, 1958.

Dale, Edgar, *How to Appreciate Motion Pictures*,* The Macmillan Company, New York, 1933.

Duerr, Edwin, *Radio and Television Acting*, Rinehart & Company, Inc., New York, 1950.

Field, Stanley, *Television and Radio Writing*, Houghton Mifflin Company, Boston, 1958.

Floherty, J. J., *Television Story*, J. B. Lippincott Company, Philadelphia, 1957.

Hodapp, W., *The Television Actor's Manual*, Appleton-Century-Crofts, Inc., New York, 1955.

————, *Television Manual*, Farrar, Straus and Cudahy, Inc., New York, 1953.

Jones, Charles Reed, *Your Career in Motion Pictures, Radio and Television*, Sheridan House, New York, 1949.

Kaufman, W. J., *Best Television Plays*, Harcourt, Brace and Company, Inc., New York, 1957.

Livingston, Don, *The Film and the Director*, The Macmillan Company, 1953.

McMahan, H. W., *Television Production: The Creative Techniques and Language of TV Today*, Hastings House, Publishers, Inc., New York, 1957.

Roberts, E. B., *Television Writing and Selling*, The Writer, Inc., Boston, 1957.

Southwell, J., *Getting a Job in Television*, McGraw-Hill Book Company, Inc., New York, 1947.

Wade, R. S., *Designing for TV*, Farrar, Straus and Cudahy, Inc., New York, 1952.

Weiss, Margaret, *The TV Writers' Guide*, Farrar, Straus and Cudahy, Inc., New York, 1952.

Wylie, Max, *Radio and Television Writing*, Rinehart & Company, Inc., New York, 1950.

# Appendix D

## CONSIDERING A THEATRICAL CAREER

The fascination of acting has existed through the ages and today probably more young people than ever are determined to seek a theatrical career. If you are one of them, take a long hard look before you make your final decision. Heed the warning "Don't" uttered in no uncertain tones by everyone who knows the actual situation in a profession overrun with more people hunting jobs than there are jobs to be found. Remember that the growing number of fine community theaters all over the country can provide the satisfactions and rewards of dramatic participation without the risks and disappointments of seeking a professional career.

However, if you are determined to take the chance, you must seriously consider your qualifications and the possibilities of making a living wage. In spite of the apparent increase in opportunities opened by television and the continuous need for new faces in the films, getting an opening in New York or Hollywood is as difficult as ever and the chances for permanent success as precarious. You should, therefore, get all the actual experience you possibly can in your own community before going to the big centers.

Many professional producers and directors strongly advise a college or university degree with a major in dramatics. A producer or director cannot train you and expects you to meet his requirements of the moment with intelligence and ability, which depend upon experience and training. Of course, the best professional schools, especially those in the vicinity of New York or Hollywood where students can be seen by agents and scouts, should afford opportunities, but none guarantee them. Because getting the breaks in the theater world is largely a matter of whom you know, you should try to meet and work with first-rate theatrical people as soon as possible after you leave school.

Beginning now, during your high school years, take advantage of every opportunity to gain stage experience. If a road company comes and needs extras, apply. If there is a summer theater near you, try to get in as an apprentice. If there are community theaters, church groups giving plays, or radio and television stations doing dramatic shows, take any parts you can get. You can learn to act only by acting and the more contrasting parts you play, the more flexible and adaptable you will become. You may also see some of the seamy side of backstage life and decide that you do not want to be a part of it.

497

Dramatic ability is only one asset needed in a professional career. In fact, very few people possess all of the qualifications upon which success in the theater depends. Remarkable talent combined with personal magnetism is a basic requirement. Your appearance is also important; you should have the faculty of dressing to accentuate your pleasing characteristics and to lessen any defects. Other essentials are an excellent speaking voice, a vivid imagination, sensitivity and responsiveness, a quick memory, and keen intelligence.

Good health, both mental and physical, will enable you to take disappointments in stride and resist excessive physical and emotional strain. This is of prime importance, for there is constant pressure upon an actor to be at his best whether he is acting, rehearsing, or hunting an engagement. The temptations of theatrical life are often exaggerated, but one does encounter unconventional standards and unstable temperaments. Avoiding dubious means of "getting ahead" demands an unusual degree of moral stamina in the world of the theater.

Sufficient funds for an indefinite period must be available or obtainable before you tackle Broadway, Hollywood, or any center away from home. While hunting theatrical jobs, you will probably have to do other work such as typing, clerking, ushering, modeling, and retail selling to support yourself. You should, therefore, prepare yourself to be efficient in a field which is fairly certain to have openings when you need them.

## Going on the Stage

Acting on a real stage before an audience in a professional theater is what is commonly meant by the term "going on the stage," and New York, for better or worse, is the actor's goal. If you have assured yourself that you have the talent and the means to support yourself, go there and find a reasonable place to live. Men can usually get into a Y.M.C.A. or Y.M.H.A., and girls into the Studio Club (a branch of the Y.W.C.A.), the Rehearsal Club, or similar places. Reservations must be made in advance. Before going to New York, you would be wise to write to the American National Theatre and Academy (ANTA), 1545 Broadway, New York 36, and request their fact sheets, "Notes on Theatre Careers" and "Schools of Theatre." Once in the city, you will find it helpful to join ANTA and take advantage of their Theatre Information Service, Placement Service, and Job Counseling Service.

The first step is to enroll in a good school of theater, but before you do so, investigate it as carefully as possible from every angle. Among the many drama schools in New York are the American Academy of Dramatic Arts, The American Theatre Wing, the Neighborhood Playhouse School of the Theatre, the Tamara Daykarhanova School for the Stage, the Herbert Berghof Studio, and Curt Conway's Theatre Studio. You will find these and many other schools listed, with their addresses, in *Theatre Arts* magazine. There are a number of excellent professional schools all over the country, but being in New York where you can see the current productions, watch the best actors in important roles, and also be seen by directors and agents is a distinct advantage.

Though you will continue to attend classes, when you feel you are ready you can begin to visit casting agencies and try to make a definite impression upon a few of the important people connected with them. Their primary interest will be in the experience that you have had. If you are lucky, in a few weeks or months an agency will send you to a casting director or producer who is looking for a person of your type. If your luck holds, you will be given a chance to read for a part. Directors and producers usually want experienced professional actors. However, if you suit a part, read intelligently, use good diction, make a good appearance, and are poised, courteous, and responsive, you may be given a role. Once you have actually appeared professionally, your future chances for auditions and readings will be considerably improved.

The beginner will be given all sorts of advice: to go on the road or work in stock before he tries New York, to play bit parts with recognized managements on and off Broadway rather than big parts with unrecognized ones, to wait until the big chance comes along, to play with nonprofessional groups where he can be seen by talent scouts or producers, or to hire a personal representative. All of these methods have worked for some successful players but not for others. Your best method is to keep your name and face constantly before theatrical agents and producers, pick up every clue to probable openings, and be ready for the chance when it comes. More and more, the summer theaters are becoming excellent proving grounds. You can get full particulars concerning them in *The Summer Theatre Directory* published yearly by the newspaper *Show Business* whose offices are in New York.

If you are given a part in a play, you must join the Actors' Equity Association at once. Actors' Equity is a powerful force in the American theater. Its leaders, including many of the foremost actors of this generation, feel a responsibility to members who are "at liberty," as well as to people who want to see dramatic performances. To serve both actors and the public, in 1943 Actors' Equity founded the Equity Library Theatre (so named because library auditoriums were used). Functioning as a showcase for Equity members, the Equity Library Theatre today produces a regular season of plays and also takes three or four offerings a season to high schools in the New York area. Prospective employers are invited to each production and many actors have obtained engagements as a result.

## Getting into Television

Los Angeles and New York are the centers for television employment, but there may be local stations where you can get experience. Large networks give auditions and many individual shows have casting directors. Advertising agencies which produce package shows have casting directors and so do many independent packagers. Your first step should be to file an excellent photograph and résumé with people or agencies that may be able to help you. The résumé should include your name, address, telephone number, age, height, coloring, professional and amateur experience, specialized training, and other significant information.

Announcements of casting and future productions can be found in such publications as the *Ross Reports*, *Variety*, and *Show Business*. If you are a girl, one advantage of living at a place like the Rehearsal Club is that you may hear of possible opportunities from others. However, it is better to make rounds to the agents, producers, and casting directors on your own.

There are many positions in television, technical and otherwise, which might appeal to you. If you are interested in engineering, producing, directing, or camera work, the School of Radio Technique (SRT) in New York has a well-equipped Studio for Television where you can get both training and practical experience. You can write to this school for detailed information concerning the courses and probable positions available. If you are primarily interested in television acting, the American Theatre Wing holds classes in television studios. These are taught by directors who are actually producing programs, so the training and contacts are valuable.

The field of television is growing rapidly and there are hundreds of men and women applying for positions as performers, technicians, writers, directors, cameramen, engineers, librarians, and announcers. Clever and resourceful young people should be able to find a number of career possibilities within this new industry. If television appeals to you, keep up with the latest developments and opportunities in whatever phase interests you most. Make all the connections you can with local studios where plays are being televised and keep abreast of the field through newspapers and magazines.

### Going on the Air

There are still many excellent radio opportunities, not only in Los Angeles, Chicago, and New York, but all over the country. These opportunities are becoming somewhat easier to obtain as the popularity of television increases. Successful experience on your local station provides good training for a professional radio position as do courses taken in an accredited radio school or college speech department. To perform professionally you must be a member of the American Federation of Television and Radio Artists.

All stations have staff performers to carry on the routine work and take part in sustaining programs; such positions are obtained through auditions. Since most directors of sponsored programs hire their own talent, it pays to keep in touch with the advertising agencies which represent big sponsors. In large cities, agents will arrange auditions with studios and business firms, but energetic and original people with good voices can also make their own opportunities. You may get an audition without too much trouble. Then you must wait for a call. If one comes and you make good, you will get a precarious hold on the first step in a radio career. However, as in all theatrical work, you can expect to be out of work a good deal of the time. Therefore, a regular income from some other source is essential for the beginner.

The chief requisites for a radio career are a pleasing, flexible, natural voice and excellent diction which is not artificial or affected. If you have a wide pitch range and a facility with authentic dialects, you may have a chance to double on shows.

## Getting into the Films

Getting into the movies is as difficult as going on the stage. The advice from everyone connected with the major studios is, "Stay away from Hollywood!" Practically all actors who are given a chance in the films have been discovered by scouts and executives on Broadway or in amateur and professional theaters elsewhere. However, thousands of young people do flock to Hollywood to attend the many dramatic schools there and join the players' groups, paying out large sums of money in the hope of making contacts. A big problem in Hollywood is that it is impossible to get through studio gates without a pass. If you go there without anyone to help you, you may have to struggle a long time to get even an interview.

If you should be fortunate enough to be selected by a scout, you would be taken to Hollywood or New York for a screen test. Your future depends entirely upon whether or not you are photogenic. This test costs the studio from $500 to $2500 and pains are taken to see whether you have "possibilities." If your test is successful, you may be given a seven-year contract on a sliding salary scale. Beginners are usually placed in studio schools and stock companies. There they are given training in speech, body control, and acting. Then they appear in plays before executives and directors. In due time, they may be given bit parts in films.

The casting director of a studio or company hires the actors for all parts other than the leads and extras, and his choice must be made from members of the Screen Actors' Guild. The Academy of Motion Picture Arts and Sciences has compiled *The Players Directory*, made up of photographs of studio-contract actors and actresses. From this directory many casting directors choose their casts.

Television films are being made in all the big studios now and the advertising companies are as important for these as they are for live shows. The problem of getting a break is the same.

As you watch the old films and see which actors and actresses are still holding their own as stars or featured players today, you may realize that actors like Fredric March, Cary Grant, Spencer Tracy, Gary Cooper, Clark Gable, Joan Crawford, Charles Laughton, and Bette Davis have had continuing careers because they are sincere artists. This is further proof of the fact that your best means of achieving success is to have sound technique as well as talent.

In the old days, being an extra was one way to get into the movies. Today, however, the officials of the Central Casting Corporation say your chances of getting a start in this way are five thousand to one, and they ought to know. "Background artists," as extras are called now, must be members of the Screen Extras' Guild and only a comparative few of the thousands of people applying are ever registered. Among these are former stars and featured players of not many years ago, so a newcomer has stiff competition. If you do succeed in being registered, your name and photograph will be placed on file with all your qualifications: appearance, talent, special ability or characteristics, wardrobe, and other details. The registrants are grouped alphabetically and in classified groupings of special types. If registered, you are expected to call in every day, to see if your type will be needed the next day. If Central Casting calls, you must be ready on one day's notice.

Orders are sent in from the studios by teletype. These orders are given to the casting directors, who listen over the loud-speaker for the names of the people calling in and inquiring about parts. When a suitable person calls, he is given verbal instructions. If no order is in for players, the operators simply say "no work" to every call that comes over the telephone switchboard, where there are sometimes thousands of calls an hour.

If you are called to report for work the next day, you report as directed and are paid by the day, according to your special assets. The daily pay is high, but a living wage over a year's period is not assured since the casting directors try to scatter opportunities among the registrants. The adjustment department of the bureau is kept busy day in and day out, with the staff giving advice and often financial relief to emergency cases. Conditions are infinitely better than before the bureau was established and hundreds of thousands of dollars have been saved would-be actors in fees to agents and in transportation and telephone costs.

Getting on the screen depends upon making good on the stage first, upon influential contacts, or upon an agent who is well known and resourceful. Because employment is based on contract, it is much more steady than on the stage. A well-established man or woman can usually count upon a long and well-paid career in normal times. Experience in the famous Pasadena Playhouse, the La Jolla Playhouse, and other first-class institutions is of great value. Such training is one of the best preparations for you if you wish to be given a chance in the films.

## For and Against a Theatrical Career

To summarize, consider carefully the disadvantages and advantages before you determine to enter any of these fields. Never forget that the local community theaters will give you a chance to be a part of the fascinating world of the stage while you lead normal home and business lives.

The greatest disadvantage of going on the stage is the uncertainty of making a living, for in this profession, luck plays a great part in keeping a steady job. Every actor has long periods of enforced idleness through no fault of his own, and every season the competition becomes greater. During the trying days, weeks, and months of seeking an engagement, an actor must be stylishly dressed and always appear at his best even though he has already gone through his savings. An excellent salary for one role has to serve for an indeterminate stretch before the next one materializes.

Some of the other disadvantages are less serious than the difficulty of getting three square meals a day the year round, but they should be considered. An actor must, through agents, managers, and critics, constantly sell himself to the public, which is, alas, sadly fickle. As a result of this self-exploitation, many actors become conceited, affected, and self-centered; they can talk of nothing but themselves.

The actor lives in a world of make-believe and a normal life is difficult for him. His day begins and ends with rehearsals, performances, enforced traveling, and job-hunting. Associations come and go, and friendships, though interesting, are seldom lasting. The gay times featured in novels and movies about stage life usually don't materialize for the earnest artist, for he finds that he must continually study to improve his technique while memorizing lines, rehearsing, acting, and keeping up his health with sufficient sleep and exercise.

The technical fields are less precarious than acting. Strong unions of theatrical employees insure a good living for young people employed in back-stage work, publicity, and other non-acting departments of the theater. Technicians are paid whether plays or programs succeed or fail, and new sets and scenic and sound effects have to be produced constantly. Television production affords more opportunities for young people to serve in technical capacities than do any of the other mediums.

The advantages of a dramatic career are obvious. They are a constant lure to talented people, both young and old. No profession offers more spectacular, profitable, and satisfying rewards to those who are physically and temperamentally equipped (and fortunate enough) to win them. The ordinary salary is higher than in most fields. The actor who is content to play average roles expertly, without striving to become a star, may possibly earn an excellent living after he once gets a foothold in any one of the mediums. The very uncertainty of engagements and the resulting variety of experience have a strong appeal for many people who dislike routine. You have only to read the autobiographies of stage personalities and talk with actors and actresses to learn what a grip the professional theater has upon them.

Success in a theatrical career is largely in the lap of the gods. Given talent and charm, sufficient funds, and a buoyant, optimistic nature, the stage aspirant may be sure of colorful adventure and a chance to get ahead in one of the most uncertain but alluring professions in the world.

# Appendix E

## GLOSSARY

**act curtain** The curtain, hung just upstage of the footlights, which opens or closes each act or scene.

**acting area** The portion of the stage used by actors during a play.

**ad-lib** To extemporize stage business or conversation.

**allegory** A moral play or story in which human qualities such as greed and love are personified.

**angel** A financial backer of a theatrical production.

**antagonist** The hero's opponent, usually a leading character.

**apron** The section of the stage in front of the curtain.

**asbestos** A fireproof curtain closing off the stage from the auditorium. It is raised just before the act curtain is opened.

**backdrop** A large piece of cloth hung at the back of the stage setting.

**backing** Flats or drops behind scenery openings to mask the backstage area.

**backstage** The part of the stage not seen by the audience; also the dressing rooms, waiting areas, and prop room.

**balance** The principle of stage design which demands equal interest on both sides of the stage.

**batten** A long piece of wood or pipe from which scenery and lights are suspended; also used for bracing a flat or weighting a curtain or drop.

**block yourself** To get behind furniture or actors so that you cannot be seen by the audience.

**blow up** To forget lines and business in a play.

**border** A width of material hung across the stage above the acting area to mask the loft from the audience.

**border lights** or **borders** Rows of lamps in long troughs which are hung by chains from pipe battens above the stage.

**box set** A two- or three-wall set composed of canvas flats representing an interior of a room, usually covered by a ceiling.

**brace** A jointed, adjustable, pole-like support for flats.

**breakdown** An analysis of everything needed for a motion-picture production, including technical needs and personnel.

**build a scene** To use such dramatic devices as increased tempo, volume, or emphasis to achieve a climax.

504

**business** Any action performed on the stage.

**business rehearsal** A rehearsal for onstage action.

**C** The symbol used to designate the center of the stage.

**cable** Heavily insulated wire for joining instruments to electrical outlets or a switchboard.

**callboy** A backstage crew member responsible for summoning actors to go onstage.

**canned television** A filmed program.

**character part** A role containing some physical, psychological, mental, or spiritual eccentricity.

**choral interlude** A discussion of the main action between chorus and leaders in an early Greek play.

**chronicle play** A secular medieval drama concerning historical events.

**CinemaScope** A motion-picture process in which a wide-angle picture is compressed onto a standard-size film and later widened in projection. Stereophonic sound is utilized.

**Cinerama** A wide-screen motion-picture process. Three cameras are used in photographing and three synchronized projectors throw the picture against a large curved screen. Stereophonic sound is utilized.

**climax** The highest point of interest in a play.

**color frame** A metal holder which fits into a lighting instrument to keep a color filter in place.

**comedy** A play which ends happily for the hero, usually contains humorous dialogue, and often deals with topics of current interest.

**comedy of manners** A critical and satirical play dealing with social customs and prejudices.

**complication** An Aristotelian term for events in a play from its opening to the critical point where the hero's fortunes change.

**conflict** The struggle underlying the plot of a play.

**constructivism** A style of theatrical design utilizing an architectural or mechanical skeleton as background. Constructivist plays usually deal with economic and social problems.

**countercross** A shifting of position by one or more actors to balance the stage picture.

**cover** To obstruct the view of the audience.

**crisis** The turning point in a play which determines the hero's future.

**cross** The movement by an actor from one location to another onstage.

**cue** The last words or action of one actor immediately preceding the lines or business of another actor.

**cue card** A large card used to prompt a radio or television actor.

**cue sheet** A chart containing the cues for light, sound effects, or curtains.

**curtain** The curtain or drapery which shuts off the stage from the audience; used in a script to indicate that the curtain is lowered.

**curtain line**  The imaginary floor line touched by the curtain when closed.

**cut**  To stop action or to omit.

**cut in**  To break into the speech of another character.

**cycle of plays**  The sequence of semi-religious dramas produced by the medieval merchants' associations.

**cyclorama** or **cyc**  A curtain hung around the three sides of the stage.

**denouement**  The events taking place from the change in the hero's fortunes to the end of the play.

**deus ex machina**  An expression literally meaning "god from a machine"; used today to describe any artificial device which resolves a problem.

**diction**  Selection and pronunciation of words and their combination in speech.

**dimmer**  An electrical device which controls the amount of current flowing into a lighting instrument, thus increasing or decreasing the intensity of the light.

**dissolve**  The momentary overlapping of an image produced by one camera with that of another and the gradual elimination of the first image.

**documentary**  Film presenting factual material in dramatic form.

**Doll Theater**  Japanese drama featuring large and elaborate marionettes with lines spoken by narrators.

**double cast**  To choose two casts for one play, to perform on alternate nights.

**down** or **downstage**  The part of the stage toward the footlights.

**dress the stage**  To set the stage with the necessary scenery, equipment, props, and furniture; also to keep the stage picture balanced during the action.

**drop**  A canvas cloth, fastened at top and bottom to battens, and hung from the grid.

**dry run**  A performance without an audience and of which no recording or filming is made.

**dub in**  To replace or add to a film's sound track.

**eccyclema**  A movable platform on which interior action and tableaux were shown in the early Greek theater.

**empathy**  Emotional identification of one person with another, a term often used in describing audience response.

**emphasis**  The principle of stage design requiring that everything onstage be subordinate to the center of interest.

**epic theater**  An episodic type of drama, usually dealing with a social or political theme. Epic theater frequently uses such devices as lantern slides, loudspeakers, and printed signs to create clear, illustrative episodes.

**episode**  A dramatic scene presenting important action in an early Greek play.

**exit** or **exeunt**  To leave the stage.

**exode**  The closing action in an early Greek play.

**exposition**  The introductory section of a play in which characters, time, place, and situation are presented.

**expressionism** A style of drama in which ideas and concepts are visualized, often by means of distortion or sensationalism in staging.

**falling action** The series of events following the highest dramatic point.

**false proscenium** A frame built inside the proscenium arch to reduce the width of the stage opening and designed to be in harmony with the atmosphere of the play.

**fantasy** An unrealistic play, sometimes serious, sometimes comic, and frequently containing poetic dialogue.

**farce** An exaggerated comedy based on humorous characters and situations.

**feed lines** To give lines and action in such a way that another actor can make a point or get a laugh.

**flat** A piece of rigid upright scenery, a wooden frame covered with canvas.

**flies** or **loft** The area above the stage in which scenery is hung.

**floodlight** or **flood** A lighting instrument in a metal box, which is open at one side. The inner surface of the box is painted a flat white to diffuse the light. Lamps used vary from 500 to 1500 watts. They can be hung from battens overhead, placed on the floor, or supported on a standard.

**floor plan** A drawing showing exactly how the scenery will be placed.

**fly** To raise or lower scenery.

**folk play** A dramatization dealing with the customs and attitudes of a particular group.

**footlights** or **foots** Trough lights along the front of the apron; used to throw light up and back toward the acting area.

**formal stage** A stage having a permanent neutral background that remains the same throughout a play.

**gauze** A large net curtain. When lit from the front, the curtain seems almost opaque; when lit from behind it is semi-transparent.

**gelatin** and **glass roundels** Transparent color media placed on lighting instruments to produce different colors.

**grand drapery** A border at the top of the proscenium used to lower the height of the stage.

**greenroom** A backstage lounge which is used as a reception or waiting room for the actors.

**gridiron** or **grid** A series of heavy beams just under the roof of the stage. To these beams are attached the sheaves or blocks through which lines pass to raise or lower scenery.

**grip** A stagehand.

**ground cloth** or **floor cloth** A canvas covering the floor of the acting area.

**ground row** A low profile of scenery which can stand by itself; used to mask the bottom of the cyc or backdrop.

**guild** Medieval trade association.

**hand props** Personal properties such as notebooks, glasses, or cigarette cases used by the individual players in the action of a play.

**hit** to emphasize a word or line with extra force.

**hold for laughs** To wait for the audience to quiet down after a funny line or scene.

**hold it** To keep perfectly still.

**house** The part of the theater occupied by the audience.

**house manager** The person responsible for the seating and comfort of the audience.

**impressionism** A style of theatrical production designed to enable the audience to actually feel and realize the emotions of characters.

**improvisation** A play based on an outline, in which actors extemporize and insert set speeches and business; also an impromptu scene with lines made up as the scene progresses.

**initial incident** The first important event in a play.

**interlude** A short bit of humorous action, usually performed between serious medieval plays.

**jog** A narrow flat, usually less than two feet in width, used to form such things as alcoves and bay windows.

**Kabuki** The popular theater of Japan, featuring highly stylized, traditional and elaborate historical and domestic plays and dance-dramas.

**kill light** Command to turn a light off.

**lash line** A sash cord used for lashing flats together.

**leading role** A long important part, through which the playwright illustrates his theme and usually arouses audience response.

**left** The term used to refer to the left of the stage from the actor's point of view, not that of the audience.

**left center** The area to the left of center stage, with reference to the actor, not the audience.

**legs** Pieces of cloth, usually hung in pairs, stage left and stage right, to mask the backstage area.

**light cue sheet** The lighting technician's guide for all dimmer readings and settings at act or scene openings and all changes within either.

**light plot** Diagrams showing the placing of the instruments and the plugging system, and the areas where the beams from all the instruments fall.

**Linnebach projector** A lantern for projecting images from a slide onto a backdrop, from the rear of the backdrop.

**live television** A program which is being performed as it is being viewed by home audiences.

**machina** A cranelike device operated from the roof of the *skene* in early Greek theaters.

**major climax** The high point in a play when action culminates.

**major conflict** The main struggle underlying a play's action.

**masking** Any piece of scenery used to conceal the backstage area from the audience.

**masque**  An elaborate European court production glorifying post-medieval nobility.

**master gesture**  A distinctive bit of action that can be repeated effectively as a clue to a character's personality.

**melodrama**  A play designed to arouse immediate and intense emotion by means of exaggeration and fast-moving action.

**the Method**  The Stanislavski approach to acting which assists the actor in using his own personality and life experiences to create a truthful character portrayal.

**mime**  A Roman farce ridiculing everyday life; also, to imitate, or one who imitates.

**miracle play**  A medieval dramatization of the life of a saint.

**mix**  To regulate volume by adjusting microphones for the sound track of a motion picture.

**montage**  A composite picture made up of several distinct pictures.

**morality play**  An ethical, medieval drama peopled by symbolic characters who represent abstract qualities.

**motivated action**  Dramatic action based on the inner natures of the characters.

**musical**  A play in which music, dance, and story are combined.

**mystery play**  A medieval drama based on a Bible story.

**naturalism**  An extremely realistic style of playwriting and production.

**Nō play**  A traditional Japanese drama of religious origin which features stylized acting and dances and is popular chiefly among intellectuals.

**off** or **offstage**  Off the visible stage.

**off-Broadway**  A term used to describe New York City theaters which are outside of the major theatrical district.

**on** or **onstage**  On the visible stage.

**open stage**  A stage which projects into the auditorium.

**orchestra**  The circular area containing altar and playing space in early Greek theaters. In modern theaters, the entire main floor is often referred to as "the orchestra."

**overlap**  To speak when someone else does.

**pace**  The movement or sweep of a play as it progresses.

**pantomime**  A dramatic performance in which actors interpret a story without dialogue by means of significant actions, gestures, and facial expressions.

**parallel**  A collapsible platform.

**paraskenia**  Wings containing doors on either side of the playing space in early Greek theaters.

**periaktoi**  Three-sided pieces of scenery placed on both sides of the early Greek stage.

**permanent setting**  A setting that remains the same throughout a play, regardless of change of locale.

**pit**   The space surrounding three sides of the open sixteenth-century stage where customers holding the cheapest tickets stood.

**pitch**   The relative highness or lowness of the voice at any given time.

**places**   An order for actors and crew to get to their positions.

**places**   The positions of the actors at the opening of an act or scene.

**plastic piece**   A three-dimensional article or structure.

**plot**   The main story of a play; the series of situations and incidents through which characters move, thereby telling a story.

**plot**   To plan stage business; also to plan a speech by working out the phrasing, emphasis, and inflections.

**point lines**   To emphasize lines vocally or through gestures.

**practical**   A term applied to such parts of the set as doors and windows which must open and shut during the action and stairs which must bear a person's weight.

**preliminary situation**   The events preceding the opening action of a play which are directly related to the plot.

**première**   The first showing of a play.

**profile**   The irregular edge of any piece of scenery such as branches of trees, shapes of rocks, and skylines.

**prologue**   An explanatory speech preceding the opening of a play.

**promptbook**   A complete script indicating plans and cues for all technical details as well as actors' lines and business.

**properties** or **props**   All of the stage furnishings, including the furniture.

**property-man**   The backstage crew member responsible for furniture and hand properties.

**proportion**   The principle of stage design demanding that the human being be taken as the unit of measurement.

**proscenium**   The arch or frame enclosing the visible stage; the opening through which the audience views the stage.

**protagonist**   The hero or leading character with whom the audience sympathizes.

**p$\overline{\text{we}}$**   The Burmese term for a play.

**quality**   The individual sound of a voice.

**rake**   To slant or set at an angle. A *raked stage* is inclined from the footlights to the rear of the stage.

**ramp**   A sloping platform connecting the stage floor to a higher level.

**rate**   The speed at which words are spoken.

**reading rehearsal**   An early rehearsal at which the director interprets the play and actors read and discuss character interpretations.

**realism**   A style of drama which attempts to show life as it really is.

**retake**   A motion-picture term meaning the rephotographing of a scene.

**returns**   Two flats set downstage right and left to mask the edges of the set from the audience.

**right**  The term used to refer to the right of the stage from the actor's point of view, not that of the audience.

**right center**  The area to the right of the center stage, with reference to the actor, not the audience.

**ring up**  To raise the curtain. The curtain is said to be *rung up* or *rung down*.

**rising action**  The series of dramatic events which lead to the high point of a play.

**the road**  The route followed by a traveling theatrical company.

**romantic drama**  A play which presents life and characters in an idealized fashion, frequently using poetic language.

**scenario**  A detailed treatment of a story for motion-picture production, showing its scene-by-scene development and giving the essential acting details.

**screen treatment**  A scene-by-scene description (not including dialogue and action) of a story being considered for motion-picture production.

**selective realism**  A modified form of realism in theatrical production, in which carefully selected details give the impression of actuality.

**sentimental comedy**  A comedy dealing with emotional subjects such as young love, patriotism, lost affection.

**set piece**  An individual piece of scenery, such as a tree, rock, or wall, which stands by itself.

**set props**  Properties placed onstage for the use of the actor.

**sides**  Half-sheets of typewritten manuscript containing the lines, cues, and business of a character.

**skeleton set**  A frame of scenery in which different doors and windows are used to change locales.

**skene**  The hut which early Greek actors used as a dressing room; later expanded into a permanent backing for the acting area.

**sky cyc**  A smooth cloth hung at the back and sides of the stage, painted to give the illusion of the sky.

**sky dome**  A quarter of a sphere built in plaster to make a permanent sky.

**soap opera**  A sentimental melodrama or comedy, popular today on radio and television.

**social drama**  A play concerned with the problems of society, such as the struggles between management and labor or the causes of juvenile delinquency.

**soliloquy**  A character's speech to himself.

**space stage**  A stage on which lights are used to define locales. When one locale is visible, the rest of the stage is dark.

**spotlight** or **spot**  A metal-encased lighting instrument which gives out a concentrated light and can be directed to a specific area. It is used to light the acting areas. In wattage, it varies from 250–400 (a baby spot) to 1500–2000.

**stagecraft**  The art and craft of putting on a production.

**steal a scene** To attract attention away from the person to whom the center of interest legitimately belongs.

**stock type** A recognizable and unvarying type of stage character such as a butler, faithful sweetheart, difficult mother-in-law, or foolish old man.

**straight part** A role in which the character resembles the actor in looks and personality.

**strike** The stage manager's order to remove an object or objects from the stage or to store the set.

**strip lights** or **strips** Lamps arranged in metal troughs; frequently used for lighting cycs or backings.

**structure (of a play)** The form, development, and method of presentation.

**style** The way in which a play is written, acted, and produced. Typical styles are realism, romanticism, and expressionism.

**supporting role** A secondary role.

**symbolism** The visualization of a play's idea or atmosphere through scenic treatment in which objects often represent ideas, relationships, or places.

**symphonic drama** A pageant-like play, usually dealing with historical subjects.

**tag line** The last speech in an act or play.

**take** A motion-picture term meaning the photographing of a scene.

**take the stage** Hold the center of interest; move over the entire stage area.

**teaser** A short drop hung behind the act curtain, regulating the height of the stage opening and masking the front batten of onstage lights.

**teleplay** A television drama.

**teleprompter** A mechanical device which enables television actors to read their lines while appearing to speak from memory.

**tempo** The speed with which speech and action move a play along.

**theater in the round** A type of staging in which the seated audience surrounds a circular stage.

**theatrical style of acting** Acting based on conscious technique rather than emotional involvement.

**theme** The central unifying idea of a play which underlies plot, action, and dialogue.

**Thespian** A term meaning actor. Thespis, a sixth century B.C. poet, is said to have been the founder of the Greek drama and the first actor.

**throw** The distance from a lighting instrument to the area to be lit.

**throw away** To subordinate words or phrases by saying them rapidly at a low pitch and with little volume.

**timing** The execution of a line or piece of business at a specific moment to achieve the most telling effect.

**Todd-AO** A wide-screen process in which the picture is thrown onto a large curved screen with a high reflectance surface. Stereophonic sound is used.

**top** To build to a climax by speaking at a higher pitch, at a faster rate, or with more force than in the preceding speeches.

**tragedy**   A play in which the leading character is defeated by life, fate, or his own failings.

**traveler**   A stage curtain which opens at the middle of the stage and moves to the right and left, rather than one which moves up and down.

**trim**   A piece cut from a motion-picture film which may be used later.

**unities**   Dramatic restrictions or conventions followed by writers of Greek drama. The *unity of time* limited action to successive events which followed each other without lapse of time. The *unity of place* limited the action to one locale. The *unity of action* restricted the play to a series of closely related events.

**unit setting**   A structural setting, or part of a setting, which is used in different ways to indicate different locales.

**unity**   The centering of all elements of stage design on the main idea of a play.

**up** or **upstage**   The area of the stage away from the footlights, toward the rear of the stage.

**upstage**   To take attention away from an actor improperly when he is the focus of interest.

**video taping**   Recording television programs on tape.

**VistaVision**   A wide-screen process which permits the image to be adjusted to all theater screens.

**volume**   The relative strength, force, or intensity with which sound is made.

**wagon**   A low platform mounted on casters on which stage sets can be built and wheeled onto the acting area.

**warn**   To notify of any upcoming action or cue.

**wing**   The offstage area to the right or left of the set; also a flat or drapery used stage right and left to mask the backstage area.

**wing setting**   A setting made with pairs of wings on both sides of the stage; used with a matching backdrop.

# Index

Cardiff, Jack, 410
*Carousel*, 96, 102, 146
Carroll, Paul Vincent, 127
Cartoons, animated, 404
Casella, Alberto, 106
Cast, announcement of, 304
  on performance night, 385
  photographs of, 315
Cast parties, 396
Casting of plays, 302–304
  double, 304
  radio, 432
"Cataract of Lodore, The" Southey,
  quoted, 193–194
Center of interest, 255
Center stage (C), 172, 253
Cervantes, Miguel de, 130
Character, keeping in, 267
  projection of, 267
Character development, 27, 36–37,
  52–53
  in television, 31–32
Character parts, 234
Characterization, 181, 231–250
  analysis of role in, 231–233
  convincing, 78
  evaluation of, 392
  keeping in character, 267
  make-up and, 372–373
  methods of, 77
  of old age, 234–235
  technique and, 255–270
Characters, 77
  grouping of, 257
  relationship between, 248
*Charley's Aunt*, 92
Chayefsky, Paddy, 443
Chekhov, Anton, 58, 102, 128
Cheney, Sheldon, 324
Cherry Lane Theatre, New York, 149
*Cherry Orchard, The*, Chekhov, 128
Children, acting by, 39
Children's films, 426
Children's theater, 151
China, theater in, 133
Choral interludes, 110
Choreography, pantomime and, 175
Chorpenning, Charlotte, 151
Christian Church, drama in, 114–115
Chronicle plays, 116
Church dramas, 115
*Cid, Le*, Corneille, 127
CinemaScope, 401
Cinematographers (*see* Cameramen)
Circle in the Square, New York, 147,
  149
Circuits, electric, 344
"Climax," 438

Climax, 27, 31, 262
  in interpretation, 213
  major, 71
Closed-circuit television, 451
Clothes for rehearsals, 269
Clurman, Harold, 143, 147
Coca, Imogene, 437
Cocteau, Jean, 128
Coe, Fred, 443
Cohan, George M., 312
Coleridge, Samuel Taylor, 221
College and university theaters, 4,
  150, 277, 331, 451
Color City, California, 436
Color frames, 344
Color mediums, 346
Color schemes, 338–339
Color television, 450
Colorado, University of, 154
Colors in scenic design, 335–339
  analogous, 337
  clashing, 338
  complementary, 337
  intensity of, 337
  lighting and, 351–352
  meaning of, 338
  primary, 335
  secondary, 335
  value of, 336
Comedians, radio, 430
Comédie Française, 127
Comedy, 89, 91–92, 95–96
  cues for, 259
  definition of, 89
  Greek, 110
  of manners, 95
  pointing lines in, 259–260
  sentimental, 96
*Comedy of Errors, The*, Shakespeare,
  92
Commedia dell' arte, 117–118
*Common Glory, The*, Green, 104
Como, Perry, 438
Complication, definition of, 70
Conflict, 27
  major, 71
Congreve, William, 95, 122, 200
Conkle, E. P., 224
Connectors, 344
Connelly, Marc, 143
*Conquest* (film), 403
Consonant sounds, 217–218
Constructivism, 128, 130, 328
*Contrast, The*, Tyler, 138
Cooke, George Frederic, 123
Cool colors, 337
Copyrights, 270

Door stop, definition of, 320
Double casting, 304
Dowden, Edward, 157
Down, Oliphant, 45, 214, 241
Downstage, definition of, 172, 253
Drama, in Asia, 130–136
  in England, 1600 to present, 122–127
  in Europe, 127–130
  Greek, 91, 109–112
  history of, 108–153
  medieval, 115–116
  realistic, 128
  Renaissance, 117–120
  Restoration, 95, 122
  in United States, 138–151
  (*See also* Plays; Theater)
Drama classes, 5, 149–151
  advantages of, 8
Drama groups, 146
Dramatic criticism, as journalism, 388
  by students, 389–391
Dramatic readings, 280, 282–283
*Dramatics*, 150
Draperies as set backgrounds, 339–340
*Dream Girl*, Rice, 94
Dress rehearsals, 315–317
  television, 448
Dressing rooms, care of, 317, 365
  visitors in, 255
Dressing the stage, 313–314
  definition of, 253
Drew, Georgiana, 140
Drew, Louisa Lane, 140
Drinkwater, John, 124
Drop, definition of, 320
Dublin, theater in, 127
Duerr, Edwin, 442
Dumas, Alexandre, 127
Dunsany, Lord, 79, 263
"DuPont Show of the Month," 439
*Dynamo*, O'Neill, 329

*Eccyclema*, 113
Echegaray, José, 130
Educational films, 404
Educational and Recreational Guides, Inc., 426
*Edward II*, Marlowe, 119
Egypt, ancient, drama in, 108–109
Elitch Gardens Company, Denver, 146
Elizabeth, Queen, 120
*Elizabeth the Queen*, 143
Elizabethan drama, 118–119
Elizabethan theater, 120, 157–158

Ellipsoidal reflector spotlights, 344–345
Emotional passages, 242
Emotions, acting and, 177–180, 250
  cultivation of, 8
Empathy, lack of, 30
Emphasis, 212
  in scenic design, 333
  stage, 255–256
*Emperor Jones, The*, O'Neill, 141
England, 115, 118–120, 327
Entrances, 255
Epic theater, 105
Epilogues, 70
Episodes, 110
Ernest, Earle, 136
Ervine, St. John, 127
Essential action, 309
Euripides, 106, 110
Europe, film festivals in, 427
  theater in, 127–130, 327
Eustis, Martin, 267
Evaluation, of plays, 26–30, 391–393
  of performances, 390, 395–397
Evans, Maurice, 146, 154
*Every Man in His Humour*, Jonson, 118
*Everyman*, 101, 115
*Everywoman*, 101
Exit, definition of, 253
  technique of, 263
Exposition of plot, 71, 73
Expressionism, 327
Eyebrow pencils, 370
Eyes, importance of, 249
  make-up for, 372

*Fabulous Invalid, The*, Hart and Kaufman, quoted, 49–51
Face powders, 369
  use of, 373–374
*Fall of the House of Usher, The*, Poe, quoted, 214
Falling, 174
Falling action, 74–75
False proscenium, 320
Fantasy, 92, 94
Farce, 92
Farnese Theatre, Parma, 324
Farquhar, George, 95, 122
*Fashion*, Mowatt, 138
*Faust*, Goethe, 128
Feature films, 403–404
Federal Communications Commission, 435
Federal Theatre, 144
"Fee" television, 450
Feeding, definition of, 253

McKenna, Siobhan, 124
Macready, William Charles, 123, 138
*Madame Butterfly* (film), 403
*Madwoman of Chaillot, The,* Girau-
doux, 94
Materlinck, Maurice, 99
*Magic Curtain, The,* Langner, 142
Magnani, Anna, 403
*Mahabharata,* 131
Major climax, 71
Major conflict, 71
*Maker of Dreams,* Down, quoted, 45–
46, 214, 241
Make-up, 367–375
    functions of, 367
    for motion pictures, 414
    principles and procedures for,
    371–374
    problems of, 374–375
Make-up kits, 369–371
Make-up people, 296, 383–385
Make-up rooms, 370–371, 384–385
*Man of Aran* (film), 404
*Man and Superman,* Shaw, 280
Managers, 140
    (*See also* Business managers; Stage
    managers)
Mansfield, Richard, 140
Marceau, Marcel, 175
March, Frederic, 146, 403
Marionettes, 135
Marlowe, Christopher, 119, 230
Marlowe, Julia, 140
*Mary Rose,* Barrie, 124
    quoted, 224
Mascara, 370
    application of, 374
Masking, definition of, 322
Masques, 116
*Master Builder, The,* Ibsen, 128
Master gesture, 232
*Matchmaker, The,* Wilder, 230
Mate, Richard, 410
Mechanical equipment, first, 122
*Medea,* Euripides, 110
Medieval drama, 115–116
Melodrama, 94–95
Memorized scenes, production of, 54–
56
    quotations for, 56–67
Memorizing, 54–56, 247, 267–268
    "whole" method of, 55
*Merchant of Venice, The,* Shake-
speare, quoted, 199–202, 209,
227, 240
"Method, the," 128, 143–144, 229–
230
Meyerhold, Vsevolod, 128, 328–329

Middle vowels, 216–217
*Midsummer Nights Dream, A,* Shake-
speare, 94, 154
Mielziner, Jo, 329
Miller, Arthur, 78, 96, 147
Miller, Henry, 140
"Millionaire, The," 438
Milne, A. A., 87
Mimes, 175
    Roman, 113
*Minna von Barnhelm,* Lessing, 128
Miracle plays, 115
Miyata, Teruaki, 136
*Moana* (film), 404
Model settings, 334–335
Mohr, Hal, 410
Molière, 91, 127
Molnar, Ferenc, 96, 102
Monologues, 245–247
Moody, William Vaughan, 140
Morality plays, 115
Morgan, Angela, 214
Morley, Christopher, 138
Moscow Art Theatre, 128, 229–230
*Moscow Rehearsals,* Houghton, 329
Mosel, Tad, 443
*Most Happy Fella, The,* 102, 146
Motion Picture Association of Amer-
ica, Inc., 404, 426
    Children's Film Library, 426
    Community Relations Committee,
    426
    International Committee, 427
Motion picture directors, 34, 409–410
Motion Picture Export Association of
America, 406
Motion picture industry, organizations
representing, 404, 406
Motion Picture Production Code, 406
Motion Picture Research Council,
Inc., 406
Motion pictures, 5, 27, 398–428
    acting in, 421, 424
    Broadway stars in, 146, 403
    choice of, 32–33
    classroom study of, 427–428
    exporting of, 406
    first, 140
    foreign, 33, 403
    internationalization of, 399, 403
    making of, 408–419
    and the school, 426–428
    of Shakespeare's plays, 154
    special categories of, 403–404
    on television, 398, 403
    wide-screen, 33–34, 400–401, 403–
    404

Motivation of action, 77
 in Shakespeare, 159
*Mourning Becomes Electra*, O'Neill,
 143
*Mourning Bride, The*, Congreve,
 quoted, 200
Movement, 248, 257–258
 unnecessary, 249, 257
Mowatt, Anna Cora, 138
Muni, Paul, 146
Museum of Modern Art, New York,
 426
Music, for motion pictures, 414–415
 on radio, 431
*Music Man, The*, 146
Musical directors, 414–415
Musical drama, 102, 146
*My Fair Lady*, 102, 124, 146, 223
Mystery plays, 115

*Nanook of the North* (film), 404
Nash, N. Richard, 66, 82
National Association of Community
 Theatres, 149
National Thespian Society, 150
Naturalism, 98, 325
*Neighbours*, Gale, quoted, 85–86, 236
New Delhi, 132
*New Theatres for Old*, Gorelik, 105
New York City, 119, 124, 128, 138,
 140, 146–147, 149, 450–451
New York Drama Critics' Circle
 Award, 27
*New York Times*, 36
*New York Times Index*, 281
New York World's Fair, 435
Newman, Paul, 146
News broadcasts, radio, 431
 television, 439
Newsreels, 404
*Night at an Inn, A*, Dunsany, 79–80
 quoted, 263
*Night of January 16th, The*, 71
*Night Must Fall*, 95
Nipkow, Paul, 434
Nō plays, 135
Nobel prize for literature, 144
Nobility and royalty as patrons, 117,
 120
Nonrealistic plays, lighting of, 350
 (*See also* Fantasy)
Norway, theater in, 128
Nose putty, 374
Notebooks, 9
*Nothing But the Truth*, 92

Oboler, Arch, 430
O'Brien, Brian, 401

O'Casey, Sean, 78, 127
Odets, Clifford, 96, 144, 238
*Oedipus Rex*, Sophocles, 110, 233
Oenslager, Donald, 329
Off or offstage, definition of, 254
Off-Broadway theaters, 147, 149
*Oklahoma!*, 102, 145, 175
 film, 401
O-Kuni, 135
Old age, characterization of, 234–235
Old Globe Theatre, San Diego, 154
Old Testament, 108
Old Vic Theatre, 125, 403
*Oliver Twist* (film), 403
Olivier, Laurence, 124, 154, 403
Olympian Academy, 323
"Omnibus," 439
On or onstage, definition of, 254
One-act plays, 101–102
 list of, 272–273
 taking part in, 269–272
One-man performances, 245–247
O'Neill, Eugene, 78, 96, 101, 141–
 144, 147, 151, 327, 329
Open stage, 70
Orchestra, 110, 297
Oregon, University of, 154
*Oresteia*, Aeschylus, 110
Oscars, 406
*Our Town*, Wilder, 77, 279, 341
 quoted, 86–87
Outdoor theaters, 154, 331
*Outward Bound*, Sutton Vane, 279
 quoted, 64
Overacting, 242
Overlap, definition of, 254

Pace, climax and, 262
 definition of, 254
*Pal Joey*, 146
Palladian, The, 323–324
Palladio, Andrea, 323
Panel shows, television, 438
Pantomime, 115, 168–189
 acting in, 175–189
 characterization in, 181
 definition of, 168
 group, 186–189
 individual, 182–186
 preparation for, 168–175
 Roman, 113
 Shakespeare in, 275
Parallel, definition of, 322
*Parascenia*, 113
*Paris Bound*, Barry, 143
Parma, Italy, 324
*Pather Panchali* (film), 403
Paulson, Flavia, 427

Promptbooks, 293, 301
Prompters, 271, 293, 295, 317, 382
Pronunciation of words, 218–219
Propaganda plays, 106
Properties or props, 364
  definition of, 254
  for motion pictures, 413
Property-men, 295–296, 383
Proportion in scenic design, 333–334
Proscenium, 70
Proscenium opening, 258
Protagonist, 77, 91
Provincetown Players, 141
Psalms, the, quoted, 209
Publicity, importance of, 296
Pulitzer prize plays, 104, 141
Punch and Judy shows, 115
Puritans, 122
*Pwe*, 133
*Pygmalion*, Shaw, 102, 124, 190, 223, 233
  film, 403
  quoted, 237

*Quality Street*, Barrie, 96, 124
  quoted, 56–58
Quality of voice, 194, 196
Quintero, José, 147
Quiz shows, 437

Rachel, 127
Racine, Jean, 127
Radio, 430–434
  history of, 434
  techniques of, 432–433
Radio serials, 430
Radio stations, school, 431
*Radio and Television Acting*, Duerr, 442
*Rainmaker, The*, Nash, 82
  quoted, 66–67
Rains, Claude, 124
Rake, to, definition of, 322
*Ramayana*, 131
*Ramona*, Jackson, 104
Ramp, definition of, 322
Rattigan, Terence, 102
Read, Thomas Buchanan, 211
*Readers' Guide to Periodical Literature*, 281
Reading of plays, 36–38
  aloud, 40
  (*See also* Play readings)
Reading rehearsals, 305–307
Realism, 98
  selective, 325, 327
Realistic plays, 128
  lighting of, 350

Recordings, improvement of diction and, 223
"Red Buttons' Show," 437
Redgrave, Michael, 124
Reed, Carol, 409
Rehearsals, 55, 265–270, 305–318
  blocking, 307–309
  crew, 312–314
  dress, 315–317
  lighting, 352–353
  polishing, 311–312
  for radio, 432–433
  reading, 305–307
  schedules, 306–307
  technical, 314
  for television, 440, 446–448
  working, 309–311
Reinhardt, Max, 154
Réjane, 127
*Relapse, The*, Vanbrugh, 95
Relaxation, 265
  laughter and, 239
  pantomime and, 168–169
Renaissance drama, 117–120
Renaissance stage, 323–324
Renaud, Madeleine, 128
Renoir, Claude, 410
Research for motion pictures, 413
Resonance, 194
  exercises for, 198
Restoration drama, 95, 122
Returns, definition of, 322
Reviews of plays, as readings, 280–282
  (*See also* Dramatic criticism)
Rhymed couplets, 157
Rice, Elmer, 94, 101, 143–144
*Richard III* (film), 154
Richardson, Ralph, 124
*Riders to the Sea*, Synge, quoted, 236
Right, definition of, 172, 254
Right center, definition of, 254
*Rime of the Ancient Mariner, The*, Coleridge, quoted, 221
Ring up, definition of, 254
Rising, definition of, 258
Rising action, 74, 158
*Rising of the Moon, The*, Gregory, 127
"Rising in 1776, The," Read, 209, 211
*Rivals, The*, Sheridan, 78, 123
*River, The* (film), 404
Road companies, 146
Roanoke Island, North Carolina, 104
*Robe, The* (film), 401
"Robert Montgomery Presents," 438
Robinson, Lennox, 127
Robson, Eleanor, 140
Rodgers, Richard, 145–146

Shakespeare, William, plays of, list of recommended scenes for acting improvement, 276
stagecraft in, 163
structure of, 157–159
study of, 157
as playwright, 157
(*See also* titles of plays)
Shakespeare festivals, 154
Shakespeare Memorial Theatre Company, England, 125, 403
*Shakuntala*, Kalidasa, 131
*Shall We Join the Ladies?* Barrie, 338
*Sham*, Tompkins, quoted, 61
Shaw, David, 443
Shaw, George Bernard, 78, 91, 102, 124, 128, 143, 190, 224, 237, 280
*She Stoops to Conquer*, Goldsmith, 123
Shearer, Norma, 154
*Sheep Has Five Legs, The* (film), 403
Sheldon, Edward, 140
Sheridan, Richard Brinsley, 78, 95, 123, 201
Sherwood, Robert, 144
*Shoemaker's Holiday*, Dekker, 118
Shore, Dinah, 438
*Shore Acres*, Herne, 140
Showmanship, definition of, 254
Show-offs, 252
Sica, Vittorio de, 403
Siddons, Sarah Kemble, 122–123
Sides, definition of, 254
Simonson, Lee, 329
Sitting, 171–172, 258
Situation, 80–81
"$64,000 Question," 437
Skeleton settings, 330
*Skene*, 113
Sketches, one-person, 245–247
*Skidding*, Rouverol, quoted, 243–244
Skinner, Cornelia Otis, 245
Skinner, Otis, 140
Sky cyc, definition of, 322
Sky dome, definition of, 322
Sladen-Smith, F., 351
Smith, Milton, 355
*Snow White and the Seven Dwarfs* (film), 404
Social drama, 96
Soliloquy, 77, 78, 159
"Song from Aglaura," Suckling, quoted, 200
Song of Songs, The, 108
Sophocles, 110
Sothern, E. H., 140
Sound, motion-picture, 414
Sound effects for television, 446

Sound synchronization, 419
Sound tracks, 417
*South Pacific*, 102, 146
film, 414
Southern California, University of, 451
Southey, Robert, 194
Space stage, 341
Spain, drama in, 130
"Spectaculars," television, 439
Speech, breath control and, 192–194
improvement of, 215
pronunciation, 218–219
rate of, 211–212
vowel and consonant sounds, 216–218
(*See also* Voice)
Spirit gum, 370
Spontaneity, 265
Spotlights or spots, 344–346
location of, 348
*Spreading the News*, Gregory, 127
quoted, 236
*Squaw Man, The* (film), 404
Stage, cleaning of, 365
open, 70
Stage balance, 255–257
Stage consciousness, 256
Stage crew, 383
*Stage Design Around the World Since 1935*, 329
Stage directions in Shakespeare, 163
*Stage Door*, 233
Stage emphasis, 255–257
Stage equipment, ancient, 113
Stage fright, 268
Stage left, definition of, 172
Stage managers, 250, 295, 312, 317, 380–381
Stage right, definition of, 172
Stage terminology, glossary of, 253–254, 320–322
Stagecraft, 322
Staging, 26, 128, 130
evaluation of, 393
in the round, 277–279
(*See also* Sets or settings)
Stallings, Laurence, 143
*Standards of Photoplay Appreciation*, 426
Standing, 170
Stanislavski, Constantin, 128, 229
Stanislavski Method (*see* Method, the)
Stanley, Kim, 144, 230
Stapleton, Maureen, 230
Stealing a scene, definition of, 254

War and Peace (film), 413
Ward, Winifred, 151
Wardrobe mistress, 296, 317, 365, 383–385
Warm colors, 337
Warn, to, definition of, 254
Washington, D.C., 146
Washington Square Players, 142–143
Wattage, 345
Way of the World, The, Congreve, 95
Wayne, David, 230
Welles, Orson, 154, 341
Westerns, television, 437
Westwood, California, 451
What Every Woman Knows, Barrie, 124
  film, 403
What Price Glory, Anderson and Stallings, 143
"What's My Line?" 438
Wide-screen motion pictures, 400–401
Wigs, 375, 414
Wilde, Oscar, 123, 227, 260
Wilder, Thornton, 77, 87, 279, 341
Wilhelm Tell, Schiller, 128
Williams, Emlyn, 245
Williams, Tennessee, 77, 78, 102, 147
Williamsburg, Virginia, 104, 138

Wing setting, 322
Wings, 322
Winters, Shelley, 230
Winterset, Anderson, 82, 233
Witness for the Prosecution, 95
Woffington, Peg, 123
Wolfe, Thomas, 236
Wonderful Town, 146
"Work," Morgan, quoted, 214
Working rehearsals, 309–311
Wouk, Herman, 279
Would-Be Gentleman, The, Molière, 127
Wrinkles, make-up for, 370, 373
Wurzel-Flummery, Milne, quoted, 87
Wycherley, William, 95, 122
Wyler, William, 409

Yale University, 151
Yearling, The (film), 403
Years Ago, Gordon, 279
  quoted, 64–65
Yeats, William Butler, 125
"Your Show of Shows," 437

"Zoom" lens, 447
"Zukettes," 136
Zworykin, Vladimir, 435

**530**   INDEX